On the Offensive

I'm not a racist, but …
You look good, for your age …
She was asking for it …
You're crazy …
That's so gay …

Have you ever wondered why certain language has the power to offend? It is often difficult to recognize the veiled racism, sexism, ageism (and other -isms) that hide in our everyday discourse. This book sheds light on the derogatory phrases, insults, slurs, stereotypes, tropes, and more that make up linguistic discrimination.

Each chapter addresses a different area of prejudice: race and ethnicity; gender identity; sexuality; religion; health and disability; physical appearance; and age. Drawing on hot button topics and real-life case studies, and delving into the history of offensive terms, a vivid picture of modern discrimination in language emerges.

By identifying offensive language, both overt and hidden, past and present, we uncover vast amounts about our own attitudes, beliefs, and values and reveal exactly how and why words can offend.

Karen Stollznow is an Australian-American linguist and author. She is a Researcher at the Griffith Centre for Social and Cultural Research and was formerly a Research Associate at the University of California, Berkeley. Her books include *Language Myths, Mysteries and Magic, Would You Believe It?*, and *God Bless America*. Karen is a host of the popular science podcast Monster Talk.

On the Offensive

Prejudice in Language Past and Present

KAREN STOLLZNOW
Griffith University, Queensland

CAMBRIDGE
UNIVERSITY PRESS

University Printing House, Cambridge CB2 8BS, United Kingdom

One Liberty Plaza, 20th Floor, New York, NY 10006, USA

477 Williamstown Road, Port Melbourne, VIC 3207, Australia

314–321, 3rd Floor, Plot 3, Splendor Forum, Jasola District Centre,
New Delhi – 110025, India

79 Anson Road, #06–04/06, Singapore 079906

Cambridge University Press is part of the University of Cambridge.

It furthers the University's mission by disseminating knowledge in the pursuit of
education, learning, and research at the highest international levels of excellence.

www.cambridge.org
Information on this title: www.cambridge.org/9781108791786
DOI: 10.1017/9781108866637

First published 2020

Printed in the United States of America by Sheridan Books, Inc.

A catalogue record for this publication is available from the British Library.

ISBN 978-1-108-79178-6 Paperback

For my son, Blade, and his generation, who are the gatekeepers of tomorrow's language.

Contents

Acknowledgments

I'd like to thank unnamed people for unwittingly inspiring this book and shaping its course.

My sincere gratitude goes to Rebecca Taylor, Isabel Collins, and the team from Cambridge University Press, for believing in this book and making it happen.

I'm deeply grateful to my friend and colleague Blake Smith for his support and his prowess with puns.

Last but not least, heartfelt thanks to my husband and son for their unfailing patience, understanding, encouragement, and love throughout the research and writing of this book.

Introduction

You Can't Say Anything These Days

You people ...
She was asking for it ...
That's so gay ...
Don't be a Jew ...
My ex-girlfriend is crazy ...
You'd be pretty if you lost weight ...
You look good ... for your age ...

These statements can be offensive to some people, but it is complicated to understand exactly why. It is often difficult to recognize the veiled racism, sexism, ableism, lookism, ageism, and other -isms that hide in our everyday language. From an early age, we learn and normalize many words and phrases that exclude groups of people and reinforce bias and social inequality. Our language expresses attitudes and beliefs that can reveal internalized discrimination, prejudice, and intolerance. Some words and phrases are considered to be offensive, even if we're not trying to be.

Disclaimers such as *It's not my intention to hurt your feelings*, and *I didn't mean to offend*, suggest that, as a rule, people do not want to be offensive. We can often assume kind intent behind the things that people say. But there is a paradox. It is also frowned upon to *be offended*. Phrases such as *don't be offended*, *don't take offence*, and *they are easily offended* tell us that being offended is viewed with disapproval in society. The responsibility for offense is then redirected from the offender to the offended. It is argued that *being offended is a choice*. That *offence is taken, not given*. It is said that in a free society people have *the right to offend* but *nobody has the right to not be offended*. If you are offended then that is your problem. Some people say that the offended should simply

1

toughen up and *get over it*. We are reminded of the childhood nursery rhyme: *Sticks and stones may break my bones, but words will never hurt me.*

And yet, when we talk about being offended we use the same metaphorical language to express emotional distress that we use to describe physical pain. According to figures of speech, we can suffer from a *broken heart* as much as a broken bone, we can nurse our *wounded pride* as much as a wounded leg, and we can talk about having *bruised feelings* as well as a bruised knee. To *offend* is to cause anger or annoyance, but it is also to make someone *feel* something bad. Contrary to the phrase *words will never hurt me*, words can indeed be said to *hurt, harm,* and *injure*. The upsetting things people say to us can *crush, burn, break, bruise, sting, sear, scar, tear,* and *cut like a knife*. An insult can be *a slap in the face* or a *kick in the teeth*. Hurtful language can *attack* and *abuse*, cause *damage*, and *destroy* or *traumatize* people. Words can inflict *pain* and *suffering*. Offensive language is something said to us that we find to be morally repulsive or personally insulting. It is language that strikes the core of our beliefs or identity and affects us on a fundamental level. We can say that insulting words and phrases *offend to the core, offend to the bone, deeply offend,* or make us feel *personally offended*.

Some people boast, *I don't get offended easily*, suggesting that this shows strength of character, while being offended shows weakness. Not being afraid to offend is also admired. Some purport to be impartial in their prejudice, that they *offend everyone equally*. Others claim their right or *license to offend* that gives them a "free pass" to be offensive or they excuse any offensiveness with *that's just how I talk*. It is said that *it's a person's right to speak their mind*. They are praised for not being *afraid to speak their mind*, for their *straight talk, truth-telling,* and for *telling it like it is*. Often, people rule that certain language is "not offensive," simply because it is not offensive to *them*, thereby dismissing the possibility that it may be offensive to other people. It can be difficult to understand why something is offensive if we're not the one who has experienced prejudice, and therefore not an authority on what is offensive or not. People who are discriminated against are the authorities on their own discrimination. Someone who is not a member of a marginalized group is said to be coming from a place of *privilege*. Privilege refers to the benefits, rights, advantages, and powers that are afforded to some people in society, simply because they do not belong to a stigmatized group. For people who've enjoyed this type of privilege their whole lives, social equality may seem scary or oppressive. Being confronted by one's own prejudices can lead to a state that has been described as *fragility*. Fragility is a resistance to acknowledging these prejudices, and it is often characterized by anger, guilt, argumentation, silence, denial, and defensiveness.

Some people are offended by people who are offended.

People who get offended are usually portrayed as emotional, vulnerable, and weak. We have a lot of popular labels to describe "the offended." It is said that offended people *take things to heart*, and they are *thin-skinned, too sensitive,* or *hypersensitive.* They are called *uptight, fragile,* and *delicate.* They are *snowflakes.* Offenses are minimized as *taunting, teasing,* a *slight,* an *insult,* or a just a *joke.* It is said that an offended person *can't take a joke*; they are *overreacting,* or *looking to be offended.* They need to *get a sense of humor,* simply *ignore it, suck it up,* or *toughen up* and *grow a thicker skin.* Offended people are accused of being self-obsessed and narcissistic. It is said they think themselves to be morally superior, educated, and "woke." They are accused of trying to look good in the eyes of others with their *virtue signaling.* They are ridiculed for their requests for *safe spaces, content notes,* and *trigger warnings* that allow them to choose whether or not to expose themselves to potentially distressing topics. (Although such warnings have been a feature of television for decades, from movie ratings and content warnings to cultural sensitivity warnings.)

People who get offended are said to be the products of *helicopter parenting,* that is, overprotective parents who, like helicopters, hover over their children overseeing every minute aspect of their lives. The offended are regarded as immature, or infantilized as whining babies having tantrums. At Kent State University in October 2017, the conservative group Turning Point USA held a protest on campus in which they argued, "Safe spaces are for children." Their publicity stunt featured students who dressed up in diapers, and drew in coloring books as they sucked on pacifiers in a playpen.[1] They displayed posters that read: "Your censorship offends me." People who are offended are said to be part of today's *outrage culture.*

Some people are outraged by people who are outraged.

Western society is thought to be in the midst of a "cultural war." People who are concerned about social justice are framed as a kind of subculture believed to be in opposition to the rest of society. They are derisively labeled *Social Justice Warriors,* a slur that is usually abbreviated to *SJWs.* According to this rhetoric, they have their own *SJW culture* or *PC culture* that has gone "too far." Social justice advocates are denounced as "progressives" who censor speech and disseminate *propaganda.* They are characterized as mobs with pitchforks on the Internet engaged in modern-day *witch hunts.* Ad hominem attacks are employed against them to shut down debate. They are delicate *snowflakes,* but also *rabid, radical, militant,* and *angry.* A popular adage on Twitter is, "What are we angry about today?" Their boycotting of celebrities who make offensive remarks is branded *cancel culture* (or *call-out culture*), and they are accused of ruining comedy, journalism, movies, books, and video games. Those who have been affected by prejudice, and survivors of harassment and abuse, are accused of casting themselves as tragic *victims,* and it is said that their *victim mentality* has created a *victimhood culture.* They are believed to be a culture of people who are offended by everything.

But we have always been offended.

Historically, people (usually men) were obliged to defend their honor by answering insults and affronts, often through the use of violence.[2] This kind of society was known as a "culture of honor." Samuel Johnson, the author of the first dictionary of the English language, said to his biographer James Boswell in 1783, "A man may shoot the man who invades his character, as he may shoot him who attempts to break into his house."[3] Ideas about what is considered to be offensive language change, sometimes dramatically, across culture, context, and time. Calling someone a *fopdoodle* or a *cumberworld* would probably be laughed at today, although in the past, besmirching someone's good name offended their honor, and the offender might be challenged to a duel. Boswell's son, Sir Alexander Boswell, would die in 1822 in such a duel with politician James Stewart after he called him a "bully", a "coward", a "dastard", and a "sulky poltroon." Stewart was cleared of murder charges, and the verdict of acquittal was received with loud cheers.[4]

Ideas about what is an appropriate response to offensive language also change across culture, context, and time. The New Testament of the Bible advocates nonviolence in the face of personal insult, "If anyone slaps you on the right cheek, turn to them the other cheek also" (Matthew 5:38–40). But God didn't always turn the other cheek. In the Old Testament it is said, "He that blasphemeth the name of the LORD, he shall surely be put to death, and all the congregation shall certainly stone him: as well the stranger, as he that is born in the land, when he blasphemeth the name of the LORD, shall be put to death" (Leviticus 24:16). There were often harsh punishments for such heretics. Until the end of the seventeenth century, blasphemy was punishable in Britain by burning or hanging. *God, Lord, Jesus, Christ, hell*, and *damn* were banned in print, cinema, television, and radio until the twentieth century, when blasphemy was replaced in offensiveness by obscene words relating to sex.[5]

Today, religious profanity has lost its punch in English, although the devout may still take offense at the use of language that they perceive as disrespectful toward their religion. However, some Islamic countries still impose severe punishments for committing blasphemy. In Pakistan, blaspheming or desecrating the Qur'an can receive life imprisonment, while the death penalty is prescribed for insulting the prophet Muhammad.[6] In February 1989, Salman Rushdie's novel *The Satanic Verses* was viewed as an insult toward Islam by Iranian clerical leader Ayatollah Khomeini, who issued a fatwa calling for the British author's death.[7] In January 2015, the offices of the French satirical newspaper *Charlie Hebdo* were attacked because the newspaper published cartoons depicting Muhammad. The attackers killed 12 people and injured 11, in their mission to "avenge the prophet."[8]

These are extreme cases of oppression, but they illustrate the importance of freedom of speech in Western society. However, in the United States, the First Amendment, which includes the right to free speech, is not absolute. Certain offensive words can be prohibited, such as *fighting words*, that is, vilifying language that is intended to incite hatred or violence against an individual or group of people. Language can be violent, and it can lead to violence.[9] Today, taboos against blasphemy and swearing have relaxed and been replaced by social sanctions against language that shows prejudice against race, gender and sex, sexual orientation, appearance, disability, and religious affiliation. These kinds of offensive language criticize an immutable aspect of people, such as their age, sexuality, or the color of their skin. Nowadays, most people would agree that racist language is especially taboo and offensive.[10] Language that attacks an individual or group on the basis of race, ethnicity, or nationality can constitute *hate speech*, which may have repercussions under criminal or civil law.

Unfortunately, the discussion of offensive language is often condemned as an *attack on free speech*. It is hyperbolized as *silencing, suppression,* and *censorship*. Social justice activists are branded the *language police* while polite, preferred, and inclusive terms are derided as *doublespeak, euphemisms,* or *political correctness*. Some people bemoan that they must tiptoe around certain hot button topics. They complain that so many words are offensive they *can't not offend*. They believe that language is such a minefield they *Can't say anything these days*. Of course, free speech is a vital part of a free society. The discussion of offensive language is not waging war on free speech, but is exercising the right to free speech. This book is not about censoring language. It does not prescribe language or tell people how to speak. It is a catalog of offensive language in Anglophone (predominately

English-speaking) countries, but is not intended to be a resource on "how to offend." It does not provide ammunition to bigots, but instead describes the language of bigotry and bias. This book identifies language that is considered to be offensive in order to answer the questions: "*What* is offensive?" and "*Why* is that offensive?"

This book unpacks the meaning and usage of offensive language by exploring various semantic phenomena. (*Semantics* is a fancy linguistics term that means "meaning.") Meaning is not always in the dictionary. Dictionary definitions can be obscure, circular, and outdated, while they do not always keep up with slang, but they can be a useful starting point, especially to uncover a word's historical meaning. Language reflects social attitudes, beliefs, and values at a given point in time, but it can also reflect those of the societies that came before us. So, we often travel back to the etymology, to the original and former meanings of a word, to trace its history, which can reveal historical baggage that it can carry to this day. But meaning is not permanent, unchanging, or stable. Meaning is fluid. It shifts, changes, and evolves. Some words that were not offensive can develop offensive meanings. A popular defense to justify the use of an offensive word is that it *didn't used to be offensive*, although it has become offensive over time. This historical process is known as *pejoration*. This occurs when a word with a neutral or positive sense develops negative connotations and becomes taboo. Taboos are powerful influencers of language, and a tabooed word often drops out of usage.

Once again, there is a paradox. We stop using tabooed words because we generally don't want to offend. Some words are thought of as "dirty" and are dropped simply because they resemble offensive words. The animal name *donkey* has replaced *ass*, *rooster* is preferred over *cock*, while *rabbit* has supplanted *coney* (formerly pronounced similar to *cunny* which was a synonym of *cunt*).[11] The negative sense of a word usually supersedes its positive sense. Ayds appetite-suppressant candy was popular in the 1980s, until the public awareness of AIDS as a life-threatening condition sullied the brand's name and led the company to withdraw the product from the market. At the time of writing, the emergence of COVID-19, also known as the Coronavirus, was falsely linked by some to the Mexican beer Corona, because of the similarity of the two names. Even the word that denotes phonological similarity, *homophone* (used for words with different meanings that sound the same, like *pair* and *pear*), has been tarnished because it sounds similar to the word *homosexual*, even though the words have nothing to do with each other beyond their prefix *homo-*. In 2014, an English teacher who penned a blog post about homophones was fired when he was accused of creating the perception that the school promoted a gay agenda.[12] Occasionally, a word actually improves in its meaning or it loses its offensiveness. For example, in Middle English *nice* meant "foolish," "silly," or "simple" before it developed favorable connotations in the 1800s to mean "kind" and "friendly."[13] This historical process is known as *amelioration*, but it is far more rare.

The emergence of *euphemisms*, words substituted for others that are considered unpleasant or embarrassing, can be motivated by a desire to not offend. However, sometimes these good intentions can backfire. The so-called "euphemism treadmill" is when a word becomes pejorative because of its reference to offensive concepts, and so a polite word is introduced to replace it.[14] As an example, *latrine* became *water closet*, which became *toilet*, which became *bathroom*, which became *restroom*. All related words will eventually stigmatize because the very subject matter is taboo. Over time, a euphemism becomes tainted by association and is also replaced. In the well-meaning search to find a stigma-free term, this cycle repeats itself. No matter how benign the euphemism appears at first, it will become offensive and be replaced by another word that in due course will also undergo the same process. However, relabeling a concept does not necessarily reduce its stigma or improve people's attitudes. As we will see, the euphemism treadmill is common in the areas of language related to race and ethnicity, disability, and disease. The fluid nature of offensive language can lead some people to think this topic is a linguistic minefield. A common lament is, *I can't keep up with what's offensive!* But we can. At any given point there is terminology that is preferred by stakeholders, that is, the people to whom the terms refer. This book aims to favor the most preferred and inclusive terms at this time, to explain which terms have been chosen and why, and also to provide additional acceptable ones.

There are many different types of offensive language, which are of varying degrees of offensiveness. Some language is not intended to be offensive, but may be interpreted as offensive. Just because someone argues they didn't mean to be offensive by what they said, or insists that what they said wasn't offensive, doesn't mean it wasn't construed as offensive by the listener. This interpretation is based on the listener's personal circumstances and experiences, which may not be shared with or understood by the speaker. Language that can be interpreted as covertly racist, sexist, ableist, and so on, is colloquially described as *hidden*, *everyday*, *subtle*, or *casual*. This kind of offensive language includes outdated labels, microaggressions, stereotypes, preconceived beliefs, assumptions, tropes, and myths that may be accidentally or unintentionally insulting. Some language is intended to be offensive. Overtly or explicitly derogatory language includes insults, slurs, name-calling, abusive epithets, and terms of abuse. Unlike euphemisms that intend to protect, offensive language is dysphemistic, and is meant to hurt. Of course there are exceptions, and some insults are instead intended as playful banter, good-humored teasing, or joking. On the other hand, jokes can also disguise disparaging attitudes. A seemingly gentle phrase such as *Bless your heart* can be a genuine expression of sympathy, or wielded as cutting sarcasm. Many of the terms in this book have multiple meanings, which are dependent on context.

Reclamation demonstrates the importance of context in language, and shows that meaning is not singular, static, or universal. Reclaiming is a process by which controversial terms that were previously used to offend are appropriated by the discriminated group. In an effort to reshape language and attitudes, insults are rejected as stigmatizing labels previously imposed on the group, but are then taken back and used by the people they had been used against. For example, the LGBTQ community reclaimed *gay*, while Australian Aboriginal people use *Abo*, *boong*, or *blackfella* among themselves. The offensive word is recast with a positive meaning within the group, as an expression of solidarity and pride in one's identity. These terms are used in defiance, and often employed in an ironic or satirical way. This can be empowering for some people, although others may continue to have strong negative associations to these words. Reclaimed words are also context-dependent, continuing to retain their negative connotations when used outside of the community that seeks to retain them.[15] While it may be appropriate for members of this *in-group* to reclaim a word due to personal experiences that allow them to understand when, why, and how to use it, and the implications of using it the wrong way, it may not be appropriate for the *out-group* to use, that is, people outside of the group.

Over the past century, progress has been made toward obtaining human rights and equality for various groups, in particular, civil rights, women's rights, disability rights, and LGBTQ rights. Many of these advances are reflected in our language and the way we now talk about these groups of people. These improvements have been hard won, although the struggle for social justice is not over yet. Modern language continues to reveal discriminatory attitudes and beliefs. This book explores offensive language in our own words, both past and present; the exclusive language that offends and hurts, and the preferred terms that are inclusive of the people to whom they refer. This book is about understanding and empathizing with the life experiences and challenges of other people, through the lens of language. It is also about recognizing prejudice in language, both against other people and ourselves, because we will all be affected by prejudice.

1 I'm Not a Racist, But . . .

In 1963, the poet Ali Cobby Eckermann was born in Adelaide, Australia. An indigenous woman of Yankunytjatjara and Kokatha descent, she was adopted as a baby.[1] But just like her mother and grandmother before her, Eckermann had been stolen from her birth family. Known as the Stolen Generations, at least 100,000 children with multiracial backgrounds were forcibly removed from their families and communities between 1910 and 1970.[2] At the time, it was believed that indigenous Australians were a *dying race*, although the *half castes* could still be rescued. Also branded *half-breeds*, *crossbreeds*, *quadroons*, or *octoroons*, terms that are now highly offensive, these children were adopted into new families or forced into institutions to assimilate them into Anglo-Australian culture. Dr. Cecil Cook, the "Chief Protector of Aborigines" in the Northern Territory, argued, "Everything necessary must be done to convert the half-caste into a white citizen."[3] Today, these policies are perceived as a type of *institutional racism*, systemic discrimination against certain groups of people through biased laws or social practices. For many years, Eckermann searched for her birth mother, but didn't find her until she was 34 years old. Most of the institutions failed to keep records of the children's parentage, so many of the Stolen Children were never reunited with their birth families.

There are many definitions of racism, ranging from narrow to broad interpretations. We return to the issue of defining racism throughout this chapter, because the task is not as simple as it might seem at first. As a working definition to begin with, racism can be described as discrimination or prejudice against a group of people based on their ethnicity, nationality, or "race".[4] Racism often involves the assumption that people's race determines who they are, and also implies a belief in the superiority of one race and the inferiority of another or others. However, the root term *race* itself is problematic. *Race* originally referred to speakers of a common language, and was later used to denote national affiliation. By the seventeenth century, race referred to physical traits, such as skin color, hair type, and skeletal anatomy.[5] This physical classification led to the theory that there are three major races of humankind: Caucasoid, Negroid, and Mongoloid. Modern scientists argue that race is a social construct without biological meaning, because all living humans belong to the same species, *Homo sapiens*.[6] Even though there is no scientific basis for the theories or ideologies of *race*, it remains a proxy or general term for categorization, although it is often replaced by less emotionally charged terms such as *people(s)*, *population*, *ethnic group*, or *community*. Even if there is no such thing as race, people often act as if there is, and racism describes acts of prejudice against groups of people. Racism usually occurs when different groups of people come into contact with each other, often as a result of immigration, forced migration, or colonialism.

Colonialism has taken its toll on all indigenous people.[7] Colonizers, often celebrated as *pioneers, pilgrims, explorers,* or *settlers,* or framed negatively as *invaders,* drove people off their traditional lands, introducing disease and imposing their culture, religion, and language on the indigenous people. Indigenous children were forced into Missions (Australia), Native Schools (New Zealand), or Residential or Boarding Schools (Canada and the United States), which had the primary task of assimilating them into the dominant culture, but where mistreatment and abuses often took place. Some names for indigenous people are now considered to be offensive because they were imposed on them and they have colonial connections. During his fifteenth-century exploration of the New World, Italian explorer Christopher Columbus believed he had reached the coast of China or Japan (which was then known as the "Indies"), so he incorrectly named the indigenous people *una hente Indios*, meaning "people of the Indies" or "Indians."[8] *American Indian* became a popular term for indigenous people in both the United States and Canada, although today, many perceive it to be offensive because it is a malapropism (a wrong name), and was bestowed upon the indigenous people rather than one they gave to themselves. *Injun*, a now dated abbreviation of American Indian, is also derogatory, because it mimics the indigenous people's pronunciation of "Indian," and it has colonial connotations. Columbus was credited with the "discovery" of America, and awarded a national holiday in October, the month of his arrival in 1492. In recent years, some US cities and states refuse to observe Columbus Day, instead celebrating the people who arrived in the country first, with Indigenous Peoples Day or Native American Day.

As original inhabitants of the land, *Native American* became one of the preferred terms for indigenous people. For some stakeholders, *Native* can also be considered offensive, given the pejorative colonial usage of "natives," as in the infamous line spoken by British colonizers, "The natives are restless."[9] Native is also related to other offensive terms that imply that indigenous people are backward, ignorant, and uncivilized, such as *primitives*, *barbarians*, *brutes*, and *savages*. This conception of non-Western people as *savage* and *native* in the colonial era led to the phenomenon of "human zoos" in which people of Asian and African descent and indigenous people were kidnapped by *man-hunters*, labeled as *exotic specimens*, and exhibited in cages with monkeys or kept in mock villages for the entertainment of Western people.[10] (See also Chapter 6.) The last human zoo was as recent as 1958, featuring "natives" from the Congo who were exhibited at the Brussels World Fair. Ironically, *Native* has since been appropriated by some white people, *nativists* who claim precedence for being native-born or established in a particular US state, as opposed to being an immigrant, or a *transplant*, someone who has relocated interstate. In Colorado, Florida, and other US states where this migration is common, "NATIVE" is a popular bumper sticker that is designed to look like a state license plate.

For some stakeholders, the names *American Indians* and *Native Americans* also pose a problem because America was so named, not for the indigenous people who had lived there for thousands

of years, but after the fifteenth-century Italian explorer Amerigo
Vespucci.[11] In light of the problems with these labels, many prefer
a name that is based on a shared language, such as the Algonquin-
speaking people, or based on their geographic region, such as the
Pueblo-dwelling people. Some older names can be problematic,
such as *Eskimo* that is still commonly used to refer to the native
people of Alaska and other Arctic regions. The name is now
considered to be derogatory because non-native colonizers
bestowed it on them, and also the folk belief arose that Eskimo
meant "eater of raw meat," which became associated with barbar-
ism and violence. The name is now believed to be an indigenous
word referring to snowshoes, but the damage has been done.[12]
Depending on where they live, stakeholders now prefer to be
called *Inuit*, *Yupik*, or by their nationality. In general, as those
who lived in these places before the Europeans arrived, some
people prefer the self-identifying terms *native*, *indigenous*, *first
nations*, *first people*, or *original people*. In Australia, *Aborigine* has
dropped out of usage, because it has racist connotations from
Australia's colonial past; so stakeholders prefer the adjective
Aboriginal, *indigenous*, or *first people*, or the specific name of
their people.

Like the Stolen Generations of Aboriginal people in Australia,
other multicultural societies stigmatized the offspring of interracial relationships. Multiracial children were often the result of
white men sexually exploiting indigenous or enslaved women.
Enslaved women in the Southern United States were deemed to
be the "property" of their slaveholders and were often victims of
sexual abuse by these people, especially in their attempts to produce more enslaved people. In this book, *enslaved people* is used
because it is becoming the preferred term to *slave*, which is seen as
a nameless, passive word that strips these people of their humanity. Similarly, the words *enslavement* and *slaving* are often preferred to the dehumanizing *slavery*. Some apologists conflate
servitude with *slavery*, and *servant* with *slave*, in an attempt to
downplay the practice. However, the former terms imply free will,

while the latter imply submission, oppression, and control. Others make the valid point that *enslaved person* is presentist and may be thought to minimize the horrific experiences of these people, whereas *slavery* is explicit and precise because the practice treated humans as pieces of property to be bought, sold, and abused at will.[13]

Despite its prevalence in the past, interracial sex was tabooed. (It still is socially prohibited for many people today.) Known by the disapproving term *miscegenation*, it was believed to be unnatural and harmful. The Racial Integrity Act of 1924 was a ban placed on interracial marriage, which was a crime in many parts of the United States until the landmark *Loving v. Virginia* case in 1967.[14] Pure races, in the sense of genetically homogenous populations, do not exist in the human species, although the concept of *racial purity* was once common. Historically, there were complicated categorizations to label multiracial or biracial ancestry. A *mulatto* was a person with one black parent and one white parent, although it broadened in meaning to refer to anyone perceived as racially ambiguous. The word is possibly derived from Portuguese *mulato*, meaning "young mule," referring to the hybrid animal resulting from the mating of a donkey and a horse.[15] *Quadroon* referred to a person who was one-quarter black, an *octoroon* was a person who was one-eighth black, and *hexadecaroon* was a person who was one-sixteenth black. These terms are now highly offensive because of their historical connections to enslavement, and their classification of people on the basis of how white they were.

Racism is not only prejudice against people because of their "race," but also because of their perceived race. While some people with black heritage were light-skinned enough to *pass as white* (also known as *invisible blackness*), being classified as *black* extended to people who had even "one drop" of "black blood." In the nineteenth century, the United States enforced the *one-drop rule*; the assertion that any person with even one ancestor of African descent was considered to be black or *Negroid* in historical terms.[16] Before the Civil Rights movement of the 1950s and 1960s, people racialized and legally defined as *black* had lower social status and lost certain civil rights, including the right to citizenship and the right to vote. At the time, there was the simplistic belief that white people had "white blood," while black people had "black blood." Personality traits were even assigned to blood; white blood was believed to be somehow superior, while black blood was deemed inferior and made a person animalistic, primitive, and savage. Until 1950 there were bans on interracial blood transfusions and the Red Cross segregated "Negro blood."[17]

Along with racial classifications, categories of people were assigned colors as arbitrary racial identifiers. Caucasoid people were described as having a *white* skin tone, Negroid people were said to be *black* or *brown* skinned, and Mongoloid people were labeled as being *yellow* skinned. In 1758, Swedish biologist and taxonomer Carl Linneaus was the first to label Asian people as *luridus*, meaning "lurid," "sallow," or "pale yellow."[18] In reference to Asian people, *yellow* has a long history of being used in a derogatory way. The *Yellow Peril*, *Yellow Terror*, and *Yellow Spectre*, were slogans of nineteenth-century propaganda that promoted the idea that Asian immigrants posed a threat to the Western world. (See also Chapter 4.) The modern slang term *yellow fever* refers to men who fetishize Asian women (make them an object of sexual attention or activity). Some stakeholders have tried to reclaim the word in positive usages, such as the Yellow Power movement of the 1960s, and the name of the popular Japanese band *Yellow Monkey*. The 2018 movie *Crazy Rich Asians* features a Mandarin-language cover of the Coldplay song "Yellow" to recast *yellow* as an empowering word. However, in reference to Asian people, *yellow* often has racist connotations because of its negative usage in the past.

Linnaeus also described indigenous North American people as *rufus*, meaning "reddish, ruddy." *Red skin* was later a form of self-identification for some indigenous people, such as the Mississippi Valley French *Peau Rouge* ("red skin") people and the Illinois *e. rante.wiroki.ta*, the name meaning, "person with red skin."[19] By the twentieth century, the name became popular as an "Indian" sports mascot, most notably for the football team the Washington Redskins. However, the term is now considered to be dated and offensive because of its colonial connections. In an attempt to cancel the trademarks held by the team in 2014, it was successfully proven during trial that *Redskin* is now associated with contempt, condescension, and sentimental notions of the "noble savage."[20] Many stakeholders consider *Redskin* to be disparaging, and it has been referred to as *the R-word*. As a mark of respect, several college teams that used the name changed it voluntarily, such as the University of Utah Redskins who became the Utah Utes in 1972; the Washington Redskins, as of July 2020, have been temporarily named the "Washington Football Team."

Other phrases related to indigenous Americans that are considered to be culturally insensitive include *Indian-giver, Indian summer, lowest man on the totem pole, they're on the warpath, circle the wagons,* and *hold down the fort,* because of their colonial connotations. It is also considered offensive for non-Native people to appropriate Native terms, such as *pow-wow* and *rain dance,* because their usage out of context trivializes these traditions. Racism and sexism intersect with the derogatory term *squaw,* which is often believed to be an indigenous word for an indigenous woman, although English colonists coined the word. The term is further controversial because it acquired a false etymology that *squaw* meant "female genitalia."[21] Despite its offensiveness, Squaw is still used in many place names around the United States.

Typically, red and yellow are not acceptable color names for people, although *white* and *black* are often considered to be acceptable, which is why they are used here as general terms. However, *black* was considered to be derogatory until quite recently when it was reclaimed as a term of racial pride during the Civil Rights movement in the United States. Racist language is in a constant state of flux. It seems almost inconceivable nowadays, but *colored* and *darky* (or *darkie*) were once considered to be mild or even polite terms, although they became derogatory through negative connotations and usage.[22] *Colored* is outdated and offensive today, given its strong association with the Jim Crow era of racial segregation (1877 to mid-1960s), and the ubiquity of the word in public signs that segregated *white* from non-white or *colored* people. It must be noted that *colored* is still acceptable in some in-group usage only, especially in older references and names such as the National Association for the Advancement of Colored People (NAACP), an organization founded in 1909.

The *white/non-white* binary paradigm is problematic because it presents white people as colorless, the norm, first, superior, and as some kind of standard against which all other kinds of people are compared. *Non-white* people are then rendered as *colored, secondary, inferior*, and pitted as the *other*. Color labels dichotomize human identity and reduce people to a color, which has negative connotations. As labels for people, *black, brown, dark, red, yellow* and *colored* are all terms that are or have been stigmatized, although *white* has never been stigmatized. The legacy of racism is reflected in the common metaphor *white is good, black is bad*, in which synonyms for white usually have positive connotations (e.g., *pure, clean, noble*), while black and dark-related sayings frequently have negative connotations; for example, *blacklist, black market*, and *black sheep*, to *darken one's door* or to *blacken someone's reputation*.[23] Similarly, *Caucasoid* and *Caucasian*, as synonyms for *white person* or *person of European ancestry* are not stigmatized terms and are still in use, meanwhile *Mongoloid* (see also Chapter 5) and *Negroid* are now considered to be highly offensive and have mostly dropped out of usage.

Negroid came from the word *negro*, which was borrowed from Spanish and is derived from the Latin *niger*, simply meaning "black."[24] From the time of its earliest usage in the English language in the eighteenth century, *Negro* was a polite and respectful proper term for African Americans and used as a self-identifying label. Negro was the term used by Dr. Martin Luther King Jr. in his celebrated "I Have A Dream" speech given in 1963. But it went out of use very quickly after Dr. King's death in 1968, when it became associated with white-imposed attitudes and was superseded by the use of *black*, the preferred term of the Black Power movement. Today, Negro is mostly considered to be derogatory, along with the gender-specific *Negress* that is considered both racist and sexist (compare *Jewess*, see Chapter 4). Younger generations consider the word to be very offensive because they don't know its history, and they often think it is the *N-word*. However, Negro is still acceptable in a historical context and is used in the names of some older organizations, such as the United Negro College Fund. The United States Census Bureau included *Negro* as a form of self-identification on the 2010 Census alongside *Black* and *African American* because some older citizens still identified with the term.[25]

As we can see, many groups have had names imposed on them by outside groups, which have since been rejected in favor of self-identifying labels that reflect their identity. There are several modern terms that are considered to be acceptable by the groups to whom they refer, although the appropriateness of these labels changes according to individual factors such as age, geographical location, and background, and who uses them. However, no term is without possible problems and limitations. Some stakeholders prefer the term *person/people of color* (often abbreviated to "POC"), and the corresponding gender-specific *women of color* and *men of color*, whereas others disfavor the terms because they resemble the now offensive *colored people*. It may be that *people of color* is acceptable because it uses person-first language, highlighting their humanity over their skin-color. (See also Chapter 5.) These pan-racial terms are inclusive in that they encompass all people who are not white, but they still represent a *white/non-white* binary. Furthermore, the terms cover such disparate groups they can be perceived to erase an individual's identity. For example, some *people of color* might prefer instead to identify specifically by their skin color, ethnicity, or nationality. In the United States, some stakeholders prefer the term *African American*, which highlights their heritage. However, others eschew the term because it perpetuates the myth that all black American people come from Africa, or implies that they are immigrants who were born in Africa. *Black* is the preferred self-identifying label for many stakeholders, and it is often capitalized as *Black* in writing. (In this book, proper nouns regarding ethnicity or origin are capitalized, such as African American, while broad descriptions of skin color appear in lowercase letters, in line with Associated Press style guidelines.) Some stakeholders avoid the term *black* because it is perceived as reductive, unrepresentative, or they consider it to be a misnomer, due to the fact that "black people" have a brown skin color.

From *niger* we derived *black*, an empowering, self-identifying label for many stakeholders, but we also acquired the slur *nigger*. The word dates back to the sixteenth century and was offensive from its earliest usage.[26] Undoubtedly, *nigger* is the most offensive word in the English language today. It is deeply offensive in all Anglophone countries, but particularly so in the United States, where the word is synonymous with the country's history of institutional and social racism, through enslavement, segregation, lynching, and other acts of violence and discrimination against black people. *Nigger* is a symbol of oppression and violence, and the word expresses extreme hostility and contempt. It is so opprobrious nowadays that some people refuse to write or utter it, but instead use the euphemism *the N-word*, or censor the word as *n—* or *n**ger*. In the early twentieth century, the word was used as a kitschy brand name for various commercial products, but today, these products have all rebranded. *Nigger Hair Smoking Tobacco* became Bigger Hair Smoking Tobacco, while *Nigger Candy* became Chocolate Babies. (*Darkie Toothpaste* also became Darlie Toothpaste.) Lakes, creeks, and points that once had names such as *Niggerhead* and *Nigger Creek* have since been changed. The taboo against the word is so strong today that it has led to the pejoration of homophones that resemble *nigger*, such as *snigger*, *denigrate*, and *niggardly*, even though they are not etymologically related at all.

Like the self-identifying label *black*, *nigger* has been reclaimed in recent decades as a positive, empowering term by some stakeholders. However, there are many important caveats for its acceptable usage, the chief among these being that the word is *only* acceptable when used by people from the in-group. When used by the in-group, the word can have many different positive meanings. It can be used in a jocular way as part of banter or good-humored teasing. It can be used to show familiarity and solidarity, and also to express a shared history and values. The reclaimed word is usually spelled and pronounced differently as *nigga* or *niggah*, in order to clearly differentiate it from *nigger* and its historical baggage. This version of the word is popularly used in hip-hop and rap music, such as the name of the 1980–1990s hip hop group, N.W.A. ("Niggaz Wit Attitudes"). Of course, it can also be used as an insult within the inside group. But even within the black community the word can be perceived as offensive in every context. Some black people consider it to be a word that should never be said or written. The word is never acceptable when used by people from an outside group.

Despite the strong social taboo against the word, *nigger* is the most commonly used racial slur during hate crimes and in hate speech. There are several infamous cases of its usage in public. In 2006, Michael Richards, better known as Cosmo Kramer of *Seinfeld* fame, was performing a stand-up comedy show at the Laugh Factory in Hollywood, California, when a group of people arrived late and ordered drinks. The latecomers interrupted his show, so Richards commented, "Look at the stupid Mexicans and blacks being loud up there."[27] Offended by the remark, one of the party replied, "My friend doesn't think you're funny," to which Richards flipped him off and said, "Fuck you, nigger." He then unleashed an outburst of personal attacks during which he shouted repeatedly, "He's a nigger!" He also referred to racial segregation and lynching, saying "Shut up! Fifty years ago, we'd have you upside-down and impaled with a fork." A member of the audience captured the two-minute tirade on video and went public with the recording. Richards later apologized on the *Late Show with David Letterman*, although his apology seemed insincere when he referred to his hecklers as *Afro-Americans*, which is an outdated precursor to *African American*.[28] Richards claimed he was "not a racist, but" he had lost his temper when trying to defuse the heckling. (Saying, *I'm not a racist, but* ... to precede racist language is a commonly used tactic to excuse or deny modern racist behavior.) As a result of the incident, the New York City Council banned the use of the word *nigger*, although the ban is symbolic because it carries no weight in law and there is no penalty for its usage.[29]

In 2013, celebrity chef Paula Deen was also embroiled in a racist scandal in which a former employee accused her of various acts of racism. The complainant was engaged to the celebrity's brother, and reported that Deen said she wanted a "true Southern plantation-style wedding" for the couple.[30] She added, "What I would really like is a bunch of little niggers to wear long-sleeve white shirts, black shorts and black ties, you know in the Shirley Temple days, they used to tap dance around." When asked in a deposition if she had used the slur, Deen replied, "Yes, of course." As a result of this negative publicity, she lost her TV show with the Food Network, and her endorsements with Kmart, Sears, and Walmart.[31] Deen was also criticized for other racist behavior, such as forcing a black female employee to dress like Aunt Jemima, the iconic symbol of the brand of pancake mix, syrup, and other breakfast foods. This was offensive, because Aunt Jemima was originally a stereotypical black caricature that appeared in minstrel shows.

Minstrel shows were a form of entertainment in the United States during the nineteenth century. They consisted of comedy sketches, dancing, variety acts, and music performances, ostensibly influenced by black African culture. Minstrel shows were performed by white people, such as the well-known singer and actor Al Jolson (who is best known for his rendition of the song "My Mammy"). Minstrels wore make-up called *blackface* to play caricatures of black people. Early performers used burnt cork and later greasepaint or shoe polish to blacken their faces and exaggerate their lips. In their time, minstrel shows were extremely popular, including among black people.[32] Today, wearing blackface is considered to be highly offensive, because it is a symbolic form of racism. In 1993, actor Ted Danson wore blackface and used the word *nigger* a dozen times during his routine at a Friar's

Club comedy roast in honor of his then girlfriend Whoopi Goldberg.[33] During the performance, some audience members hid their faces in their hands, while others left in protest. Paula Deen was further criticized when a photo emerged on Twitter of her dressed as Lucille Ball from the 1950s TV comedy show *I Love Lucy*, while her son Bobby Deen was dressed in brownface as the character Ricky Ricardo, played by Cuban actor Desi Arnez.

Minstrel shows are considered to be offensive today because they are perceived to ridicule African American people and reduce them to a set of racial caricatures. These unflattering stereotypes were also popularized in books, theater, songs, and movies. Some caricatures appeared on collectibles and memor-abilia, including postcards, ashtrays, souvenirs, toys, and house-hold products.[34] Common caricatures included the *sambo* or *coon* (an abbreviation of *raccoon*) character, which represented black people as variously lazy, unreliable, unintelligent, inarticulate, dishonest, disrespectful, happy-go-lucky *darkies*. (*Coon* is not to be confused with *coon-ass*, an insult toward a person of Cajun ethnicity.) The *pickaninny* was the racial caricature of black chil-dren. (In the United States, *niglet* is a modern racial slur for a black child, based on *piglet*, the term for a young pig. Compare *jewlet* in Chapter 4.) Black children were portrayed with bulging eyes, unkempt hair, red lips, and wide mouths, wearing ragged, torn, old, or oversized clothes, if they were not entirely nude. In many cartoon images of pickaninnies, the children were grossly sexualized. Pickaninnies were frequently shown on postcards and trinkets as "live bait" to lure alligators and crocodiles for hunting. This depiction was inspired by anecdotal events reported in American newspapers and in movies such as *Alligator Bait* (1900) and *The Gator and the Pickaninny* (1900).[35]

Another caricature was that of the lighter-skinned *tragic mulatto*. Suffering from an identity crisis and ashamed of their *mixed blood*, they struggled to find a place to belong in society because they were never fully accepted into the *white world* or the *black world*. Being *near-white*, they resented their *one drop of Negro blood* and tried to *pass as white*. The *Jezebel* caricature was a seductive, lascivious, lewd woman, who was promiscuous, and even predatory of white men. The *brute* caricature depicts black men as savage, animalistic, violent criminals; as dangerous beasts who were crazed with lust for white women. In depicting black people as unintelligent, worthless, aggressive, and inferior, these caricatures were conceived to justify enslavement, lynching, segregation, and the other brutalities and atrocities that had been committed against them.

Other enduring caricatures are argued to be "positive" stereotypes, but they are still loaded with racist connotations. The *Mammy* (an alteration of *mamma*) was an archetype maternal figure. An obese woman with a big grin and hearty laugh, she was a cook, maid, and nanny. Mammy is depicted as strong, kind, religious, superstitious, and a loyal *servant*, rather than as an enslaved woman. The male counterpart to the Mammy is the *Tom* caricature. He is a smiling, subservient cook, butler, or waiter who is also a loyal servant or part of the family, rather than an enslaved man. Tom is named after the main black character from Harriet Beecher Stowe's 1852 novel *Uncle Tom's Cabin*. The idea of *Mammies* and *Toms* arose in Antebellum America from the eighteenth century until the Civil War. Faithful and content in service to their white *masters*, these caricatures were created in defense of enslavement, although they were a nostalgic yearning for a time that had never existed.[36]

As servile and subservient terms of address during the days of enslavement and segregation, *master* and *sir* are often considered to be offensive today. *Boy* is also derogatory, because it was used to address black adult men, implying they were of a lower social status. As a slur, *boy* inspired the catchphrase of the abolitionists, "Am I not a man and a brother?" As a declaration of civil rights, "I am a man!" became a response to this cry. Today, *Uncle Tom* or *Tom* are strong insults used in-group to refer to a black person who is perceived as subservient or overly respectful toward white people. Such a person is also known as a *sell-out*, *race-traitor*, or a *white-man's nigger*. Related terms include *Oreo*, a black person who *acts white*, which is a reference to the Nabisco-brand cookie that is "black on the outside and white on the inside," while *wigger* is a slang term for a white person who appropriates Black culture and language.

Similar to the use of *Tom* as an insult, other proper nouns are used as racial slurs. The quintessential Irish nicknames *Paddy* (the diminutive form of Patrick) and *Mick* (from Michael) have been used as insults for hundreds for years, reflecting anti-Irish senti-ment in Britain, which was also imported to its colonies, notably America, Australia, and Canada. These names are inscribed with rigid ethnic characterizations and stereotypes about Irish people. (For example, the belief that all Irish people are poor, unculti-vated, or drunkards.) Stereotypical nicknames might be used as banter to express friendship, but more often they are offensive because they are dismissive, and they make cultural assumptions about an entire group of people. In Anglophone countries, min-ority groups are often "othered" with these types of slurs. *José* is a common derogatory name for Latino men, while *Guido* is a disparaging term for Italian American men. *Dago* is an older offensive term for people of Italian (and also Portuguese and Spanish) origin, which is derived from the Spanish name *Diego*.[37] (See also Chapter 4.)

Prominent historical names are also a source for terms of abuse. US President Donald Trump has repeatedly used the name *Pocahontas* as a slur for political adversary Senator Elizabeth Warren, in his claims that she lied about her self-proclaimed Cherokee and Delaware Indian ancestry. The historical figure Pocahontas was a Native American girl who was captured and held for ransom by the English in 1613.[38] She was the daughter of the powerful Powhatan, the Chief of the Powhatan tribal nation in Virginia. During her captivity, Pocahontas converted to Christianity and chose to remain with the English people, among whom she was touted proudly as a *civilized savage*. In response to Trump's comments, the Alliance for Colonial Era Tribes released a statement saying, "The name becomes a derogatory racial reference when used as an insult."[39] Senator

Warren later released the findings of a DNA test that "strongly support" her claim.[40] (Although it must be noted that heritage and cultural identity entails more than just genetics.) Trump doubled down on his insult, adding, "I can no longer call her Pocahontas because she has no Indian blood."[41]

Proper nouns for nationality and ethnicity are also wielded as slurs by members of the out-group. Using the noun form to say, *They are Blacks* (Asians, Mexicans, etc.) can seem more derogatory and harsh than the corresponding adjective, *They are Black* or *Black people*, because using the names as descriptions appears more humanizing. Nouns can also be suggestive of negative stereotypes and generalizations, for example, *Asians are . . .* or *Mexicans are . . .* In 2016, Donald Trump was criticized for tweeting the message, "Happy #CincoDeMayo The best taco bowls are made in Trump Tower Grill. I love Hispanics!", which was accompanied by a photo of him eating a taco bowl.[42] Some people found this comment to be offensive for a number of reasons, including his use of the noun *Hispanics* instead of the humanizing adjective *Hispanic people*. (Furthermore, some Latin American people identify as Latino/Latina or by the gender-neutral term Latinx, but not as Hispanic, while others identify instead as their national origin, such as Mexican or Cuban.) This comment also implied that Trump only connects Hispanic people to the stereotype that they all work in the service industry, while the comment reduced their culture to a "taco bowl." Furthermore, Trump took the opportunity of a Mexican cultural holiday to make it about him by advertising his business, while this was viewed as a clumsy attempt to ingratiate himself with a group of people that he had already alienated with previous remarks. (See below.)

Proper nouns are also transformed into racial slurs when they are coupled with an abusive modifier, such as *fucking Mexicans*, *dirty Mexicans*, or *stupid Mexicans*, the insult Michael Richards used at the Laugh Factory. When the Denver Nuggets basketball team were on a losing streak in 2001, coach Dan Issel was taunted by a ticketholder with "Issel sucks!", to which he responded, "Go drink another beer, you Mexican piece of shit."[43] Issel was suspended for four games without pay for using abusive language. The phrasing, *you Mexican* is also offensive, because it is a form of *othering*. The phrases *you people* and *those people* are exclusive and divisive, because they divide people into groups of *us* versus *them*. People like *us* are generally perceived as superior, while people like *them* are inferior. Othering is an alienating process that underlies racism in general. During his presidential campaign in 1992, Ross Perot addressed the NAACP and offended his audience when he used the phrases "you people" and "your people" when talking about communities that suffer the most from economic problems and crime.[44]

Some abbreviations of proper nouns have become terms of abuse, including *Abo* from *Aboriginal*, *Lebo* from *Lebanese*, *I-tie* or *Eyetie*, as mispronunciations of *Italian*, *Chink* from *China*, and *Paki* from *Pakistan*. (See also Chapter 4.) Conflict and war generates an *enemy* or *other* and is a rich source for the creation of racial slurs, especially those based on common names. During World War I, German soldiers called English soldiers *Tommy*, which was short for the generic name Tommy Atkins, although this was often an affectionate term that was used by the allies too. (During WWII, American soldiers were dubbed *G.I. Joe* after the comic strip by Dave Breger. Like Tommy, G.I. Joe was mostly affectionate when used by the allies, although some usage was sarcastic, implying that soldiers were mass-produced products of the government. This sentiment was somewhat fulfilled when in 1964, Hasbro debuted "G.I. Joe," a military-themed line of action toys for boys.)[45] Names for the Axis powers weren't so friendly. During World War II, *Jap* from *Japanese* became derogatory, as did *Nip*, short for *Nippon*, the Japanese name for Japan. During World Wars I and II, the British referred to German troops as *Fritz*, which was short for Friedrich. English soldiers also called German soldiers *Jerry*, the name possibly coming from the *Jerry can* gas cans, which were designed in Germany. Alternative theories suggest that *Jerry* is an abbreviation of *German*, or that the name arose because their military hats looked like a *jerry*, which was slang for a chamber pot. The name is mostly archaic but is clearly still offensive to some groups. For this reason, the 2014 BBC4 documentary, *World War One's Forgotten Photographs*, was renamed from the original title, *Tommy and Jerry's Camera.*[46]

During the Vietnam War, American soldiers referred to Viet Cong communist forces as *VC*, which are represented as *Victor Charlie* in the NATO phonetic alphabet. This gave rise to the further shortened nickname *Charlie*. During the Korean and Vietnam Wars, US soldiers referred to the inhabitants of those countries by the slurs *slant eyes* and *slopes*, in reference to appearance, and also as *gooks*. The term *gook* dates back to the Philippine–American War (1899–1902), and is possibly imitative of the sound of Asian languages to American ears.[47] Today the term has broadened to become an insult toward people of East and Southeast Asian descent. During the 2000 Presidential campaign, veteran John McCain condemned the North Vietnamese prison guards who held him captive during the war with, "I hate the gooks. I will hate them as long as I live."[48] Some commenters excused his use of the slur because he was "old school" in his thinking and had suffered as a prisoner of war. Others argued that this was not appropriate language for someone running for office. McCain said he intended the insult specifically for his captors, although today, using the term reveals negative attitudes toward all Vietnamese people, and possibly all Asian people.

As a stereotypical food of German cuisine, the Allies also referred to German people as *Cabbage eaters* or *Kraut*, short for *sauerkraut*. During this time, sauerkraut was renamed *Liberty Cabbage* and frankfurters renamed *hot dogs* in patriotism, which is reminiscent of when *French fries* were renamed *Freedom fries* by some in the United States in response to France's opposition to the proposed invasion of Iraq. Some racist insults are based on dietary stereotypes, known as *foodways*. Chinese food is often blamed for a series of vague symptoms, which have been informally linked to the ingredient monosodium glutamate (MSG). This alleged condition is colloquially named *Chinese Restaurant Syndrome*, a name that is steeped in stigma against Chinese immigrants who opened restaurants that used MSG in their cooking. Watermelon and fried chicken are mainstays in racist portrayals of black people.[49] Writing in *The Telegraph* in 2002, now UK Prime Minister Boris Johnson referred to African people as having "watermelon smiles." In kitschy memorabilia, black people were often depicted as dirty, lazy, and shiftless, as they greedily devoured slices of watermelon. Historically, watermelons were linked to the diet of enslaved people, while farming the fruit was popular among some free black people. This racist stereotype is captured in Harry C. Browne's 1916 song, "Nigger loves a watermelon. Ha! Ha! Ha!" This tune borrowed the "Turkey in the Straw" melody that is still played by some ice cream trucks in the United States.[50] *Watermelon Contest*, a two-minute silent film produced by the Edison Manufacturing Company in 1897, shows four Black men wolfing down enormous slices of watermelon. This movie is believed to have contributed to the watermelon stereotype.[51] The 1915 film *Birth of a Nation*, which is about the founding of the Ku Klux Klan, is believed to be the origin of the fried chicken stereotype, because one scene shows a black elected official eating fried chicken in a crude manner. These racist stereotypes are still common. In 2013, when asked if he would invite rival Tiger Woods to his house, professional golfer Sergio Garcia replied, "We'll have him 'round for dinner every night. We will serve fried chicken."[52]

Another racist stereotype is that groups of people supposedly "smell like" the staple foods of their culture. Asian people are stereotypically believed to *smell like rice* and have been called *rice eaters*; Indian people supposedly *smell like curry* and have been called *curry munchers*, while Italian people are said to have *garlic breath* and have been called *garlic eaters*. Korean people have been labeled *Kimchi* after the national staple dish made from fermented cabbage, the French have been called *Frogs* for their penchant for eating frog's legs, while British people have been called *Limey* from lime fruit, because citrus juice was added to sailors' rations of rum to prevent scurvy during long voyages. In the United States, Mexican people have been called various names based on popular cuisine, including *taco, nacho, jalapeño, chili-eater, pepperbelly*, and *beaner*. In 2018, when a Latino man received his espresso drink from a Starbucks in Los Angeles, the word *Beaner* was typed on the label instead of his name, Pedro, which he had provided when he ordered.[53] Mexican-American comedians George Lopez and Carlos Mencia have reclaimed *beaner* in their jokes, but it is never appropriate for someone from an outside group to do so.

Minority groups of people are often targeted with negative social stereotypes. In Australia, Aboriginal people are often stereotyped as lazy alcoholics who sniff petrol, and as *dole bludgers*, welfare cheats. Prejudice is learned, and social stereotypes can often lead to discriminatory attitudes. Some social stereotypes are said to be *positive*, because they are complimentary, such as the pervasive beliefs that *Asian people are good at math*, and that *Black people are naturally better at sports*. However, positive stereotypes can have negative effects because they are distorted truths that are fixed, limiting simplifications that do not account for variation within a group or individual differences. Social stereotypes are based on images represented in mass media, or reputations passed on by parents, friends, and society. They are concealed in popular idioms, sayings, and expressions, and hidden in racial slurs and jokes. Some social stereotypes are so deeply engrained in our culture and normalized that we are unaware they exist. For this reason they are called *unconscious biases*. These biases are resistant to change. People have the tendency to embrace anecdotes and stories that reinforce these biases, but reject experiences that contradict them. For example, the saying, *Some of my best friends are* ... (Black, Asian, Muslim, immigrants, etc.) captures this tendency to allow for some exceptions to the "rule" without changing our bias.[54]

In the United States, people of Hispanic, Latino, and especially Mexican origin are targeted by persistent social stereotypes. They are often assumed to be illegal immigrants, and are branded *aliens, illegals, border bunnies, border rats, border hoppers, wetbacks* and *Mojado* (Spanish for "wet"), the latter two terms being a reference to Mexican migrants who cross the United States border illegally via the Rio Grande river. Some stereotypes conflict with each other, such as the belief that Mexican people are lazy, which contradicts the belief that Mexican immigrants are *stealing* jobs from other Americans. The Mexican government faces an ongoing *War on drugs* against various drug-trafficking syndicates, leading to the stereotype that many Mexican immigrants are *drug lords*, *drug dealers*, and *criminals*. In 2015, Donald Trump began his US presidential bid by reinforcing this stereotype. He accused Mexico of, "Sending people that have lots of problems, and they're bringing those problems with us. They're bringing drugs. They're bringing crime. They're rapists. And some, I assume, are good people."[55]

Immigrants are often targets of racism in their adopted country. Some citizens fear that supposed "hordes of foreigners" will consume *their* resources, including housing, welfare, education, healthcare, and employment. It is argued they will *steal our jobs* and *steal our welfare*. Misinformation and panic is spread about immigrants; it is said that they are *terrorists* trying to infiltrate the country, or they are guilty of introducing infectious diseases. During waves of immigration to the United States in the nineteenth and twentieth centuries, some people called cholera *the Irish disease*; polio was named the *Italian disease*; the Chinese community was blamed for leprosy, venereal diseases, and the bubonic plague; and tuberculosis was dubbed *the Jewish disease*. (See also Chapter 5.) In more recent decades, HIV/AIDS, malaria, and Ebola have all been called *the African disease*. Immigrants are often portrayed as the bogeyman that *natives*, *old stock*, *real* and *true* citizens must fight against, while xenophobia, nationalism, and jingoism are minimized as *nativism* or *patriotism*. In the United States, an offshoot of the "NATIVE" bumper stickers and license plates mentioned above reads, "No Vacancy," communicating that immigrants and migrants are not welcome.

Negative attitudes toward immigrants have negatively affected labels relating to migration. People who have been forcibly displaced from their country due to conflict, persecution, or natural disaster, and seek resettlement in another country are called *refugees*, a term which has developed negative connotations. Stakeholders tend to eschew *refugee* as a self-identifying label, because it is perceived as dehumanizing and distancing, and it carries with it the stigma and trauma of their experiences. The media instill a sense of panic about refugees by referring to a rise in numbers of displaced people as a *refugee crisis*. Before receiving refugee status in a new country, displaced people are regarded as *asylum seekers*, a term which has similar negative connotations. (*Asylum* has acquired additional negative associations because of its use in the now dated phrases *lunatic asylum* and *insane asylum*. See Chapter 5.) In Australia, asylum seekers are often accused of being *queue jumpers* who supposedly *jump the line* to achieve resettlement ahead of refugees. The hundreds of thousands of refugees who fled Vietnam by boat or ship after the Vietnam War became known as *boat people*, which is now used as a slur for any person seeking resettlement.

Before World War II, *alien* was used to refer to migrants in the United Kingdom, but the term has since fallen out of usage. *Alien* is perceived as dehumanizing because of its more common pop culture sense of *extraterrestrial*. However, *alien* remains official terminology used by the United States government to refer to noncitizen residents. *Alien* has negative connotations because it is strongly associated with unauthorized immigration due to the common phrase *illegal alien*, while a study found that *illegal* was the most common descriptor for the word *immigrants*.[56,57] Immigrants are often assumed to be illegal, especially if they are people of color and do not speak English. *Wop*, the older slur used toward Italian Americans, is popularly believed to be an acronym for *Without Papers* or *Without Passport*, although this is a folk etymology.[58] (The origins of *wop* are uncertain, although it may be derived from Neapolitan *guappo*, roughly meaning "thug," "hooligan," or "ruffian."[59]) In 2019, New York City banned the term *illegal alien* when used "with intent to demean, humiliate or harass a person."[60]

In the United States, undocumented or unauthorized immigrants are also demonized as *border jumpers*, or simply *illegals*. Labeling people as illegals is dehumanizing and minimizes their plight, meanwhile delegitimizing their petitions for asylum. They are characterized as criminals who *sneak into the country illegally*, often in large numbers. Unauthorized immigrants are told to *Get in line* by citizens who do not understand the complexities of immigration. In 2018, Donald Trump compared unauthorized immigrants to pests, saying of the opposing Democratic party, "They don't care about crime and want illegal immigrants, no matter how bad they may be, to pour into and infest our country."[61] The Trump administration called for stronger immigration laws, resulting in thousands of families being forcibly separated at the US border. Almost 70,000 children, referred to as "Unaccompanied Alien Children," or UAC in bureaucratic jargon, have been detained in detention centers under inhumane conditions while their parents, labeled *detainees*, faced criminal prosecution or were deported separately. This is in stark contrast to the policies of the Obama administration, under which young non-citizens were instead called *Dreamers*, with reference to the "American Dream," as a positive way to describe people who met the conditions of the Dream Act (Development, Relief, and Education for Alien Minors).

In general, the euphemism treadmill has affected the language of immigration. Even the seemingly neutral terms *immigrant* and *migrant* have acquired negative connotations, tarnished through association to words such as *alien* and *illegal*. That immigrant is stigmatized is supported by the fact that it is less likely to be used to describe people from Western countries. Australian, American, British, Canadian, and other Anglophone people who live abroad tend to self-identify as *expats* or *expatriates* instead, terms that have positive connotations. Immigrant and migrant have further negative connotations that the person or group is culturally *different, unfamiliar, unknown, strange, weird,* and *foreign*.

Given their cultural differences, immigrants are often believed to pose a threat to their new country's national values and culture.

Many citizens expect that immigrants should immediately assimilate to their country's culture, and adopt their food, clothing, religion, language, and accent. If they do not, they are accused of being un-American (un-British, un-Australian, etc.). (See also Chapter 4.) Immigrants are socially conditioned to enforce this expectation within their cultural enclaves. There are several Asian-American slurs that are used in-group to describe an immigrant's degree of assimilation into American society. An *FOB* ("Fresh Off the Boat") is someone who is unassimilated and therefore considered to be *too Asian*. Someone who is *whitewashed* is culturally assimilated, but is considered to be *too white*, and is therefore accused of being a race-traitor, like the *Uncle Tom* or the *Oreo*. These terms are similar to the epithet *banana*, an Asian person who is *yellow on the outside, but white on the inside*, and *apple*, a Native American who is *red on the outside, but white on the inside*.

As we have discussed, some racial slurs dehumanize people through their allusions to food. Other slurs do so through animal metaphors. As we will discuss in Chapter 4, the insults *rats* and *vermin* have been used to dehumanize the Jews for centuries. During World War II, the Japanese were described as *yellow monkeys*, while anti-Irish sentiment led to the British referring to Irish immigrants as *Irish monkeys*. In particular, there is a very long history of the simianization of black people, that is, portraying people as non-human primates.[62] The 1854 book *Types of Mankind* was the leading text on racial differences of the day, and it included illustrations that compared black people to chimpanzees, gorillas, and orangutans.[63] Depicting humans as non-human primates is offensive because it renders them less than human. For hundreds of years, black people have been referred to as *monkeys*, *jungle monkeys*, *porch monkeys*, *chimps*, and *apes*. As discussed above, "human zoos" showcased black people in locked cages alongside monkeys, chimpanzees, and other apes. There are many contemporary examples of simianization. In 2013, Indigenous Australian footballer Adam Goodes was called an *ape* by a 13-year-old girl. He admitted this was not the first time he had been called *ape* or *monkey* on the football field.[64] The practice of throwing bananas in front of black sportspeople is a common racist provocation even today. In 2016, Pamela Taylor, a West Virginia nonprofit director, posted on Facebook, "I'm tired of seeing an ape in heels," in reference to then First Lady Michelle Obama.[65] Taylor was removed from her position for the act. In 2018, Roseanne Barr's TV comedy *Roseanne* was canceled after she tweeted, "muslim brotherhood & planet of the apes had a baby=vj," which was a reference to Valerie Jarrett, a black woman born in Iran who served as the senior adviser to former US President Barack Obama.[66] When Prince Harry and Meghan Markle's son Archie was born in May 2019, he was Britain's first royal multiracial baby. In reference to the birth, Danny Baker, a veteran broadcaster in the UK, posted to Twitter a vintage photo of a well-dressed couple holding hands with a chimpanzee wearing a bowler hat and jacket, with the caption "Royal baby leaves hospital." Baker was dismissed from his job for the tweet, although he claimed it was a joke and that he failed to see its racist connotations.

While the infamous white supremacist hate group the Ku Klux Klan has gone underground in recent decades, modern racism has escalated online. It is so prevalent that the term *Cyber racism* was coined to capture this unique phenomenon. The easy anonymity of the Internet provides a protective forum for racist language, and gives racists a collective voice. Cyber racism has experienced a surge on social media platforms, including Twitter, Facebook, 4chan, and Reddit.[67] Cyber racism typically involves the usage of slurs, while other racist content comes in the form of shareable memes that reveal hateful ideas in humorous words and imagery. For example, one meme shows a photo of black talk show host Montel Williams with the caption, "This would be racist ... if black people could read."

Internet forums are also places where racist ideology is shared, including the white nationalist, white supremacist, and Neo-Nazi websites Stormfront and Daily Stormer. These sites promote racist events, such as the Unite the Right rally (also called the

Charlottesville riots), the white supremacist rally that occurred in Charlottesville, Virginia, during August 11–12, 2017, where marchers chanted racist slogans and carried Nazi flags and semi-automatic rifles to intimidate others. This rally was reminiscent of the historical cross burnings and mass parades of the Ku Klux Klan. This online environment of normalizing extremist ideas has also emboldened public displays of racism. The day after the US presidential election in 2016, Melissa Johnson was walking out of a supermarket in San Diego when a BMW pulled up beside her and the driver shouted through the open window, "Fuck you, nigger, go back to Africa. The slave ship is opening up. Trump!"[68]

The catch cries ordering people to, *Go back to where you came from*, *Go back to your country*, *Get out of my country*, *Get out of here*, and *Go home* are variants of a racist trope that implies that members of minority groups do not belong in Anglophone countries. The phrases are blatantly anti-immigrant, although ironically, they are often said to birth citizens. In 2019, Donald Trump stated that a group of four minority congresswomen should "go back" to the countries they came from rather than "loudly viciously telling the people of the United States" how to run the government.[69] He referred to US Representative Ilhan Omar, a naturalized citizen, but also three other congresswomen who were birth citizens. Trump followed up with a comment revealing a stereotypical perspective, "Why don't they go back and help fix the totally broken and crime infested places from which they came?" This echoed his 2018 comment, "Why do we want all these people from shithole countries coming here?" with reference to African countries and Temporary Protective Status nations, especially Haiti.[70]

In the United States today, enslavement and segregation are in the past, although institutional racism against black people is still prevalent. In particular, racial profiling, police brutality, and racial inequality still exist within the criminal justice system. In 2012, 17-year-old African-American Trayvon Martin was walking home in Sanford, Florida, when resident George Zimmerman reported him to local police as "suspicious." Martin was innocent of any crime, although Zimmerman confronted the young man and fatally shot him, claiming the act was in self-defense. He was acquitted of his crime.[71] Following this incident the hashtag #BlackLivesMatter began appearing on social media, in support of Martin and in protest of institutional racism. This inspired the Black Lives Matter movement. The phrase "All Lives Matter" soon sprang up in response to the movement, ostensibly to argue that all lives matter because we are all human beings. The Black Lives Matter slogan does not mean that other lives do not matter, although All Lives Matter derails the specific conversation about racism against black people. The motto dismisses, ignores, or denies the problem of justice for black people, and effectively shuts down the debate about racism. There are similar common phrases that also stifle this discussion. When black people identify racial bias in language, they are often accused of *playing the race card*. This implies that black people invoke race as a ploy simply to win the argument at hand and gain sympathy.[72] In response to former President Barack Obama and Attorney General Eric Holder's suggestions that racism was a motivating factor in criticisms against them, former Vice President Dick Cheney responded by saying, "I think they're playing the race card."[73]

This language is implicitly racist, although another type of racist rhetoric is said to be both conscious and deliberately concealed. *Dog whistle politics* is a colloquial term for the use of coded language in the political arena that appears to have a surface meaning to the general public, but also communicates a veiled racist message.[74] The name is an analogy to a dog whistle, whose ultrasonic sound is audible to dogs, but inaudible to humans. The *dog whistle* is an implicit racial message that maintains plausible deniability that it is not racist by avoiding explicitly racist language. For example, *thug* is defined as a violent person or criminal, although in the United States it is used specifically to refer to black males, invoking the image of the dangerous "brute" caricature. Today, thug is a nominally polite way of using the N-word. In 2015, hundreds of demonstrators protested the death of 25-

year-old African American Freddie Gray, who died following an incident of police brutality. Following these so-called "Baltimore riots," CNN host Erin Burnett, who is white, asked why *thug* is not an appropriate word to describe predominately black protesters and rioters. City Councilman Carl Stokes, who is black, reacted with a blunt description of how black people interpret *thug* when it is used against them when he replied, "Come on. So calling them thugs? Just call them niggers."[75]

These racist messages, which some people may not interpret as explicitly racist, reveal that racism in language can be much more indirect and implicit than using the N-word. People have become sensitive to not appearing racist, and so new code words and phrases have emerged to camouflage racist attitudes. In contrast to the overt racism of the Jim Crow era, racism has become less socially acceptable. Post civil rights era racism has gone more underground, in what has been called *everyday, casual, hidden, subtle, color-blind,* or *new* racism. This kind of covert racism includes the use of *microaggressions.* These are common words, phrases, statements, and questions that reveal prejudice on a subtle or indirect level. For example, saying, *I'm not a racist, but* . . . as a shield to avoid being labeled a racist when expressing racist views.[76] Some people argue that the term microaggressions is imprecise and minimizing because it presents this problem as small, inconsequential, and unimportant. However, microaggressions are a widespread problem, and are often experienced by people on a regular, if not daily, basis. They can have an accumulative effect, which leads to a marginalizing experience over a lifetime. Microaggressions often reveal unconscious bias. They are not usually intended to be discriminatory or rude, so some people are unaware of exactly why they are considered to be offensive.

As an example of more covert forms of racism, in Anglophone countries, the physical differences of people belonging to minority groups are often described as *exotic*. Racism and sexism intersect when Asian women are said to be exotic because of their *almond-shaped eyes* and *jet black hair*, while black woman are considered exotic because of their dark skin color or body shape. These descriptions may be intended as compliments, although this kind of *exotification* can portray people as novelties and objectify them. The term *exotic* also has colonial connotations. Exotic was initially used to describe flora and fauna, not people, although in the West, Asian women came to be stereotyped as exotic, sub-servient, child-like, docile, and delicate flowers, as a *Lotus Flower*, or an evil, erotic *Dragon Lady*.[77]

Asian women are further stereotyped as hyper-sensual, and typecast as *mail-order brides* or prostitutes. Stanley Kubrick's film about the Vietnam War, *Full Metal Jacket*, famously exploits the *Asian hooker* stereotype when a Vietnamese woman proposi-tions herself to two American GIs with the words, "Me so horny. Me love you long time." As mentioned above, Asian women are also fetishized in what has been called *yellow fever*. Some white men objectify Asian women as sex objects. In a scene in the movie *Wedding Crashers*, Vincent Vaughn regards intercourse with an Asian woman as a rite of passage when he brags, "That was my first Asian!" Like the *Jezebel* caricature, black women are stereo-typed as hyper-sensual and portrayed as *hos*, *skeezers*, and *bitches* with an insatiable appetite for sex.[78] Describing human groups as *minorities* or *ethnic* can be offensive too, because these are mar-ginalizing labels that suggest these people are insignificant or peripheral. In Anglophone countries, classifying humans as *exo-tic*, *ethnic*, and *minority* also suggests they are the *non-white* other, and imply foreign, different, rare, and unusual. But on a global population level, these people are not exotic, ethnic, or minorities, because they belong to the majority.

Other examples of covert racism can be found in common questions and statements. For example, the remarks, *You're not really black*, *You don't act like a normal black person*, and *I don't see you as a black person* are backhanded compliments that imply that the person *acts white* in their behavior, and that this is somehow superior to *acting black*. Comments intended to be flattering such as, *But you're so well spoken*, and, *You're articulate*, omit the assumed clause ... *for a black person*, and imply by

default that black people are typically not well spoken or articulate. They suggest that *an articulate black person* is some sort of
exception or counter-stereotype. In 2007, presidential candidate
Joe Biden said of his running mate Barack Obama, "He's the first
mainstream African American who is articulate and bright and
clean and a nice looking guy."[79] By implication, Biden suggested
that African American people are usually inarticulate, unintelligent, dirty, and unattractive. The descriptions *articulate, smart,*
and *bright* are often applied to culturally assimilated immigrants
too, exceptionalizing them compared to their counterparts who
speak *accented* English and are, therefore, presumed to be
unintelligent.[80] Similarly, the description *uppity* has racial connotations, suggesting that a black person is arrogant, stuck up, and
doesn't know their place. In 2008, Republican congressman Lynn
Westmoreland described then President Barack Obama and his
wife Michelle as members of an "elitist class ... that thinks they're
uppity."[81]

Some comments and curious questions are intended to show
interest but they are offensive because they are intrusive and they
make assumptions about a person's identity. These include the
remarks, *No, you're white, You're not really Asian,* and *Why is your
daughter white?* as spoken to multiracial people who *pass as white*
or *look white.* The related questions, *Where are you from?* and
What are you? are invasive and personal, while the latter is also
dehumanizing because it implies the person is a *what* rather than
a *who.* These interrogatives force people to explain and defend
themselves to curious strangers. They also demand a succinct
answer, although human identity does not fit into neat boxes.
Where are you from? also seems to anticipate that the person came
from an *exotic* location. When the question is responded to with
an unexpected, mundane answer such as, *I'm from California,* this
may be met with surprise and challenged with, *No, where are you
really from?*

Some multiracial people report being asked the question, *Are
you mixed?* Today, *mixed* is still a common self-identifying label
preferred by some stakeholders. It appears in the terms *mixed*

blood or *mixed babies*, although some argue that mixed has negative connotations of being confused, defective, or suffering an identity crisis. Mixed can also be perceived as dehumanizing because the word is tied to animal breeding, where *mixed* dogs, cats, and horses are seen as barriers to being *pure bred*. This metaphor of impurity or contamination is revealed by other derogatory terms for multiracial people, including *mixed-breed*, *half-breed*, *cross-breed*, *mongrel*, and *mutt*. In a 2006 interview, American rapper Kanye West referred to multiracial women as *mutts* when he was quoted as saying, "Me and most of my friends like mutts a lot. Yeah, in the hood they call 'em mutts."[82]

Another common example of covert racism is mislabeling a person's nationality. For example, assuming all people of Asian descent are *Chinese* because the speaker is most familiar with China and otherwise unfamiliar with Asian geography. Alternatively, indiscriminately labeling people as *Asian* instead of identifying them by their specific country of origin can also be considered offensive. Many stakeholders self-identify as Asian, although some believe that the term lumps together as a single identity diverse groups of people with cultural, political, and social differences. *Asian* also has different meanings in different countries. In Australia, *Asian* refers to people from East Asia and Southeast Asia, including Korean, Indonesian, Malaysian, Vietnamese, Japanese, Chinese, and Cambodian people. But in the United Kingdom, *Asian* is more commonly associated with people of South Asian origin, particularly people of Indian, Pakistani, Bangladeshi, and Sri Lankan ancestry. Historically, people of East and Southeast Asian descent were called *Orientals*. When referring to people, this term is now dated and has negative connotations of colonialism, harking back to a time when Asian people were perceived as subordinate and "exotic". (Although the word is still used to describe objects, such as *oriental furniture* and *oriental rugs*.)

Indiscriminate labeling is related to problems with cross-racial identification, having difficulty distinguishing between individuals within a different race. This is known as the *other-race effect* and is caused by the lack of meaningful exposure to people of other racial groups.[83] The belief that all people belonging to one race are identical in appearance is exemplified by the phrases, *all Asians* (Mexican, black people, etc.) *look the same* and *they all look alike to me*. During the time of minstrel shows, Ernest Hogan had a hit in 1896 with the song, "All Coons Look Alike To Me." These statements deny and dismiss the experiences and expression of individuals within a race. In 2014, actor Samuel L. Jackson was offended when a TV entertainment reporter confused him with actor Laurence Fishburne. He replied, "We may all be black and famous, but we don't all look alike."[84] The other-race effect can also have serious social and legal repercussions. In 2015, a white New York City police officer tackled James Blake, the retired tennis star, and arrested him in a case of mistaken identity, because he mistook him for another black man who was suspected of credit card fraud.[85]

In contrast to the explicitly racist belief that all people of one group look the same, some harbor the implicitly racist attitude that they are *color-blind*. A common assertion is, *I don't see color*. *Colorblindness* is often a well-meaning attempt to be perceived as non-racist and inclusive. People who use this phrase mean that they *see past* a person's skin color to focus on the individual. However, *not seeing color* can be offensive, because it is not acknowledging the identity and heritage of people. It is said to *erase* them and to render them *invisible*. The *Asian Pride* and *Black Pride* movements were created to celebrate the culture and heritage of these groups and to increase their visibility. The term *White Pride* arose as a response to these movements; however, it is not an equivalent term. Advocates argue that having pride in being white is valid because of the existence of minority pride groups, although these movements were a reaction to the dominant culture and ideologies of white people in the West, who have not experienced prejudice based on the color of their skin. Minority pride groups exist to overcome their history of oppression and inequality and to address their continued struggles. They are meant to be empowering and inspiring to marginalized groups.

Conversely, White Pride is antagonistic to these groups and is synonymous with historical racism. White Pride has now become the motto of groups that preach white solidarity and modern racism, such as neo-Nazi, white separatist, white nationalist, and white supremacist organizations.

Some white people perceive the discussion about racism as a personal attack. The very existence of modern racism is minimized, dismissed, and even denied, while it is often claimed that we live in a *post-racial society*. This resistance to acknowledging and challenging racism has been called *white fragility*. White fragility is characterized by anger, fear, denial, guilt, argumentation, silence, and the use of other defensive moves by white people when they are challenged about their racism.[86] Similar to the reaction toward the Black Power and Asian Power movements, the empowerment of minority groups has been interpreted as a threat to the social privileges of white people. This has led to a backlash. The "It's okay to be white" campaign was launched in 2017 via the online chat space 4chan.[87] This slogan soon appeared on posters and stickers in city streets and on college campuses across the United States, Canada, Australia, New Zealand, and the United Kingdom. The phrase reveals the guilt of white fragility, while it has also been interpreted as covertly racist in tone. Saying *it's okay to be white* therefore implies that it is not okay to be *non-white*. The motto is further divisive and vilifying, because the slogan was adopted by neo-Nazi and white supremacist groups.

Minority groups standing up for their civil rights and equity, and the push back against racism, have been construed as *anti-white racism*. This alleged change of direction of racism, in which some white people see themselves as the victims, is often labeled as *reverse racism*. (Affirmative action has often been branded as *reverse discrimination*.) Technically, racism is racism. However, these ideas imply that specific types of discrimination, such as racism against black people, is expected or *normal*, while racism against white people is unexpected or *abnormal*. Moreover, minority groups of people are stigmatized in Anglophone countries, while white people are *not* stigmatized. This is because white people have *white privilege*. That is, they are afforded social privileges because they belong to the advantaged racial group that enjoys dominance, status, control, prestige, and power. White people continue to benefit from this current social structure that disadvantages minority groups of people.

A less talked about area of racism is linguistic discrimination or *linguicism*. This refers to prejudice against people because of the language, dialect, or accent they speak.[88] Linguicism is common in Anglophone countries. Accents can offer clues about a person's class, education, nationality, or geographical location, although many people make positive or negative judgments about regional and social accents based on their associations with groups of people.[89] For example, British English is often perceived as prestigious in the United States because it is associated with education and intelligence. Conversely, some Southern US accents have low prestige outside of their group. Revealing classism, the "Southern drawl" is described as *hick, country,* or *uneducated,* while poor, white, Southern people are labeled *rednecks* or *white trash.* In popular culture, Southern accents are often synonymous with racism. In linguistics, *dialect* refers to a variety of a language, although among the general public it is also a slang term meaning a *substandard* version of a language. Standard English is often perceived as *proper English* or *normal,* while Nonstandard dialects are labeled as *bad English* or *broken English* and are thought of as being *wrong, corrupt, poor, lazy, uneducated,* or *inferior.* However, Standard English is only the idealized version of the language, because it is the variety used by the politically and economically dominant group, and it is the language of status, power, and prestige. Criticism of other languages, dialects, and accents can reveal prejudice against the groups that speak them.

Linguicism is an extension of racism, as revealed by negative attitudes toward Nonstandard dialects of English spoken by minority groups. African American Vernacular English (AAVE, which is also known as *Ebonics* meaning "black speech" or "Black English") is often thought of as uneducated and ungrammatical by speakers of Standard English, even though it has been demonstrated to be a systematic, rule-driven variety of English. The dialect was mocked in minstrel shows with the crude, pidgin-style language of black caricatures, and the "butchered" English spoken by black characters in books, such as *Uncle Tom's Cabin*, *Huckleberry Finn*, and *Gone With The Wind*. The dialect was also mimicked in advertising for household items, especially beverages and breakfast foods. The Cream of Wheat brand used the image of an Uncle Tom caricature named Rastus with the slogan, "Dis sho'am good." In a 1921 advertisement, a smiling, barely literate Rastus holds a sign that reads, "Maybe Cream of Wheat aint got no vitamines. I dont know what them things is. If they's bugs they aint none in *Cream of Wheat* but she's sho' good to eat and cheap. Costs 'bout 1¢ fo a great big dish."[90] In the early 1900s, Aunt Jemima breakfast foods featured a Mammy caricature who uttered catchphrases such as, "Shonuff! Everybody loves dee-licious Aunt Jemima pancakes at any meal!" and "I'se in town honey!" Australian Aboriginal English has also been parodied in older advertisements. In a racist play on the *civilized savage*, 1920s advertisements for Pelaco shirts featured Pelaco Bill, a character based on Australian Aboriginal Fred Wilson, who was a renowned buckjumper, expert at stockwhip-cracking and boomerang-throwing, and was affectionately known as Mulga Fred. Advertising signs showed Fred wearing a crisp white dinner shirt with a red tie, but nothing else, with the slogan, "Mine tinkit they fit!"[91]

In popular culture, Nonstandard dialects of English are often portrayed as simplistic and halted, and they reveal racial stereotypes. As we have seen, indigenous people are often depicted as primitive and backward, and *Tonto*, the Native American companion of the Lone Ranger, spoke a crude English, in phrases such as, "Me think so," and "Him say man ride over ridge on horse."[92] Similarly, Spanish-inspired phrases used by English speakers are often intended to be humorous, but are interpreted as racist because they misuse or ridicule Spanish and often invoke negative stereotypical views.[93] This "Mock Spanish" includes features such as botched Spanish syntax (e.g., *no problemo* or *el cheapo*),

Spanish borrowed words (e.g., "Hasta la vista, baby" from the movie *Terminator 2: Judgment Day*), exaggerated parodies of a Spanish accent (e.g., *Es no my yob*), and a hyper-Anglicized accent (e.g., "grassy-ass" for *gracias*). Ironically, some Anglo people mock the Spanish accent in this way but are themselves highly critical of the accents of English-speaking Hispanic and Latino people. Donald Trump has been accused of repeatedly using Mock Spanish, borrowing the Spanish word *loco* (to mean "crazy") and referring to Mexican immigrants as "bad hombres," effectively turning *hombre* ("man") into a racial slur.[94] To Spanish speakers, Mock Spanish implies that "real Americans" do not speak Spanish and do not have respect for the language.[95]

Linguicism is often a negative judgment of how speakers of English as a second language use and shape the English language. *Engrish* is a slang term for the "misuse" of English by speakers of Asian languages. The term comes from their tendency to transpose /l/ with /r/. (A popular parody is to spell or pronounce *fried rice* as "flied lice.") Engrish includes inaccurate translations of English in restaurant menus and on signs, or quirky phrases of borrowed English used for decoration or fashion purposes on t-shirts and in advertising to make them seem glamorous. A famous example is the quote, "All your base are belong to us," which is an inaccurate English translation found in the 1989 Japanese video game *Zero Wing* that became the source of an internet meme. Websites such as Engrish.com are devoted to collecting humorous examples of this "corrupt" English, especially those than have crude or sexual connotations. (For example, one Chinese menu translates *steamed crab* as "steamed crap.") In a parody of the phenomenon, British fashion brand Superdry uses simple automatic translation programs such as Babelfish to create nonsensical Japanese phrases including, "Clever Weather Company" and "Membership Certificate" that appear in Japanese kanji characters on their clothing.[96]

A common expression of linguicism is mimicking how another language "sounds" to naive ears. On the television show *The View* in 2006, Rosie O'Donnell used the phrase *Ching chong* to describe

Chinese people discussing actor Danny DeVito's recent drunken appearance on her show. Imitating Chinese newscasters, she said, "You can imagine in China it's like: 'Ching chong . . . ching chong. Danny DeVito, ching chong, chong, chong, chong. Drunk. *The View.* Ching chong.'"[97] O'Donnell apologized for making fun of Chinese accents, but explained that she didn't know the phrase was offensive. *Ching chong* is a playground taunt that dates back to a nineteenth-century nursery rhyme, "Ching Chong Chineeman, clear right out of here," whose lyrics revealed anti-Chinese sentiment on the goldfields of California. In 2013, General Motors pulled an advertisement for their Chevrolet Trax SUV that featured women singing, "Ching-ching, chop suey" and referring to China as "the land of Fu Manchu."[98] (Dr. Fu Manchu was a stereotypical Chinese villain who appeared in a series of novels written by the British author Sax Rohmer.) The song in the advertisement was based on the 1938 "Oriental Swing" by Lil Armstrong, the original lyrics also referring to Japanese geisha girls who want to "swing it like Amelicans." This kind of mispronunciation, and phrases like *Ching chong*, are crude imitations of what people think Mandarin or Cantonese sound like.[99]

Several Asian languages are tonal, which means a word's meaning can change with the tone or pitch in which it is spoken, giving the language a song-like quality that is mimicked by *Ching chong.* Imitating Chinese to sound simplistic further reflects a belief that the language is inferior to English, and by extension, that the people who speak it are also inferior.

As discussed above, regional and social English accents can attract positive or negative stereotypes, depending on their associations with groups of people. Similarly, positive or negative judgments are also made about other languages, based on their popular associations. English speakers often describe the German language as sounding *harsh, angry, grating,* and *aggressive.* These opinions may reflect longstanding negative attitudes toward German people as the *enemy* during World Wars I and II. In the United States, the Spanish language is often associated with racist generalizations about Hispanic, Latino, and Mexican people, who are stereotyped as stupid, dirty, lazy, violent, and amoral, and as we have seen, are often assumed to be illegal immigrants. In stark contrast, the Italian language is often thought to sound *sexy* and *romantic*, based on the stereotype of the passionate *Latin lover*.

In Anglophone countries, a commonly held misconception is that *I don't have an accent*. An accent is often perceived to be relative to the speaker; and something only had by other people from other places. English spoken with a *foreign accent* is often considered to be *exotic* and can invite unwanted compliments, conversation, and harassment from strangers. Accents are sometimes fetishized, and immigrants, tourists, and speakers of different accents may be told their accent sounds *charming, cute,* or *sexy.* They may be asked to say particular words in their accent, or their accent may be imitated. People with different accents may be told, *Your accent is hot,* or they may be propositioned with, *I've got a thing for accents.* Some people overhear a different accent and play a guessing game to speculate about a person's origins. This can be offensive, because it is intrusive, and the guess is often incorrect. Asking, *Where are you from?* or *Where's that accent from?* is usually intended to be a friendly display of interest, or simply seen as making small talk, but it can force an unwanted conversation, while the question itself can be perceived as invasive and exclusionary. People with different accents often feel they should not have to educate other people about language and geography or divulge personal information simply because a nosy stranger is curious. However, they are asked these questions frequently, which can lead to feelings of alienation and isolation, and that they are being treated like a novelty or as entertainment. They may feel self-conscious, uncomfortable, and excluded. Assumed to be tourists, they are made to feel like outsiders, and that they do not belong in the place they call home. Foreign accents hold fascination in Anglophone countries because the language is still comprehensible; however, speaking an entirely different language is not always tolerated.

There is an expectation that people in Anglophone countries "should" speak English. This position is held by the English Only movement, a group that advocates the establishment of English as the only official language in the United States. This attitude often underpins anti-foreign language sentiment and anti-immigrant sentiment. A fear of multilingualism has led to people removing foreign language books from shelves in libraries, grassroots attempts to ban business signs in languages other than English, and even attempts to pass state and federal laws prohibiting the use of other languages. Anti-foreign language sentiment often manifests as negative reactions toward people speaking other languages in public. Bilingual people report being abused with, *Don't talk your fucking language around me!* There have been several cases of employees being fired for speaking a foreign language in the workplace. In 2018, the manager of a Dunkin' Donuts in Baltimore posted a sign asking customers to report employees speaking in a foreign language in exchange for free coffee or donuts.[100] Some people fear that any utterance they hear in a different language must be about them, and is probably insulting. It is a common belief that Asian women working in nail salons gossip in their mother tongue about their English-speaking customers. This stereotype is explored in an episode of the TV comedy *Seinfeld*, when Elaine visits a nail salon run by Korean manicurists. She suspects that they are making fun of her in Korean, and so she takes along a Korean-speaking friend to spy on them, discovering that they are indeed gossiping about her.[101] Being excluded from a conversation can make some people feel uncomfortable, insecure, and even threatened. (See also Chapter 4.)

While it is expected that people should speak English, it is often assumed that immigrants, tourists, or racialized people who simply *look foreign* cannot understand or speak English. The slur *spic* is popularly believed to be derived from the phrase *No speak English*, although it is probably an abbreviation of *spiggoty* ("speak-a the") representing learner English.[102] Not speaking English is frequently linked to undocumented immigration. As noted above, in the United States, it is often assumed that Hispanic, Latino, and Mexican immigrants are undocumented workers. In 2018, a lawyer in Manhattan, New York, threatened to call Immigration and Customs Enforcement (ICE) on workers in a restaurant; in his belief they were illegal immigrants because they were speaking Spanish. He complained to the store manager, "Your employees are speaking Spanish to customers when they should be speaking English."[103] Further to the New York City ban on the use of the term *illegal alien*, the city has also banned threats to call immigration authorities on someone based on a discriminatory motive, and discrimination against someone based on their English proficiency.

The United States has the world's second-largest Spanish-speaking population, although resentment and hostility toward Spanish-speaking people has led to a spate of hate speech incidents across the country. In 2016, a woman's rant in a shopping mall in Louisville, Kentucky, was caught on camera when she yelled at shoppers speaking Spanish, "Go back to where you belong," and, "Speak English. You're in America."[104] In 2017, a teacher at Cliffside Park High School in New Jersey urged her students to "Speak American," arguing that "brave men and women" are "not fighting for your right to speak Spanish – they're fighting for your right to speak American."[105] (In 1923, a bill was drafted that proposed to call the national language *American*, to differentiate American English from English spoken in England, although the bill did not pass in Congress.) In increasing hate crimes across the United States, anti-immigration sentiment has turned deadly. In 2019, 21-year-old Patrick Crusius opened fire in a mall in El Paso, Texas, killing 22 people and injuring dozens more. The shooter penned a manifesto in which he railed against immigration and announced, "This attack is a response to the Hispanic invasion of Texas."[106]

In the United States, anti-immigrant, anti-foreign language memes are found on shop signs that demand, *This is America. When ordering speak English.* Bumper stickers and t-shirts say, *This is America. Speak English or get the fuck out!*, *Welcome to America. Now Speak English!*, and *I'm tired of pressing 1*. This latter slogan is in reference to automated customer service hotlines that instruct callers to *Press one for English. Para Español, oprima dos.*

(However, this motto is a myth, because most welcome messages do not typically ask English speakers to press a number, but instead ask this of Spanish speakers.[107]) For many Americans, speaking English is an important part of their identity. A 2016 study found that 7 out of 10 Americans believe that it is important to speak English to be *truly American*.[108] Language is often viewed as the cornerstone of national identity, and there is extreme social pressure placed on immigrants in Anglophone countries to *sound American* (or *sound Australian, sound English*, etc.) by not only speaking English, but also adopting the local accent. Those who do not assimilate in this way are often viewed as outsiders who *don't fit in* or *don't belong*. They are branded Un-American, or even Anti-American. They are accused of threatening the *American way of life*. It is said they are not *one of us*. They are told they are not welcome.

In the past, anti-immigration sentiment was often enshrined in government policy as a form of institutional racism. In the late nineteenth century, concern was growing in the Australian colonies about the level of *non-white* immigration to Australia. A political slogan at the time was "White Australia: Australia for the Australians."[109] When the colonies united in 1901, one of the first pieces of legislation passed was the Immigration Restriction Act. Commonly known as the White Australia Policy, it aimed to limit non-British immigration to Australia. A new feature of this policy was the Dictation Test, a language test that non-European applicants were required to pass. The test was given in any European language as chosen at the discretion of the immigration officer, so it was easy to ensure failure if the applicant was considered to be "undesirable." A person who failed the test was deemed a prohibited immigrant and deported. White British migrants did not have to sit for the test at all.[110] In 1934, the Australian government attempted to exclude Jewish Communist and anti-war activist Egon Kisch from entering the country. To outwit Kisch's fluency in several European languages, a police inspector asked him to recite the Lord's Prayer in Scottish Gaelic. Kisch failed the test and was sentenced to six months hard labor. He appealed to the High Court, and the decision was overturned when the demand was shown to be unreasonable because the inspector who administered the test was unable to understand Scottish Gaelic.[111]

As part of the Immigration Act of 1917, the United States also had a literacy test to exclude "undesirables." The test required immigrants to read and write a short passage of the US Constitution.[112] But when it was actually implemented, the test required reading only short passages in *any* language, and few people were excluded on the basis of literacy. There is a persistent myth that immigrants entering through New York's Ellis Island had their names changed against their will because the clerk misunderstood the name, decided it was too complicated, or the immigrants spoke little or no English and couldn't answer the question, *What is your name?* However, clerks worked from lists created by shipping companies, while many translators were employed, so language problems were rare.[113] Instead, it was the immigrants who changed their names for reasons of convenience, to help them seek employment, or so they could assimilate into the American culture.

Many Hollywood actors have Anglicized or even changed their names for this reason. Actor Natalie Wood was born Natasha Nikolaevna Zakharenko,[114] actor Kirk Douglas was born Issur Danielovitch,[115] actor Bruce Lee's birth name was Lee Jun-fan,[116] and KISS musician Gene Simmons was born Chaim Witz.[117] Prejudice against foreign-sounding names is still common. In 2018, Dear Abby columnist Jeanne Phillips advised a reader of Indian descent to avoid choosing a "foreign" name for his children, but to instead select a "Traditional Western name". She wrote, "Not only can foreign names be difficult to pronounce and spell, but they can cause a child to be teased mercilessly. Sometimes the name can be a problematic word in the English language. And one that sounds beautiful in a foreign language can be grating in English."[118] But some people have indeed had name changes imposed on them. As we have seen, Residential or Boarding Schools were established in the United States and Canada, to assimilate indigenous children into the dominant culture. In these

institutions, speaking their indigenous languages was strictly forbidden, and their birth names were replaced with European names
to *civilize* and *Christianize* them.[119]

The extreme consequence of linguicism is linguistic genocide.
This is the deliberate oppression of a language, often with the
intention of eradicating it to replace it with a dominant language.
In the British Isles during the eighteenth and nineteenth centuries,
Scottish Gaelic, Irish, Welsh, and other indigenous languages
were considered to be "problems" and were banned in schools.
Children were forced to speak English, which was thought to be
the language of progress and opportunity. Children were admonished for speaking their native tongues in an effort to stigmatize
and suppress the minority languages. In Welsh schools, *cwstom* or
"Welsh sticks" were commonly used to discourage the use of
Welsh and shame any child who was overheard speaking the
language.[120] *Welsh Not* or the initials *WN* were carved onto
a wooden board, which was tied around the child's neck. The
student would be forced to wear the sign until another child was
caught speaking Welsh, and the board was then passed on. At the
end of the school day, the child left wearing the board would be
beaten or punished by the schoolteacher. As a result of this stigma,
the Welsh language became endangered. Modern revitalization
efforts have led to a resurgence of the language, although Welsh is
still considered to be vulnerable.[121]

During the time of the British Empire, the English language was
imposed on the colonies to assert the authority of the ruling power
and achieve linguistic unity. This often involved prohibiting the
use of native languages in order to assimilate the indigenous
people. As we have discussed, Aboriginal children, the Stolen
Generations in Australia, were forcibly removed from their
families by the government and placed with new families or in
church missions. In these institutions, they were forced to abandon their identities and culture. The assimilation "training" often
involved punishment if they dared to speak their indigenous
languages, such as depriving them of food or washing their
mouths out with soap and water.[122] Before 1788, there were

approximately 700–800 languages spoken throughout Australia.[123] Today, Indigenous Aboriginal languages have dwindled to only 20 viable languages. As a result of the dominance of the English language around the world, thousands of indigenous languages are on the brink of extinction, while many more have died. When we lose a language, we lose the worldview, knowledge, and culture of the people who spoke it, which is a loss to humanity.[124]

As we can see, racism comes in many different guises. Ironically, despite its prevalence, racism is viewed negatively in society. No one wants to be called a *racist*. Insults condemn them as *bigots* and *xenophobes*, while they are further socially reproved as being *intolerant, prejudiced,* and *narrow-minded*. People resist and deny the label with protestations such as, *I'm not a racist, but* ... to avoid being labeled a *racist* when expressing racist views. *Racist* and *racism* are viewed as blunt and inflammatory terms that make people defensive. To avoid them, some people reframe their racist ideology as *white nativism, ethno-nationalism, culturalism, racialism, racial anxiety,* or *racial resentment*. Racist language is reinterpreted euphemistically as *divisive, controversial, patriotic, racially freighted,* or *racially charged*. Our modern language shows that racism is as widespread as ever, and in order to stay alive, it is always changing.

2   Boys Will Be Boys

Vintage advertisements seem rife with sexism nowadays. In a 1930s advertisement for Kellogg's PEP cereal, a woman wearing a figure-hugging dress, high heels, and an apron, and holding a feather duster, is embraced by her husband who says, "So the harder a wife works, the cuter she looks!"[1] A World War II advertisement from the United States Department of State shows a female factory worker who pleads, "The soldiers need our help! Gather 'round, American women!" The tagline reads, "Turns out you gals are useful after all!"[2] A 1950s advertisement for Schlitz beer features a tearful housewife clutching a scorched, smoke-filled skillet as her husband consoles her with, "Don't worry darling, you didn't burn the beer!"[3] These advertisements promoted traditional gender roles, especially among white, middle-class families. Today, the explicit sexism of this bygone era seems shocking, offensive, or even amusing. Some people believe that sexism is now a thing of the past. But our modern language reveals that sexism is still prevalent, while it has also taken on new forms.

Sexism can be defined broadly as attitudes, beliefs, and behaviors that reflect negative evaluations of people on the basis of sex or gender.[4] *Sex* and *gender* are often used interchangeably, although there is a distinction between the two. Sex refers to biological identity based on physical characteristics such as genitalia, genes, and hormones, while gender refers to identity based on behavioral, cultural, or psychological traits. In a scientific sense, sexism originally referred to the categorization of an organism as male or female, but by the 1960s the term became used to parallel racism.[5] Sexism can involve the unequal treatment of people based on their sex, and includes institutional and cultural practices that treat people unfairly, such as the gender gap in hiring and the gender pay gap. Sexism can also promote the belief that one sex is inherently superior; therefore implying that the other is inferior. Sexism includes the objectification of people in the media and advertising, and also sexist language, such as insults, jokes, and speech that abuses, belittles, or undervalues people based on their sex or gender. Sexist attitudes also underpin sexist behavior, including sexual harassment and sexual assault. Sexism is often referred to as *chauvinism*, although in usage, chauvinism almost exclusively implies *male chauvinism*.

Sexism can affect anyone, but it primarily affects women and girls. This is borne out in our language, both past and present. According to the way we talk, men are usually represented as the default sex, while women are talked about as subordinate, secondary, second-class citizens, or the "other."[6,7] Men are said to be *the first sex*, while women are *the second sex*. According to the Book of Genesis (2:21–22) in the Old Testament of the Bible, woman was made from man.[8] To be a companion for man in the Garden of Eden, God created Eve from one of Adam's ribs. (This is the basis of the urban legend that men have one less rib than women because of God's act, and is also the source of the jocular term *rib* to refer to women.) Tempted by an evil serpent, Eve committed a sin by eating fruit from the forbidden tree, and goaded Adam to do so. (*Forbidden fruit* is often interpreted as a metaphor for sex.) God was displeased. He banished Adam and Eve from Paradise, and cursed women with the pain of childbirth and subordination to their husbands. Many other scriptural readings also subordinate women. Titus (2:5) states that woman are "to be busy at home, to be kind, and to be subject to their husbands," while Ephesians (5:23) says, "the husband is the head of the wife as Christ is the head of the church." 1 Timothy (2:11–12) declares, "A woman should learn in quietness and full submission. I do not permit a woman to teach or to assume authority over a man; she must be quiet." Colossians (3:18) asserts, "Wives, submit to your husbands, as is fitting in the Lord." Throughout the scriptures, God is characterized in exclusively masculine terms. "He" is described as "Lord," "King," "Father," "Judge,"

"Master," and the "God and Father of our Lord Jesus Christ."[9] In contrast to the world's other religious traditions in Egypt, Greece, Rome, India, and Africa, female deities are completely absent from Christianity, Judaism, and Islam.

In light of the Adam and Eve narrative and other subordinate representations of women in the Bible, some people interpret the scriptures as promoting the idea of a male-centered, patriarchal society. A *patriarchy* is a social system in which men hold the majority of positions of power and influence, and where cultural values and norms favor men.[10] In such a male-centric or andro-centric society, men control most aspects of the cultural, political, legal, and religious spheres in society. Several anthropologists claim that early human societies were matriarchies, female-centric or gynocentric societies.[11] It is believed that these "queen-doms" worshipped a "Great Goddess" or "Mother Goddess" and were peaceful, idyllic societies, until they collapsed with the "rise of the patriarchy."[12] Some authors report that several modern-day matriarchal societies still exist in remote parts of the world. However, the consensus is that historical societies were patriar-chal, while in practice, contemporary societies are still patriarchal.[13] Popular figures of speech remind us that we live in a *male-dominated society*, that *men rule the world*, and *it's a man's world*.

The existence of a patriarchy in Western society is reflected in historical inequalities between the sexes. During the nineteenth and twentieth centuries, women did not have the same rights and privileges in society as men. Women were disenfranchised in that they were not allowed to vote. Women were also not permitted certain legal rights; for example, a married woman's property was considered to be owned by her husband. Education and employ-ment opportunities for women were also severely limited. These inequalities inspired the creation of the Women's Rights move-ment to achieve social reform. During this era, known as the "first wave of feminism," the "suffragettes" campaigned for the women's vote and were granted this right at different times in different countries (as early as 1893 in New Zealand, but not until

1928 in the United Kingdom).[14] Property and custody laws were eventually abolished. Women were finally granted access to higher education and greater job opportunities. During the World Wars, millions of men went away to fight, and this saw many women entering the workforce, where they worked in factories and shipyards producing munitions and supplies for the war effort. The iconic female factory worker, now dubbed "Rosie the Riveter" with her motto "We Can Do It!" represented these working women. But post-war, women were urged to return back to the home, to create stability after those times of uncertainty, and so many women did.[15]

At this time, it was widely believed that the only way a woman could achieve fulfillment in life was through marriage and motherhood.[16] It was warned that a woman did not want to end up an *old maid* or a *spinster*, or to be *always a bridesmaid, never a bride*. (See also Chapter 7.) Like the advertisements mentioned at the start of this chapter, advertising in newspapers and women's magazines and women's education focused on marriage, family, and the home, perpetuating this view. Within the family dynamic, men and women were socialized into traditional gender roles. The role of the man was to be the *provider*, to support the family financially. The husband was the *breadwinner, the meal ticket*, and the one who *brings home the bacon*. The woman's domain was the home, and she was the *homemaker*. It was said that *men make houses, women make homes*. But the husband was the *head of the household*, and *a man's home is his castle*. Like the title of the 1950s television sitcom, *Father Knows Best*, the father was the family *leader* and the family's *protector*. Well into the twentieth century, America still had "Head and Master laws" that permitted a husband to have the final say regarding all household decisions and jointly owned property, without his wife's knowledge or consent. In an infamous Head and Master case in Louisiana in 1974, Harold Feenstra was imprisoned for molesting his young daughter. He mortgaged his home to pay for his lawyer, an act that did not require his wife Joan's permission, despite the fact that she had paid for the house.[17] Women too are often portrayed as the property of men. At her wedding, a woman is *given away* by her father, and the married couple is pronounced *man and wife*. According to older social values, a woman was defined by her marriage, but the relationship was not equal. She was second to her husband, and *the woman behind the man*, because *behind every great man there's a great woman*. Women were raised to *stand by your man*, despite his shortcomings and faults.

There was the idea that the "natural role" of a woman was as a wife and mother, which was reflected in language. A wife was a dependent to her husband, the *kept woman* or *kept wife*, and she was his possession, the *little woman*, *the missus*, or *the wife*. She was the guardian of morality, the *good wife*, but also her husband's warden, as the *old lady*, the *old ball and chain*, *jailer*, *trouble and strife* (rhyming slang for "wife"), his *mother*, *the boss*, or *the chief*. She was a helper to her husband, a domestic goddess, and a servant, a *homemaker*, *housewife*, *housekeeper*, *maid*, *cook*, or *dough-beater*. The housework was considered to be *women's work*, although a *woman's work is never done*. Historical advertisements encouraged women to view housework as a career, and one that required specialized products. A 1960s Kenwood Chef advertisement displays a wife wearing a chef's hat as she leans happily against her husband who says, "The Chef does everything but cook – that's what wives are for!"[18] Women were reminded, *the way to a man's heart is through his stomach*. There was also the idea of a *woman's place*: That a woman *belongs* in the home, *a woman's place is in the home*, and specifically, *a woman's place is in the kitchen*. (Although there is no equivalent "man's place.") If a woman impinges on a man in some way, she may be reminded of her social *place* and ordered to *get back into the kitchen, make my dinner*, or *go make me a sandwich*. During a 2008 speech given by American politician Hillary Clinton, a man in the audience heckled her with a sign that read, "Iron my shirt!" as he chanted the phrase at her.[19]

Upon marriage, a wife typically adopts her husband's last name, as do any children born to them. A wife's *maiden name* is supplanted by her husband's last name, and even her first name when she is addressed as Mrs. John Doe. For some women, to be referred to in relation to a man is to experience a loss of identity, and so more married women are opting to retain their birth names, to hyphenate the birth name with the married name, or for both parties to hyphenate their last names. In 1969, John Lennon married Yoko Ono, and they changed their names to John Ono Lennon and Yoko Ono Lennon.[20] In a reversal of tradition, artist Marco Saldana took on actor Zoe Saldana's name when they married in 2013.[21] Honorifics, the titles prefixing a person's name, are unequal for men and women. *Mrs.* is inflected to show that the woman is married; *Miss* is used to address an unmarried woman, while *Ms.* emerged to avoid any guesswork of the age or marital status of a woman. However, there are no equivalent terms that reveal whether a man is married or single. *Mr.* is an abbreviation of *Mister*, which is derived from an earlier form of *Master*, that meant "one having control or authority."[22] *Mrs.*, *Ms.*, and *Miss* are all derived from *Mistress*, which was once the female equivalent term for *Master*, but now refers specifically to the extramarital lover of a married man.

Honorifics for men that once had equivalents for women are no longer equal. *Governess* was once the equivalent of *governor*, but it has now narrowed to mean a woman employed to teach children in a private home. Several terms for women have developed negative connotations in a way that those for men have not. *Madam* was once the female equivalent of *sir*, but it now means the female manager of a brothel. *Courtesan* was once the equivalent of *courtier*, an attendant at a royal court, but it now it means a mistress to a royal or noble man, or a high-class prostitute. *Dame* originally meant a woman of high social position, and it is still the female equivalent to the rank of *knight* in Britain, but as a synonym for woman, *dame* is mostly archaic and slightly derogatory. *Hussy* comes from *husewif*, an early version of *housewife*, but it now means a disreputable woman. *Wench* once meant a female infant or young unmarried woman, but later referred to a server or prostitute. *Tart* was once just a contraction of *sweetheart*, but now means a prostitute or a sexually provocative woman. Honorifics for men still speak of high power and status, while terms for women that were once equivalents now suggest a subordinate status, or sexual service to men.[23]

When people think about sexist language, they traditionally think of words and phrases that show gender bias toward men. This kind of sexism is entrenched in the English language, in which women seem to be left out of history. Those who led the American Revolution (1775–1783) are known as the *Founding Fathers,* while the United States Declaration of Independence (1776) states that, "All men are created equal." Neil Armstrong, the first person to walk on the moon, famously said, "One small step for man; one giant leap for mankind." More recently, technology entrepreneur Elon Musk has been dubbed "the savior of mankind."[24] The rules of grammar once dictated the use of the masculine pronouns *he, his, him,* and *himself* to refer to both men and women, which is known as generic *he.* Everyday language refers to *man* as the generic sex for "human," in words such as *mankind, manmade, manpower, man-eating,* and *man-hours.* Older titles favored the masculine suffix, such as *chairman, mailman, policeman, fireman,* and *congressman.* Gender-specific nouns imply that a woman is a lesser version of her male counterpart, in the terms *author* versus *authoress, comedian* versus *comedienne, hero* versus *heroine,* and *actor* versus *actress,* and they are now often considered to be inappropriate and demeaning. There used to be many more feminine nouns in use, although they sound strange today, including *neighboress, singeress, friendess, farmeress, spousess,* and *soldieress.*

Using unmarked words for men (e.g., *editor*) but marked forms for women (e.g., *editrix*) suggests that men are the "default human," the norm, or archetype, while women are less important or inferior. This kind of excusive language is also said to promote an androcentric worldview. For this reason, some feminists prefer alternative spellings to *woman,* such as *womyn, womon,* or *wimmin* (old AAVE), to avoid the word ending -*man.* Using gender-biased language was considered unremarkable in Anglophone countries until feminists challenged it during the "second wave of feminism" in the 1960s and 1970s. Today, many organizations have guidelines for using inclusive language, recommending gender-neutral alternatives for job titles, roles, and turns of phrase. *Humankind* is suggested instead of *mankind*, *spokesperson* instead of *spokesman*, and *server* instead of *waiter* or *waitress*. *Emcee* is preferred to *master of ceremonies*, *maintenance hole* is preferred to *manhole*, while *limbo* is preferred to *no-man's land*.

However, the use of male-centric language is still common in ways we don't think of immediately, such as the exclamations *Oh, boy!* or *Oh, man!* (Note that we don't say *Oh, girl!* or *Oh, woman!*) Some everyday phrases suggest it is favorable to be masculine, but insulting to be feminine. Calling a group of women *you guys* or *dudes* is acceptable and common, although to flip this and refer to a group of men as *ladies* or *girls* is considered to be humorous, or an insult to their masculinity. Complimenting a woman as *just one of the guys* implies that being a *guy* is the height of achievement as a woman, while calling a man *just one of the girls* is humorous, or questions his sexuality and manhood. *Guys, dude,* and *bro* are not gender neutral and their use can imply that maleness is more natural and universal. Instead of using group terms that specifically address men, gender-inclusive terms are gaining popularity, such as *people, everyone, friends, folks, you, y'all* (Southern US), or *youse* (Australia and New Zealand). But overall, gender-biased language presents a narrow view of sexism. Everyday language reveals even more sexist attitudes and a lack of equality between the sexes.

The first wave of feminism tackled legal reform, but there were still social issues to address regarding the inequality of women. As well as being a *wife*, the other part of the *natural role* of a woman was motherhood. With the renewed domesticity of women after World War II, there was an increase in birth rate that is known as the *baby boom*, while the children born in that era are called *baby boomers*. Stereotypes surrounding the social expectation that women should become mothers are still around today. Women are dubbed *the softer sex* and *the gentler sex*. They are described as *nurturing* and *motherly* and are believed to have an inherent *maternal instinct*. When a couple marries, they are encouraged to *be fruitful and multiply*, while it is expected that the mother will become the primary childcare provider. It was (and occasionally still is) believed that a woman should not work outside of the home, and that she should be kept *barefoot and pregnant* during her reproductive years because her *biological clock is ticking*. (See also Chapter 7.)

The second wave of feminism broadened the sexism debate to include a wider range of social issues that women face. Seminal books such as Betty Friedan's *The Feminine Mystique* (1963) and Germaine Greer's *The Female Eunuch* (1970) challenged the idea of the "natural role" of women as wife and mother.[25,26] Groups such as the National Organization for Women (NOW) were founded to seek equality for women in the family unit, to secure their reproductive rights, and to fight against discrimination in the workplace. During this time, women began entering the workforce in greater numbers. However, laws known as *marriage bars* forced women to quit their jobs once they got married, or became pregnant. To this day, women are told they have to make a choice between having children *or* having a career, because they *can't have it all*. Women who choose a career over motherhood are often stereotyped as *selfish* or are said to have made a *sacrifice* they may regret.

However, those early *working women, career girls, career ladies*, and *career women* (there is no equivalent *career men*) faced inequality in the workforce. For the most part, their employment options were limited to low paid, low status jobs. It was believed that women were naturally suited to certain *feminine* professions. Known as *pink-collar* jobs, these included nurse, waitress, teacher, sales lady, cleaning lady, secretary, or an assistant with the title *girl Friday*. Today, when a woman holds a position in a male-dominated profession, her title is often qualified unnecessarily, such as *female doctor, female lawyer, female soldier, female senator, female CEO*, or *female President*, implying that these women

are exceptions to the norm. Similarly, the titles of jobs traditionally viewed as feminine are often qualified when held by men, such
as *male nurse*, *male secretary*, or *male teacher*. Women are criticized whether they choose career, motherhood, or to *juggle* both
as a *working mother*. (We don't say *working father*.) In the past,
career-driven women were taught that they had to be a wife and
mother to be fulfilled in life, while today's women are asked, how
can you possibly be fulfilled if you're just a *stay at home mom*?
Modern mothers are often belittled and stereotyped in phrases
such as *housewives*, *single moms*, *soccer moms*, and *stage moms*.
They are mocked by "yo momma" jokes and sexualized as *yummy
mummies* and *MILFs* ("Mother I'd Like to Fuck"). (See also
Chapter 7.)

Gender discrimination is still common in the workplace.
Women are less likely to be hired than men, and women earn
lower wages than men worldwide, which is a form of institutional
sexism that is known as the *gender wage gap*.[27] A woman's career
is limited by the *glass ceiling*, but if she becomes successful, she
may be accused of *sleeping her way to the top*. In the workplace,
women are often stereotyped as less capable, competent, or intel-
ligent than men. The perspective that *men are better than women*
underpins the modern concept of *mansplaining*. In popular culture, mansplaining is when a man attempts to explain something
to a woman (or an audience of women) in an oversimplified
manner, often adopting a condescending tone, and making the
insulting (and often incorrect) assumption that he has more
knowledge. In the workplace, leadership is still male dominated,
and men are often stereotyped as preferred candidates to fill
higher status positions. (As the saying goes, the *best man for the
job*.) During the 2016 US presidential election, former Mayor of
New York City Rudy Giuliani stated his preference for candidate
Donald Trump over Hillary Clinton and revealed gender bias
when he said, "Don't you think a man who has this kind of
economic genius is a lot better for the United States than
a woman and the only thing she's ever produced is a lot of work
for the FBI checking out her emails?"[28]

Throughout history, feminists have been mocked and attacked by those with opposing views. During the first wave of feminism, Susan B. Anthony and other suffragists were depicted as unfeminine, insulted as *spinsters*, and considered to be a danger to family life. Well-known activists received hate mail and death threats, while the police and even members of the public physically abused protestors during their demonstrations.[29] In the 1960s and 1970s, second-wave feminists were commonly ridiculed as *women's libbers* (the term coming from the "Women's Liberation movement") and *bra burners*. (The idea of bra burning was actually a media-generated myth, although this titillating story has served to further marginalize feminism and feminists as ridiculous and irrational.)[30] Feminists were labeled *crazy, mad,* and *insane* for their beliefs that defied traditional gender roles. In the 1970s, Hugh Hefner launched a campaign to expose the "highly irrational, kookie trends" of feminism, that he argued were "unalterably opposed to the romantic boy-girl society" promoted by his *Playboy* magazine.[31] Second-wave feminists were stereotyped as unladylike "lesbian" women who didn't wear make-up or shave their legs.[32] These stereotypes of feminists have persisted throughout the decades.

The *third wave of feminism* began in the 1980s, while beyond 2000 is loosely characterized as the *fourth wave of feminism*. This contemporary feminism is concerned with a range of ongoing issues, including sexual liberation, sexual harassment and violence against women, and reclaiming sexist language. Within modern feminism there are various branches of feminist ideology and intersectional movements that have specific concerns and goals, such as Black feminism and Native American feminism (whose issues often overlap with classism and racism). All feminists share a common goal, to achieve gender equality, although there is some infighting and disagreement within the movement today. Some commentators (both inside and outside of the movement) argue that the first wave of feminism was valid, along with various aspects of the second wave, but that modern feminism is not justifiable or necessary. Some people believe that sexism in the

West ended decades ago, and that equality has been achieved. They accuse modern feminists of exaggerating the problems experienced by women today and hyperbolizing that men are behind the *domination, subjugation,* and *oppression* of women.

In some usage today, the word *feminist* has been demonized and carries negative connotations. Critics of modern feminism characterize feminists as *angry, extreme, radical, rabid,* and *militant.* They are labeled *femtards* and *feminazis.* Some people reject the label *feminist* because of the negative stereotypes attached to the term. Authors known for critiquing the contemporary feminist movement distance themselves from the name. Christina Hoff Sommers instead identifies as an *equalist*,[33] while Camille Paglia calls herself a *dissident feminist*.[34] (Although some feminists would argue that these authors are "not feminists.") Critics of contemporary feminism argue that the movement has gone too far. Some perceive feminism as a threat to the order of society. So-called *female supremacists* are said to have a *feminist agenda* to *overthrow society* and bring about *matriarchal domination.* Some claim that modern feminism has abandoned the cause of gender equality to become antagonistic toward men in a mission to *dismantle, fight,* and *smash the patriarchy,* as the mottos say. It is argued that having a feminist awakening has *destroyed* or *ruined* women and that modern feminism has pitted the sexes against each other in a *battle,* creating *the war of the sexes, the gender wars,* and the *war against men* in which men are perceived as the *enemy.* Feminists are accused of being *anti-male, man haters, man bashers,* and *misandrists.*

Misandry, the "hatred of males,"[35] was modeled after the earlier term, *misogyny,* which is often defined as the "hatred of women."[36] Today, the meaning of *misogynist* has broadened to refer to someone who dislikes or is prejudiced against women. In modern usage it has become a synonym for *sexist.* In 2012, then Australian Prime Minister Julia Gillard, Australia's first female leader, called the opposition leader Tony Abbott a "misogynist" for his repeated use of sexist language.[37] (Abbott had also allowed himself to be photographed with placards bearing the slogans,

"Ditch the bitch" and "Ditch the witch.")[38] Gillard's opponents staunchly denied that Abbott was a *woman hater*. They accused her of exaggeration, and of not understanding the meaning of the word misogynist. The incident inspired the *Macquarie Dictionary*, Australia's most authoritative dictionary, to update its definition of *misogynist* from the former "pathological hatred of women" to "entrenched prejudice against women." However, certain groups of men are accused of having a pathological hatred of women and are branded *misogynists*, *anti-feminists*, and *women haters*.

The controversial Men's Rights movement, the title modeled after the Women's Rights movement, appeared in the 1970s as a countermovement to feminism. Men's rights advocates have some serious concerns, including the conscription of men, sexual violence against men, and the discrimination of men in family courts with regard to child custody after divorce. (Ironically, in many of these instances of sexism against men, the perpetrators are not women but other men.[39]) These issues are not central to feminist theory; however, some components of the movement are anti-feminist. For example, Men's Rights Activists, popularly known online as *MRAs*, state that women have rights and advantages in society that men do not, and that men are oppressed by women. They say that "the system" favors women, and argue that the concerns of men are considered to be less legitimate than the concerns of women. Some claim that affirmative action and similar attempts to correct institutional sexism constitute *reverse sexism*. (This term poses the same problems as *reverse racism*, implying that sexism against women is somehow expected or "normal," whereas sexism against men is unusual or strange.) Not all MRAs are men, such as former feminist Bettina Arndt, who says there is a pervasive "anti-male bias" in society, and that modern feminists are guilty of "manshaming."

Many so-called MRAs belong to an online network of blogs, forums, and websites that discuss issues related to men and is known collectively as the *Manosphere*. One popular online movement is called MGTOW (Men Going Their Own Way). These various groups tend to have a focus on community and anti-feminism, rather than activism of men's rights. This environment has bred contempt and hostility toward women, with many MRAs behaving in an abusive or harassing manner online, and often anonymously, although the community denies they are sexist or misogynistic. (Similar to *racist*, when accused of being a *sexist* (*chauvinist* or *misogynist*), many people tend to reject these labels and deny the accusation. The comparable phrase *I'm not a sexist, but …* is used as a shield to avoid being labeled *sexist* when expressing sexist attitudes.) MRAs appear to have a complicated relationship with women. They are said to be critical and abusive of women, but on the other hand, to also desire women sexually (although usually in an objectifying way). Some MRAs present themselves as *Pick Up Artists* (PUA) and seducers, who devote their time to seducing as many women as possible, and operate websites offering advice on how to pick up women. If they don't prefer visiting sex workers, MGTOW tend to be celibate. They call this *going monk*, and tend to avoid relationships with women, in their fear of false rape accusations and *gold-diggers*, and their general dislike of women, or belief that women dislike men. This *Manosphere* subculture has its own vocabulary. A *Chad* is a popular and attractive man who has no problems finding girl-friends, while *Stacy* is his female counterpart. According to their lingo, someone who has swallowed the *red pill* has woken up to the "fact" that society discriminates against men, not women. A *blue pill* is a person who "hasn't woken up to this fact." These terms are a nod to the 1999 film *The Matrix*, referring to a red pill that the main character must swallow in order to become aware of the "dark truths" about the world.

A related online community of youths is known as *incels*. Unlike MGTOW, incels ("involuntary celibate") do not want to be celibate. These young people (usually men) blame society, feminism, and women for their unwanted celibacy and believe that women owe sex to men. Incels have a reputation for violence as revenge for their perceived sexual and social rejection. A self-identified 22-year-old "incel," Elliott Rodger, posted a series of

YouTube videos titled "Elliott Rodger's Retribution" and penned his "manifesto," a lengthy autobiography describing his wishes for violent retribution against women because he was a virgin and had "never even kissed a girl."[40] On May 23, 2014, he went on a stabbing and shooting rampage near the University of California, Santa Barbara, where he injured 14 people and killed 6. He then killed himself with a gunshot wound to the head. In the final pages of his manifesto he declared, "I am the true victim in all of this. I am the good guy."[41] Rodger is idolized as a "hero" within the incel community, where he is referred to as "Saint Elliot." Rodger has inspired other killing sprees, including the Toronto van attack of April 23, 2018. This is attributed to 25-year-old Alek Minassian, who allegedly went on a vehicle ramming attack through the streets of Toronto, Canada, killing 10 pedestrians and injuring 16. In a Facebook update posted prior to the spree, Minassian declared the "Incel Rebellion" and praised Rodger with, "All hail the Supreme Gentleman Elliot Rodger!"[42]

Men's rights activists, MGTOW, incels, and related groups have a traditional view of masculinity that is based on stereotypical gender roles, which they call *Neomasculinity*. Outside group labels tend to have more negative connotations. Gender scholars refer to this ideology as *hegemonic masculinity*, while in popular culture it is known as *hypermasculinity* or *toxic masculinity*. Many of these stereotypes of manhood and womanhood are reflected in language. Traditionally, a woman is expected to be polite, delicate, docile, and feminine. She must be *ladylike* and *act like a lady*, and then men will *treat her like a lady*. As the *fairer sex*, she is expected to be attractive and to take care of her appearance. Young girls often hear the comments, *You're pretty*, and *She's so beautiful*, which teaches them that being good-looking is a woman's worth and value in society. They learn that if they are not beautiful, they can be smart instead, but they must have either *beauty or brains*. According to traditional roles, men are said to be the *dominant sex*. Men are expected to be physically strong, whereas women are referred to as *the weaker sex*. Traditional etiquette requires that women have doors opened for them, chairs pushed in for them, and heavy objects carried for them. A traditional man should be a gentleman and chivalrous toward women. However, Neomasculinity declares that *chivalry is dead*, because feminists have killed courtship and romance. It is argued that if a woman shouldn't be expected to make a sandwich, a man shouldn't be expected to pay for dinner on a date. Neomasculinity states that women can either enjoy special treatment from men, *or* equality, but *women can't have it both ways*.

According to sexist ideology, women need to be protected but also controlled and *kept in their place*. They should be submissive, passive, quiet, and even-tempered. Women who are not are branded *difficult* and *dramatic* or as *drama queens* and *bitches*. Ex-girlfriends and ex-wives are commonly dismissed as *crazy* or *psycho*. Wives are described as *shrews* or *shrill*, and their voices *nagging* and *grating*. Women in general are described as *emotional, irrational, irritable, neurotic, hormonal,* and *hysterical*. Until quite recently, *female hysteria* was pathologized as a disease. Since ancient times, Egyptian and Greek societies believed that women could develop a "wandering womb," wherein her uterus migrated around her body, placing pressure on other organs and causing disease. By the eighteenth century, hysteria was viewed as a mental disorder that caused a woman to become anxious, depressed, and emotional. Over time, treatments have included exercise, smelling salts, hysterectomy, sex (or abstinence), pregnancy, or gynecological massage until *paroxysmal convulsion* was achieved (that is, an orgasm).[43] Hysteria was considered to be a mental disorder and was listed in the *Diagnostic and Statistical Manual of Mental Disorders* until it was removed in 1980, while hysterical is still used to describe a woman who is considered to be *overly emotional* or *deranged* (see also Chapter 5).[44]

Women are still said to suffer from *mood swings*. Their emotional state is blamed on *PMS*, it being *that time of the month* or *she's on the rag*. Conversely, when a woman behaves *like a man* by displaying dominance, independence, and assertiveness, her behavior is reinterpreted negatively as controlling, aggressive, domineering, and unfeminine. Politicians such as Hillary

Clinton and Elizabeth Warren are often described as "not like-able," because they defy traditional gender roles in their behaviour. Strong women are often accused of having *penis envy*; that is, that they are envious of the power and status of men. Conversely, some men's rights activists say that men having all the power in society is only an illusion. They argue that women control and exploit men through the power of their sexuality. Women are said to manipulate men by engaging in or withholding sex. In a relationship where a strong woman is considered to be the dominant partner, the man is derided as *hen pecked, pussy whipped, limp-dicked*, a *eunuch*, or *dickless*, while *she wears the pants in the relationship*. If a husband shares the *women's work* in the home, then it is said his wife must have him *well-trained*.

From a young age, children are socialized into gender roles that dictate their expected social behavior, from their choice of toys to their clothing and its colors. Boys are conditioned to prefer the so-called "masculine" color blue, while girls are conditioned to favor the "feminine" color pink. Ironically, this is nothing more than a more recent fashion trend. Prior to the mid-nineteenth century, the opposite was thought to be true. Pink was perceived as a "stronger" color suitable for a boy, while blue was viewed as delicate and dainty, and therefore more appropriate for a girl.[45] Pink is also used metaphorically to refer to women, in the phrases *pink-collar jobs*, relating to work traditionally associated with women; *pink wave*, an increase in female political candidates in the United States; and the *pink tax*, the extra amount paid for goods and services marketed toward women and girls because of gender-based price discrimination.

Children, as well as adults, are expected to conform to rigid gender roles that are diametrically opposed; girls are emotional, gentle, and submissive, while boys are logical, tough, and dominant. It's a compliment for a boy to be like his dad; *like father like son*. Comparisons of boys to girls are often negative. A boy is told to not *throw like a girl, hit like a girl*, or *run like a girl*. He should not be *girly* or *sissy*. Even for adult women, being too *girly* is often perceived as a bad thing. Gendered stereotypes of adults tell us that women are inherently *bad drivers* and *bad at computers*, while men supposedly cannot cook or clean. Traditional gender roles dictate that women and girls should be *feminine*, while men and boys should be *masculine*. Gender roles demand that a man should be *macho* and *manly* and not reveal a *feminine side*. Feminists are often accused of defying this structure by making women more *mannish* and *man-like*, but also of *feminizing* society, and especially men.

Emasculating insults are popular among men's rights activists (in the vocabulary of the Manosphere) to describe and humiliate male feminists, feminist allies, and pro-feminist males. Like a modern form of chivalry, a *white knight* is a man who *comes to the rescue* of a *damsel in distress* to defend her honor when it is attacked on the Internet. (He is accused of only wanting to have sex with her.) Other terms insult men who are perceived as unmasculine, submissive, and womanish. A *mangina*, a portmanteau of *man* and *vagina*, is a man with a weak masculine side. A *soy boy* (or *soyboi*) is a man who is woman-like or not manly enough. The term comes from the urban legend that consuming soy will lower testosterone and increase estrogen production in men, thereby making them more effeminate. Soy is a meat alternative eaten by many male vegetarians and vegans, who are stereotyped as *wimps*, while eating (red) meat is perceived as masculine, as shown by the tropes *Real men eat meat* and *Real men don't eat quiche*. (Some foods are gendered. There is the idea that men eat meat and other manly, hearty foods, while women eat salads and sweets, foods that are considered to be dainty and feminine.)

A *beta male* (or *beta*) is a man who is weak, meek, timid, and not assertive, as opposed to his counterpart, the dominant, aggressive *alpha male* (as borrowed from animal etiology.) The *Chad* of the MRA vocabulary is viewed as an alpha type male. *Cuck* or *cuckold* (literally referring to a submissive man sexually cuckolded by a woman) is an insult for a weak, emasculated man. Many of these terms have entered mainstream language. During a presidential debate in 2015, Donald Trump complained that moderator Megyn Kelly asked tough questions of him because "there was blood coming out of her whatever." (Harking back to the PMS trope.) Radio host Rush Limbaugh later remarked, "If Trump were your average, ordinary, cuckolded Republican, he would have apologized by now."[46] This term has also given rise to the vulgar portmanteau *Cuckservative* to refer to a political conservative considered to be excessively moderate or too willing to compromise.

According to popular culture, and the Manosphere in particular, there is a trope that women prefer a *bad boy* type, a *bastard*, *asshole*, *jerk*, or *player*, to a *Nice Guy*. This stereotype holds that women are more interested in a man if he is unkind to her. *Treat 'em mean, keep 'em keen* goes the adage. *Nice Guys* are viewed negatively as overly sensitive, vulnerable, boring, needy, and weak, when a woman wants a strong man to lean on. The related acronym *SNAG* (Sensitive New Age Guy) mocks a man who is seen as having feminine characteristics. It is feared that a woman only ever wants a platonic relationship with *The Nice Guy* who is relegated to the *friend zone* with the dreaded rejection, *let's just be friends.* Alternatively, he is rejected with the backhanded compliment, *You're like a brother to me.* This attitude is borne out by the saying *nice guys finish last.* Within this community, a woman who is *man-like* in her behavior is welcomed as a *chill girl, just one of the guys*, or even an *honorary man*, whereas a man who is *woman-like* is rejected as a *wimp*, a *wuss*, a *pansy*, or a *pussy*. If he does anything seen as *unmanly* by his peers his *man card* will be revoked.

By promoting the traditional gender role of a man as rational, unemotional, and in control of his feelings, toxic masculinity limits the emotions "allowable" for boys and men to express. Society encourages men to show emotional restraint. There is cultural pressure for a man to be stoic, self-reliant, and tough; a *tough guy*. Men (especially white, middle-class, straight men) are socially conditioned to repress their feelings. From an early age, boys are taught to hide their emotions, to *grow up* and *be a big boy*, because *boys don't cry* like a *little girl*. A popular understanding of masculinity is that *men don't cry, women do.*[47] A masculine man is expected to restrain or hide his tears or pretend to have something in his eye. Men are told to *suck it up, grow a pair of balls, stop being a princess, man up, take it like a man, act like a man, be man enough, be a man,* or be *a real man.*

In some contexts, gender labels can become insults. Referring to an adult male as a *boy* is demeaning and has racial implications. (See Chapter 1.) However, it can be considered endearing to call a boy a *little man*, while *little woman* is an (often belittling) term for a wife. Similarly, referring to an adult woman as *girl, little girl,* or *little lady* can be disparaging and infantilizing. In 2012, UK Labour MP Austin Mitchell abused his former colleague Louise Mensch when she disagreed with something her husband had said. In a message that appeared on Twitter, Facebook, and his official website, Mitchell wrote, "Shut up Menschkin. A good wife doesn't disagree with her master in public and a good little girl doesn't lie about why she quit politics."[48] There is also a recent tendency for *female* to be used as a synonym for *woman*, but in a derogatory way.[49] *Female* is used as a noun, often to show contempt, as in the stereotype, *Females are too emotional.* Using the adjective as an identifying label, *a female* is comparable to calling someone *a black* as opposed to *a black person.* Replacing *woman* (which specifically means "female human") with *female* (which non-specifically means "female species of animal") can be a dehumanizing way of talking about people, and it is noted that *man* is rarely replaced with *male* in this way. As we have seen, some older synonyms for *woman* have also become derogatory, such as *wench, hussy, dame,* and *broad.* *Woman* can be wielded as an insult too, especially when paired with disparaging qualifiers such as *old woman, stupid woman,* or *difficult woman.* During the 2016 US presidential election, Donald Trump referred to his opponent Hillary Clinton as, "such a nasty woman."[50] *Nasty woman* was quickly adopted as an empowering label for women who do not adhere to traditional gender roles. The phrase became an Internet meme, and a popular motto on mugs, t-shirts, and buttons.

Some of the most offensive insults and swearwords in the English language are related to women. Many of these terms of abuse invoke female body parts. When the word emerged during the thirteenth century, *cunt* referred literally to "the female genitals; the vulva or vagina,"[51] but it was not considered obscene at the time. Today, it is generally accepted that *cunt* is the most tabooed swear word in English. It is so offensive that it is often referred to as the *c-word*, or censored with asterisks or dashes. The lexicographer Samuel Johnson omitted the word from the first *Dictionary of the English Language* (1755),[52] while it appears as **** in *A Classical Dictionary of the Vulgar Tongue* (1796), where it is defined as, "a nasty word for a nasty thing."[53] Despite its offensiveness (particularly in US English), *cunt* is in common usage as a strong insult to describe a despised person. It is equally used in a jocular, familiar sense in Australian English, in phrases such as, *How are you going, you old cunt?* In a literal sense, *cunt* is a dysphemism for "female genitals," while *twat, cooch, beaver, muff, quim, minge, fanny*, and *pussy* are just some of the dozens of euphemisms. There have been some attempts to reclaim *cunt* as a positive term by those who resent the use of a female-related word as profanity. The revulsion for the word and its referent is often thought to reflect contempt for women. As general terms of abuse, *cunt, twat, pussy*, and the related insult *douche* are all used toward both sexes, although predominately toward men. They imply that a man is weak, like a woman, and insult men by association with women and femininity. Some profanity refers to male genitalia, but these terms are often considered less offensive, including *dickhead, bollocks, dick, prick, cock*, and *knob*.

Many terms of abuse for women refer negatively to their appearance, such as *witch, crone, battle-axe*, or *bag*, while these insults further imply age and are often paired with *old*, such as *old hag, old biddy*, or *old bat*. (See also Chapter 7.) *Bimbo* implies youth and beauty but insults a woman's intelligence. It is interesting to note that in the early twentieth century, *bimbo* originally meant "an unintelligent man," but it shifted in meaning to refer to a woman who is "sexually attractive but of limited intelligence."[54] Animal metaphors are commonly used as dehumanizing insults, in which a woman is likened to the stereotypical traits ascribed to the creature. A spiteful woman is described as *catty*, an evil woman is a *dragon* or a *bat*, a larger woman is a *cow* or *pig*, while an ugly woman is a *horse* or *dog*.

Bitch is one of the most common insults used against women. Derived from Old English, bitch literally meant "a female dog". Since the fourteenth century, it has been used as an insult toward women, especially "a malicious or treacherous woman."[55] In modern use, bitch can have either negative or positive connotations, depending on the context. When used in a negative sense, *bitch* refers to a woman who is variously considered to be mean, bossy, cold, domineering, aggressive, intimidating, or masculine; qualities that are usually valued in men. As such, *bitch* is a common insult used to attack women in spaces typically dominated by men, such as politics. *Bitch* is also used as a general term of abuse for women, to express hostility and contempt. Since the 1960s, there have been ongoing efforts to reclaim *bitch* as a positive word to describe a woman who is assertive, strong, competitive, and independent.[56] *Bitch* can also be used in a jocular way among friends, to show familiarity. There are many euphemisms for *bitch*, including *biotch*, *beyatch*, and *biznatch*, which can all be used humorously. *Bitch* is also applied to men; in this sense it is an emasculating insult that likens a man to a woman. But there is no masculine equivalent to *bitch* as used against a woman to show anger and derision. *Son of a bitch* and *SOB* are male-specific insults, although they are less offensive than *bitch*, while they still relate back to women. Similarly, *motherfucker* describes an unpleasant person, and usually a man, but the insult relates back to women.

According to traditional gender roles in our society and the way we talk, women are expected to be the *moral guardians* or gatekeepers of sexuality. By this thinking, a young woman must be virtuous, wholesome, and sexually pure. But there is a sexual double standard. A young man is encouraged to *play the field* and *sow his wild oats*, that is, to have sex with as many women as possible before he settles down. In contrast, premarital sex is considered to be unacceptable for a young woman, who is expected to remain a virgin until she is married. Her virginity is talked about as a precious *gift* that she should only give to her husband. Only a *good girl* is considered to be *wife material.* There is the saying that *men only want sex, while women want love.* But if a woman does *sleep around* before marriage, she is considered to be *used goods* or *damaged goods.* The woman is blamed if she *gets herself into trouble* and *gets herself pregnant,* and she may be accused of trying to *trap* or *trick* the man into marriage. Then the father-to-be must *do the right thing* by marrying her to *make an honest woman of her.* In what is known as the Madonna–Whore Dichotomy, women are cast as "either 'good', chaste, and pure Madonnas, or as 'bad', promiscuous, and seductive whores."[57]

Many terms of abuse for women imply promiscuity, including *tart, tramp, slag, skank, moll, slut, floozy, Jezebel, whore, ho* (derived from *whore*), *thot* ("that ho over there"), and *loose.* Women are *slut-shamed* by these terms for their real or presumed sexual activity, which attack a woman's right to say "yes" to having sex. In stark contrast, promiscuous men are instead praised as a *stud, playboy, ladies' man, lady killer, Don Juan, Casanova,* and *Lothario;* labels that have positive connotations of handsomeness, charm, and virility. This difference in attitudes and labels across gender implies that when a woman has sex, her worth decreases, but when a man has sex, his worth increases. If a man has an ongoing extramarital affair, *the other woman* or *adulteress* is his *mistress* or *bit on the side,* and branded a *homewrecker,* while his spurned wife might be described as bitter and vengeful. As the saying goes, *hell hath no fury like a woman scorned.* However, there is no equivalent term for an adulterous male partner, so this kind of behavior does not define or condemn the unfaithful man in the same way it does the woman.[58]

Similarly, there are comparatively few names for men who provide sexual services in return for payment, including *male prostitutes* or *male escorts.* These are the marked forms of each label, suggesting that a prostitute or escort is typically a female. In contrast, there are many words for female sex workers: *whore, harlot, hooker, call girl, working girl, trollop, lady of the evening, streetwalker,* and *strumpet,* that all have negative connotations.

Labels for sex workers often make a comment on a woman's morality, including *fallen woman, loose woman, scarlet woman, woman of ill repute*, or a *woman of easy virtue*. To avoid the negative overtones of these labels, the sex industry now favors the euphemism *provider*. Meanwhile, the male customers of providers are known by non-judgmental slang terms, including *john, buyer, trick*, and *hobbyist*, while their pastime is referred to as a *hobby*.

Prostitution, pornography, exotic dancing (stripping), and other types of sex work are often viewed as objectifying, along with the portrayal of people, especially women, as sex objects in advertising, music videos, television, movies, and beauty contests. Objectifying language only values a woman as *eye candy* and an object of male desire, rather than as a person with thoughts and feelings. A woman is often talked about as an object; a *doll*, a *dish*, a *skirt*, a *bit of skin*, a *bit of crumpet*, or a *piece of tail*. She is referred to by her body measurements, such as the so-called *perfect vital statistics* of *36–24-36*. She is reduced down to a specific body part, such as the character "Hot Lips Houlihan" from the TV show *M*A*S*H*. In 1989, *Time* magazine bestowed Australian model Elle Macpherson with the nickname *The Body* (of Our Time).[59] Images of women are fragmented and fetishized in film, TV, on book covers, and in advertisements. In 2016, comedian Marcia Belsky began a social media project to document the "Headless women of Hollywood," in which she collected the numerous movie posters that feature the faces of men but only a faceless woman's legs, cleavage, or other body part, except her head.[60]

Some men profess to have a preference for a particular female body part, describing themselves as a *breast man, butt man*, or *leg man*. A self-styled *boob man* may have a preference for a specific bra cup size. Women are often identified metonymically by the color of their hair, as *the brunette, the redhead*, or *the blonde bimbo with the big tits*. Often they are referred to specifically as sexual body parts; as *Double D, tits and ass* or *T&A, pussy*, or a *piece of ass*. In a 2004 interview, Donald Trump allowed shock jock Howard Stern to refer to his daughter Ivanka Trump as a "piece of ass."[61] Women are sexualized and talked about as possessions or playthings; as objects to be used for sexual gratification. They are perceived as conquests or prizes to win, such as a *sugar baby* or a *trophy wife*. A man can be said to *score* with a woman, but then she becomes just another *notch on his bedpost* or number in his *little black book*. A woman's worth is often based on her desirability, which is then pitted against other women. Facemash, the forerunner to Facebook, was a site that placed photos of female college students beside each other and asked users to choose the *hotter* woman.[62] Women's appearance might be rated on a scale of 1–10. In the movie *10*, the bride-to-be played by Bo Derek is rated an "11" by Dudley Moore's character, who proceeds to stalk her on her honeymoon to Mexico. In the above-mentioned conversation with Stern, Trump said, "You know who's a great beauty? My daughter Ivanka. Now she's a 10."

There is the idea that, in an exclusively male setting, men often talk differently among themselves. When women are not present, men are free to engage in crude and vulgar talk about women and to boast about their sexual conquests. This is called *locker room talk*, named after the sports locker room-style environment where it stereotypically takes place. This behavior is often excused, normalized, or even encouraged as *male bonding*, *men's club*, and *boy's club*. It is brushed off as *boys will be boys*, *it's just a guy thing*, and *that's just how men talk*. During the 2016 US presidential election, a recorded conversation between Donald Trump and Billy Bush surfaced. In this *Access Hollywood* videotape recorded in 2005, Trump bragged about forcibly kissing and groping women. Two widely shared quotes were, "I moved on her like a bitch, but I couldn't get there. And she was married. I did try and fuck her," and also, "You know, I'm automatically attracted to beautiful – I just start kissing them. It's like a magnet. Just kiss. I don't even wait. And when you're a star, they let you do it. You can do anything. Grab them by the pussy. You can do anything."[63] Trump shrugged off his talk about assault and adultery as "locker room banter."

The use of objectifying language can lead to or accompany objectifying behavior. Women are subjected to *street harassment* in public areas such as streets, shopping malls, restaurants, and on public transportation, and to *sexual harassment* in the workplace or community. Sexual harassment can include lots of different kinds of non-verbal behavior. Women feel uncomfortable under the *male gaze*, when men *stare*, *leer at*, or *ogle* them. A man eyes a woman up and down, known as *elevator eyes*, or he *undresses her with his eyes*. Non-verbal harassment includes honking at or following someone, blocking their path, or making facial expressions at them, such as winking, throwing kisses, licking lips, making sexual gestures with the hands or body movements, or exhibiting (flashing). There is the stereotypical scenario of the construction workers *wolf-whistling* at or *catcalling* women passing by. Harassing verbal behavior can include making kissing sounds, howling, smacking lips, calling someone *honey*, *dear*, *doll*, *sugar*, *sweetheart*, *darling*, or *baby*. Referred to by the innocuous-sounding *diminutives*, *terms of endearment*, or *pet names*, these names imply familiarity and affection, although they can be interpreted as condescending, patronizing, and even contemptuous. Sexual harassment can involve making sexual comments about a person's body, such as *nice legs*, *nice rack*, or *nice ass*, or telling a woman to *smile*, *loosen up*, or not be *so serious*. Sexual harassment can also include physical behavior, such as standing close to or touching another person or touching oneself sexually around a person.[64]

The woman is expected to respond positively to this harassment; to smile, giggle, blush, bat her eyelashes, or reply in kind. But in actuality, she often feels uncomfortable, fearful, intimidated, powerless, ashamed, embarrassed, or humiliated. She sees the man as a *creep*, a *pervert*, or a *sleaze*, and his behavior as *rapey*. (Derived from the word *rape*, *rapey* is a contemporary term that describes a man who acts *creepy* by giving unsolicited hugs or kisses, leering, making sexually suggestive remarks, or in general, giving off a *creepy vibe*. The word is deliberately exaggerated, describing inappropriate behavior that is a *red flag* for a would-be rapist.) A woman who is harassed may feel like she is being *treated like a piece of meat*. But if she ignores the man's advances, she is accused of not having a sense of humor or she is branded a *prude, lesbian, bitch,* or *slut.* When a woman rebuffs a man in a bar, a common face-saving response is, *You don't want to go out with me? You're ugly anyway.* She is expected to interpret the behavior, not as harassment but as flattery, attention, or playfulness. He may defend himself with, *But I was just trying to give you a compliment.* Or he may argue that he was just admiring, appreciating, or flirting with her. But women often interpret this behavior as threatening, and fear for their safety. If she complains or reports the incident, she may be accused of *over-reacting,* because it is just a trivial or small matter. However, sexual harassment can escalate. In November 2019, 19-year-old college student Ruth George was catcalled by a man in Chicago but she ignored him. Angry that he was being ignored, the man followed her into a parking garage, where he put her in a chokehold from behind and dragged her into the back seat of her car. He proceeded to sexually assault the unconscious woman. The force with which he choked George caused her to be strangled to death.[65]

In general, sexual harassment refers to "unwanted conduct of a sexual nature which has the purpose or effect of violating someone's dignity, or creating an intimidating, hostile, degrading, humiliating, or offensive environment for them."[66] Sexual harassment also extends to sexual assault, which involves forced sexual acts, including inappropriate touching, kissing, or grabbing a person's genitals. Rape is defined as a type of sexual assault that involves sexual intercourse or other sexual acts committed without consent. Throughout much of history, forced sex in marriage, known today as *spousal rape* or *marital rape,* was not considered to be a crime due to the belief that the husband enjoyed *conjugal rights,* which could be taken by force against the will of his wife. Marital rape was not completely outlawed in the Western world until the 1990s.[67]

The modern perception of sexual harassment is broadening, and transforming in line with new technology. Sexual violation can be digital as well as physical, including unwanted *sexting* (a portmanteau of *sex* and *texting*), which refers to the sending of sexually explicit messages or photos via phone. Sending *dick pics* is a common form of digital harassment in which a man sends an unsolicited candid photo of his penis to an unwilling recipient (also known as *cyber flashing*). Digital harassment includes sending unwanted messages of a sexual nature via email or social media, abusing people with sexually offensive language, or stalking people online. Nonconsensual pornography or *revenge porn*, which is the distribution of sexually explicit images of individuals without their permission, is an increasing problem online. On August 31, 2014, more than 500 celebrity photos, most of them nude, were leaked onto the imageboard website 4chan.[68] The incident was dubbed "The Fappening," which is a portmanteau of *fap*, a slang term for masturbation, and the title of the 2008 movie *The Happening*.

Sexual harassers are overwhelmingly male.[69] According to traditional gender roles, men are supposed to be potent, virile, and sexually aggressive. This belief is borne out by common figures of speech. It is said that men are preoccupied with sex; *Men have a higher sex drive than women, men only have one thing on their minds, he's thinking with his dick*, and *men are all the same*. A man feels he *deserves* and is *entitled* to sex from the women he is attracted to, and especially from his girlfriend or wife. Sex may be *just another chore* for a woman, but it is her *wifely duty* to be available and ready for sex, to *put out* and *please her man* at any time, whether she wants to or not. It is argued that there is a biological dimension to the aberrant sexual behavior of men, that it is not a result of social or cultural conditioning; it is *male instinct*. With all of that *testosterone pumping through their veins*, *hot-blooded* and *red-blooded* men have *needs* and *urges* that are *uncontrollable*. Urban legend states that *men think about sex every seven seconds*. It is said that a man simply cannot resist sexual temptation, *he can't keep it in his pants*, and if he does not have sex when he wants it, he will get *blue balls*. Men are told that *no means yes*, so *don't take no for an answer*. A man's belief that he is entitled to a woman's time, conversation, affection, or body is known as *male entitlement*.

The term *sexual harassment* did not exist until the 1960s, but even without a name for the behavior, it was extremely common, as it is today. In some sections of society there is a minimization of and complicity in sexual harassment. Traditional views still hold that sexism and sexual harassment are *normal* and *a part of life for women*. They are told they should just *accept it, deal with it, put up with it,* and *toughen up*. It is spoken of as a rite of passage to womanhood. Some older women culturally accept and perpetuate harassment by saying, *I went through it, and I turned out okay.* They are complicit in harassment when they state, *It's the price you pay for being a woman.* Women are groomed to accept bad behavior from men from an early age. It is said that girls are *sensible,* whereas boys are *silly, naughty,* and *immature,* while girls *mature faster than boys.* Girls are taught that teasing and bullying are forms of flirting and affection; *He picks on you because he likes you.* They are taught that men are predators; *Your dad will have to chase the boys away when you're older.* They are taught that (*dirty old*) men prey on younger women, even women in their own families, with the *creepy uncle* trope of a male relative or family friend who behaves inappropriately. Girls learn that sexual attention from boys and men is supposedly their fault when they are told, *don't wear that to school, you'll distract the boys.*

Victim blaming is holding victims and survivors responsible for the sexual harassment, sexual assault, or rape that is committed against them. Women's feminine performance is often used against them. Sexual harassment in the workplace may be blamed on the fact that the victim wore clothing that was *revealing* or *distracting* because it exposed her cleavage or legs. Date rape might be blamed on the victim for *dressing like a whore,* or being an *attention whore* who posts sexy selfies on social media. Victims are made answerable for their abuse with remarks such as *she wants it, she asked for it, she is asking for trouble, she is begging for it,* and *she deserved to get raped wearing those clothes.* When a woman reveals that she has been abused, she may be interrogated with questions like, *What were you wearing that night?* or

How much did you have to drink that night? It will be said that she *brought it on herself* because she was drunk or high. It will be said that she *led him on* by flirting with him, so she was a *prick teaser* or a *cock tease*. It is argued that women secretly desire nonconsensual sex because they *fantasize about rape*, and because many women enjoy reading *bodice-rippers*, a genre of romance novels that feature sex and violence. Acts of domestic violence are defended by perpetrators with the victim-blaming refrain, *See what you made me do?* In February 2020, following a domestic violence murder-suicide in Queensland, Australia, a police detective commented that this was a case of a "husband being driven too far" when he burned his estranged wife and their three young children to death in the family car.

Sexual harassment or assault is often denied. Assumptions are made about its rarity and it is trivialized. The panicky adverb *alleged* precedes claims of harassment to undermine their legitimacy. Survivors are accused of lying. It is said that a woman's accusations are *false*, she is *making it up*, or that she has *false memories* of what really happened. She is said to be experiencing guilt or shame after consensual sex; that she has *buyer's remorse*. She is accused of being a *slut*. As part of her *anti-slut defense*, she will be accused of saying she was too drunk to say *no*, so she could not be labeled a *slut* or have to take responsibility for having consensual sex. Some survivors who speak out are accused of being *vindictive*. It is said that she accused the man out of petty revenge, jealousy, or she is seeking money or attention. Survivors of sexual harassment experience lifelong negative effects, but their suffering is overlooked, and they are branded *career destroyers*. They are accused of having *ruined a man's life*, and his *reputation*, and of *dragging his name through the mud*. But if the claims were true, they ask, *why didn't she report the incident earlier?* Women are often too afraid, ashamed, or confused to report incidents of harassment. One study found that only one in five women report sexual harassment. Of these, 80 percent found that nothing changed as a result, while 16 percent said the harassment worsened.[70] Women are reluctant to report harassment, assault, and rape because of prevailing social attitudes and the existing legal system. When a woman stands up to accuse a man, she ends up being the one placed on trial in the court of popular opinion, and charged with a lack of credibility.[71] These attitudes are said to have created a *rape culture*; a society that excuses, normalizes, and tolerates sexual violence.

Sexual harassers are often in a position of power.[72] In October 2017, *The New York Times* published a story detailing decades of allegations of sexual misconduct against Hollywood producer Harvey Weinstein.[73] More than 80 women accused him of sexual harassment, assault, or rape, and making promises to advance their careers in return for sexual favors. In 2006, activist Tarana Burke began using the phrase *Me too* on social media to promote empowerment through empathy among women who have experienced sexual abuse. Following the Weinstein revelations, actor Alyssa Milano reinvigorated this *Me Too* movement by tweeting, "If all the women who have been sexually harassed or assaulted wrote 'Me too' as a status, we might give people a sense of the magnitude of the problem."[74] This inspired an international conversation in which countless women responded with "Me Too" (and the hashtag #MeToo) and shared their personal stories of sexual harassment. In 2020, Weinstein was convicted of rape and sentenced to 23 years in prison. Prominent politicians, comedians, actors, athletes, scientists, and other public figures, many of whom have been sexually abusing women and men for years, are finally beginning to face consequences for their actions.

There are many different reactions to the Me Too movement. It is said to be a *scary time for men*. Some see this social change as a form of persecution; saying it is an *attack against men*, and a *witch hunt*. They fear that women conflate flirting with sexual harassment, or construe behavior as harassment if they don't find the man to be attractive. There are complaints that *you can't talk to women anymore, you can't compliment women anymore, you can't flirt anymore*, and *you can't so much as look at a woman anymore*. The Me Too movement prompted the response on

Twitter, "Not all men are like that" from some feminist allies, which led to the hashtag #NotAllMen and *that's not me*. This is not an unexpected reaction; although similar to the All Lives Matter argument in response to Black Lives Matter, Not All Men is not a helpful reply to Me Too. Women know that not all men are rapists, murderers, or violent; they do not need to be told this.[75] However, when a woman encounters a man while walking down the street, or she goes on a blind date, she does not know which category the man belongs to: *the good men* or *the bad men*. Not All Men is a defensive argument that distracts from the topic at hand: sexism. Another common reaction to Me Too expresses apparent sympathy: *I have a daughter and I wouldn't want this to happen to her*. However, it is important to have empathy without having to think about how other people exist in relation to oneself. Not All Men was soon replied to with, "Yes All Men," arguing that even *the good men* are complicit in the behavior of *the bad men*, and that all men benefit from male privilege.

Male privilege describes the viewpoint that being a man, especially a straight white man, means being granted a lot of inherent privilege in society. That is, unearned advantages, opportunities, benefits, or rights which are afforded to men, solely on the basis of their sex. Men live without the fear of walking alone day or night, or being harassed on the streets and in the workplace. Men can dress how they want to and not worry that it will be used as a defense if they are raped. Men are not asked in job interviews how they will balance a career with a family, or not be hired because an employer assumes they will have children in the near future. Men who rise to prominence in their jobs will not be accused of sleeping their way to the top. Men can have promiscuous sex and be viewed positively for it. Men are not labeled *bossy* or *domineering*, or told to *loosen up* or *smile*. Men can use expressions and conventional language that reflects their sex. Men are not expected to change their last names when they marry. Men are treated better in society in most of the areas discussed in this chapter, because they belong to the non-stigmatized group. Male privilege has parallels to *white privilege* (see Chapter 1), the inherent benefits that white people enjoy in society. Women face prejudice, injustices, and fears that men might not even think about, recognize, or accept.

The idea of *male fragility* has parallels to *white fragility* and involves the anger, fear, denial, guilt, argumentation, silence, and use of other defensive moves by men when they are challenged about their sexism. (See Chapter 1.) Male fragility can involve the refusal to acknowledge the existence of modern sexism. It may be argued that a sexist phrase, *wasn't sexist back then*, or that sexism *isn't as bad in America* (or the UK, or Australia, etc.), or that sexism today *isn't as bad it used to be*. Sexism is often minimized, and it is argued that Westerners exaggerate women's issues. Sexism in the Western world is compared favorably to sexism in other countries, such as the plight of women in Muslim countries, gendercide (the preference for sons in India and China leading to female infanticide), child marriage, female genital mutilation, or the former practice of foot binding in China. These arguments imply that Western women, *have it easy in comparison*, and so they have *no right to complain*. However, sexism is still sexism at any level, and there is no hierarchy of what is valid sexism and what is not. Despite the advances in equality over time, social inequalities and power imbalances still exist between the sexes. As we can see, many of these biases are reflected in the English language. Sexism is still typically against women, but our modern language reveals that both men and women endorse and perpetuate sexist beliefs about each other and themselves. Maintaining strict gender roles can be harmful, although we belong to a culture that often demands gender and sexual conformity.

When a baby is born, the first question usually asked is, *Is it a boy or a girl?* But not all humans are born fitting into the male or female binary. Biologically, some people are not one or the other sex, but perhaps neither, or both. *Intersex* people are born with a combination of male and female biological characteristics.[76] They may have variations of sex chromosomes or sex hormones, or ambiguous genitalia, genitals that do not fit the typical definitions for male or female bodies. This is a naturally occurring variation in humans; with up to 2 percent of people having intersex traits, or 1 in 2,000 children.[77] However, intersex people are often stigmatized for their physical difference. Some cultures in African countries believe that intersex babies are *bad omens*, a sign of witchcraft, a punishment from God, and a curse on the family and community.[78] In these instances, the midwife kills the child and the parents are often told the child was stillborn and not to ask further questions.

The current medical name for intersex conditions is Disorders of Sex Development (DSDs), although some stakeholders find this term to be offensive, because it implies that having these traits is a defect or disorder. Others feel that the popular term *intersex* sensationalizes the condition. In the past, the term *hermaphrodite* was used, although it is now offensive. The name derived from Hermaphroditus, the character from Greek mythology who possessed both male and female physical traits. In scientific fields, hermaphrodite now describes an organism that has both male and female sets of reproductive organs.[79] When used to refer to humans the term is stigmatizing and also inaccurate, because it implies that the person is both male *and* female.

In the Western world, when a baby is born with a body that is deemed to be sexually ambiguous, parents and medical staff are forced to identify the newborn as either male or female on birth certificates and other official paperwork, so a gender is assigned. To support this gender assignment and in the hopes of avoiding future social ostracism, it is standard medial practice to surgically alter these infants and children to *fix*, *normalize*, or *correct* their genital appearance that is perceived as abnormal, unnatural, or deformed.[80] This *genitoplasty* or cosmetic genital surgery to reflect the sexual anatomy associated with "standard" male or female bodies is controversial. It is often criticized as *Playing God*. These irreversible procedures can cause scarring, sterilization, loss of sexual sensation, the need for lifelong hormone replacement therapy, and possible psychological harm.[81] The procedure also poses an ethical dilemma, because the person is too young to give informed consent for the surgery and may later reject the sex assignment. They may be assigned to be one sex, yet identify as another. They may also identify as a different gender.

Since the fourteenth century, *gender* has referred to grammatical categories (typically masculine, feminine, and neuter) of nouns and pronouns as used in languages such as Latin and Greek.[82] From the 1940s, gender has also been used to mean a person's internal sense of being a boy or a girl, or a man or a woman, as expressed by social or cultural factors, rather than biological ones. Gender is not genitalia; gender is determined by the brain rather than biology. There are several components to gender. A *gender role* is the social expectation of how people "should" behave, dress, and present themselves, based on their actual or perceived sex of male or female. *Gender expression* is how people express their gender through their name, behavior, mannerisms, clothing, hairstyle, voice, and other outward appearances. *Gender identity* is one's internal sense of being a woman, a man, or neither. Gender exists on a spectrum.[83] Some people do not fit neatly into one of two categories and instead identify as *non-binary, gender non-conforming, genderqueer,* or *transgender.* It is estimated that there are 1.4 million transgender people in the United States alone, and that number is on the rise.[84]

Transgender, trans, or *trans** are the preferred terms for people whose gender identity or gender expression is different than the sex that was assigned at birth. It is now offensive to use transgender as a noun, to refer to someone as *a transgender;* or a verb, *he is transgendered,* which is comparable to calling a gay person *a gay* or saying they have been *gayed.*[85] Other outdated terms include *tranny* (or *trannie*) as a slang term for transgender, while *transsexual* is now considered derogatory. Transgender is not to be confused with *transvestite,* an outmoded term for a *cross-dresser,* a person who wears clothing associated with the opposite sex. Dressing in *drag* is also different from transgender. *Drag queen* describes a man who *dresses as a woman,* while a *drag king* is a woman who *dresses as a man,* often for the purposes of entertainment. Transgender people are not in costume, acting as a character, playing a part, or pretending to be a man or a woman.

Transgender is contrasted with *cisgender*, which means "not transgender." *Cis-* comes from the Latin preposition meaning "on this side."[86] Often abbreviated to *cis*, a cisgender person's gender identity corresponds to the sex they were assigned at birth. The behavior, appearance, clothing, and genitals of cisgender people "match" how they feel about themselves. Non-binary gender describes any gender identity that does not fit inside the traditional male or female categories. Non-binary people have created their own self-identifying labels, and there are hundreds of unique identities for gender. Some of the more common non-binary identities include perceiving oneself as: *androgyne* (or androgynous), both masculine and feminine; *intergender*, in between male and female; *agender*, *no gender*, or *genderless*, having neutral gender; or *bigender*, *polygender*, *pangender*, or *all genders*, having multiple gender identities. Some indigenous North Americans use the term *two-spirit* to describe intersex, transgender, and non-binary people. (See also Chapter 3.) Two-spirit is a recent name that replaced the colonial-imposed label *berdache*, and is now used as an umbrella term for LGBTQ+ indigenous Americans. Two-spirit people are seen as a third gender, similar to *muxe*, a term used in Zapotec cultures of Oaxaca for a person who doesn't identify as a man or a woman, but as someone in between. These terms describe the fluidity of gender. Gender identities can be fixed or fluid, while *gender fluid* people have a gender identity that varies over time. Gender fluidity is the idea that gender is dynamic and can change over the course of a lifetime.

There is a naive belief that if a transgender person has not undergone surgery they are not really transgender. However, being transgender does not necessarily mean that the person has undergone gender-affirming surgery, which is costly and invasive. Not all transgender people undergo surgery, because there are many non-medical ways to transition. Social transitioning can include making changes to hairstyle or clothing to more accurately express one's gender. It can involve adopting a preferred first name, or using a non-gender-specific honorific such as *Mx* (usually pronounced "mixt"), *Ind.* (which stands for "Individual"), and *Misc.*, which are used in place of *Mr.*, *Mrs.*, *Ms.*, and *Miss.* Instead of the gender-specific pronouns *she/her* and *he/him*, transgender people may prefer the new gender-neutral pronouns *xe/xem/xir* or *ze/zem/zir* (corresponding to "they"/"them"/"their"). Many people have a preference for singular *they* as used in, *If someone hugged me, I'd hug them back.* This usage emerged in the fourteenth century and has been in common use ever since, even by revered authors such as Chaucer, Shakespeare, and Jane Austen, because this was Standard English until the Victorian era when grammarians imposed the use of generic *he*. Grammarians still prescribe the use of *he*, as in, *If someone hugged me, I'd hug him back.* Singular *they* is criticized by some style guides as substandard or "wrong." As we have seen, generic *he* is not gender-neutral and is perceived as sexist for promoting masculine gender as the default or norm. In 2019, Merriam-Webster announced the personal pronoun *they* as "word of the year" for its increasing usage by non-binary people.[87] The use of gender-neutral nouns is also becoming more popular, such as *all genders* instead *of men and women*. Both the London Underground and New York City subway no longer address *ladies and gentleman* in their announcements, but instead opt for *passengers*, *riders*, or *everyone*.[88]

Some transgender people do seek to transition medically, to bring their bodies into alignment with their innate gender identities. This is done by way of hormone therapy and/or surgery, which is called *sex reassignment surgery* (SRS) or *gender-affirming surgery*. (These are the preferred terms instead of the outdated and now derogatory *sex change operation*.) For these transgender people, feeling that their bodies do not reflect their gender can cause severe distress, depression, and anxiety. This state is called *gender dysphoria*, which may be a diagnosis to help them to receive medical treatment to assist in making a transition.[89] In psychiatry, gender dysphoria was formerly called *gender identity disorder*, but it was reclassified when the condition became better understood, and to remove the stigma associated with the label *disorder*. However, there are still many misconceptions about transgender people, with some believing that it *is* a disorder, a mental illness, a disease, or deviant behavior. There are some who believe that transgender people are sick, confused, or misled. They are told that they should *get over* the feeling that they *hate their bodies* or that they are *stuck* or *trapped in the wrong body*. Being transgender is often dismissed as just a *phase*, a current *trend*, or a *fad*. Transgender people are warned they will regret transitioning or will later change their minds. They are abused as *weird*, *strange*, *crazy*, or *perverts*, and dehumanized as *freaks*, *creatures*, *monsters*, and an *abomination*.

Transphobia and *cissexism* refer to the fear, dislike, or hatred of transgender, non-binary, or intersex people and the everyday discrimination and harassment they face in society. According to this prejudice, cisgender people are perceived as *normal* and *natural*, while transgender people are represented as *abnormal* and *unnatural*. Some cisgender people say they feel awkward and uncomfortable around transgender people, or they are even afraid of them. As a result of this ignorance, transgender people are stared at, whispered about, pointed at, and laughed at in public. Transgender people report various microaggressions. Curious strangers ask invasive and inappropriate questions about transgender people's bodies, genitalia, and lifestyle, including: *What's your sex?*, *How do you have sex?*, and *Do you have a penis or a vagina?*[90] They are asked personal questions about their medication or surgeries: whether they take hormones and have they had "the surgery" to "turn" them into a man or woman? Some transgender people are disagreed with, or accused of lying, when completing forms that ask for their sex.

Transgender people often experience a lot of negative judgment from others, whether they are recognized as transgender or not (at first). There is a stereotype that transgender people with a very feminine gender presentation who "pass" as women are only men *pretending* to be women in their attempts to *deceive* other people (or alternatively, women who *masquerade* as men). A transgender woman might be represented as *really a man disguised as a woman*. Having one's transgender identity *found out* or revealed can be dangerous for the person, and the representation of transgender people as *deceivers* has promoted and excused acts of transphobic violence. In Newark, California, in 2002, transgender woman Gwen Araujo was beaten, killed, and then buried in the Sierra wilderness. The slaying occurred at a party, after Araujo was subjected to forced genital exposure, and it was announced *he was really a man*.[91]

In contrast, a transgender person may see herself as a woman but be categorized as a man by others (or a transgender man categorized as a woman). If a transgender person is not viewed as "convincing" in their gender performance to be able to "pass" as a woman (or a man), they may be asked by strangers, *What are you really?* Transgender people may be accused of not looking "enough" like a woman (or a man) or of not appearing *womanly* (or *manly*). In 2009, Germaine Greer, who was a powerful feminist voice in the 1970s, referred to transgender women as "ghastly parodies" of femaleness.[92] It is often argued outside the group that transgender people are not *real* women (or men). In particular, there is the belief that only *women born women* are authentic, *real women*, and that a trans woman is really a man. This is a position held by a subgroup of "gender critical" feminists who have been labeled *trans-exclusionary radical feminists* (TERFs).[93] (People with this point of view consider the label to be a slur.) However, for transgender people, *transgender* is just an adjective used to describe a part of their identity, and they see themselves as no less of a woman (or a man). It is often said among the community, *a transgender woman is a woman* and *a transgender man is a man*.

Related to the belief that a person's sex assignment at birth is their *real sex* is the belief that a birth name or given name is that person's *true* or *real name*. Transgender people who have changed their names as part of their social transition may be asked, *What is your real name? The one you were given at birth?* Undergoing a name change can be an affirming step in the transition process and alleviate the suffering associated with one's former name.[94]

But friends, family, and colleagues may struggle to adhere to a transgender person's new name or even refuse to acknowledge the change altogether. *Deadnaming* is the practice of, intentionally or not, referring to a transgender person by the name they used before transitioning. This is invalidating and disrespectful to transgender people and can effectively "out" them, and expose them to discrimination and harassment.

Some transgender people are addressed by titles or pronouns that reflect how they identified before transition. This is known as *misgendering*, and it might involve mistakenly referring to a transgender woman as *sir*, *he*, or calling her *a guy*. Misgendering might be unintentional, but it can be avoided by asking for a person's preferred pronouns. Conversely, misgendering may be intentional, to show disproval for a *man pretending to be a woman*. As a form of social reproval, cisgender people are also misgendered deliberately for being a *gender bender* when they defy expected gender roles with respect to dress or behavior. For example, a man with long hair might be addressed contemptuously as *ma'am*, while a woman wearing boyish hair and clothing might be mockingly called *sir*. Transgender people report being addressed by the impersonal pronoun *it*, when they are deemed to be of indeterminate gender. This is dehumanizing, because *it* is typically used to refer to things, or non-human animals, but not to people. Related insults include *shim* and *heshe*, which are slang blends of pronouns that imply that a person's gender is unidentifiable. *Shemale* and *chicks with dicks* are abusive terms specifically used against transgender women, especially those who have undergone breast augmentation but still have a penis, while these labels are typically associated with the pornography industry.

Being cisgender, that is, having a gender identity that matches the sex assigned at birth, has social advantages and benefits. This is known as *cis privilege*. Transgender, non-binary, and intersex people face social stigma and everyday challenges that are not faced by cisgender people. In most countries, birth certificates, driver's licenses, passports, and other forms of government identification only offer *male* or *female* as gender options. Public spaces are not always inclusive, such as restrooms and change rooms, where transgender people using them have experienced verbal and physical abuse for not being a "real" woman (or man). Various states in the US have tried to pass "bathroom bills" to force transgender people to use the restroom associated with the sex assigned to them at birth, making it illegal for them to use the restroom appropriate to their gender identity, even though there is no legal or ethical way to enforce such a law. The need for gender-neutral restrooms has been met with scaremongering that sexual predators will exploit nondiscrimination laws by sneaking into women's restrooms to commit sex crimes, although this has been repeatedly debunked.[95] A large number of transgender people have experienced anti-trans discrimination, harassment, homelessness, and violence, and they are at a higher risk of suicide.[96] Our modern language reveals that transgender, non-binary, and intersex people are still feared, mocked, hated, and misunderstood in society and accused of "blurring the lines" of traditional gender roles.

3 Not That There's Anything Wrong with That

At the beginning of 1895, Oscar Wilde was the toast of London. Flushed with the success of *The Importance of Being Earnest*, the Irish playwright was known for his sharp intellect and sparkling wit. He was married with two children, and he had powerful friends among the social elite, including poet Lord Alfred Douglas, who was better known as "Bosie." But Bosie's father, John Douglas, the 9th Marquess of Queensberry, suspected this was more than just a friendship. He insulted Wilde publicly by leaving a calling card at his club that read, "For Oscar Wilde, posing as somdomite" (sic).[1] Sex between men was illegal at the time. Wilde sued for libel, although Queensberry's attorney located several male prostitutes who were ready to testify that they had had sexual relations with Wilde. Wilde dropped the charge, but then he was arrested and charged with committing sodomy. Wilde was convicted of "acts of gross indecency with men" and sentenced to two years hard labor, the maximum penalty for his crime. He lost his marriage and children, his wealth, his reputation, his desire to write, and his freedom. After serving his time in jail, Wilde left the United Kingdom in self-exile, never to return. He died in France in 1900; living his final years in poverty, humiliation, and shame, a social pariah because of his sexual orientation.

Same-sex attraction or *homosexuality* is the state of "being sexually or romantically attracted to people of one's own sex."[2] *Gay, lesbian, bisexual,* and *queer* are the main preferred terms to describe people who are attracted to members of the same sex. This sexual orientation is the opposite of *heterosexuality*, a "sexual attraction to individuals of the opposite sex,"[3] which is known colloquially as being *straight*. (This is contrasted with *bent* as slang for gay.) Same-sex attraction is universal; it is a natural variation that is found in all human cultures around the world.[4] Estimates suggest that between 1 and 4 percent of the population is gay or lesbian.[5] Same-sex behavior is a nearly universal phenomenon in the animal kingdom too and is common across species, from worms to frogs to birds.[6] Same-sex attraction has a very long history. It is written about and depicted as far back as ancient Greece and Rome, where it was commonplace for adult men to keep an adolescent boy as a lover, known as a *catamite*. However, attitudes toward same-sex attraction have changed over time. Some people believe that heterosexuality is the natural order, and *homosexuality* is then relegated to *unnatural, abnormal*, and *deviant*. Heteronormativity is the belief that heterosexuality is the *normal, standard*, or even *superior* sexual orientation. This attitude can underpin homophobia, which is a dislike, fear, or hatred of gay, lesbian, bisexual, and queer people; and heterosexism, which is prejudice against this community. Our modern language reveals that heterosexism and homophobia are still pervasive in society; however, the community has successfully reclaimed some slurs as a badge of pride.

Before the word *homosexuality* emerged, sexual relationships between men were labeled *sodomy*. Sodomy is derived from Latin *Sodoma*, the name of the town in the biblical tale of Sodom and Gomorrah.[7] The Book of Genesis (19:1–29) describes these cities as depraved, and their destruction by fire as divine judgment from God. Sodom has become synonymous with homosexuality. As a result of this association, there is a long history of the criminalization of gay sexual activity. Historically, *Sodomy laws* condemned sexual acts other than heterosexual intercourse, but especially oral sex and anal sex between men. Performing an act of sodomy made one a *sodomite*, and brutal punishments have been meted out in the past. In medieval Christian Europe, sodomites were burned at the stake, based on the fire and brimstone fate of Sodom and Gomorrah in the Bible. During the European colonization of the Americas, the Spanish conquistadors subjected "Indian sodomites" to severe punishments, including public execution or being torn to pieces by dogs.[8]

In 1533, King Henry VIII of England passed the Buggery Act, making gay sex a capital offense that was punishable by hanging.[9] *Buggery*, which was described as an "unnatural sexual act against the will of God and man," referred specifically to anal intercourse between males, and also to bestiality. In practice, buggery meant any sexual activity between two men. In more recent times, sodomy and buggery laws were repealed and replaced with *gross indecency*, like the offense of which Oscar Wilde was convicted. Those charged with this so-called "worst of crimes" faced fines, imprisonment, or spending many humiliating hours in a pillory, where members of the public could throw things at them, such as eggs, potatoes, mud, dung, dead cats, and slurs.[10] In recent decades, same-sex acts are finally being decriminalized around the world. Oscar Wilde was one of about 50,000 men pardoned for "homosexual crimes" that no longer exist under the Policing and Crime Act of 2017.[11] However, same-sex sexual activity is still illegal in over 70 countries, where it can result in fines, flogging, castration, incarceration in a psychiatric institution, or imprisonment.[12] In Iran, Yemen, Sudan, and Saudi Arabia, it is still punishable by death under Sharia law.

Homosexuality is no longer considered to be a crime in many countries, although some people still consider it to be a sin. In part, this is based on the biblical tale of Sodom and Gomorrah. Ironically, these passages do not explicitly identify gay sex as the "sin" for which the cities were destroyed.[13] Conservative Christians believe that God made men and women to complete each other and to procreate. Gay sex is not reproductive, so they perceive it as sexual deviancy. It is branded *immoral, depraved,* and *perverse.* There is a trope in which Evangelical Christians blame gay people for disease, acts of terrorism, and natural disasters, such as hurricanes, flood, and fire. They say that gay sex is not the *normal* kind of sex, and that such sexual relationships do not create a *normal* family. Gay sex is described as the *creation of the devil* that goes *against God's law* and is an *abomination.*

Several key passages from the Bible are interpreted as prohibitions against same-sex acts. Leviticus (18:22) says, "You shall not lie with a male as with a woman; it is an abomination," while Leviticus (20:13) adds, "If a man lies with a male as with a woman, both of them have committed an abomination; they shall surely be put to death; their blood is upon them."[14] The following passages of Scripture are also invoked to support the belief that gay sex is a sin: 1 Samuel 18:1, 2 Samuel 1:26, Judges 19:22, Peter 2:6–10, 1 Kings 14:24, 1 Kings 15:12, Jude 1:7, Matthew 8:5–13, Luke 7:1–10, 1 Timothy 1:8–10, Romans 1:-18–32, and 1 Corinthians 6.

However, this is open to interpretation. In the First Epistle to the Corinthians (6:9–10), Paul the Apostle refers to wrongdoers who "will not inherit the kingdom of God" using the Greek words *malakoi* and *arsenokoitai*. These are translated in the New Revised Standard Version of the Bible as "male prostitutes" and "sodomites" respectively, but their original meanings are highly debated. *Malakoi* literally meant "soft" and is used in the Bible elsewhere (Matthew 11:8 and Luke 7:25), where it has nothing to do with any kind of sexual behavior.[15] *Malakoi* was never used in reference to same-sex sexual behavior, while the word appears in writings contemporary with the Epistles of Paul in reference to straight people and activities.[16] *Malakoi* may instead refer to a man who is morally weak, lacking in courage, or effeminate. The precise meaning of *arsenokoitai* is not known. It appears for the very first time in 1 Corinthians, although it is speculated that it referred to the sexual abuse or exploitation of individuals. At the time, names for people who engaged in same-sex behavior already existed, including *paiderastes*, *pallakos*, *kinaidos*, *arrenomanes*, and *paidophthoros*, but these words are not used, while *malakoi* and *arsenokoitai* were never used specifically to refer to gay people.[17]

Despite these spurious interpretations, modern translations of this passage make explicit references to *homosexuality*. The English Standard Version (2011) translates both *malakoi* and *arsenokoitai* as "men who practice homosexuality." The book states, "Or do you not know that the unrighteous will not inherit the kingdom of God? Do not be deceived: neither the sexually immoral, nor idolaters, nor adulterers, nor men who practice homosexuality, nor thieves, nor the greedy, nor drunkards, nor revilers, nor swindlers will inherit the kingdom of God."[18] However, the concept of same-sex attraction as a sexual orientation is relatively new, and the words *homosexual* and *homosexuality* did not emerge until 1869, when they were coined by Hungarian journalist Károli Mária Kertbeny.[19] *Homosexuality* did not appear in any Bible translation until 1946, when the Revised Standard Version of the Bible collapsed *malakoi* and *arsenokoitai* into one word: *homosexuals*.[20] Other versions of the Bible provide judgmental translations. The 1973 edition translates these words as *sexual perverts*, the Jerusalem Bible uses *catamites* and *sodomites*, and the New International Version (NIV) favors the terms *male prostitutes* and *homosexual offenders*.[21]

In light of negative usages such as these biblical references, *homosexual* is not a neutral term; it is a slur. Through its association with anti-gay attitudes, *homosexual* has acquired negative connotations of disapproval and judgment.[22] The early gay rights movement was instead called the *homophile movement*, because activists rejected the word *homosexual* and its negative implications.[23] *Homosexual* is further sensationalized because it contains the word *sex*. This places an emphasis on sex, although for gay people, their sexuality is merely an attribute of their humanity. *Homosexual* also contains the prefix, -*homo*, which has been used as a slur. *Homo* is often coupled with descriptors that portray same-sex attraction as something disgusting, unclean, or impure, such as *dirty homo* and *filthy homo*. As a result of these negative associations, *homosexual* is considered derogatory when referring to people. Same-sex oriented people eschew the use of *homosexual* as a self-identifying label, instead referring to themselves by a range of preferred terms, most commonly *gay, lesbian, bisexual,* or *queer*. In most usage today, *homosexual* is perceived as old-fashioned, distancing, and clinical.

Historically, the word *homosexuality* had medical implications. Until quite recently, same-sex attraction was pathologized as a *disease, sickness, defect, disorder,* or as a mental illness. (This is still the case in some communities, as we will discuss.) Same-sex attraction has been presented as a danger to society, to families, and to children in particular. It has been associated with sexual perversion, such as pedophilia, child abuse, incest, and bestiality (harking back to the earlier definition of *buggery*). This theory held that *homosexuality* had a psychological or physiological basis, such as a trauma to the brain, sexual abuse, having had a dominant opposite-gender parent, or absent same-gender parent. It has also been linked to the effects of watching pornography or eating foods containing soy (see also Chapter 2).[24] The idea that *homosexuality* had a cause led to the belief that it could be *cured* by psychiatrists, psychologists, or physicians. Psychiatric treatments included cognitive behavioral techniques, hypnosis, aversion therapy, electroconvulsive therapy, and lobotomy. Medical and surgical attempts to change sexual orientation included hormone treatments, hysterectomy, vasectomy, and castration. During the Holocaust, thousands of gay men were imprisoned in Nazi concentration camps, while some were experimented upon in an effort to "cure" their sexuality.[25] It was not until 1973 that the American Psychiatric Association removed the diagnosis of *homosexuality* from its list of mental disorders in the second edition of its *Diagnostic and Statistical Manual (DSM)*.[26]

Today, it is understood that people are *born gay* or *born this way* (although human sexuality is complex and can be fluid). Same-sex desire is recognized as a natural difference among a minority of people, like left-handedness.[27] Sexual orientation is inborn and unchangeable, although some people still believe that *homosexuals choose to be that way*. The older phrases *sexual preference* and *alternative lifestyle* are offensive because they imply that sexual orientation is a choice. According to some conservative religious groups, the *homosexual lifestyle* is a choice that can (and should) be "cured," if the person wants to go to Heaven and not to Hell. Gay conversion therapy, "homosexual healing," and reparative therapy are all religious approaches to sexual orientation change efforts that purport to re-orient "practicing homosexuals" into heterosexuals, through prayer, confession, forgiveness, and self-discipline. Renouncing one's sexual orientation in the name of religion is known colloquially as to *pray the gay away*. Exodus International was an "ex-gay" ministry that promised to rid people of their unwanted same-sex urges. The organization was dissolved in 2013 when then-president Alan Chambers declared there was no cure for same-sex orientation and that reparative therapy offered false hopes and is potentially harmful.[28] In 1999, McKrae Game founded Hope for Wholeness Network, a faith-based conversion program that promoted the idea of "freedom from homosexuality through Jesus Christ." In 2019, Game renounced the practice and revealed that he is gay.[29]

In some cases, homophobia appears to be a facade to conceal or deny one's own repressed homoerotic feelings.[30] Several prominent political and religious figures who formerly campaigned against gay rights have been exposed for suppressing their same-sex desires. Pastor Ted Haggard preached that same-sex attraction was a sin, and he was a vocal critic of same-sex marriage. In 2006, a scandal erupted when it was revealed that Haggard had been engaging in sex with a male prostitute and had had an inappropriate relationship with a young male member of his congregation.[31] Glenn Murphy Jr., an anti-gay advocate and former president of the Young Republican National Federation, was sentenced to six years in prison after he was found guilty of sexual assault for performing oral sex on an unwilling man at a party in 2007.[32] Former Idaho Senator Larry Craig had vociferously campaigned against same-sex marriage. In 2007, he was arrested for "lewd conduct" in a men's restroom at the Minneapolis-St. Paul International Airport.[33] (In older British gay slang, seeking or obtaining sexual encounters in public restrooms is known as *cottaging*. A public restroom used for this encounter is called a *cottage*, the term coming from the lavatories in British parks that were often built in the style of a Tudor cottage.)

Throughout the nineteenth and mid-twentieth century, same-sex desire was taboo and illegal, so many euphemisms developed to talk about "the subject." During the Victorian era, following Wilde's conviction for *the unspeakable crime, Oscar* became a euphemism for a gay man.[34] His friend Bosie had written "Two Loves," a poem in which the last line is often taken to refer to same-sex attraction, "the love that dare not speak its name."[35] Early euphemistic words and phrases for a gay man included: *invert, unnaturalist, indorser, different, that way, odd, a bit funny, curious, artistic, extraordinary, earnest,* and *finger-twirler.* Within the community, a gay man might be called a *lavender lad, lavender boy,* or a *man with a dash of lavender.* Cole Porter's 1929 song "I'm a Gigolo" includes the lyrics, "I'm a famous gigolo. And of lavender, my nature's got just a dash of it."

At the time, the scent of lavender was often associated with effeminate men, while the colors lavender, violet, mauve, lilac, and purple came to symbolize flamboyance, art, the aesthetic, and same-sex desire.[36] Oscar Wilde once wrote to a friend about the time he spent with male sex workers who were called *rent boys*; "How evil it is to buy love, and how evil to sell it! And yet what purple hours one can snatch from that grey slowly moving thing we call Time."[37] The Lavender Panthers was a gay rights group in the 1970s, while the modern gay rights movement is often referred to as the *Lavender Revolution.* Southern Baptist Reverend Jerry Falwell (1933–2007) once claimed that Tinky Winky from the children's TV show *Teletubbies* was gay because the character carries a handbag, wears a purple tutu, and has an antenna shaped like a triangle, the symbol of gay pride.[38] The color pink is often symbolic of women and girls (see also Chapter 2), and so it has also became associated with effeminacy and gay men. Actor Rudolph Valentino was rumored to be gay, and his masculinity was questioned in a 1926 edition of the *Chicago Sunday Tribune,* in which he was famously called a "pink powder puff."[39] In Nazi concentration camps, gay inmates were identified by pink triangles on their prison clothes, which were a badge of shame.[40] The triangle has since been reclaimed by the community as a symbol of gay pride.

To avoid persecution, and as a form of signaling, the gay community created secret signs, symbols, and other subtle forms of non-verbal communication that were recognizable to insiders. At the 1892 premiere of his play *Lady Windermere's Fan*, Oscar Wilde gave a curtain speech wearing purple gloves and a green carnation in his buttonhole, while the flower was also worn by his friends in the audience.[41] After this act, green carnations became a covert identification through which gay men could recognize each other. (*The Green Carnation* was a scandalous novel by Robert Hichens, first published anonymously in 1894, the characters based on Wilde and Douglas.) In the late nineteenth and early twentieth centuries, gay men wore red-colored neckties, cravats, and other red accessories to signal their sexuality. In the 1930s, dark brown and gray suede shoes were worn as gay signifiers. In the 1970s and 1980s, there was the *hanky code*, a form of flagging in which gay men wore different colored handkerchiefs in the back pockets of their pants to broadcast their sexual tastes.[42]

Using code words and slang was another method for gay men to communicate with others in the know. Polari was a secret language (a *cant* or *jargon*) that was spoken by some people within the gay community in Britain between 1900 and the 1970s, allowing them to hide and to reveal at a time when same-sex sexual activity was outlawed.[43] An eclectic mix of Italian, Romani, Yiddish, and London slang, Polari was spoken in gay pubs, in the theater, in circuses, and on merchant ships. In the Polari language, gay men were known as *omee-palones*, meaning "men-women." (The above-mentioned *cottage* and *cottaging* are also Polari words.) The use of Polari declined following the introduction of the Sexual Offences Act in 1967, which decriminalized gay sex, while the gay liberation movement of the 1970s found the jargon to be old-fashioned and sexist. Polari reached the general public through the 1960s BBC radio comedy show *Round the Horne*, in which the characters Julian and Sandy (played by Hugh Paddick and Kenneth Williams) were camp, out-of-work actors. Through this show, some well-known Polari words entered mainstream English slang, including *camp*, *butch*, *mince, drag, trade,* and *fruit. Friend of Dorothy* is another code term for a gay man, the term dating back to World War II. The phrase is taken from the name of the character Dorothy Gale in the film *The Wizard of Oz* (1939), played by gay icon Judy Garland.

Hollywood had its own jargon too, including the terms *passion fruit, wolves,* and *trade* which referred to straight-acting gay men. These men kept their sexual orientation a secret because of the legal, religious, and social stigma at the time. When lesbian, gay, bisexual, and queer people have not disclosed their sexual orientation, this is known as being *closeted* or *in the closet.* (Today, this is also called *on the down-low* or *DL,* which is an African American slang term.) During the Golden Age of Hollywood, male gay actors had a fear of being publicly *outed,* having someone else expose their undisclosed orientation. Gossip about a gay actor's sexuality could ruin his career and the film studio with which he worked. To avoid public scrutiny and the disapproval of fans, movie moguls placed morality clauses in their actors' contracts, ordering them to hide their sexual orientation and to "pass as straight," to maintain the appearance of being heterosexual. For this reason, some straight-acting gay actors entered into marriages of convenience that became known as *lavender marriages.*

It is said that actor Rudolph Valentino's marriages to Jean Acker (1919) and Natacha Rambova (1922) were lavender marriages.[44] In 1955, Rock Hudson married Phyllis Gates, his agent's secretary, as a cover, hearing that *Confidential* magazine was planning to out him.[45] And in 1954, Liberace announced his engagement to actor Joanne Rio, but they never ended up marrying and she later revealed that the relationship was a publicity ploy.[46] During the twentieth century, *He never married* was a code phrase used by obituary writers in the UK to signify that the deceased had been gay. During the late nineteenth to the early twentieth century, two women living together in a romantic but asexual relationship was known as a *Boston marriage,* the term coming from the ambiguous cohabitation of two women as portrayed in Henry James' 1886 novel *The Bostonians.*[47] Today, *bearding* is a slang term for gay men or lesbian women who hide their sexuality by appearing to date or marry someone of the opposite sex. Related terms include *fag hag, queen bee, fruit fly, fruit loop,* and *fairy princess,* which are (often) derogatory names that all refer to a straight woman who keeps company with gay men.

Straight people are never expected to pretend to be gay, although historically, many gay people have led double lives to avoid harassment and discrimination. Throughout the 1950s and 1960s, the US Federal Bureau of Investigations (FBI) and police departments kept lists of *known homosexuals*. Gay people were physically and verbally harassed, denied housing, institutionalized in psychiatric hospitals, blackmailed, or jailed. Many people were persecuted by the federal government, fired from their jobs, or discharged from the military for being *suspected homosexuals* in a witch hunt known as the *Lavender Scare*.[48] "Flaunting" gay behavior in public was illegal, which precluded men from holding hands, kissing, or dancing with other men, while a person could be arrested for wearing gender-inappropriate clothing. Cities routinely performed sweeps to rid neighborhoods, parks, beaches, and bars of gay people, while entrapment by undercover police and raids were common. In the early hours of June 28, 1969, the police raided a popular gay bar, the Stonewall Inn, in Manhattan's Greenwich Village, New York City.[49] In the spirit of the civil rights movements of the era, the patrons stood up to the police, aided by neighborhood residents, and the police were soon overpowered by hundreds of people. This incident led to six days of violent protests and street demonstrations by lesbian, gay, bisexual, and transgender people united behind a common cause. Known as the Stonewall Riots, these events are largely regarded as a catalyst for the gay rights and gay pride movements in the United States and around the world.

As the social stigma against same-sex attraction decreased, gay people began *coming out of the closet* or *coming out*, revealing their personal sexual orientation to friends, family, co-workers, or society. Historically, *coming out* was a reference to young women "coming out into society," being introduced to society and the world of eligible bachelors. During World War II, gay men *came out* to other gay men at drag balls, modeled after debutante balls, which were held in New York, Chicago, New Orleans, and other major cities.[50] This was not so much coming out of the *gay closet* but rather a *coming out into* what they called *homosexual society* or the gay community. Coming out to the general public once labeled the person an *admitted homosexual* or *avowed homosexual*. These are now outdated terms that are offensive because they suggest that being gay is somehow shameful or inherently secretive.[51]

Today, same-sex orientation is more socially acceptable than it has ever been. Many gay people are *out* and identify as *openly gay, openly lesbian,* or *openly bisexual.* (Note that heterosexual people never have to identify as *openly straight.*) Over the past few decades, a societal shift has taken place in which sexuality is now viewed as a social identity, rather than a behavior, as suggested by older terms such as *practicing homosexual.*[52] Covert terms and euphemisms have been replaced by a new set of identities for sexual orientation. Since the 1980s, *LGB* (Lesbian Gay Bisexual) was used as an umbrella term to refer to the community beyond gay men. Since the 1990s, *LGBT* has been used as a common abbreviation that includes gender identity and stands for "Lesbian, Gay, Bisexual, and Transgender." This term is sometimes expanded to *LGBTQ* (Lesbian Gay Bisexual Transgender Queer), *LGBTQ+,* or *LGBTQIA* (Lesbian Gay Bisexual Transgender Queer Intersex Asexual) to be as inclusive as possible.

Gay is a borrowing from the twelfth-century Old French word *gai,* which meant "joyful, happy; pleasant, cheerful."[53] Some people believe that *gay* is an acronym for "Good As You," although this is a folkloric etymology. Over time, *gay* has had many different meanings, including "bright or lovely looking" (1225); "finely or showily dressed" (1387); "excellent person, noble lady, gallant knight" (1400); "full of joy, lighthearted, carefree; cheerful, merry" (1400); and "uninhibited; wild, crazy; flamboyant" (1597). Since the twelfth century, *Gay* (and variant spellings *Gaye*, etc.) has also been both a given name and family name. By the eighteenth century, *gay* had acquired connotations of immorality. A *gay woman* was a prostitute and a *gay house* was a brothel. A *gay man* was a womanizer, like the "gay Lothario" character in Nicholas Rowe's 1703 book *The Fair Penitent*.[54] Until the last century, a synonym for a philanderer was a *gay dog*. The 1890s were known as *The Gay Nineties* in the United States, because this was a period of optimism, prosperity, and extravagance. Within a few decades, *gay* became slang for a same-sex oriented person.

By the 1960s, *gay* had become established as the preferred self-identifying label for many stakeholders. In the 1970s, *gay* pejorated in some usage outside the community, becoming slang for "foolish, stupid, socially inappropriate or disapproved of; 'lame'."[55] (See also Chapter 5.) This sense of *gay* refers to someone or something considered to be inferior, undesirable, or uncool, which is commonly expressed as, *That's so gay*. This usage is considered to be offensive, because it stigmatizes gay people and uses their identity to describe something as bad. Today, the dominant sense of *gay* is "a same-sex oriented person, especially a man," and the word cannot be used in its earlier senses of "happy" or "cheerful" without implying a double entendre, such as the double meaning behind the phrase, *You're looking very gay today!*

Some same-sex oriented women also identify as *gay*, whereas others identify instead as *lesbian*, or as both. Some reject *gay* as a label for lesbian women, because they are frustrated at the domination of the community by men, and their invisibility in the movement and in society in general. Compared to gay men, lesbian women are often invisible in history, because historical writings and records focus primarily on men.[56] Prior to the period when lesbian relationships were defined, romantic and sexual relations between women were often erased as *friendships*.[57]

This invisibility is reflected by the fact that there are fewer historical terms for lesbian women than gay men. In the Middle Ages, sodomy occasionally applied to women too. The medieval theologian St. Thomas Aquinas interpreted sodomy as, "copulation with an undue sex, male with male, female with female."[58] In 1736, author William King referred to lesbians as women who "loved Women in the same Manner as Men love them."[59] *Lesbian* has been in use since at least the eighteenth century. Lesbian originally related to an inhabitant of Lesbos, the Greek island in the Aegean Sea. This was the home of the seventh-century poet Sappho, whose erotic verse referred to women as well as to men.[60] Sappho became a symbol of love and desire between women, while *sapphic* is still used to refer to women who are sexually or romantically attracted to other women. Borrowed from French, *tribade* is an older term for a lesbian woman. It emerged in the sixteenth century and meant, "a woman who engages in sexual activity with other women," or more literally, women who rub their genitals against one another.[61] Today, *lesbian* is the most popular self-identifying label for a same-sex oriented woman.

There are many insults for lesbian women, reflecting the social stigma of the past and present. *Lesbo*, *les*, and *lezzie* are abbreviations of *lesbian* that are usually offensive because they are belittling. Some slurs refer to lesbian sexual acts, and particularly cunnilingus: *muff diver*, *carpet muncher*, *bean flicker*, *pussy puncher*, and *kitty puncher*, with *pussy* and *kitty* used as euphemisms for the vagina. *Dyke* is probably a shortening of *bull dyke* or *bulldyker*, which is a variant of *bulldagger*.[62] These terms date back to the 1930s, when they were gay slang for a lesbian woman, especially one who was tough and mannish. *Dyke* became offensive when the general public seized it as a derogatory term for a lesbian, or any woman who is masculine, with the implication that she is a lesbian. *Dyke* has since been reclaimed within the LGBTQ community, as shown by its use in the lesbian pride parades *dykes on bikes*, *dyke marches*, and *dykes with tykes*, a term that describes lesbian motherhood. Today, *dyke* is adopted affirmatively by some lesbians, but they might take offense if a straight person called them that.

Butch is another term for a masculine lesbian, which comes from the Polari language. There is a stereotype that lesbians must be either masculine-identified, as *butch* or *dyke*, or feminine-identified, as *femme* or *lipstick lesbians*. (A *Chapstick lesbian* is someone who is sporty and athletic.) The older terms *bluff* (from *butch* and *fluff*) and *kiki* referred to a lesbian who refused the opposing *butch* or *femme* roles. It is often assumed that same-sex oriented people defy traditional gender roles in their gender performance; that lesbian women act masculine while gay men act feminine. Older euphemisms reveal this assumption, such as *long-haired men and short-haired women* and *lisping boys and deep-voiced girls*. An early theory claimed that a lesbian was a man's spirit trapped in the body of a woman, while a gay man was born with a woman's spirit trapped inside his body.[63] An effeminate man might be called a *girly boy* or a *pretty boy*.

Since the sixteenth century, *tomboy* has been a term for a girl who acts or looks like a boy, while in the eighteenth century, *Tommy* became a name for a masculine lesbian. At the same time, a *Molly* was a man who was perceived as effeminate in the way he walked, talked, and dressed. (Still in use today, *mollycoddle* is a compound of the words *Molly* and *coddle*, which originally referred to a pampered, overprotected, effeminate man.) *Molly* was an insult for an unmanly man, but also was used as a self-identifying label for a man who might today identify as gay, bisexual, transgender, or queer. The name came from seventeenth-century slang *Molly* or *moll* for a low-class woman or a female prostitute.[64] (*Moll* is still a general insult for a woman in Australian and New Zealand English.) At that time, a *Molly house* was the equivalent of the modern gay bar or club. It was a safe space for men to drink, socialize, and often to have sex with other men. Mollies adopted female personas; attended stage performances in drag; and performed "marriage" ceremonies, mock birth rituals, and other pageantry.

In the past, many female names referred to effeminate men. These were used as either insults outside the group or as affectionate terms within the gay community: *Nellie, Marianne, Mary, Margery, Madge* (from the obsolete term *madge cull* for a gay man), *Angelina,* and *Lacy. Miss Nancy, Nancy, Nancy Boy, Old Nancy, Nance,* and *Nan* were also common insults for an effeminate man or boy. These names come from "Miss Nancy," the nickname of eighteenth-century actor Anna Oldfield who was known for her vanity and fine dress.[65] An effeminate man who was excessively devoted to style, fashion, and appearance was also known as a *fop, dandy,* or *beau* (which came from the iconic figure George Bryan "Beau" Brummell, a nineteenth-century Englishman who became famous for his decadent sense of fashion). Today, a (usually straight) man who is meticulous about his grooming and appearance might be called a *metrosexual.*

There are many terms that have been used to describe a man perceived as feminine in his appearance or behavior, used by those both inside and outside of the community. Late Victorian homoerotic writing often referred to gay men by the names of various types of flowers, while Oscar Wilde's nicknames for Lord Alfred Douglas included *Hyacinth* and *Narcissus* (which is the scientific name for a daffodil).[66] As we have seen, green carnations, and the colors lavender, lilac, and violet, were adopted as emblems by the gay community. Flower names have often been used as a metaphor equating gay men with effeminacy, including *daisy, daffodil, buttercup,* and *lily.* (*Lily law* was a Polari term for the police.) On the 1950s British radio comedy program *The Goon Show,* Peter Sellers played the character of Flowerdew, a flamboyant gay man. As part of their female personas, Mollies adopted flower names that are only given to women, such as Petunia, Rose, and Blossom.

Pansy is still a common insult today and is used as slang for a gay man, or a man considered to be weak, cowardly, or effeminate. Over the decades, *pansy* has been reclaimed in some usage within the community, including Robert Scully's 1933 novel *The Scarlet Pansy,* in the 1970s slogan *Pansy Power,* and the name of the 1990s gay punk rock band "Pansy Division."[67] Other effeminate names that have been adopted by the gay community include female kinship terms: *mother, aunt, sister, sissy,* and *girlfriend*; feminine diminutives: *darling, sweetheart, love*; and female titles: *duchess, princess,* and most notably, *queen.* Since the eighteenth century, *queen* was a derogatory term used to describe a gay man who was ostentatiously effeminate. In recent decades, the gay community has reclaimed *queen.* Singer Freddie Mercury said he was "aware of the gay connotations" when he changed the name of his rock band from "Smile" to "Queen."[68] *Queen* appears in many labels used within the gay community, such as *drag queens* (men who dress up in women's clothing for entertainment or pleasure), *leather queens* (effeminate men who like to wear leather), and *gym queens* (gay men who are into bodybuilding and working out).

Fairy also emerged as a slur for an effeminate man in the eighteenth century but has since been reclaimed as a badge of pride, particularly since the 1970s when gay rights activist Henry "Harry" Hay formed the "Radical Fairies" movement. *Fruit* was originally a Polari term for a gay man (which described a gay man as soft and tender, like a woman), but the term entered popular slang and became an insult. In 1956, *Daily Mirror* columnist William Connor famously described pianist Liberace as, "The pinnacle of masculine, feminine and neuter. Everything that he, she and it can ever want ... a deadly, winking, sniggering, snuggling, chromium-plated, scent-impregnated, luminous, quivering, giggling, fruit-flavoured, mincing, ice-covered heap of mother love."[69] At the time, same-sex sexual activity was still illegal in the United Kingdom. Liberace sued the newspaper for libel, his case hinging on the term *fruit-flavoured* as slang for a gay man. In court, Liberace denied he was gay and was awarded £8,000 in damages. For the rest of his life, he continued to maintain that he was not gay. Liberace died of AIDS-related pneumonia in 1987, at a time when HIV/AIDS was heavily stigmatized and gay men were blamed for the disease. (See also Chapter 5.) Throughout his life, Liberace was described as *flamboyant* for his extravagant costumes and performances. Ostentatious gay men are often portrayed as flamboyant and showy: *camp*, *fabulous*, *flaming* or a *flamer*.

The terms *poof*, *poofter*, *pouf*, *pooftah*, and *poove* (probably all derived from *puff*) are used in Australia and the UK. They may be used in a jocular sense, but they can also be anti-gay slurs that are the equivalent of US *faggot* in offensiveness. *Faggot* dates back to the late thirteenth century, when it originally referred to "a bundle of sticks or twigs tied together for use as fuel."[70] Some people believe that the modern use of *faggot* refers to gay men who were burned at the stake as punishment, although this is a false etymology. In the eighteenth century, *fag* was British public school slang for a junior student who performed certain duties for a senior student (with suggestions of being a *catamite*). (*Fag* also emerged as nineteenth century slang for *cigarette*, which is still used in Britain and Australia.) The modern sense of *faggot* dates back to early 1900s American English slang for a gay man, especially one considered to be effeminate, but more generally, a man considered to be weak or cowardly. The slur is probably derived from a sixteenth-century term of abuse for a woman deemed to be old, lazy, or troublesome.[71]

Today, *faggot* and its abbreviation *fag* are the most offensive anti-gay slurs in the United States. They are occasionally used to describe lesbian women, and also modified as *she fag* or *lady faggot*. When used by the outside group, *faggot* and *fag* are instilled with hatred and contempt for gay people. Formerly led by Pastor Fred Phelps, the Westboro Baptist Church of Topeka, Kansas, is known for picketing gay pride parades with the slogan, "God Hates Fags," which is also the name of their website.[72] *Fag* has been reappropriated by some gay men as an identity, but attempts at reclaiming this emotionally charged word have been less successful than related terms, such as *queer*. In "The F-Word," a 2009 episode of the TV animated comedy *South Park*, the characters attempt to change the definition of *fag* from an anti-gay slur to a term describing obnoxious Harley Davidson bikers.[73] The show attempted to disempower the word, although it was still used in a negative context, therefore reinforcing its status as an insult.

Similar to insult terms that refer to lesbian sexual acts, there are many slurs that describe gay sexual activities. Some refer to anal sex: *arse bandit, bum bandit, bum boy, butt pirate, butt boy, butt pilot, turd burglar*, and *fudge packer. Pillow biter* refers to receptive gay sex. The term entered the lexicon after the 1979 scandal in which British MP Jeremy Thorpe stood trial for the attempted murder of his lover. He was accused of having an affair with model Norman Scott, who claimed he had to "bite the pillow" to keep quiet so Thorpe's mother wouldn't hear him being penetrated in the next room.[74] Scott said, "I just bit the pillow, I tried not to scream because I was frightened of waking Mrs. Thorpe." (*Screamer* and *squealer* are also slang for a gay man, while *screaming queen* refers to an ostentatiously effeminate gay man.)

In gay slang, a *top* is the partner who assumes a penetrative role, while a *bottom* is the partner who prefers to be penetrated or to take a more submissive role during sexual interactions. In US English, the penetrator is called the *pitcher*, while the penetrated partner is the *catcher*. While these terms arose from baseball terminology, they are derogatory, because the outside group typically uses them. Older insults include *sod*, from *sodomy*, and *bugger*, from *buggery*, although both are now more popularly used as swearwords to express anger or annoyance. *Shirt-lifter* is another outdated insult, which refers to a man who lifts his shirt in order to be able to penetrate his partner. Several insults refer to fellatio, including *cock jockey* and *cocksucker*. In October 1961, Lenny Bruce was arrested for obscenity at the Jazz Workshop in San Francisco because of his copious use of the word *cocksucker* during a stand-up comedy routine, although a jury later acquitted him of the charges.[75] In his 1972 monologue, comedian George Carlin listed *cocksucker* as one of the "Seven words you can never say on television."[76] At these times, *cocksucker* literally implied a man who performs fellatio, although today it is a generalized term of abuse.

Gay and lesbian refer to same-sex orientation, while modern labels for sexuality transcend this binary. *Queer* dates back to the sixteenth century, when it originally meant something strange, odd, peculiar, or eccentric.[77] Its first usage in reference to sexual orientation was recorded in 1894, when Bosie's father John Douglas, the Marquis of Queensberry, referred to gay men in a personal letter as "Snob queers."[78] In this context, it was a derogatory term meaning "sexual deviant." *Queer* was reclaimed as a self-identifying label by gay men in New York in the early twentieth century, about a decade before *gay* was adopted. But it became offensive again for the most part until the late 1980s when *queer* was reclaimed again as an umbrella term for the LGBT community and as a label that refuses traditional sexual orientation. (See also Chapter 2.) People with sexual identities outside of gay, lesbian, or bisexual feel represented by *queer*. Some universities have developed degree programs in Queer Studies, while the term is used in the names of organizations such as the activist group, Queer Nation. In the 1990s, Queer Nation used the slogan, "We're here. We're queer. Get used to it!" Between 2003 and 2007, *Queer Eye* (originally titled *Queer Eye for the Straight Guy*) was a TV series about a team of gay (queer) men, the "Fab Five," who performed makeovers on straight men.[79] *Queer* is a success story in reclaiming derogatory language; however, it can still be offensive when used by people outside of the LGBTQ community (e.g., *fucking queers*) because of its long history as a term of abuse.

There are many other contemporary terms for labeling the spectrum of sexual attraction, or even a lack of sexual attraction. *Asexual* refers to a lack of sexual attraction to others, or a low or absent desire for sexual activity. *Pansexual* people (the prefix *pan-* meaning "all") experience sexual attraction to other people regardless of their sex or gender identity. *Polysexual* people (the prefix *poly-* meaning "many") are attracted to people of multiple sexes and genders, although not necessarily all. *Men who have sex with men* includes men who choose to have sex with other men, whether or not they identify as gay, including sex workers, prisoners, and sailors. The term arose during the emergence of HIV/AIDS and refers to a man's sexual history rather than his sexual orientation. Some indigenous Native American people use *two-spirit* to describe gay, lesbian, and bisexual people (and also intersex, non-binary, and transgender people). Historically, these people were honored for having two spirits, both that of a man and that of a woman, and they were often revered in their communities as religious leaders, teachers, and traditional healers. Feminine males were branded *berdache* (an alteration of French *bardache*, meaning "catamite") by early French explorers in North America, a term that is now derogatory, while the Spanish and English colonists condemned them as *sodomites*.[80] *Two-spirit* was adopted in the 1990s to replace the negative associations of *berdache*. (However, it is often offensive when non-Native people appropriate the term, because they have not experienced the struggles of Native two-spirit people.)[81]

Bisexual refers to individuals who are attracted to people of either sex. *ACDC* is an old Polari term for bisexual people (taken from AC/DC, devices that are able to operate with either alternating current or direct current). In the United States, bisexual or *bi* people are colloquially called *switch hitters*, who *swing both ways*, terms coming from baseball terminology for a player who bats both right-handed and left-handed. Bisexual people have experienced prejudice and *biphobia* within both straight and gay and lesbian communities. Bisexual people are often perceived as *gay* by straight people, but *straight* by gay people, who often view them as *not gay enough*. There are many negative stereotypes about bisexual people. Bisexuality is often dismissed as a valid sexual orientation, and it is argued that bisexuality does not truly exist.[82] It is thought by some that people are either straight or gay, so bisexual people must be on their way to coming out as gay.[83] Bisexual people are commonly described as *confused*, *going through a phase*, *just experimenting*, or *bicurious* (i.e., curious about having same-sex relations). This perception of being wild and adventurous is reflected in *LUG*, a slang term for bisexual women, the acronym standing for "Lesbian Until Graduation." Bisexual people are also stereotyped as promiscuous, in the belief that they will have indiscriminate sex with anyone. Woody Allen once joked that being bisexual, "doubles your chances for a date on Saturday night."[84] Bisexual people are a smaller part of the mainstream narrative, although one study shows that bisexual people make up the largest share of the LGBTQ community in America (in which 46% identified as bisexual, with 32% gay, 16% lesbian, and 5% as queer or another sexual orientation).[85]

There are many harmful stereotypes, myths, and assumptions about LGBTQ people. Gay culture is more prominent than lesbian culture, so some falsely believe that lesbians do not really exist (especially older lesbians).[86] There is the conflicting stereotype that *all* women are bisexual or lesbian and that none are truly straight. The homophobia experienced by lesbians is often an extension of sexism. Lesbianism is a preoccupation of straight male pornography, promoting the idea that lesbian relationships only exist because they are titillating for men, making lesbianism (and its apparent rejection of men) palatable for straight men.[87] There is also the misconception that all lesbians are butch, mannish, hairy, or ugly. There is the myth that within a lesbian couple, someone has to play the role of "the man," while the other partner must be "the woman." Some people wonder how lesbian women have sex, or consider lesbian sex to not be "real sex," because female sexuality is typically defined in terms of men, with sex being perceived as male penetration and male orgasm. Lesbians are also accused of being *man haters*, which is often a backlash against them for their perceived sexual "rejection" of men. Another assumption is that women became lesbians because men have mistreated them. It is often thought that lesbianism is just a passing phase that women will outgrow; that they are just "fooling around" but will go back to men. There is the belief that lesbian women have just not found the right guy yet, and that they can be *turned* into straight women. The disturbing practice of so-called *corrective rape* is the sexual assault of lesbian women in order to *cure* them of their sexual orientation.

Stereotypes about gay men include the belief that they are promiscuous, that they are interested in having sex with *all* men, and are out to *seduce* or *turn* straight men gay. There is a belief that gay men are involved in *homosexual recruitment* to enlist more men, and even plot to turn children gay. A popular myth is that gay men have defined behavioral traits and mannerisms and that they *act gay*. Some purport to have *gaydar*, an intuitive ability to detect a gay man by his behavior. *Mince* is a Polari word for a gay man who walks affectedly, as described by the phrases *light in the loafers*, *light on his toes*, and *twinkle toes*, meaning "light on his feet". (This latter term may come from *Twinkletoes*, the title of the 1926 silent movie about an aspiring dancer, starring Colleen Moore.) Stereotypical postures and hand gestures are associated with gay men, such as limp wrists, as in the term *limp-wristed*. A postcard from 1910 shows a limp-wristed gay man circling a policeman and uttering, "Sweet perfume of violets! What a charming policeman!"[88] Some gay men have co-opted these stereotypical mannerisms as a way to signal their sexual orientation. Another subcultural signifier for gay men to recognize other gay men includes the use of certain linguistic features, such as the marked pronunciation of /s/ and /z/, known as the *gay lisp*.[89]

Other generalizations of gay men include that they are fashion savvy and always well dressed. The premise of the TV series *Queer Eye* relied on the stereotype that gay men are experts in matters of fashion, style, and grooming. Another assumption is that gay men do not know they are truly gay if they have never had sex with a woman, or that they are too lazy to find a woman. In the Middle East, where same-sex sexual activity is still criminalized, some countries ignore or deny the existence of gay people. During a speech at Columbia University in 2007, Iranian President Mahmoud Ahmadinejad claimed there are no gay people in his country, "In Iran, we don't have homosexuals like in your country. In Iran, we do not have this phenomenon."[90]

A common lament is that a gay man (especially a handsome one) is a *waste of a man*, while a lesbian is said to be a *waste of a woman*. Although usually intended as a joke or compliment, this can be offensive, suggesting that being straight is somehow superior, and implying that a person's sole purpose is to have children. In gay slang, *breeder* can be a joking or disparaging term for straight people who have children. The term comes from Jonathan Swift's 1729 satirical essay "A Modest Proposal (For preventing the Children of Poor People From being a Burthen to Their Parents or Country, and For making them Beneficial to the Publick)," in which he refers to women as "breeders," humorously proposing that women should breed children for cannibalistic purposes to tackle social problems of poverty and hunger.[91] Breeders has expanded in meaning to refer to heterosexual people in general (and is even used to describe LGBTQ people who have children.) Some people consider *breeders* to be dehumanizing for its animalistic connotations; dogs and pigs are "bred," not humans. The term can also have racial undertones, implying that some groups of people *breed like rats*. In 2018, US President Donald Trump tweeted about California's "sanctuary" laws affecting undocumented immigrants, which he characterized as "this ridiculous, crime infested & breeding concept."[92]

Some phrases superficially appear to be supportive of LGBTQ people, but can reveal underlying prejudice or internalized homophobia. The assertions, *I'm not homophobic, some of my best friends are gay*, and *I love gay people*, are often used to excuse or deny anti-gay sentiments. (See also Chapter 1.) In a 2013 interview, US politician Ben Carson compared "homosexuality" to pedophilia and bestiality. He later apologized with, "I love gay people", which was criticized for appearing disingenuous.[93] (He also referred to gay people as *gays*, which is comparable to the derogatory racial terms *blacks* or *Mexicans*. See also Chapter 1.) In a famous episode of the TV comedy *Seinfeld*, characters Jerry and George are mistakenly outed as a gay couple. They strenuously deny being gay, but with the condition, "Not that there's anything wrong with that."[94] This comment can be offensive, because it reveals a fear of being seen as gay but also a fear of being seen as homophobic. It reveals the covert homophobia of people who are progressive but heterosexual. Such remarks are characteristic of well-meaning people who see themselves as *gay friendly* but still covertly consider it bad to be thought of as gay.[95] A related phrase is *No homo*, which is used by straight men as a caveat after

expressing their emotions, to rid them of any possible gay implications. For example, *Dude, you're so awesome. No homo*. This tag
arose from East Harlem slang in the 1990s, and then spread via the
hip-hop lyrics of rappers Cam'ron and Lil Wayne. *No homo* has
been criticized as homophobic, but it is also argued that the phrase
allows for emotional expression in communities where there is
stigma attached to boys and men expressing their feelings.[96]

Even in countries where same-sex sexual activity has been
decriminalized, sex that involves minors is illegal. As we saw
earlier, in ancient Greece and Rome, a *catamite* was a boy in an
intimate relationship with a man. *Ganymede* was another historical term for a boy who was the sexual partner of an older
male, the name coming from the Greek mythological character
Ganymede (the Latin form of the name was Catamitus) who was
Zeus's cup-bearer and, in many versions, his lover.[97] These
liaisons are known as *pederasty*, a sexual relationship between
an adult male and a pubescent or adolescent boy. In modern
times, sexual interactions between men and boys are perceived
as predatory and exploitative. An adult engaging in sex with
a minor is classified as *pedophilia*, which can constitute child
sexual abuse or statutory rape. Sexual abusers often describe
themselves as *boy lovers* and appeal to ancient practices as
justification for their interest. Regardless of whether they are
consensual, these relationships are illegal if either party is under
the age of consent. Some organizations advocate the removal of
this legal protection for children, such as the North American
Man/Boy Love Association (NAMBLA). The LGBTQ community is sometimes conflated with pedophilia, but in fact,
staunchly condemns the practice.

Consensual same-sex relationships between people over the age
of consent are legal, regardless of any age gap. Within the LGBTQ
community, there are several terms to describe young gay men.
Coming from the Polari language, a *chicken* is a young boy, while
a *chickenhawk* is an "older man who prefers chickens." Some slang
terms are used to describe a younger man's appearance for sex and

dating purposes. Since the 1960s, *twink* has been used to describe an attractive, boyish-looking, hairless younger man, while a *twunk* is a more muscular twink. *Twink* is thought to be related to *twinkie*, an older term for a young gay man that was inspired by the cream-filled Hostess Twinkie cupcake.[98] (It may also be related to *twinkle toes*.) A *pup* is a slender young gay man, while a *cub* is a young or younger-looking gay man who is *husky*, that is, hairy and heavy. (As opposed to an older, rugged, masculine gay man known as a *bear*.)

Same-sex sexual activity is decriminalized in Anglophone countries, although LGBTQ people continue to fight for their civil rights. (Conservatives often reframe this battle as the *homosexual agenda*, portraying the pursuit of equality as something sinister.) Historically, gay men and lesbian women were banned from military service in the United States. From 1993, they were subjected to a Don't Ask, Don't Tell, Don't Pursue policy, in which they would not be discharged from the military, but only as long as they did not reveal their sexual orientation.[99] In 2011, the bill was repealed, and gay people now have the freedom to serve in the armed forces openly (although the same rights for transgender people are now tenuous). Same-sex marriage has only recently been legalized in Canada (2005), New Zealand (2013), the United Kingdom (2014, but not until 2020 in Northern Ireland), the United States (2015), and Australia (2017).[100] Conservatives fought against these laws, arguing that *marriage*, as defined by ancient tradition, *is between a man and a woman*, and that same-sex marriage ruins the *sanctity of marriage*. Before same-sex marriage was recognized, same-sex couples often used euphemisms such as *partner, significant other, roommate, special friend*, or *close friend* to refer to their life partners.[101] Adoption for same-sex couples is still illegal in many places, because it is argued, *children need both a mother and a father to raise them*.

The *Gay Pride* movement (or LGBTQ pride) arose out of these historical and contemporary struggles in an effort to promote the dignity and equality of LGBTQ people. But there has been a backlash. Some straight people believe there should be a *straight pride* movement simply because there is a gay pride movement. This idea is offensive, because straight people have not struggled to achieve civil rights and overcome shame in the way that LGBTQ people have had to do. That straight people are allowed to marry, adopt children, join the military, and enjoy other kinds of social opportunities as a given is known as *heterosexual privilege*. Similar to the white privilege and male privilege discussed in previous chapters, this encapsulates the personal, social, economic, and legal benefits afforded to straight people in a heteronormative society.[102] These advantages are often unconscious or taken for granted. Unlike LGBTQ people, straight people do not have to worry about being identified by their sexual orientation, or being ridiculed for it. They do not have a fear of being labeled *deviant* or *perverse*, of being *outed* or being excluded from certain professions because of their sexuality. They can reap legal benefits and rights in their relationships. They can receive social acceptance from neighbors, colleagues, friends, and family. They can walk with a partner in public, hold hands, kiss, or express affection without fear of disapproval, laughter, hostility, or even the threat of violence. They will not be harassed, beaten, or killed because of their sexuality.

As we have seen, *gay* was adopted from an older term for "joyful" and "happy," although these people have been the victims of violence throughout history. In more recent times, many LGBTQ people have suffered physical violence, colloquially known as *gay bashing*. Gay bashing includes verbal abuse, bullying, physical assault, and even murder. One of the most infamous homicides thought to be fueled by homophobic hatred is the case of Matthew Shepard.[103] On October 6, 1998, 21-year-old Shepard was at a gay bar in Laramie, Wyoming. He left the bar with two men, but when he climbed into their truck, he was robbed of his keys, wallet, and shoes and beaten repeatedly. He was taken to a field where he was tortured, then tied to a fence, set on fire, and left unconscious. When he was found, his face was covered in blood, aside from tear tracks streaming down each cheek. Six days later, he died from severe head injuries. Shephard's murder was allegedly due to his sexual orientation, and his story is now synonymous with anti-gay hate.

The word *homophobia* expresses the social condemnation of prejudice against LGBTQ people. Those accused of being homophobic will often deny the charge, while phrases such as *I'm not a homophobe, but ...* are an attempt to resist the accusation, meanwhile ironically expressing homophobia. Despite this social disapproval, homophobia is still prevalent in modern language, as we can see. Anti-gay prejudice is evident in the vast amount of insults, slurs, stereotypes, and myths related to LGBTQ people. To their credit, the community has successfully reclaimed many offensive words that have been used against them for hundreds of years. However, these words are still wielded as weapons by those who are unsympathetic to the community's ongoing struggle against prejudice.

4   Don't Be a Jew

Anti-Semitism has been a reality throughout Jewish history. In Ancient Greece, Jewish religious ceremonies were banned and their temples destroyed, while possessing Holy Scriptures was a capital offence.[1] In medieval Europe, Jews were segregated into ghettos and forced to convert to Christianity. Others were expelled or killed in massacres.[2] During the middle ages, the Jews became scapegoats for misfortune and disease. They were accused of unleashing the Black Death by poisoning the wells of Europe with a mixture of frogs, spiders, lizards, and Christian hearts, in order to stamp out Christianity.[3] In the Middle East, heavy taxes were imposed on Jews, their holy relics were destroyed, and many were exiled, if they were not the victims of pogroms.[4] In more recent history, Nazi Germany committed genocide against the Jews during World War II, murdering approximately six milion people across Europe.[5] More than 70 years after the Holocaust, prejudice against Jews is not only a historical fact, it is a current event.[6]

Religious discrimination is intolerance, fear, or hatred of an individual or group because of their faith, creed, or beliefs. Religious discrimination often involves prejudice against people based on their ethnicity, race, or national origins, so there are overlaps of xenophobia and racism. Unlike racism or sexism, there is no -ism for prejudice against religious groups, although specific forms of religious discrimination are so prevalent that they have their own labels, including *Anti-Semitism* and *Islamophobia*. Many Anglophone countries have laws in place against religious discrimination, for example, freedom of religion is protected under the First Amendment of the US Constitution. However, religious discrimination is on the increase globally.[7] An estimated 84 percent of people are religious worldwide,[8] but some people are only respectful of the religion they belong to, while they are intolerant of others.

As opposed to disagreement or criticism that is a part of legitimate debate, religious discrimination involves the persecution or mistreatment of religious people, usually those belonging to minority religions, by individuals, groups, or governments. Religious discrimination can take many forms. It can involve the unequal treatment of a person or group with regard to employment, education, and housing. It can also include violence and hate crimes, such as physical assault, arrest and detention, the desecration of holy sites and objects, and verbal abuse.[9] Discriminatory language is significant, because slurs and insults often precede or accompany the above actions. Our modern language reveals negative attitudes and beliefs about minority religious groups. In particular, there has been a global increase in anti-Semitism, while anti-Semitic language has reached an all-time high since the 1930s.[10, 11]

The term *anti-Semitism* comes from the name *Semite*, a mythological race of people mentioned in the Bible as descended from Shem, one of the three sons of Noah in the Book of Genesis (10:21–30).[12] *Semite* referred to Jews, but also Arabs, Arameans, and Assyrians.[13] *Anti-Semitism* can be viewed as a misnomer because it implies that it is directed toward all Semitic people, although the term specifically means prejudice against Jews as a religious and ethnic group. Today, *Semitic* specifically refers to a group of languages originating in the Middle East, including Arabic, Amharic, and Hebrew, rather than referring to the diverse ethnicities covered by *Semite*. For these reasons, some scholars prefer using the terms *anti-Judaism* or *Judeophobia* to anti-Semitism, although these words haven't been popularized.[14] The term *anti-Semitism* emerged in nineteenth-century Germany, at a time when *Judenhass* ("Jew hatred") was common, and anti-Jewish people freely self-identified as *antisemitisch* ("anti-Semites"). Today, *anti-Semite* has become a pejorative. As we have discussed for other forms of intolerance in previous chapters, there is a tendency to resist the label by using caveats such as, *I have Jewish friends, but . . .* or *I'm not an anti-Semite, but . . .* to precede making anti-Semitic comments.

Many believe the roots of anti-Semitism go back to the beginnings of Christianity and the charge of *deicide*, the accusation that Jews were responsible for the death of Jesus. For centuries, it has been said that *the Jews killed Jesus*, and they have been demonized as *Christ-killers*. The source of this canard is the Gospel of Matthew, in which it is told that the Jews accepted liability for the crucifixion of Jesus. Pontius Pilate washed his hands of the matter, "'I am innocent of the blood of this just person: see ye to it.' Then answered all the people and said, 'His blood be on us, and on our children'" (Matthew 27:24–25). [15] This has been called the *blood curse*. The belief that Jews were collectively guilty of killing Jesus remained Catholic doctrine until 1965, when Pope Paul VI formally repudiated the belief. He stated that the accusation could not be made, "against all the Jews, without distinction, then alive, nor against the Jews of today."[16]

Jews have long been dehumanized as beings that personify evil, such as demons, devils, Satan, sorcerers, or the anti-Christ.[17] Grotesque caricatures depict Jews as monsters or vampires with exaggerated features, such as a hooked nose, horns, and pointed teeth. Jews have been vilified by urban legends, including the belief that Jews drink the blood of non-Jews, and murder people so they can harvest their organs. The most infamous myth is that of the *blood libel*, the belief that Jews kidnap and sacrifice Christian children in order to use their blood in rituals during Passover, the Sabbath, and other religious holidays. Allegations of ritual murder date back to ancient Greece and have often been the pretext for the historical persecution of Jews.[18] The accusations still happen today. In 2014, a spokesperson for the Palestinian resistance group Hamas said, "We all remember how the Jews used to slaughter Christians, in order to mix their blood in their holy matzos. This is not a figment of imagination or something taken from a film. It is a fact, acknowledged by their own books and by historical evidence."[19]

The world's 14 million Jews comprise only 0.2% of the global population although they are one of the most discriminated against religious groups.[20] Modern acts of anti-Semitism against Jewish communities and individuals have included terrorist attacks, bomb threats, property damage, cemetery desecration, physical assault, and verbal abuse. In 2009, two men with baseball bats beat a teenage Orthodox Jew in Melbourne, Australia, as they yelled, "Fucking Jew, you deserve to die."[21] Overtly anti-Semitic language is not widely tolerated, although it flourishes in the anonymous environment of the Internet. In 2018, it was revealed that over 4.2 million English-language anti-Semitic tweets were posted to Twitter that year, despite steps that the site has taken to remove hate speech.[22]

There are many anti-Semitic slurs, including the older insult *Heeb* (or *Hebe*) derived from *Hebrew*, and *Yid*, which is an abbreviation of *yidish* ("Jewish").[23] Originally, *Yid* (or *Yit*) was used by Jews to mean "buddy," "mate," or "fellow." Today, *Yid* is highly offensive when used outside of the group, although it has been reclaimed by Jews, along with *Yiddo*. In the 1970s, both terms became football chants used by the Jewish fan base of the English club Tottenham Hotspur, in response to anti-Semitic chanting from opposing supporters.[24] The group call themselves the *Yid Army*. The chant has provoked hissing from opponents, intended to resemble the sound of gas used by Nazis to murder Jews during the Holocaust. Anti-Semitic chants, shouts, and songs are still common at soccer events. In recent years, European soccer fans have chanted "Gas the Jews," "Let's go Jew hunting," and "Auschwitz is back" at Jewish teams.[25]

As we saw in Chapter 1, common or famous first names have been used as insults for people belonging to an ethnic or racial group. Several derogatory nicknames for Jews are based on this pattern, such as *Moses*, *Abe* or *Abie* (from *Abraham*), and *Ikey* or *Ike* (from *Isaac*). Before he became a famous Hollywood actor, Errol Flynn was said to be a spy for Britain and the Allies prior to World War II. In now declassified files held by the CIA, Flynn wrote to German intelligence agent Hermann Erben in 1933, "A slimy Jew is trying to cheat me . . . I do wish we could bring Hitler over here to teach these Isaacs a thing or two."[26] *Hymie* is another common name-based insult, which comes from *Hyman* (based on Yiddish *Khaym*).[27] In 1984, the Reverend Jesse Jackson made an off-handed remark in a private conversation with a reporter, referring to Jews as "Hymies" and New York as "Hymietown."[28] Though Jackson initially denied the comments, he later acknowledged and apologized for them.[29] New York City is known for having a high population of Jews, while *Jew Yorker* is a derogatory term for New Yorkers of Jewish stock.

Of all the ethnic slurs for Jews, *Kike* is the most common. Its etymology is contested, and it is not known whether the word came into use among the Jews, or among their persecutors.[30] One theory is that *Kike* was first used by German-American Jews in reference to newcomers from Poland and Russia, because their names commonly ended in -*ki* or -*ky*.[31] Another popular theory is that *Kike* comes from Yiddish *kaykl* or *kikel* meaning "circle." According to this story, illiterate Jewish immigrants signed their entry forms with a circle, eschewing the "X" that they associated with the Christian cross. Ellis Island immigration officials began calling these people *kikels*, and the term shortened to *Kike* as it came into popular use.[32] *Kike* had become somewhat dated, although the current wave of anti-Semitism has led to a resurgence of the insult.[33]

Negative attitudes toward Jews have led to many stereotypes and misconceptions about the group, one of the most common being that all Jews are affluent. In the nineteenth century, the Rothschilds of Germany established banking and finance houses across Europe and grew to become a wealthy, preeminent Jewish family. Along with the knowledge of other influential Jewish families and figures, this birthed the conspiracy theory that all Jews are rich and powerful, and they control global businesses, finances, banks, and the economy.[34] There is a folk etymology that *Jew* comes from *jewelry* (although the word comes from *Y'hudah* "Judah," the name of a Hebrew patriarch and the people descended from him).[35] As a result of this misconception, Jews around the world have been kidnapped and held for ransom, and even murdered for their assumed wealth. In 2018, 85-year-old Mireille Knoll, a Holocaust survivor living in Paris, was stabbed and set alight by two men, one of whom had told the other, "She is a Jew, she must have money."[36]

Jews are not only believed to be well-off, but also miserly with their money. In the Bible, the disciple Judas Iscariot betrayed Jesus to the rabbis in exchange for "thirty pieces of silver."[37] (Matthew 26:15) Historically, Jews had worked as bankers, tax collectors, and money lenders. This is due to persecution in many countries, wherein their means of earning a living was confined to a restricted range of occupations, mainly in trading and finance.[38] As a result of this reputation, Jews have been labeled as *misers, stingy, cheap, scrooges, penny pinchers, tight-fisted, greedy, avaricious, money-obsessed,* and *money-grubbing.* These beliefs were given expression by Shakespeare in the character of Shylock, the Jewish moneylender in *The Merchant of Venice.* Colloquially, to be stingy or cheap is said *to be Jewish.* There are equivalent terms in other languages, such as the Hungarian phrase *ne légy zsidó!* ("Don't be a Jew!") and the Italian phrase *che rabbino!* ("What a rabbi!").[39]

There are many negative social stereotypes of Jews that characterize them as *the sly Jew* who is devious, dishonest, pushy, manipulative, and lying. This is contrasted with the neurotic, *guilt-ridden Jew* who suffers from the stereotypical *Jewish guilt,* which is a humorous trope featured in jokes (and is a feature of Woody Allen movies). It is often believed that Jews don't integrate or assimilate well into other cultures, but instead they *stick to their own kind.* Jews have been accused of having *dual loyalty,* of being more loyal to Israel or the Jewish population worldwide than to their own home countries.[40] In London in 2006, 12-year-old Jasmine Kranat was riding home on a bus when a group of girls confronted her and demanded to know, "Are you English or Jewish?" Before she could answer, they subjected her to a brutal beating; stomping on her head and chest, and knocking her unconscious.[41] No one on the bus offered her assistance during the attack.

There are also many conspiracy theories about Jews. It is often believed they are a sinister force that controls the media and governments and conspires to conquer the world. Some fear there is a worldwide *Jewish alliance* that is responsible for all global misfortune, including acts of terrorism, and even diseases and natural disasters. Many of these theories have their basis in *The Protocols of the Elders of Zion*, a twentieth-century literary forgery from Russia that describes a Jewish plot to achieve global domination.[42] The book also presents Jews as warmongers, claiming that Jews are behind all conflicts, and that they orchestrate wars for profit. This is still a commonly held belief. In 2006, Australian actor Mel Gibson was arrested in California for driving under the influence of alcohol while speeding. When he was not permitted to drive home, Gibson exploded into an obscenity-laced tirade in which he said to the (Jewish) arresting officer, "Fucking Jews . . . the Jews are responsible for all the wars in the world. Are you a Jew?"[43] Gibson later apologized for his "despicable" remarks.[44]

But this wasn't Gibson's only anti-Semitic comment on record. Actor Winona Ryder told an anecdote in which she met Gibson at a Hollywood party years before. Upon learning she was Jewish, he referred to Jews as "oven-dodgers."[45] *Oven-dodger* is an insult for a Holocaust survivor, a reference to the mass crematoria used by the Nazis to dispose of the bodies of the Jews they murdered. This is a common theme in anti-Semitism. In 2017, a neo-Nazi website unleashed a terror campaign on a Jewish woman in Whitefish, Montana, in which she received a barrage of over 700 anti-Semitic letters, texts, postcards, social media comments, and emails, one of which read, "Thanks for demonstrating why your race needs to be collectively ovened."[46] Slurs such as *firewood, German oven mitt, oven baked,* and *oven dweller* are all offensive because they invoke painful imagery of the Holocaust. The related insults *candle, soap, Dial* (a brand of soap), and *lampshade* refer to the urban legend that the Nazis made these products out of the skin of

Jewish victims. In response to an article she wrote about US First Lady Melania Trump, Jewish journalist Julia Ioffe was barraged with death threats and crank callers, one of whom played recorded speeches of Hitler on her voicemail, and another who said that Ioffe's face would "look good on a lampshade."[47]

Further to the anti-religious aspects of anti-Semitism, the Nazis' persecution of the Jews took on a distinctly racial quality. They perceived the Jews to be an inferior race in comparison to the "superior" northern Europeans or *Aryans*. When Adolf Hitler came to power as Chancellor of Germany in 1933, the Jews were quickly denied basic civil rights, such as using parks and public swimming pools. They were then stripped of their German citizenship. They soon became the victims of violence, such as the infamous pogrom of November 1938, in which Jewish homes, hospitals, schools, and synagogues were destroyed, and many Jews were murdered.[48] Known as *Kristallnacht*, ("The Night of Broken Glass"), the name comes from the shards of glass that littered the streets after windows in Jewish-owned stores and buildings were smashed.[49] Following these events, Jewish persecution intensified. Jews were deported, forced into ghettos, or incarcerated in concentration camps, where many were murdered by mass shootings, if they did not succumb to starvation or disease. In 1941, a plan was initiated to "solve" the "Jewish Question." The *Final Solution* became a euphemism for the systematic genocide in which millions of Jews were herded into extermination camps and suffocated in gas chambers. *Zyklon B*, which is the name of the cyanide-based pesticide used in the killings, is also a slur used against Jews.

During the Holocaust, the Nazis targeted Jews, but also Communists, LGBTQ people, Slavic people, and Romani people (who are also known colloquially as Roma, while the outdated term *gypsy* is now considered pejorative because of its connotations of illegality and itinerancy). The Nazis branded these people *Untermenschen* ("subhumans"). The phrase *Lebensunwertes Leben* ("life unworthy of life") was also used to refer to people with physical or intellectual disabilities. They used the terms *extermination, annihilate, eliminate,* and *eradicate,* which typically refer to killing pests, not humans, suggesting that Jews were viewed as less than human, or even non-human. Jews were talked about in dehumanizing language that denied their human qualities in order to justify their mistreatment. They were characterized as "unclean" animals: *cockroaches*, *rats*, *pigs* and *swine*; or as "pests": *insects*, *vermin*, *parasites* and *bloodsuckers*.[50] Jews have also been described as a "sickness": *plague*, *disease*, *infection*, *virus*, and *boils*; or as "dirty": *filth*, *shit*, *scum*, *trash*, and *garbage*. Today, these metaphorical insults are still commonly used, especially online, where Jews are attacked anonymously.[51]

Today, one of the most prevalent forms of anti-Semitic talk is Holocaust denial.[52] *Holocaust* was originally a Bible word for "sacrifice by fire, burnt offering," then it evolved to mean "massacre, destruction of a large number of persons" before it came to refer specifically to the Nazi genocide of European Jews in World War II, which was earlier known in Hebrew as *Shoah* "catastrophe." Despite the overwhelming evidence and eyewitness testimony of the genocide of the Jewish people at the hands of Nazi Germany during World War II, some people minimize its scale, or deny that it happened at all. In what they dismiss as the *Holohoax*, denialists claim that Nazi Germany did not devise a Final Solution, establish extermination camps, or use gas chambers to commit mass murder. They believe that the victims instead died of disease, and that the number of deaths was greatly exaggerated, the death toll being considerably lower than six million people. Some believe that the Jews fabricated the Holocaust for financial gain in the form of reparations, and for political gain in the acquisition of the State of Israel, and that they spread this myth via their control of the media. Mel Gibson's father, Hutton Gibson, once said that "most of" what historians say about the Holocaust is "fiction." He claimed that six million people weren't murdered, they simply moved elsewhere. In his opinion, the concentration camps were merely "work camps," while Holocaust museums are "just a gimmick to make money."[53]

Holocaust denialism seems to attract anti-Semites. English author and convicted Holocaust denier David Irving once claimed that Auschwitz is "hugely inflated and hyped up. It's like Disney. I don't go there. It has no part in history."[54] Holocaust denial is illegal in many European countries, because it is considered to be hate speech. Irving spent a year in prison in Austria, charged with "trivializing, grossly playing down and denying the Holocaust," and was banned from returning to the country.[55] He is also banned from Canada, Italy, and Germany. Holocaust denialism is often renamed *historical revisionism* by its proponents, to give their pseudoscientific theories an academic veneer. In 2006, the Iranian foreign ministry hosted the "International Conference to Review the Global Vision of the Holocaust," a convention in Tehran that aimed to further the theories of holocaust denialism. *Hamshahri*, an Iranian newspaper owned by the Municipality of Tehran, hosts an annual Holocaust Cartoon contest that mocks the Nazi genocide of Jews during World War II.[56]

Certain symbols and imagery are associated with age-old forms of anti-Semitism. In Nazi Germany, Jews were forced to wear a yellow six-pointed star sewn onto their outer garments. This *Magen David*, the "Star of David" with *Jude* ("Jew") printed in the middle, was to render them identifiable in public. As stated in the *Reich Gazette*, this "Star decree" was a warning to "save the Germans from contact with the Jews."[57] There are historical precedents to this law, and while Rabbinical rules often regulated the appearance of Jews, in many countries non-Jewish authorities forced Jews to wear a particular hairstyle or color of clothing, or to attach bells to their clothes as a way of humiliating them and demonstrating their lowly position in society.[58] In medieval Germany, Jews were forced to wear a cone-shaped hat, which was a kind of dunce cap that was designed to make them look ridiculous.[59]

The *Hitler Salute* is another symbol associated with anti-Semitism. During Nazi Germany, this gesture was a social greeting and an oath of allegiance to party leader Adolf Hitler that was mandatory for civilians and military.[60] The salute was performed by extending the right arm from the neck into the air with a straightened hand, and it was usually accompanied by the phrase, *Heil Hitler!* ("Hail Hitler!") or *Sieg Heil!* ("Hail victory!"). At the time, the salute was thought to simplify the elaborate system of German etiquette and to bring social equality (although obviously not for the Jews).[61] Today, if not used ironically, the salute is seen to mock Jews or show sympathy to anti-Semitic thinking. As a hate crime, it is a criminal offense to perform the gesture and utter these phrases in some European countries, including Germany and Austria.[62] In 2016, US presidential candidate Donald Trump triggered a controversy when he called on supporters at campaign rallies to swear to vote for him by raising their right hands. The gesture was criticized as reminiscent of the Hitler Salute. The incident inspired white supremacists at other Trump rallies to chant "Hail Trump!" while performing the Hitler salute.[63]

The swastika, a cross with clockwise projecting limbs, is another symbol associated with Nazi Germany. The word *swastika* is Sanskrit for "well-being, fortune, luck," and the symbol has been used in many different cultures.[64] To the ancient Mesopotamians, it stood for prosperity and good fortune, while it is a sacred symbol in Buddhism, Hinduism, and to the Navajo people of North America. In the twentieth century, the swastika was used by adherents of the *völkisch* ("folkish") movement, a group dedicated to uncovering a romanticized Aryan past. In Germanic myth, it became a symbol for the *sun worshippers*, a race of white-skinned people of innate superiority.[65] Inspired by this folklore, Hitler adopted the swastika as the emblem of the Nazi party. The legacy of the Nazi regime and the Holocaust has converted the swastika into a symbol of hate and anti-Semitism in the West. In 2005, Prince Harry, a member of the British royal family, was criticized for wearing a Nazi costume to a fancy dress party, complete with a swastika armband.[66] The swastika is a common symbol of white supremacy and appears in tattoos and graffiti, and is used to vandalize Jewish schools, cemeteries, and places of worship. In 2007, Jewish graves in a cemetery in Wellington, New Zealand, were defaced with swastikas and other anti-Semitic messages, including "Hitler RIP," "Rot you filth," and "Juden swine."[67]

In Nazi Germany, *Jude* ("Jew") was wielded as a slur, and it became an insult with serious consequences for the civil rights of Jewish people.[68] Long used in the context of extreme prejudice, the exonym *Jew* has acquired a harsh ring of anti-Semitism.[69] Today, *Jew* is still used as a term of abuse. Jew is synonymous with the negative stereotypes mentioned above, while the verb form of *jew* means "to cheat, to drive a hard bargain."[70] As an insult, the word is intensified with disparaging adjectives, including *fat Jew, old Jew,* or *dirty Jew.* Jew is also used in epithets such as *Jew boy, Jew girl,* and *jewlet,* a derogatory term for a Jewish child. (Also compare *niglet.*) *Jewess,* the archaic female form of *Jew,* is now perceived as an ethnic slur and also as sexist. (Also compare *Negress.*) For writing about the election of Donald Trump emboldening his anti-Semitic supporters, Jewish reporter Bethany Mandel was attacked as a "slimy Jewess" and told she deserved "the oven."[71] The use of the noun seems more offensive, so to some, *Jew* and *Jews* seems more derogatory than the corresponding *Jewish.* Jewish-American comedian Lenny Bruce once said, "I'll say 'a Jew' and just the word Jew sounds like a dirty word and people don't know whether to laugh or not."[72] Trying to be respectful, some non-Jews favor the adjective, *Jewish* people, although many stakeholders find it offensive that *Jew* itself can be considered derogatory, and so they prefer to use the noun as a self-identifying label. (For this reason, *Jew* is preferred in this chapter.)

In various forms, anti-Semitism has existed for thousands of years. It has sometimes been called *the world's oldest hatred,* and it continues to not only exist but also evolve. The *new anti-Semitism* or *anti-Zionism* is said to involve the unfounded criticism of Israel or Israeli policies as veiled attacks on Jews. New anti-Semitism often manifests as anti-Jewish prejudice that is presented as opposition to the Jewish state, or that challenges its right to exist. Ironically, the Israeli government has often been compared to Nazi Germany. The Israeli treatment of Palestinian territory in the Gaza Strip has been likened to Jewish ghettos or concentration camps.[73] The Israeli claim to being the *Chosen People* is compared to the Nazi theory of the Germans as the *Master Race*.[74] Other criticisms blame Jews and the Jewish state for the current world crisis. Osama bin Laden, founder of Al-Qaeda, the militant organization behind the 9/11 attacks on the United States, cited the government's support for Israel as a motivating factor of anti-American terrorist activities.[75] This type of new anti-Semitism has led to the resurgence of anti-Jewish violence around the world.

The targets of religious discrimination, and its manifestations, differ across time and space. Some religions that are now viewed favorably were once the focus of prejudice and intolerance. For most of the nineteenth and twentieth centuries, Buddhists faced persecution in the United States.[76] There was fear that the country was *under attack* from the increasing numbers of Asian immigrants, a *threat* that was known variously as *the Yellow peril, the Yellow terror,* or *the Yellow specter*. This prejudice was racist in origin, their different religion perceived as a marker of their foreignness. The *heathen Chinese* and the *heathen Japs* were perceived as primitive, unchristian, and uncivilized. Some racism against Chinese people, known specifically as *sinophobia*, was institutional. The 1882 Chinese Exclusion Act was a US federal law that prohibited all immigration of Chinese laborers. This was the first law preventing the immigration of an entire ethnic group, and it was not repealed until 1943. People of Japanese origin were also targeted in the United States, especially after the bombing of Pearl Harbour in 1941. In 1942, Executive Order 9066 authorized the removal of 110,000 Japanese Americans into concentration camps for the duration of World War II.[77] People of other Indic faiths have also experienced prejudice in Anglophone countries. In the early twentieth century, the immigration of Punjabi Sikhs to California was referred to as "The Tide of Turbans" and, inaccurately, as "The Hindoo Invasion."[78]

Today, there are 500 million Buddhists worldwide.[79] In modern Western societies, Buddhism is often perceived favorably, especially by New Age spiritualists, and the community is associated with peace, pacifism, wisdom, and meditation. The Buddha did not consider himself a deity, so Buddhism is often viewed as a philosophy instead of a religion. Buddhism has experienced periods of being fashionable, and its ideas permeate Anglophone culture, from the spiritual themes in movies such as *Seven Years In Tibet* and *Star Wars*, to the professed faith of celebrity converts including Angelina Jolie, George Lucas, and Richard Gere. A recent Gallup poll suggests that Americans are less prejudiced against Buddhism than other religions.[80] However, as a minority religious group, Buddhists have experienced some instances of discrimination that are usually racial in origin. In a school in Louisiana in 2014, a sixth-grader of Thai descent was harassed when a teacher denigrated the student's Buddhist faith as "stupid," while school officials suggested he should transfer to a school with "more Asians."[81]

There has sometimes been a tendency, particularly in the West, to confuse Buddhism with Hinduism and to lump together all "Eastern Religions" into one category.[82] Hinduism is the world's oldest religion. It is also the third largest, with over 1 billion Hindus worldwide, although it is still a minority religion in the Anglosphere.[83] Like Buddhism, Hinduism often has a positive image in the West, where it is perceived as a peaceful religion, while Hindu teachings such as yoga and meditation are popular. Hinduism too is often seen as more of a way of life than a religion. Since the 1960s, there have been many celebrity endorsements of various Hindu belief systems, for example by American actor Julia Roberts and British comedian Russell Brand. Most famously, in the 1960s, the English rock band The Beatles dabbled in Transcendental Meditation under the tutelage of its founder, the Maharishi Mahesh Yogi. This inspired Beatle George Harrison to become a lifelong follower of the International Society for Krishna Consciousness (ISKON). His religious beliefs influenced his music, such as his solo song "My Sweet Lord" that was written in praise of the Hindu god Krishna.

ISKON was founded in 1966 by Swami Prabhupada, as an off-shoot of Hinduism. Devotees, colloquially called the *Hare Krishnas*, are often recognizable for wearing saffron-colored saris, having shaved heads, burning incense, soliciting donations in exchange for flowers, dancing, and chanting the Hare Krishna mantra in public places, such as airports. Followers are often disparaged as *weirdos*, *hippies*, or *tree-huggers*, while the religion is denigrated as a *sect* or a *cult*. These terms are often used to imply that a religious group is heretical, extreme, or dangerous, and *not a real religion*. ISKON has been accused of indoctrinating its members. In a landmark 1976 case in the United States, the parents of two Hare Krishna devotees alleged that the group "brainwashed" their children and used "mind control" on them. However, the court found that they had entered the movement voluntarily and were exercising their right to freedom of religion. There are several different branches of Hinduism and the court further determined that ISKON is an orthodox Hindu tradition (it is classified as a Gaudiya Vaishnava Hindu religious organization).[84]

Mainstream Hinduism is not free from prejudice either. Non-Hindus often harbor misconceptions about the religion, believing that Hinduism endorses the caste system in India, that Hindus are *idol worshippers*, or that they *worship cows*. In an episode of the TV show the *700 Club*, Evangelist Pat Robertson made numerous anti-Hindu statements, labeling Hinduism a "demonic" religion.[85] Robertson's son Gordon added, "Whenever [Hindus] feel any sort of inspiration, whether it's by a river or under a tree, on top of a hill, they figure that some God or spirit is responsible for that. And so they'll worship that tree, they'll worship that hill or they'll worship anything."[86] This kind of disdain for Hinduism has led to anti-Hindu violence.

In 1998, Rishi Maharaj was walking through the Ozone neighborhood of Queens, New York, when he was set upon by three youths wielding baseball bats and shouting anti-Hindu slogans. They attacked him, and he ended up in hospital in critical condition.[87] Other hate crimes are more organized. In the fall of 1987, a hate group calling itself "Dot Busters" terrorized Pakistani and Indian people across Jersey City, New Jersey. Named after the *bindi* (decorative mark) that some Hindu and Jain women wear on their foreheads, the group verbally abused, physically attacked, and occasionally killed their victims. A local newspaper published a letter from the Dot Busters that threatens, "We will go to any extreme to get Indians to move out of Jersey City. If I'm walking down the street and I see a Hindu and the setting is right, I will hit him or her."[88] Gang members revealed that they selected their victims by looking up the common Indian last name Patel in the phone book.[89]

Hinduism and Buddhism have influence and prestige as "world religions," but historically, religions that did not fall into this category were labeled *tribal religions* or *primitive religions*.[90] Now called *traditional religions*, these include Native American, Australian Aboriginal, and traditional African religions. Traditional religions are different from world religions in that they usually do not have central institutions such as churches or mosques, and they do not have sacred texts with a fixed system of beliefs. Traditional religions may be romanticized as *mysterious* and *exotic*, or belittled as *quaint* and *strange*. Alternatively, they may be dismissed as *primitive*. African religions such as Santeria and Voodoo are often demonized as *wicked* or *witchcraft*, because practitioners participate in magical rituals and practice folk medicine and veneration of the dead. *Voodoo* is also used colloquially to mean something that is nonsense or superstition. Traditional religions are often marginalized in Anglophone countries, even though they predate the major religions introduced by colonizers. To more conservative attitudes, traditional religions may not even be perceived as "real" or valid religions.

Not holding religious beliefs is not protection against religious discrimination. People who identify as *atheist, non-theist, non-believer, non-religious, freethinker, agnostic,* or *humanist* also suffer discrimination and prejudice. In the United States, atheists enjoy the same protection as religious people in the workplace, even if their "religion" is the lack of any religious belief at all.

Equal Employment Opportunity Commission guidelines state that employers are prohibited from, "subjecting employees to harassment because of their religious beliefs or practices – or lack thereof."[91] In 2010, Abby Nurre was fired from her job teaching math at a Catholic school in Des Moines, Iowa, for filling out a Facebook survey in which she revealed that she did not believe in God, although she had no recourse for the action against her.[92] Much like age discrimination (see also Chapter 7), religious discrimination is notoriously difficult to prove or regulate.

Atheists experience social prejudice too. Not being religious is often stigmatized, while the self-identifying label *atheist* is wielded as an insult. American magician and atheist activist Penn Jillette once remarked, "When Christians are showing their disapproval of me, they call me 'atheist'. It's the word I use for myself, and to them, it's a bad thing."[93] *Godless, heretic, heathen, pagan, infidel,* and *Satan* are insults used to demonize atheists as bad people. Some religious people assume that if someone does not believe in God, by default they must worship Satan. Many Christians think that a belief in God is essential to morality. Colloquially, *Christian* is used as a synonym for *good* or *kind,* as in the phrase *He is a Christian person.* Therefore, it is often believed that people who are not religious simply cannot be moral. Atheists are stereotyped as immoral, depraved, wicked, sinful, or evil. In 2012, 16-year-old Jessica Ahlquist petitioned to have a prayer plaque removed from the wall of her high school auditorium in Rhode Island because it excluded atheists and other non-Christians. On a popular radio show, State Representative Peter G. Palumbo branded her, "an evil little thing."[94]

For their lack of belief, atheists encounter hostility, death threats, and even curses. Religious believers threaten atheists with punishment in the afterlife: *You're going to hell* or *Go to hell.* These are intended to be insulting, because those who make the threats believe in the concept of *Hell.* In 2018, at a county meeting in Wichita, Kansas, an atheist asked to deliver an invocation at commission meetings. However, Commissioner David

Unruh denied the request and said, "If you don't believe in God, that's fine with me. I don't care. Go to hell."[95] The United States is predominately Christian, *In God We Trust* is the country's official motto that appears on all US bank notes, while *God Bless America* is a common axiom. Atheists are an unpopular minority. A 2014 poll showed that atheists are the second most negatively viewed group in the United States, ranking only slightly higher than Muslim people.[96] Atheism is on the rise, but the vast majority of people in the Anglosphere are still Christian.

Worldwide, Christianity is the largest religious group, with a population of 2.2 billion adherents.[97] Globally, Christians are the most discriminated against religious group.[98] Even though they are the majority group in the United States, some members of the "Christian right" or "religious right" argue that there is a *War against Christianity* that is being waged by liberals. They believe there is an assault on the religious liberties of modern Christians, which manifests as the elimination of prayer in schools, the eradication of Christian content from textbooks, and the tendency of the media to ridicule Christian politicians.[99] Some conservative Christians expect a tolerance for their beliefs that is not extended to other religions. In 2012, Louisiana State lawmaker Valarie Hodges tried to rescind her vote for a bill authorizing public funds for religious schools because Muslims wanted to benefit from the bill too. Hodges admitted that she had mistakenly assumed that "religious meant Christian."[100]

The Christian right further contends that there is a *War against Christmas*. Some Christians believe that big corporations are censoring Christmas, like Starbucks, whose seasonal cup designs emphasize winter weather or social harmony over Christmas greetings.[101] They further argue that the religious sentiment of Christmas is ignored by the replacement of *Merry Christmas* with the more inclusive *Happy Holidays*, which also recognizes minority holidays such as the Jewish festival Hanukkah and the African American celebration Kwanzaa. However, *Happy Holidays* has been used in the United States since the nineteenth century, and so the phrase is not the recent creation of anti-Christmas secular liberals.[102] In 2012, the American Atheists organization was criticized for a series of Christmas billboard campaigns that ridiculed Christmas, including the slogans, "Keep the merry! Dump the myth!" and "Who Needs Christ during Christmas? Nobody."[103]

Some Christians are stereotyped as overzealous evangelists. This view is influenced by the door-to-door and street proselytizing that is the hallmark conversion tactic of the Jehovah's Witnesses and members of the Church of Jesus Christ of Latter-day Saints (LDS). (Members of the LDS are known colloquially as *Mormons*. This was the name of an ancient American prophet said to have engraved their holy scripture, the "Book of Mormon," on plates of gold. Followers once called themselves *Saints*, while *Mormons* became a term of derision used by outsiders. In 2018, Church President Russell M. Nelson requested that people stop using the nickname.)[104] Christians are often derided as *God botherers*, *Bible thumpers*, *Bible-beaters*, or *Bible-bashers*. Evangelical Christians are disparaged as *Fundies*, an abbreviation of "fundamentalist," with negative connotations of extremism, zealotry, and fanaticism. Evangelical Christians are sometimes labeled *crazy* or *mentally ill* for their literal interpretation of the Bible and supernatural worldview. On an episode of the TV show *The View*, co-host Joy Behar came under fire for criticizing Vice President Mike Pence's belief that Jesus tells him what to say. Behar said, "It's one thing to talk to Jesus. It's another thing when Jesus talks to you. That's called mental illness, if I'm not correct, hearing voices."[105]

The United States does not have an official religion, so it is not formally considered to be a "Christian state." The First Amendment states that, "Congress shall make no law respecting an establishment of religion, or prohibiting the free exercise thereof."[106] However, the United States is often informally called a *Christian nation*, because the majority of residents (78.3%) identify as Christian. A 2012 study revealed that the following percentages of people identify as Christian in Anglophone countries: 92% of Irish people, 81.2% of South Africans, 71.1% of people in the United Kingdom, 69% of Canadians, 67.3% of Australians, and 57% of New Zealanders.[107] Therefore, Christians comprise the majority religious group across these countries. In any society, it is the minority religions that are stigmatized, while the majority religion is privileged. Although there is some prejudice within Christianity across denominations, Christians are generally privileged in Anglophone countries and experience less discrimination than other religious groups, such as Muslim communities.

Islam is the second most popular world religion after Christianity, with 1.8 billion adherents, and it is also the second most discriminated against religious group worldwide.[108] Islam is the religious system revealed by the prophet Muhammad. The religion arose in the early seventh century in the community of Mecca (which is in present day Saudi Arabia).[109] The name *Islam* dates back to the seventeenth century in English and is a borrowing from Turkish *islām* ("the Muslim religion") and also Arabic *islām* meaning "submission or resignation (to the will of God)."[110] It is often said that Islam means "peace" in Arabic. While this is not technically correct, the word is related to *salaam*, literally meaning "peace," which is a Muslim greeting (compare Hebrew *shalom*). A follower of Islam is called a *Muslim*, which comes from Arabic *muslim*, "one who submits" (to the faith).[111] *Muslim* is both a self-identifying label and the exonym used outside of the community.

Conflicts such as the Iran Hostage Crisis (1979–1981), the Gulf War (1990–1991), and US military operations in Kuwait, Afghanistan, and Iraq, have led to stigma against Islam and Muslim people. Since the end of the Cold War (1947–1991) between the Soviet Union and the United States and its allies, Islam and Muslim people have become perceived as the current *menace, threat, danger,* or *enemy* of the West.[112, 113] Anti-Muslim language has become even more rampant since the "9/11" attacks of September 11, 2001, perpetrated against the United States by Osama bin Laden and his organization Al-Qaeda. The sentiment has been further exacerbated following the actions of the Taliban and the Islamic State of Iraq and the Levant (ISIL). Anti-Muslim prejudice often overlaps with racism and xenophobia, because it can include bias against race (Middle Eastern people are often perceived to be *black* or *brown*), ethnicity, nationality, culture, and language.

Given the current and historical conflicts between the Western world and the Middle East, Islam is arguably the most discriminated against religion in the Anglosphere. Discrimination against Muslim people goes back as early as the Crusades (the medieval religious wars between Christians and Muslims that were sanctioned by the Latin Church to retake the Holy land from Muslim control).[114] Anti-Muslim sentiment is so common that a specific term has been created for the phenomenon: *Islamophobia*. This is so widespread in Anglophone countries that it is referred to as "everyday Islamophobia," which describes the discrimination and bias that are daily experiences for Muslim people living in the West, and anyone perceived to be Muslim. Islamophobia is not a recent name; it has been in use since the 1920s.[115] It was probably modeled after *Germanophobia* ("a strong dislike of Germany or Germans"),[116] *Francophobia* ("a strong dislike of France or the French"),[117] and *xenophobia* ("a deep antipathy to foreigners"), which are terms that can be traced back to the nineteenth century.[118]

As we have seen, the suffix *-phobia* has since been used to label other forms of prejudice, including *homophobia* and *transphobia*. However, *-phobia* often implies a clinical disorder involving an extreme or irrational fear of an object or a situation (e.g., claustrophobia, agoraphobia). Islamophobia is not purported to be a psychological condition, nor does it refer to legitimate political or theological criticisms of Islam, but instead describes a dislike, fear of, intolerance for, or prejudice against Islam and Muslim people. To delegitimize the term, some detractors argue that they are criticizing Islam as a religion, not Muslim people, and that *Islamophobia* is an accusation that shuts down debate.[119] Criticizing Islam and Muslim people is variously defended as *freedom of speech, artistic expression*, and *democracy*. *Islamophobe* is often considered to be a slur, in the same way that we have seen people reject the labels *racist, misogynist,* or *homophobe*. To deny the accusation of Islamophobia, some appeal to the fallacy, *I have Muslim friends, but . . .* or, *I'm not Islamophobic, but . . .* to precede anti-Muslim rhetoric. Given these ambiguities surrounding the use of *Islamophobia*, and the manner in which criticizing Islam as a religion has been used to justify criticizing Muslim people, this term is often dispreferred by stakeholders. For these reasons, this book favors *anti-Muslim prejudice* over *Islamophobia*.

It is popularly believed that Islam and its religious text the *Qur'an* (or *Koran*) actively encourage violence, war, and terrorism. In the mainstream Western media, Islam is demonized as an inherently violent religion, a view that is shared by influential public figures. In 2006, on *The 700 Club*, Evangelist Pat Robertson warned that Americans need to "wake up" to the "danger" that Islam presents and added, "Who ever heard of such a bloody, bloody, brutal type of religion? But that's what it is. It is not a religion of peace."[120] This negative perception of Islam and Muslim people is borne out by collocations (co-occurring words) commonly used by the media, including: *violent Islam, radical Islam, Islamic fanaticism, Islamic bombs, dangerous Islam, militant Islam, Muslim extremists,* and *Islamic threat.* Ironically, vilifying Islam and Middle Eastern people as *violent* has escalated anti-Muslim violence and hate crimes.

One such incident occurred on March 15, 2019, when 28-year old Australian Brenton Tarrant stormed the Masjid al Noor Mosque and Linwood Islamic Centre in Christchurch, New Zealand.[121] Armed with semi-automatic weapons and shotguns, he opened fire on the peaceful worshippers, killing 50 people and injuring 50 more. These events occurred during the *jummah* (or *jum'ah*) prayers and sermons held on Fridays at noon, which are particularly important for Muslims and involve large numbers of worshippers. The first 17 minutes of the attack were live-streamed on social media in a graphic video. Prior to the attack, Tarrant posted to Twitter and 8chan an 87-page manifesto filled with anti-immigrant and anti-Muslim rhetoric. He revealed himself to be a white supremacist and part of the *alt-right*, while he cited US President Donald Trump as a "renewed symbol of white identity."[122] During the media coverage and political commentary that followed, the events were often characterized as a "mass shooting" rather than a "terrorist act," while Tarrant was described as a "gunman" instead of a "terrorist."

This highlights a disparity in the terminology used in the news coverage of terrorist attacks. The word *terrorism* is typically ignored in the context of non-Muslim violence, although used liberally in news reports covering crimes committed by Muslim people. This has led to an increased fear of *Islamic terrorism* and *Muslim terrorists* and a reduced empathy for Muslim victims. Furthermore, when a crime is committed by a non-Muslim, the perpetrator's religion is generally not invoked, even in cases of domestic terrorism. For example, the Irish Republican Army has carried out many acts of terror over the decades, although the media does not refer to them by their religious affiliation (the group is rooted in Irish Catholic nationalism). But in the case of violent acts committed by people with a connection to Islam, their actions are invariably linked to their religion.

The Western concept of terrorism is currently linked to Islam, maligning the religion itself as *terrorism*. In response to attacks on Muslims in the aftermath of 9/11, British Prime Minister Tony Blair stated, "What happened in America was not the work of Islamic terrorists, it was not the work of Muslim terrorists. It was the work of terrorists, pure and simple."[123] However, any terrorist act linked to Islam is often attributed to all Muslim people. There is an Internet meme showing a bowl of M&Ms (or Skittles, etc.) that says, "Not all Muslims are terrorists? Some of these M&Ms are poisoned. Would you eat a handful?" This is a false equivalence, and crimes that are complex politically, historically, and socially are blamed naively on Islam and Muslim people. On an episode of ABC's *The View*, Bill O'Reilly claimed that, the "Muslims killed us on 9/11!"[124] In response to the events of 9/11, then United States President George W. Bush declared the

War in Afghanistan, which became known colloquially as the *War on Terror*, although much of the general public interpreted this as a war against Islam and Muslim people.

In the West, there is a simplistic dichotomy that Muslims are either *good* (moderate) or *bad* (extremist). By and large, stereotypes of Islam and Muslims are negative, which is revealed by the way the religion and its people are talked about. Commonly used adjectives describe them (especially men) as "violent": *hostile, terrorists, war-mongering, dangerous, threatening, evil, inhuman,* and *cruel.* They are portrayed as "fanatical": *fundamentalist, militant, maniacs,* and *extremist.* Islamic society is thought to be "chauvinistic": *patriarchal, sexist, misogynistic, oppressive,* and *hypermasculine.* And Islamic countries are believed to be "opposed to modernity": *barbaric, backward, primitive, medieval, uncivilized, undemocratic,* and *archaic.* Some of these negative stereotypes are based on fearmongering, conspiracy theories, and misconceptions about the Qur'an and Islamic concepts such as *Sharia law* that have been disseminated via anecdotes, jokes, news items, and chain emails. There are many myths about Islamic doctrine; for example, *jihad* is often mistranslated as "holy war" or "terrorism," although it is more accurately understood as a struggle on behalf of Islam.[125]

In comparison to these negative images of Islam and Muslim people, the West sees itself favorably as: civilized, sophisticated, democratic, modern, progressive, enlightened, and promoting freedom and humanity. This is a type of ethnocentrism, the conviction of the superiority of one's own culture, that has been called *Orientalism.*[126] According to this representation, the West is rational, developed, humane, and superior, while the Middle East is portrayed as irrational, undeveloped, inhumane, and inferior. In this "us and them" mentality, Muslim people are positioned as the "other." The Middle East is pitted against the West in a battle of good versus evil. Muslim people are cast as the enemy in what has been called *Islam's War against the West.*

It is often said that Islam represents a cultural clash with the West, and that Muslim immigrants to Western countries are unwilling, if not unable, to assimilate or integrate socially. It is further thought that Muslim people do not share the same values as Westerners; that they are reluctant to adopt Western values, and that Islamic culture is ultimately "incompatible" with Western society.[127] Invoking the "Muslim friend" fallacy, US politician Ben Carson once said, "I had a lot of Muslim friends and playmates and schoolmates. Nothing wrong with Muslims, as long as they accept our culture and our Constitution."[128] In a subsequent interview, Carson denied that Islam is consistent with the Constitution. Islamic values are perceived as not only dissimilar to Western values (Un-American, Un-British, Un-Australian, etc.), but also in opposition to Western values (Anti-American, etc.). It is believed that Islam endangers freedom and threatens the Western "way of life." There is a fear of *Islamization*, that Islamic culture will *take over* Western culture, and a fear of *Muslim domination*. These attitudes often reveal a thinly veiled racism. Nick Griffith, leader of the British National Party, who called Islam "a wicked, vicious faith," also accused Muslims of having transformed Britain into a "multi-racial hell hole."[129] In the 1990s, England's capital city was dubbed *Londonistan* by those who resented the growing Muslim population (based on the names of countries that end in *-stan*, like Afghanistan or Pakistan, the suffix meaning "land" in Persian).

Opposition is shown to Islamic religious and cultural practices that are transported into Anglophone countries. In particular, the practice of women wearing headscarves is heavily criticized. The three styles of veils most known to Westerners are the *hijab*, the *niqab*, and the *burka*. *Hijab* means "modest dress" but also refers to a scarf that covers the head and neck. The *niqab* is a veil that leaves the area around the eyes clear. The one-piece veil that covers the head and body is called a *burka* (or *burqa*). The burka is the namesake of the "burka ban," a prohibition of face-coverings introduced in Quebec (Canada), Belgium, France, and Denmark, and which is the subject of ongoing debate in the United Kingdom and Australia. These headscarves are worn for modesty, and religious and cultural purposes, although it is argued by critics, under the guise of women's rights, that they are sexist, or that they are dangerous because they conceal the identity of would-be terrorists. Women wearing veils are simultaneously feared and mocked. British Prime Minister Boris Johnson once defended Muslim women's right to wear the burka, but joked that they look like "bank robbers" and added, "It is absolutely ridiculous that people should choose to go around looking like letter boxes."[130] In the United Kingdom, Muslim women have had their headscarves pulled off by attackers in the streets.[131] However, Muslims are not the only people to wear veils or scarves in Western countries. Post 9/11, Sikhs who wear turbans and Indian women and others who wear headscarves often experience harassment, because they are mistaken for being Muslim.

Former US President Barack Obama was the first African American to be elected to the presidency. During his two terms in office, numerous conservative conspiracy theories developed to discredit him, and many of these involved the belief that Obama secretly practiced Islam.[132] During his presidential campaign, it was rumored that Obama took his oath of office as a US senator while placing his hand on a Qur'an instead of a Bible.[133] It was said that Obama's wedding ring is emblazoned with the Islamic declaration of faith: "There is no god except Allah."[134] A chain email circulated with the fabrication that Obama's middle name is Mohammed. (His actual middle name is Hussein, which was also deemed to be suspicious and linked incorrectly to former President of Iraq Saddam Hussein.)[135] It was alleged that Obama went undercover as a CIA agent to facilitate the transfer of cash and weapons to the Afghan guerilla fighters known as the *mujahideen* (who would later become the Taliban). Another popular conspiracy theory claimed that Obama schemed to bring 100 million Muslim people from the Middle East into the United States to convert the country into an Islamic nation.[136]

Anglophone countries pride themselves on being "multicultural" and claim to embrace diversity, although some people rail against Muslim immigrants, who are referred to disparagingly as the *Muslim presence*. There is an inflated perception of the number of Muslim people living in Anglophone countries, which is described as an *Islamic takeover* of countries being *swamped* with Muslims. In fact, Muslim people only represent a small population. A 2014 British study revealed negative attitudes toward Muslim people, and 35 percent of the respondents agreed, "Muslims are taking over our country."[137] They also believed that Muslim people made up 36 percent of the population, as opposed to the accurate figure of only 5 percent. Muslim immigration supposedly heralds *the end of Britain* (or America, Australia, etc.) and the *changing face* of the country, while Muslim people are accused of *replacing* white people. Brenton Tarrant, who carried out the terrorist attacks in Christchurch, New Zealand, mentioned above, named his manifesto "The Great Replacement" (after an anti-immigrant tract by French writer Renaud Camus). He referred to Muslim immigrants as those who "invade our lands, live on our soil and replace our people."[138] Ironically, many Muslim immigrants are fleeing Western-backed invasions, occupation, or persecution in their home countries.

Muslim immigrants in Anglophone countries are abused with *Go home!*, *Go back to your own country*, and *Go back to where you belong*, revealing a strong belief in the illegitimacy of the Muslim presence. (See also Chapter 1.) In July 2019, US President Donald Trump criticized four "Progressive" Congresswomen (known derisively as "the Squad"), tweeting that they should "go back and help fix the totally broken and crime infested places from which they came."[139] He referred specifically to Democratic Representatives Alexandria Ocasio-Cortez, Ayanna Pressley, Rashida Tlaib, and Ilhan Omar, who are all women of color. However, the initial three Representatives are US born. Representative Omar is a Somali-born American citizen, and one of the first two Muslim women (along with Tlaib) to serve in Congress. She is a practicing Muslim and distinctive in her appearance for wearing the hijab. Trump's "Go back" comment was followed by a rally in Greenville, North Carolina, where at the mention of Omar, the crowd broke into an extended chanting of "Send her back!"

That Muslim people *do not fit in* or *do not belong* in Western countries is a recurring theme. On an institutional level, proposed government policies promote the belief that Muslim people need to be feared and driven out, or refused entry in the first place. This push to deny entry to Muslim people is informally known as *the Muslim ban*. Following the 2017 terrorist attacks in London, Australian politician Pauline Hanson called for a ban on Muslim immigration to Australia, tweeting, "Stop Islamic immigration before it's too late."[140] US President Donald Trump had also been calling for a travel ban, a "total and complete shutdown" of Muslim immigrants and tourists to the United States.[141] In general, Trump called for a greater scrutiny of Muslims, including legal residents, and proposed a registry to track all Muslims in the country. In doing so, Trump appealed to the "Muslim friend" fallacy: "I have friends that are Muslims. They're great people, but they know we have a problem." Islam is often positioned as a *problem* for Western countries. In general, how governments should interact with Muslim people around issues of immigration, integration, religious freedom, and identity, is posed as "the Muslim question". (Which is reminiscent of the "Jewish Question" discussed above.)

Muslim immigrants are blamed for the marginalization they feel, although critics of their alleged failure to integrate are also often advocates of measures that would further isolate and marginalize them.[142] In a statement issued on the day of the 2019 terrorist attacks in New Zealand, former Australian Senator for Queensland, Fraser Anning, issued a statement saying, "the real cause of bloodshed on New Zealand streets today is the immigration program which allowed Muslim fanatics to migrate to New Zealand in the first place,"[143] He added, "Muslims may have been the victims today, usually they are the perpetrators," and "Just because the followers of this savage belief were not the killers in this instance, does not make them blameless." In August 2018, Anning invoked a Nazi euphemism in his inaugural speech as

Senator, when he called for a ban on Muslim immigration, which he recommended as a "final solution to the immigration problem."[144]

There are many anti-Muslim slurs, including self-identifying labels. As we saw with *Jew*, exonyms are used as insults when they are uttered with contempt, including *Muslims* and *Arabs*. However, many Westerners do not differentiate between *Arab*, *Muslim*, and *Middle Eastern*, although there are significant differences. Some Middle Eastern people do not necessarily identify as *Arabs*, such as Iranians (Persians) who speak Persian, although Islam is the state religion in Iran (Persia). Many Persians are Indo-Europeans and are ethnically distinct from most Arabs, who are Semitic. Furthermore, not all Muslim people are of Middle Eastern descent. Islam originated in the Middle East, but it has spread across the globe. In fact, the country with the largest Islamic population is not in the Middle East but in Southeast Asia. Indonesia has over 202 million Muslim people.[145] There are half a billion Muslim people in the other South Asian countries of India, Pakistan, and Bangladesh, while Africa has a large population of Muslim people. Many Muslim people are born or raised in Western countries too, but frequently, they are still treated like foreigners or outsiders.

Anti-Muslim insults often draw parallels with existing racist epithets, such as *sand niggers* and *sand monkeys*. Other common terms of abuse are also racial in nature, including *camel jockeys*, *camel fuckers*, *ragheads*, and *towelheads*. Some anti-Muslim slurs target national origin, such as the abbreviations *Leb* or *Lebos* to refer to people with a Lebanese background, and *Paki* for people with a Pakistani background. In the 1980s, gangs in Britain and Canada engaged in *Paki bashing*, violent attacks against Pakistanis and others who bore a resemblance to South Asians.[146] Paki is highly offensive in many Anglophone countries, although Americans are not always familiar with the abbreviation as a slur. Trying to defuse tensions between India and Pakistan in 2002, US President George W. Bush said, "We are working hard to convince both the Indians and the Pakis that there's a way to deal with their problems without going to war."[147] Similar to the Paki bashing of the 1980s is the recent emergence of *Punish a Muslim Day*. This phenomenon began in 2018, when flyers were delivered to homes and businesses across the United Kingdom inciting people to commit hate crimes against Muslim people on April 3.[148] The flyers encouraged a point system for committing various hate crimes, awarding 10 points to "Verbally abuse a Muslim," 25 points to "Pull the head-scarf off a Muslim 'woman'," 100 points to "Beat up a Muslim," 1,000 points to "Burn or bomb a mosque," and 2,500 points to "Nuke Mecca." The flyers went viral online and have encouraged hate crimes against Muslim people globally.

Other slurs ridicule Islamic religious practices, such as *pigs*, *swine*, and *bacon*, as a reference to the fact that consuming pork and pig derivatives is *haram* ("forbidden"). This religious restriction has been mocked in growing numbers of hate crimes against Muslim people, in particular in the desecration of mosques. In January 2016, Michael Wolfe broke into a mosque in Titusville, Florida, where he vandalized the building, smashing windows, cameras, and lights with a machete, and then left a slab of raw bacon at the scene.[149] As we saw with Jewish names, common Middle Eastern first names are wielded as insults, including *Abdul*, *Omar*, *Mohammed*, and also infamous names: *Saddam Hussein* or *Osama bin Laden*. In 2015, a Sikh-American man in Chicago was mistaken for being Muslim because of his turban and beard. He was called "terrorist" and told, "Go back to your country, Bin Laden," then he was brutally beaten.[150] Non-Muslim people become targets of anti-Muslim prejudice when they are perceived to be Muslim because of their appearance or dress. Other terms of abuse are based on the names of terrorist groups, including *Al Qaeda*, *Taliban*, and *ISIS*. In the United States, there has been an increase in anti-Muslim hate crimes in schools, with students being bullied and branded as *terrorists*. In 2015, in Vandalia, Ohio, a seventh-grader got into an argument on a school bus with a sixth-grade Muslim student, accusing him of being responsible for 9/11. He threatened to bring a .40-caliber handgun to school the next day to end the argument, and called him a "terrorist," "towelhead," and "the son of ISIS."[151]

A significant contributor to the demonization of Islam and Muslim people is that various terrorist organizations purport to have links to the religion, namely the Taliban (Pashto for "students") and Al-Qaeda (Arabic for "the Base"). Since 1999, the extremist group ISIL have been responsible for human rights abuses and war crimes worldwide, including killing civilians, forcing captured women into sexual slavery, and beheading foreigners in Iraq and Syria. The media initially reported the group by the acronym ISIS ("Islamic State of Iraq and Syria"). Isis is also the name of an ancient Egyptian goddess, the name borrowed from ancient Greek Ἶσις.[152] Despite this etymology, the name has pejorated by association, and Isis has become synonymous with the terrorist organization. This has been to the detriment of the many people and businesses that share this moniker. In 2015, ISIS Books and Gifts in Denver, Colorado, a store which sells New Age books, music, and art, became the target of multiple acts of vandalism because it was believed to be associated with the terrorist group.[153] In 2016, the owner of Facets of Isis, a bead and jewelry boutique in the suburbs of Chicago, Illinois, was harassed with death threats and voice messages telling her, "Go back where you came from."[154]

Both businesses opted to retain their long-standing names and fight the stigma, although the terrorist attacks prompted the Californian company Isis Pharmaceuticals to rebrand to Ionis Pharmaceuticals, because they didn't want to have that negative association.[155] In light of stories such as these, an online petition gathered almost 70,000 supporters to call on the news media to stop using the acronym.[156] Today, most officials refer to the group as ISIL or IS ("Islamic State") instead. However, ISIS, IS, and ISIL offend many Muslims who disapprove of *Islam* and *State* appearing in the name because the group is neither Islamic nor a state. There is a push to call the group *Daesh* instead, which is an acronym of their full Arabic name *al-Dawla al-Islamiya fi al-Iraq wa al-Sham* (Islamic State in Iraq and Syria (or the Levant)). It is also an insult to the group. Depending on how it is conjugated in Arabic, Daesh means "to trample down and crush," or, "a bigot who imposes his views on others."[157] The group has threatened to cut out the tongues of anyone who uses the name.

ISIL's attacks, and the copycat incidents they have inspired, have reinvigorated the anti-Muslim prejudice ignited by 9/11, and also reinforced the stereotype that Islam is a violent religion. In 2016, the assassination of a priest in Rouen, France, was an attack claimed by ISIL. In response to a reference to "violent Islam," Pope Francis responded that it is wrong to equate Islam with violence. "Not all Muslims are violent. Just like not all Catholics are violent either. I don't like to talk about Islamic violence because every day when I look at the papers I see violence here in Italy. Someone killing his girlfriend, someone killing his mother-in-law. These are baptized Catholics. They are violent Catholics. If I speak about Islamic violence, I need to speak about Catholic violence."[158] Although they claim to carry out their attacks in the name of Islam, the actions of these organizations are not representative of the religion and the worldwide Muslim community. In fact, multiple Muslim leaders have denounced the actions of ISIL as *haram* (forbidden or proscribed by Islamic law), while Sheikh Abdullah bin Bayyah issued a *fatwa* (an authoritative legal pronouncement) against the group.[159] In general, terrorist attacks have made Muslim people scapegoats and provided individuals and groups with an excuse to malign the community as a whole.

A significant contributor to anti-Muslim prejudice is a fear of what appears "foreign" and what is not understood. As discussed in Chapter 1, linguicism is language-related discrimination; prejudice against people based on their language, dialect, or accent.[160] Linguicism can reveal racist attitudes and religious discrimination. Anti-Muslim prejudice has led to a spate of linguicism, particularly a fear of spoken and written Arabic. Modern Standard Arabic is the universal language of the Arabic-speaking world, while there are many colloquial varieties. There are approximately 420 million (native and non-native) speakers of the language worldwide, making it the sixth most spoken language.[161] Classical Arabic is the language of Islam's scripture, the Qur'an, and classical literature. However, for some Westerners, the Arabic language and writing system are solely associated with extremist groups, such as Al-Qaeda and ISIL. In the West, immigrants and travelers often avoid speaking Arabic in public so that they do not invite suspicion and harassment from strangers.

With the stereotype of Muslim people as "terrorists" and the memory of 9/11, this fear of spoken Arabic is particularly evident at airports, where there have been many incidents of airport security personnel overreacting to its use. In 2016, Iraqi student Khairuldeen Makhzoomi was removed from a Southwest flight for speaking Arabic on the phone with his uncle. He had uttered the word *Inshallah*, which means, "If God is willing," which is used as an exclamation by all native speakers of Arabic, irrespective of religious affiliation.[162] A fellow passenger overheard the conversation and reported Makhzoomi to airline staff who escorted him off the plane, where he was interrogated by police and FBI agents. There have been several cases of Muslim people being removed from flights for merely speaking Arabic. Inspired by this racial profiling that many call *Flying while Muslim*, Iranian-American comedian Maz Jobrani joked that when speaking Arabic on planes or at airports, people should code-switch occasionally, randomly inserting innocuous English words, such as *strawberry, rainbow* and *tutti frutti*, to put worried passengers at ease.[163]

Written Arabic also provokes fear among members of the general public and government agencies in the West. Seen on the flags, murals, banners, and bandanas of extremist organizations, the Arabic writing system has become synonymous with terrorism in the West and has occasionally inspired hysteria. In 2009, Nicholas George was detained at the Philadelphia airport for five hours, when his pockets were found to contain Arabic flash cards because he was a student of the Arabic language. During his ordeal, a supervisor asked him, "Do you know who did 9/11?" He replied, "Osama Bin Laden." Then she asked if he knew what language Osama Bin Laden spoke. "Arabic," he said. "So do you see why these cards are suspicious?" she asked as he was arrested. George sued the Philadelphia Police Department and eventually won a settlement against them.[164]

The mere sight of the Arabic language, or any writing resembling the Arabic script, has occasionally resulted in panic. In 2015, alarmed residents of Gardner, Louisiana, alerted the sheriff's office when they discovered a banner that bore an "Arabic terror message." It was later discovered that the sign read, "Welcome Home, Yamit" in Hebrew.[165] In 2016, the Department of Homeland Security was contacted when a flag with Arabic writing was discovered hanging from a building in downtown Lubbock, Texas. The flag was feared to be a terrorist message from ISIL. The mayor shut down traffic and removed the flag before it was discovered that it bore the Arabic expression, "Love is for all" across a red heart, displayed in honor of Valentine's Day.[166]

In 2016, a gas station was temporarily closed, a nearby daycare center was evacuated, and a bomb squad was called in when a box of cookies, which had Arabic script on the side, was discovered near a gas pump in Marshalls Creek, Pennsylvania. A customer discovered that the *maamoul* cookies (a kind of shortbread filled with dates, walnuts, or pistachios) had Arabic writing on the box and immediately called the police to report it.[167] At Gay Pride celebrations in London in 2015, a CNN reporter identified a flag as "very distinctively the ISIS flag." It was some time before it was realized that this was a satirical Islamic State flag festooned with images of adult sex toys.[168] This fear of Arabic writing (and similar-looking symbols) arises from its associations, and not knowing what it says. To demonstrate this fear from ignorance, the Israeli graphic design company Rock-Paper-Scissors created a provocative tote bag that reads in Arabic, "The only goal of this text is to spread panic among those who fear the Arabic language."[169] In response to Donald Trump's 2016 statements against Islam and Muslims, a billboard appeared on Interstate 94 heading into Dearborn, Michigan, the city with one of the largest Arabic communities in the United States. The sign said, "Donald Trump" followed by Arabic script that translates as, "He can't read this, but he is afraid of it".[170]

Religious groups that are a minority in the West are often seen as a threat to national identity, and even national security. Overall, criticisms of these religions are usually simplistic and uninformed, while differences are exaggerated, oversimplified, and caricaturized. The religious "other" is feared. They are positioned as alien, dangerous, and the enemy. Religious discrimination in language represents not only radical ideology or extremist views, but also everyday biases and prejudices. It is a message of intolerance that can lead to exclusion, harassment, persecution, and ultimately, genocide. This leap is not as great as it seems. It begins with slurs, negative stereotypes, and other expressions of hate speech that call into question the basic humanity of others, making it easier for society to justify persecution. Countries in the Anglosphere are multicultural and, therefore, multireligious, while most religious people are simply trying to lead their lives in accordance with the understanding, compassion, and peace promoted by their religions.

5 That's Crazy

In 1887, American journalist Nellie Bly went undercover as a patient to investigate reports of cruelty and neglect at a mental institution for women on Blackwell's Island, New York.[1] Her exposé, *Ten Days in a Mad-House*, revealed that the patients were subjected to severe physical and psychological abuses in the hospital. They were segregated from society and involuntarily committed for an indefinite period, but often for the rest of their lives. Many women were brought here, not because they were sick, but because their husbands or families wanted to get rid of them. Others ended up in the hospital because they had fallen through the cracks in society, as women who were homeless, unemployed, disabled, poor, elderly, or they were immigrants who were unable to speak English. In Bly's nineteenth-century book, the terminology of psychiatric disorders is offensive by today's standards. Patients were branded *lunatics, insane, idiots, demented, deranged,* and *hysterical,* and were confined to *insane asylums, lunatic asylums,* or, as called in the title of her book, *madhouses.* Language that is considered appropriate to refer to mental illness today is very different from that used back then. But even language that was acceptable a few decades ago is already considered ableist.

Modeled after racism and sexism, *ableism* is prejudice against people because of their different physical, intellectual, or psychological status. Ableist language; words and phrases that are intentionally or inadvertently derogatory toward a person with a disability, disease, or mental illness, is an often-ignored area of discrimination. Like racist and sexist language, ableist language is considered a form of language that excludes people with disabilities and casts them as inferior, irrelevant, or invisible. But there is probably greater consensus among the general public about what could be considered racist or sexist language than what is considered ableist.

In part, this may be because some people do not perceive ableist words and phrases in terms of their origins and implications.

Many words that are considered ableist today were once diagnostic terms, such as *lunatic*. Lunatic originally referred to a condition believed to be caused by the changing phases of the moon that was named after the Roman goddess of the moon, Luna.[2] Similarly, Old English *monseoc* meant "moon-sick," a person who was "affected with periodic insanity that was supposed to depend on the changes of the moon."[3] From the late thirteenth century, *lunatic* was widely acceptable to refer to people with mental illness and the place where they resided, the *lunatic asylum*. Around this same time, the word *mad* emerged. While it was never a diagnostic term, *mad* informally referred to mental illness, meaning "mentally unbalanced, deranged."[4] In the seventeenth century *crazy* appeared; it originally referred to "diseased, sickly" or bad health in general, but later meant "of unsound mind, insane."[5] A demonology theory prevailed as late as the nineteenth century, in which demonic possession, witch-craft, or punishment from God were blamed for mental illness.[6]

By this time, *lunatic* had acquired negative connotations. Beliefs about the cause of mental illness had advanced from astrological and demonological theories, so lunatic was sup-planted by *insane*, while lunatic asylums were renamed *insane asylums*. *Insane* was derived from Latin *insanus*, which meant "mentally unsound," because people with mental illness were thought to have lost their sense of reason.[7] By the 1950s, a more scientific approach was taken toward mental health, and *insane* became offensive too. Psychiatric terminology was reformed to reshape the negative image of the profession and to promote the idea that people with mental illness were sick, although able to be treated and cured. *Patient* and *mental illness* came into usage, while lunatic and insane lost their diagnostic status. They do not appear in the modern official guide, the *Diagnostic and Statistical Manual of Mental Disorders*.[8]

Lunatic and *insane* became subject to the euphemism treadmill whereby they became offensive and were replaced with euphemisms that in turn also became offensive, necessitating the creation of new terms.[9] (See Introduction.) As we will see, this phenomenon is common to the terminology of mental illness, disability, and disease.[10] Although they were substituted with more acceptable language and are no longer part of the clinical vocabulary, in a legal context, *insanity defense* and *temporary insanity* are still used, although the terms are being replaced by *mental disorder defense* or *defense of mental impairment. Lunatic* and *insane* remain in everyday language in such phrases as *You're a lunatic!* and *That's insane!* The abbreviation *loony* is popularly associated with the Warner Bros cartoon *Looney Tunes.* Some modern usage has even developed positive connotations. At an Apple shareholder's meeting in January 1984, co-founder Steve Jobs described the first Macintosh computer as, "Insanely great."[11] However, these words are disparaging in most usage, as derogatory descriptions of people with mental illness and as general terms of abuse.[12] They are commonly used as insults in political rhetoric, such as the *lunatic left* and *loony left.* In July 2016, the front cover of *The Atlantic* showed an image of Uncle Sam wrapped in a straightjacket slumped on the floor of a padded room, with the title, "How American Politics Went Insane."[13] The vocabulary of mental illness is often relied upon to label what is perceived as irrational, ignorant, incompetent, or lacking reason and sense.

Mad and *crazy* also linger in modern language. Similar to the phenomenon that occurred with words like *wicked* and *bad* that have acquired antonymic senses, *mad* and *crazy* have developed positive connotations in colloquial usage. They appear in numerous idioms, such as *mad good* and *crazy in love* that suggest excitement or infatuation. *That's crazy!* can mean something that is strange or outlandish. But the stigma associated with mental illness has left its mark on these words, in particular *crazy,* rendering it offensive in usages such as *batshit crazy* or *You're crazy!* Although they are ubiquitous words that people use all the time without even noticing, *mad* and *crazy* are increasingly regarded as offensive because they perpetuate mental health stigma and are considered to be *casual ableism*. This is the use of commonplace language that can be interpreted as derogatory to people with disabilities, disease, or mental illness.[14] Casual ableism reinforces stereotypes and continues to stigmatize and marginalize already vulnerable groups. Many people use ableist language without consideration, because they are desensitized to its past and present implications. Similar to racist and homophobic language, some stakeholders seek to reclaim ableist language. The Mad Pride movement, a group of activists who educate the public about mental health myths, attempts to reclaim words such as *mad* and *psycho*.[15]

Not only are outdated clinical diagnoses used as insults, but also modern ones. Mental health metaphor is a common form of hyperbole used to talk about behavior. The neighbor whose house is neat and tidy is called *OCD* (Obsessive-Compulsive Disorder), while someone who is worried or self-conscious is *paranoid*. Mood swings are described as *bipolar*, an egotistical politician is a *narcissist*, a person who cannot pay attention or concentrate is *ADHD* (Attention-Deficit/Hyperactivity Disorder), and the hated ex-girlfriend is a *psycho bitch*. These clinical terms and also *psychotic, paranoid, schizophrenic, schizo, depressed,* and *hypochondriac*, are used conversationally to describe undesirable traits or character flaws, or to speculate about the mental health of public figures.

Pop psychology labels are also used as terms of abuse. *Sociopath* and *psychopath* are not clinical terms, but are used colloquially to refer to someone considered to be dangerous and lacking in shame, empathy, or remorse. (*Antisocial personality disorder* is the actual clinical term for the disorder which is characterized by disregard for other people.) Although widely accepted in society, psychiatric name-calling is often offensive to people who have been diagnosed with mental illness, because terms used to describe their medical conditions are instead being used to describe bad behavior. This colloquial usage of mental health terminology is perceived to trivialize conditions that are complex and debilitating and to perpetuate harmful and misleading stereotypes and myths. This is part of the process of creating stigma around mental illness, while stigmatizing language drives people away from seeking help for these conditions.[16]

The use of recently outdated or obsolete medical terms can also be considered offensive, because they are associated with stereotypes about the conditions. For example, *manic* and *mania* refer to obsession and frenzy and have become associated with phrases such as *Manic Monday* and *homicidal maniac*, so what was previously called *Manic depression* is now *Bipolar Disorder*. *Multiple personality disorder* was stigmatized through the book and TV mini-series *Sybil* and other fictional portrayals of the condition as a kind of demonic possession, so it was renamed *Dissociative Identity Disorder*. Brain damage is now referred to as *brain injury*, while an *epileptic fit* or *attack* is instead a *seizure, episode,* or *event*. Some purported psychiatric conditions have disappeared altogether, such as *female hysteria*, a mental disorder that affected only women, which was characterized by extreme emotion, anxiety, fainting, nervousness, irritability, and sexual desire. (See also Chapter 2.) Perceptions of other conditions have evolved over time to become more sympathetic. Before it became known by its modern name *Post-Traumatic Stress Disorder* (or PTSD) in the 1970s, the condition was referred to in turn as *exhaustion, soldier's heart, shell shock, combat fatigue, war neurosis,* and *battle fatigue*, moralistic terms that blamed traumatized soldiers for their own suffering.

The language of mental illness is surrounded by taboo and shame. The terminology used to talk about suicide is a good example of this stigma. People who die by suicide are labeled *victims* and depicted as *cowards, weak, selfish,* or *attention seeking*. There are trivializing names for people who attempt suicide, such as *jumper*, a person who attempts suicide by jumping from a high place, such as a bridge or skyscraper. The act of suicide itself carries historical connotations of dishonor, moral sin, and illegality. In the past, suicide was a criminal act in many countries, which is still reflected in the phrase *committed suicide*. This presents a problem, because the term continues to imply criminality through its resemblance to phrases such as *committed murder*. Advocates campaign for the use of more accurate and compassionate terminology, such as *died by suicide*, because the phrase avoids judgment. Some offensive language comes from within the mental health industry. *Unsuccessful suicide* means the patient survived a suicide attempt, while *successful suicide* means the patient died, both terms portraying suicide as "success." *Failed attempt at suicide* presents survival as failure; so *attempted suicide* is now the preferred term.[17] It is also considered disparaging to label someone *suicidal*, so the preferred term is *a person with thoughts of suicide*.

Labeling someone with a mental illness is a controversial matter. Using the noun form of a condition such as *a schizophrenic* can be dehumanizing, because this defines people by their diagnosis. The preferred form of language when discussing mental illness is *person-first language* or *people-first language*. This is intended to be a humanizing way of talking that acknowledges the person first, before naming the disability, disorder, or condition. Using person-first language, *a person living with schizophrenia*, or *he has a diagnosis of schizophrenia* are the preferred terms for many stakeholders. Person-first language aims to decrease the stigma attached to negative labels. For example, *a person with a substance use disorder* is now preferred over the negative connotations of *substance abuse*, *addict*, *abuser*, and *junkie*.[18] The purpose of this language is also to promote the idea that someone's condition is just a label and not the defining characteristic of the person. Some people use quotation marks around medical terms to emphasize that it is a diagnosis; *a person diagnosed with "schizophrenia"*. This is hoped to be an objective way of talking about disabilities, disorders, or diseases that eliminates stereotypes by focusing on the person or patient rather than the condition.

Some argue that the euphemism treadmill has already affected the term *patient*. A number of other terms are considered appropriate replacements, including *a person seeking treatment for mental health*, *a person receiving mental health services*, *mental health client*, *user of mental health services*, *mental health consumer*, and *consumer*. Unlike *patient*, all of these modern labels are perceived as empowering, with a greater focus on the individual as a consumer rather than a passive experiencer, and also connoting choice and autonomy in treatment. *Psychiatric survivor* and *survivor* are also used to imply that a mental illness is a condition that is treatable, and a state that is more likely to change than to be permanent.

Everyday language reveals negative social attitudes and beliefs about mental illness. Common phrases such as *off his meds, off her rocker, delusional, barking*, and *bonkers* represent people with mental illness as out of control, unpredictable, and unstable. In September 2003, English tabloid newspaper *The Sun* came under fire for calling former boxer Frank Bruno "bonkers" when he was sectioned under a British Mental Health Act and taken to a psychiatric hospital for his depression. The front-page headline read, "Bonkers Bruno Locked Up," while the article branded him a "nutter" and reported that he was "put away in a mental home."[19] Phrases such as *put away, locked up, committed, institutionalized*, and *sent away* portray people as weak, helpless, and passive, and suggest incarceration against their will, while labels like *inmate* and *ward* liken patients to prisoners. *Quacks, witch-doctors, head-shrinkers*, and *shrinks* reveal a fear and mistrust of therapists and doctors and the psychiatric industry in general.

Mental health facilities have long been stigmatized with derogatory nicknames, including *booby hatch, snake pit, bat house, nuthouse, padded palace, cuckoo's nest, loony bin*, and *funny farm*. *Asylum*, which once had positive connotations of refuge, retreat, and sanctuary, became associated with abuses, such as those described by Nellie Bly. They were re-named *institutions* or *hospitals*, although they continued to be stigmatized. Bellevue Hospital in New York was the first psychiatric hospital in the United States. Entrenched in popular culture, *Bellevue* became a metonym for *psychiatric hospital* and a metaphor for *mentally ill*. (This is the American equivalent of *Colney Hatch* in London, England.) Some towns were stigmatized when they become synonymous with their mental institutions, such as Byberry, the location of Philadelphia State Hospital, which became infamous following a 1946 issue of *Life* magazine that profiled the facility's inhumane conditions.[20] *Bedlam*, the colloquial pronunciation of London's notorious Hospital of Saint Mary of Bethlehem, became associated with chaos, confusion, and madness.

A colloquial sense of mad is *angry*, and *stark raving mad, maniac, berserk, psycho, deranged*, and *disturbed* all portray someone with mental illness as wild, aggressive, and violent. Everyday language reveals a discomfort with mental illness, while individuals with psychiatric conditions are often demonized as evil, sick, or criminal. There is a stereotype that mental illness is to blame for mass murders, gun massacres, serial killings, and other acts of violence.[21] People with mental illness are stigmatized as the perpetrators of these kinds of crimes, although generally speaking, they are more likely to be victims of violent acts than to commit violence.[22] Straightjackets, restraints, padded cells, barbaric-sounding procedures such as lobotomy and Electroconvulsive Therapy (ECT), and other popular imagery of psychiatry instill a sense of fear toward people with mental illness and imply that they pose a threat of danger to themselves, and to others.

The language used to talk about mental illness often invokes abnormality. A mental illness is perceived as a peculiarity, oddity, eccentricity, or quirk. Insults portray the person with mental illness as unusual or strange, such as *weirdo, basket case, whackjob*, and *wacko*. In the 1980s, wild stories circulated about American musician Michael Jackson. Newspapers claimed that he had purchased the Elephant Man's bones, that he slept at night in an oxygen-rich tank, and that he had undergone extensive plastic surgery and skin bleaching. Jackson's unconventional behavior earned him the nickname "Wacko Jacko" in the tabloid press.[23]

Modern metaphorical expressions also reveal popular perceptions of mental illness. Some idioms invoke loss: *losing one's marbles, losing one's mind,* or *taking leave of one's senses.* Others suggest deficiency: to be *a few cards short of a deck, a few sandwiches short of a picnic,* and similar phrases that follow this formula. *Nervous breakdown, crackpot, unhinged, falling to pieces, to have a screw loose,* and *not firing on all cylinders* imply that the person with mental illness is somehow broken, faulty, or defective. In the late sixteenth century, *crazy* also meant, "Full of cracks or flaws, damaged," while in the seventeenth century, the meaning of *cracked* was "mentally unsound."[24]

The word *demented* goes back to Latin *de* "out of" and *mens* "mind." Modern idioms depict people with mental illness as blank, empty, withdrawn, or overmedicated, including *out of his mind, out of his tree, away with the fairies, zombie, not all there, there's no one upstairs, the lights are on but nobody's home, in a world of her own,* and *gone in the head.* Mental illness is associated with the mind, and there are many head-related metaphors that are used as insults, such as *head case* and *mental case,* while the predominant sense of *mental* has become *a disorder of the mind.*[25] As slang for head, nut metaphors appear in many terms of abuse, including *nutter, nutjob, nutcase, nutcake,* to be *off one's nut,* or *nutty as a fruitcake.* Other insults involve food metaphors, such as *fruitcake, fruit loop, bananas,* and *crackers.* Animal metaphors and similes are also common, including *bats in the belfry, crazy like a fox, mad as a March hare,* or to be *buggy, batty, squirrely,* or *cuckoo.* A cuckoo bird is said to be ridiculous because of its monotonous call and its habit of laying eggs in the nests of other birds. As we can see, mental health-related terms are often contemptuous or mocking in tone, portraying people with mental illness as objects of ridicule and scorn.

There is a lot of overlap between the language of mental illness and the way that people talk about intellectual disabilities. Again, we find that modern insults were once medical terms for people historically labeled as "subnormal." *Idiot, imbecile,* and *moron* were part of a now disused classification system of intelligence that was used by doctors to describe what we call *intellectual disabilities. Idiot* dates back to the fourteenth century, when it meant a "person so profoundly disabled in mental function or intellect as to be incapable of ordinary acts of reasoning or rational conduct."[26] *Village idiots* were tolerated by their communities for the purposes of amusement, cruelty, or charity, or they were cast out of society, becoming tramps and vagrants.[27] As a technical term, *idiot* referred to the greatest degree of intellectual disability, to describe an adult with an IQ of 25 or below, with the mental capacity of a 3-year-old or younger. *Imbecile* emerged in the sixteenth century, when it meant "weak, feeble."[28] As a technical term it indicated an adult with an IQ of 26–50, with the mental capacity of a 4- to 7-year-old. *Moron* is a relatively new term. In 1910, psychologist Henry H. Goddard coined the word from the Greek word for "fool" to replace the older terms *simpleton* or *feeble-minded*.[29] The American Association for the Study of the Feeble-minded adopted moron to label adults with an IQ of 51–70, with the technical definition of an "adult with a mental age between 8 and 12."[30]

Cretin is another historical term for someone with intellectual disabilities. The word comes from *crestin*, an eighteenth-century Swiss French word meaning "Christian."[31] This euphemism served as a reminder that people with intellectual disabilities were humans, as distinguished from the beasts, though they were different physically and mentally. In contrast to one theory that people with mental illness or intellectual disability were suffering punishment by God, figures such as the *holy fool* and the *Fool for Christ* were believed to have compensating divine blessings, while describing someone as *touched* suggests intervention by the hand of God.[32] *Cretin* was borrowed into English as a medical term specifically for a person with a congenital deficiency of thyroid hormones (known as *hypothyroidism*). In infants, this condition results in stunted growth, physical deformities, and cognitive impairment. No longer a medical term, *cretin* became a term synonymous with *idiot*, although today it is mostly considered an old-fashioned insult.

Idiot, *imbecile*, and *moron* are no longer used as clinical terms, but they still exist as ableist insults. Despite their offensiveness, they are very common. Their usage is often defended by the argument that the original meaning has changed, so they no longer apply to people with intellectual disabilities, who have no reason to feel offended by their usage. However, they are still perceived as offensive, not only for insulting intelligence and insinuating intellectual disability, but also for their sinister history. During the early twentieth century, the eugenics movement flourished in the United States. Due to its political influence, more than half of the states passed laws calling for sterilization of the mentally "unfit," resulting in an estimated 60,000 non-consensual surgeries.[33] This was a time of record high immigration, and numerous immigrants branded *morons* were either institutionalized or deported from the country. The Nazi regime also participated in the eugenics movement. Theories of racial purity and supremacy led to the forced sterilization of approximately 400,000 people and the "involuntary euthanasia," by starvation, poisoning, or gassing, of 300,000–400,000 disabled and sick children and adults in Germany and countries under Nazi rule.[34]

Mentally handicapped was introduced to replace *idiot*, *imbecile*, and *moron*. *Handicapped* had already been around since the seventeenth century. According to legend, the word comes from begging with "cap in hand," dating back to a time when people with disabilities were forced to beg for a living. This is a folk etymology, because it was originally a gambling term that was not used in reference to people with disabilities until the twentieth century. *Handicapped* became the standard term for someone with physical and intellectual disabilities, until it developed negative connotations in the 1960s. However, the term is still used in horseracing, golf, and other sports to describe a disadvantage placed on a superior competitor to make it a fairer race or game. *Handicapped* is mostly outdated and derogatory when used in reference to people, but it is still accepted in some contexts, when referring to parking spaces and bathroom stalls, although *accessible* or *disabled* are now preferred in many places. *Mencap*, the name of the UK charity for people with learning disabilities, is a portmanteau of the phrase "Mentally Handicapped." Despite public criticism over the modern connotations of the phrase, the organization has, so far, decided not to change its name.[35]

In the mid-twentieth century, *mental retardation* and *mentally retarded* were also introduced as diagnostic terms to replace the offensive outdated words. These phrases labeled a person with an IQ of lower than 70 who had limited social and practical skills. Almost immediately, these words fell prey to the euphemism treadmill. *Retarded* and the abbreviation *retard* became strong insults, especially when used to describe people with disabilities. The recent abbreviation *tard* is also highly offensive, which is commonly used as a suffix to form new insults, such as *fucktard* ("fucking retard"), *libtard* ("liberal retard"), and *glutard* ("gluten retard") to refer to someone with a gluten-intolerance.

It is often argued that *retard* and related insults, while technically describing disability, are not being used to refer to disability specifically, and so, therefore, are not offensive. Ironically, the argument that a word cannot possibly be insulting because it no longer retains its original meaning is also used in defense of *retard* as an insult. It is noted that Latin *retardare* originally meant, "make slow, delay, keep back, or hinder,"[36] so it is argued that *retard* must be innocuous and is not intended to be offensive toward people with disabilities. When certain words or phrases cause a group of people to feel stigmatized, marginalized, or excluded, the intention behind using this language is largely irrelevant. The words remain offensive, because they suggest the negative way that speakers feel about the individuals whom these words represent. *Retard* is still used in a scientific context, to mean "delay" or "slow down," but it is offensive when used in reference to people. Despite this, it is prevalent in pop culture and everyday language, although it is now considered to be the most offensive disability-related word. Drawing parallels to *nigger* and *the N-word*, *retard* is often censored as *the r-word*.

In an effort to convey a more positive image, *special* was adopted in place of *mental retardation*, especially with regard to children with intellectual disabilities. The word was chosen to imply positive connotations, that people with intellectual disabilities are somehow exceptional, distinctive, and unique. However, the word has been criticized for singling out people with disabilities when they want to be treated as equals, not as special. *Special* soon developed negative connotations and is now perceived as patronizing. It is a euphemism for unintelligent, and it is used as an insult to imply sarcastically that someone must be intellectually disabled. However, *special* is still acceptable in some contexts in which the word has been institutionalized. Founded in 1968, the Special Olympics is the world's largest sports organization for people with intellectual disabilities. *Special education* refers to students whose learning is impeded by mental or physical disability, while *special needs* is a diagnostic term for individuals who require assistance for disabilities.

From the 1960s, *disabled* superseded *handicapped, mentally deficient, mentally retarded,* and *special,* becoming the inclusive term to refer to people who have difficulties with intellectual abilities. Today, *intellectual disability, cognitive disability, developmental disability, processing disorders,* and *learning difficulties* are all considered to be appropriate terms. These cover a broad range of conditions that make it difficult for people to learn at the rate expected of their age group. Intellectual disability is now based on the following criteria: an IQ that is below 70–75, significant limitations existing in two or more adaptive skill areas, and that the condition manifests before the age of 18.[37]

While *disabled* is an accepted term, *the disabled* is not. As a collective term it is perceived as dehumanizing, because it reduces people with a disability to the disability itself. Moreover, it ignores the individuality and diversity of these people by lumping them together in an undifferentiated group whose members are only defined by their disability. (See also Chapter 7.) It is preferable to refer to *the disability community* instead, or to use people-first language, *people with intellectual disabilities,* because this recognizes that the disability is only one characteristic of the individual or group. The alternative phrasing, *intellectually disabled people,* is called *identity-first language,* because it places the disability or disorder before the person. This phrasing can be viewed as offensive, because it is perceived to highlight and focus on the disability. However, some people prefer this terminology, because they consider person-first language to be too verbose. They also believe that it suggests that people without disabilities are anxious and uncomfortable about dealing with disabled people. If it is necessary to draw comparisons, *people without disabilities* or *non-disabled* are preferable to *normal*, *healthy*, or *whole*, which imply that a person with a disability is somehow abnormal, unhealthy, or broken. The terms *neurotypical* and *neurodiverse* have also emerged recently, the latter implying that intellectual disabilities are natural variations or differences that form a part of human diversity, rather than being "defects."

Other intelligence-related insults were never medical terms. *Stupid* has been a derogatory term since the sixteenth century when it meant, "lacking ordinary activity of mind, slow-witted, dull."[38] Today, *stupid* still mocks a person based upon perceived mental acuity. It is used to put down or undermine someone who is viewed as mentally slow, of low intelligence, lacking common sense, uniformed, or ignorant. *Stupid* is an extremely common word, but it is another example of casual ableism. Given the connection of the word to people with intellectual disabilities, *stupid* is becoming increasingly derogatory, in part because it is often interpreted as a euphemism for *retarded*.[39] For these reasons, many people avoid the use of this term.

Dictionaries often provide *silly* as a synonym of *stupid*. *Silly* has traveled a long semantic journey from its origins in Middle English *selly*, when it evoked a positive sense of "happy" or "blessed." *Silly* then started to acquire negative meanings, such as "wretched," "unfavorable," or "weak" before arriving at its modern definition of "foolish" in the sixteenth century.[40] *Foolish* comes from *fool*, a thirteenth-century term that has had several different meanings, including "weak-minded or idiotic" and "jester, court clown."[41] Today, both *silly* and *foolish* imply a lack of common sense or judgment. They are less opprobrious than *stupid*, probably because neither word has modern connotations of intellectual disability or mental illness.

Dumb is another synonym for *stupid*, but this was not its original meaning. The word goes back to the eleventh century, when it meant "mute, speechless" in Old English.[42] In the eight-eenth century, *dumb* referred to a lack of function in any part of the body, not just the voice, so that a *dumb arm* meant an injured or non-functioning arm.[43] *Dumb* did not acquire its modern sense of "unintelligent" until the 1820s, when it was probably influenced by German *dumm*, meaning "stupid." Today, *dumb* and *dumbass* are considered to be mildly insulting, although they are used com-monly. In the United States, *dumbocrat* is a slur against supporters of the democrat political party. *Dummy* is also a frequently used mild insult, although it also appears in the title of the "For Dummies" series of instructional books, which are intended to transform "the hard-to-understand into easy-to-use."[44] The offen-siveness of *dumb* is intensified when it is used as a modifier of other insults, including *dumb bitch, dumb blonde, dumb shit,* and *dumb fuck.* Today, *dumb* generally implies "unintelligent." As a result, using *dumb* to mean "non-verbal," as in *deaf and dumb,* is now considered to be highly offensive.

Intelligence is connected to the head, so many metaphorical insults invoke the head, mind, or brain to imply low intelligence or abnormality, including *dickhead, bonehead, soft in the head, featherbrained, numbskull, halfwit, nitwit,* and *fuckwit.* Some insults suggest delay; *slow, slow learner, slow-witted, slow on the uptake, dopey, behind,* and *backward.* As a reminder of how quickly the euphemism treadmill affects stigmatized areas of language, it is interesting to note that the abovementioned charity Mencap was formerly known as the Association of Parents of Backward Children when it was founded in 1946. Other intelligence-related metaphorical insults imply thickness: *dense, blockhead, fathead, thick,* and *thick-headed;* or a lack of brightness or sharpness: *dull, dull-witted, dim, dim-witted, not the brightest light on the Christmas tree,* and *not the sharpest tool in the shed.* They suggest naivety, child-like innocence, and a lack of complexity: *simple, simple-minded,* and *simpleton;* or suggest immobility or a lack of control over their bodies: *drooler, dribbler, mouth breather,* and *vegetable.* Some metaphorical insults refer to animals stereotyped as unin-telligent: *ass, donkey, dodo, monkey, turkey, goose, harebrained, birdbrain*, and *dumb as an ox*, or unintelligent characters: *fool*, *twit*, *buffoon*, and *clown*. Intelligence-related insults and idioms often suggest emptiness: *airhead*, *brainless*, *mindless*, *empty-headed*, and *not much between the ears*. Some terms that insult intelligence imply deficiency: *missing a few screws* and *one brick short of a load*, which are phrases that also overlap with mental illness-related idioms.

Just as mental illness diagnoses are used as insults, clinical terms for intellectual disabilities and learning difficulties are also used as hyperbolic ways of speaking about behavior. Someone who makes a reading or spelling mistake may be referred to jokingly as *dyslexic*. *Autistic*, *Asperger's*, and *on the spectrum* are used as slurs implying that a person is socially inept, awkward, or lacking empathy. In 2006, the National Autistic Society criticized British politician George Osborne when he said that Chancellor Gordon Brown lacked personal skills and suggested that he could be "faintly autistic."[45] The figurative use of clinical terms perpetuates myths about intellectual disabilities and implies that a diagnosis can be blamed for bad behavior. In 2017, Australian television personality Don Burke offended the Autistic community when he attributed his actions of sexual harassment to undiagnosed Autism Spectrum Disorder (ASD) because he "missed body language and subtle signs."[46]

Autism Spectrum Disorder refers to a group of neurodevelopmental disorders that affect social communication and interaction. Typically, *Autism* is capitalized as a proper noun to represent the community and identity, although individuals have personal preferences for self-identifying labels. Some prefer using person-first language; to be called *a person with Autism* or *a person on the Autistic spectrum*, because they see their diagnosis as something that does not impact their identity on a fundamental level.[47] Using identity-first language, many prefer to be called *Autistic people*, *Autist*, or *Autistic*. They consider Autism to be an inseparable part of who they are, and not a "disability," "disease," "disorder," "deficit," or something to be cured or fixed. Autism is embraced as a defining aspect of their identity, in the same way that we refer to *black people*. (Which is why this term is favored here.) This position holds that person-first language portrays Autism as something negative, which can and should be separated from the person.[48]

Some Autistic people have reclaimed the insults *Autie* and *Aspie* (an abbreviation of *Asperger's Syndrome*, a milder subtype of Autism that is now subsumed under the single diagnosis of ASD). The terms *high functioning* and *low functioning* are medical diagnoses that label the severity of Autism, but they can be offensive because they oversimplify the condition, while the categorization of degrees of human "functioning" is considered to be dehumanizing. Furthermore, *low functioning* can imply non-functioning, not working, or malfunctioning. *High functioning* suggests that the goal of Autistic people should be to "pass" or present the appearance of being neurotypical, or *allistic*, that is, not Autistic or neurodiverse.

Just as some mental illness terminology has become outdated, some disability-related labels have dropped out of usage, because they are now considered to be offensive due to their origins. For example, *Down Syndrome* was originally called *Mongolism*. The term dates back to the 1860s, when doctor John Langdon Down published the paper, "Observations on an Ethnic Classification of Idiots," in which he claimed that it was possible to categorize different types of conditions by ethnic classifications.[49] He thought that people with this disorder shared facial features with people of Mongolian ethnicity, so he named it *Mongolism*. Down further believed that this condition was a reversion to an inferior race. In 1959, French geneticist Jerome Lejeune discovered the cause of the condition, which is an extra copy of Chromosome 21.[50] Lejeune petitioned the medical community to find a new name, because *Mongolism* was a misnomer. In 1965, the World Health Organization withdrew the name after a request by a delegation from the Mongolian People's Republic who wanted to reclaim the name of their native people. The condition was re-named Down Syndrome, while the term *Trisomy 21* is also used. (*Down's Syndrome* is no longer appropriate in the USA, though still widely used in the UK.) It is now perceived as misleading and offensive to use *Mongoloid* to refer to people with this condition. In November 2017, nutritionist Libby Weaver issued an apology and recalled 20,000 copies of her book *What Am I Supposed To Eat?* following complaints of her use of *Mongolism* to refer to Down Syndrome.[51] *Mongoloid, Mongol, mong,* and *mongy* are still used as insults toward people with intellectual disabilities and as general terms of abuse. In October 2011, English comedian Ricky Gervais came under fire when he shared the joke, "Two mongs don't make a right" on Twitter. He refused to apologize and even added a sketch about "mongs" to his comedy routine. Eventually, after much public pressure, he backed down and apologized, admitting that he had offended people by using the term and did not realize that it was still used as a derogatory term for people with Down Syndrome and other disabilities, or to imply disability.[52]

Disability and *disabled* are also the preferred terms for many people with physical, movement, and processing impairments. If a comparative term is needed, *non-disabled* or *abled* are acceptable, although *able-bodied* can be offensive, because it implies that people with disabilities are disabled in all physical respects. However, some people regard *disability* as problematic, because the prefix *dis-* is negative, meaning "not, opposite, or absence of." It implies a deviation from what is "normal" or "typical," while *disabled* is also used in computing and electronics to indicate dysfunction. The prefix produces many words with negative connotations, including *disagree, dishonest, dishonor,* and *dislike.*

Another issue lies with definition. Those working in medical, legal, and political sectors often define disability, rather than those people who are directly affected. In what is known as the *medical model* of disability, medical definitions of disability cast human variation and difference as deviance from the norm and portray disability as abnormality, incapacity, disadvantage, dependence, deficiency, and as an individual burden and personal tragedy.[53] People with disabilities are often represented as poor, unfortunate, sad, and pitiful. Alternatively, the *social model* of disability is the idea that disability is a social construct, while it is the environment that fails to appropriately accommodate the needs of people with disabilities who face obstacles such as limited physical access in public spaces and limited access to resources.[54, 55] According to this model, a student with dyslexia is not "unable" to do her homework, the lack of provision for dyslexia-friendly texts and learning opportunities disables her from doing so. From the perspective of the social model, it is environmental barriers and negative attitudes that disable people.

These concerns with *disability* and *disabled* led to a search for more empowering terms. In the 1980s, *differently-abled* was proposed as an alternative, on the grounds that it supposedly conveys a more positive message. The term aimed to humanize people with disabilities by focusing on their abilities rather than on their impairments.[56] However, the term has been criticized as overly euphemistic and condescending, and it never enjoyed widespread acceptance among disability communities or the general public. *Differently-abled* is perceived as highlighting difference and reinforcing the idea that there is only one normal way to be human. Instead of implying that all people are different, it suggests that people with disabilities are deviant from a subjective "norm." (This is comparable to describing people who are not white as *differently-colored* or people who are not men as *differently-gendered*.)

Other terms have been created as alternatives to disabled, including *diffability, other abled,* and *specially abled. Handicapable* was intended to be a pun on *handicapped* to refute the implications of inability. These phrases were all well-meaning and intended to protect those who perceive *disability* or *disabled* as hurtful or offensive. But being "politically correct" does not make them automatically inoffensive, instead, many of them are offensive to stakeholders. They are often perceived as patronizing and suggest that the term *disability* is or should be uncomfortable, which further increases the stigma against people with disabilities. The creation of euphemisms often stems from the discomfort of abled people, and should not be confused with respect for or acceptance of people with disabilities.[57]

The appearance of some of these terms coincided with ground-breaking civil rights legislation in the United States. The Individuals with Disabilities Education Act (IDEA) of 1990 ensures that students with a disability are provided with free education that is tailored to their individual needs. The Americans with Disabilities Act (ADA) of 1990 is a civil rights law that prohibits disability-based discrimination. These laws helped to increase awareness of and public sensitivity toward people with disabilities. This environment also led to the creation of the terms *challenged, physically challenged,* and *mentally challenged. Challenged* was intended as a positive alternative to *disabled,* but it was construed as yet another clumsy attempt at euphemism. It was argued that disabilities are impairments, not *challenges* that may be overcome. *Challenged* is now considered derogatory. The word was parodied mercilessly, leading to the creation of humorous and ironic terms, including *follicularly challenged* ("bald"), *vertically challenged* ("short"), *calorically challenged* ("overweight"), and *cerebrally challenged* ("low intelligence"). Using this formula, it is joked that people without disabilities should be called *disability challenged.*

Physically disabled has superseded several terms that are now considered to be outdated and derogatory, such as *cripple. Cripple* has been in existence since Old English. The first recorded usage of *cripple* as "one who is disabled (either from birth, or by accident or injury) from the use of his limbs" dates back to 950.[58] Using *cripple* to refer to people with movement disorders is now highly offensive and it has dropped out of usage. As a metaphor, *crippled* has remained prolific in usage to describe someone severely damaged or harmed, such as *crippled by debt* or *crippled by anxiety.* Some people with physical disabilities have reclaimed *cripple,* but usually in the abbreviated form *crip* to distinguish it from the insult. The *Wry Crips* are a theater group from Berkeley, California, featuring women with disabilities who perform poetry, skits, and dramatic readings that express their feelings about their lives. Artist Chun-Shan Yi created *Crip Couture*, avant-garde wearable art that confronts society's impulse to ignore or avoid looking at disability and seeks to redefine standards of beauty and normalcy. *Crip* is also a term for a member of the Los Angeles gang The Crips. The name dates back to the 1960s and may be related to *cripple*, because some leaders carried canes to mark their status as "pimps," although the etymology is debated.

Unlike *cripple*, *spastic* was originally a medical term, which was first used in the 1890s. *Spastic paralysis* initially referred to spasms in the muscles and then to cerebral palsy and other disabilities affecting motor coordination. By the 1950s, *spastic* had become an insult to refer to someone regarded as physically awkward, clumsy, lacking coordination, or behaving erratically. Today, it is also used to insult intelligence and imply disability. From *spastic* arose the abbreviations *spaz*, *spazzo*, *spasmo*, *spazzing*, and *spaz out*. In a 2006 interview, American professional golfer Tiger Woods drew ire with his comment, "I was so in control from tee to green, the best I've played for years ... But as soon as I got on the green I was a spaz."[59] *Spastic* featured widely in the names of charitable organizations until it became unmistakably derogatory. The UK-based charity The Spastics Society wanted to make a strong statement that attitudes toward people with disabilities need to change, so it rebranded its name to Scope in 1994. *Scope* was chosen in the belief that it was a neutral term. However, the euphemism treadmill has already affected it, and *scopers* is an insult that is used in the same way as *spastic*.[60]

Certain terms reflect negative attitudes about people with physical disabilities. They portray people with disabilities as inferior to those without disabilities and as less valued members of humanity, less than human, or even monstrous. *Freak*, *circus freak*, *deformed*, *mutant*, *reject*, *invalid*, *lame*, *gimp*, and *gimpy* represent people with disabilities as abnormal, broken, useless, deformed, misshapen, or less than whole. However, people in the disability community have reclaimed some of these terms, most notably *gimp*. Actor Teal Sherer is the star of *My Gimpy Life*, a comedy web series about her experiences as a person who uses a wheelchair.

Lame dates back to Old English, when it was first recorded as *lama* in the year 725. An early meaning was "disabled through injury to, or defect in, a limb, specifically disabled in the foot or leg, so as to walk haltingly or be unable to walk."[61] A figurative use emerged in the fourteenth century, meaning "imperfect or defective, unsatisfactory as wanting a part or parts" in reference to an argument, excuse, or story. The literal sense of *lame* as "unable to walk normally because of an injury or illness affecting the leg or foot" is now derogatory in reference to people, although it is still acceptable in referring to non-human animals, such as *the horse is lame*. In the 1940s, the modern sense of *lame* developed to mean someone who is "naïve, unfashionable, or socially inept."[62] Using phrases such as *That's so lame* to mean boring or uncool is considered to be casual ableism, because the literal term references disability, while the figurative sense describes negative behavioral traits. Many related words, such as *bent, limp*, and *warped* are used to describe disability or deformity but also have negative figurative meanings. In a metaphorical sense, *twisted* means perverted, cruel, or immoral. *Crooked* refers to someone who is dishonest or corrupt, such as a *crooked lawyer* or a *crooked politician*. In contrast, society values an *upstanding citizen*, a *stand-up person*, or an *upright person*, while someone who is *straight as an arrow* is considered to be honest and of good character.[63]

People with sensory disabilities have preferred terminology, while some terms have become outdated. Members of Deaf communities usually prefer identity-first language, that is, *a Deaf person*, rather than *a person who is deaf*. Stakeholders with this preference dislike person-first language, because they consider their disability to be an inseparable part of who they are. It is argued that putting the person before the disability portrays the disability as something negative, which can and should be separated from the person. Capitalized *Deaf* is also preferred to *deaf* with a lowercase "d". The rise of the Deaf Pride ("Deaf Power") movement in the 1980s (with their slogan "Deaf is dandy") introduced a distinction between *deaf* and *Deaf,* with the capitalized form referring to membership and affiliation with respect to Deaf culture and Deaf communities, while *deaf* refers to being physically deaf.[64, 65] Some stakeholders prefer *hard of hearing, person with hearing loss,* or *hearing impaired,* although these terms can be considered offensive if the individual referred to has profound hearing loss. Just like the problems with the term *the disabled, the deaf* is also perceived as offensive, because it reduces Deaf people to their disability, so the adjective must always be accompanied by a noun. As discussed above, the archaic term *deaf and dumb* is an offensive label for people who are unable to hear and unable to speak. *Dumb* is no longer acceptable to refer to non-speaking or non-verbal people, because it has been superseded by the sense of unintelligent. *Deaf-mute* and *mute* are also inappropriate, because they imply that people who have not developed any spoken language skills are unable to communicate in any way. *Deaf without speech* is currently the preferred term for many stakeholders.

There are parallels with appropriate language for Blind people. Members of the Blind community generally prefer capitalized *Blind* to *blind,* the latter referring to the state of being physically blind (e.g., *He has been blind since birth*). While some stake-holders prefer person-first language in their belief that *a person who is blind* focuses on the whole person rather than the disability, many favor using identity-first language, *Blind person,* because they perceive their disability to be entwined with their identity. Some are of the opinion that *blind* is too blunt or harsh, so they prefer *people with visual impairments* or *people with low vision.* However, these phrases can be offensive if the individual is totally blind and, therefore, the term is inaccurate. Similar to *Deaf person, Blind* is also preferred as an adjective that needs an accompanying noun, such as *the Blind community* or *Blind people.* Just like the collective phrase *the deaf, the blind* is interpreted as dehumaniz-ing, because it groups diverse people together solely on the basis of their disability. In 2007, the British organization The Royal National Institute of the Blind changed its name to The Royal National Institute of Blind People.[66]

While these adjectives need an accompanying noun to be respectful, referring to a person's disability unnecessarily, such as *the blind musician* or *the deaf actor* can be offensive, because it over-emphasizes and draws undue attention to the person's disability. In general, disability does not need to be referenced, unless it is relevant to the discussion. Sensory disability-related terms are also used as a source of metaphor and imagery without giving thought to the literal meaning.[67] However, this can be considered casual ableism when these idioms equate disability with negative traits or behavior; for example, *to rob someone blind*, to be *blind drunk*, or *blinded by ignorance*. Deafness-related idioms often infer that someone is unwilling or refusing to listen or help, such as to *turn a deaf ear to* or to be *deaf to their screams*. Figurative expressions that invoke the senses may be considered inappropriate when used in conversation with people with sensory disabilities; for example, *listen to reason* and *I can't see what you mean*. Invoking disability as a metaphorical tool can also be considered appropriative; for example, to say, *I was paralyzed with fear*, because this minimizes the experiences of people with these actual disabilities.

Regarding spinal cord conditions, person-first language, *a person with paraplegia*, is typically favored by stakeholders rather than using the condition as a designation, such as *the paraplegic* or *the quadriplegic*. Terms such as *cripple* and *wheelchair jockey* are obviously offensive, but some insulting phrases are less overt. Common sayings such as *He is wheelchair bound*, *confined to a wheelchair*, or *restricted to a wheelchair* represent the person as incapacitated, immobilized, and powerless. These are perceived as judgmental terms that define the disability as a limitation and imply that the wheelchair takes away someone's freedom. The preferred phrase is a *person who uses a wheelchair*, which indicates that the wheelchair is an assistive tool that provides an individual with independence. A wheelchair enables a person to get around and is considered to be liberating, not confining, despite society's barriers. Common descriptive phrases such as *He was left blind by the accident, left disabled by an illness,* and *left paralyzed by a stroke* can also be disempowering because they portray the person with a disability as helpless and weak.

Ableist language takes not only the form of insults and the use of outdated terms, but also of negative stereotypes and attitudes. These can manifest as the impolite, disrespectful, and demeaning questions that strangers ask of people with disabilities. It can reflect a sense of entitlement to demand to know how a person became disabled by asking invasive questions such as, *What happened to you?*, *What's wrong with you?*, or *Were you born that way?* It is also offensive to make assumptions about how someone's disabilities were acquired. In one exchange, a person who uses a wheelchair reported that a stranger approached him and said, "Thank you for your service," making the incorrect assumption that he had been injured while serving in the military.[68]

Other offensive interactions include asking highly personal questions of strangers with disabilities, such as, *What's it like to be disabled?* or *Can you have sex?* There is a tendency for people to believe they are entitled to ask intrusive questions about the bodies of people with disabilities and to expect them to reveal personal information about themselves for the benefit, education, or curiosity of others. This phenomenon has been called *forced intimacy*, which is explained as the "common, daily experience of disabled people being expected to share personal parts of them-selves to survive in an ableist world."[69] In this way, people with disabilities are often made to feel as though their bodies are public property.

Remarks such as the observation, *But you look so normal* can also be offensive. Society has preconceived ideas about how disabled people are supposed to look or act. However, not all disabilities are readily apparent to others. Many people have hidden or non-visible disabilities, including epilepsy, rheumatoid arthritis, brain injuries, or learning difficulties such as dyslexia. The lack of a visual cue, such as a wheelchair or a cane, can raise suspicions when people with hidden disabilities seek accommodations. As a result, some people are expected to prove their disabilities. In September 2017, war veteran Andy Grant was boarding a London train but when he was asked to produce his disability card, he discovered that he had lost his wallet. An employee asked, "How do we know you are even disabled?" "Because I got blown up in Afghanistan," Grant replied, as he lifted up his trouser leg, revealing a prosthetic limb. His right leg had been amputated following an explosion.[70] This kind of forced intimacy obliges people with disabilities to share personal information to gain accommodations and have their access needs met, and this can feel humiliating, exploitative, and violating.

More overtly offensive behavior includes the imitation of physical disabilities. In November 2015, US presidential candidate Donald Trump was accused of mocking Serge Kovaleski, a *New York Times* reporter with a physical disability. Kovaleski has arthrogryposis, a congenital disability that limits the function of his joints. (Note that *congenital disability* is the preferred term rather than the outdated *birth defect*.) Trump launched into an impression of Kovaleski, pointedly flopping his right arm around with his hand held at an odd angle.[71] This is not the first time that Trump has appeared to ridicule a person with disabilities. Also in 2015, in response to criticisms from columnist Charles Krauthammer, Trump called him, "a guy that can't buy a pair of pants."[72] Krauthammer is paralyzed from the neck down following a diving accident. Trump has also been accused of mocking actor Marlee Matlin, calling her "retarded," mimicking her voice, and treating her as if she was intellectually disabled, although she is deaf.[73]

Physical disability is often conflated with intellectual disability. It is mistakenly assumed that people with physical disabilities have intellectual disabilities too, or that they are of lower intelligence. For this reason, some people use condescending and patronizing language when talking to a person with a physical disability. They may raise their voices and speak slowly and deliberately, or ignore the person altogether by talking to their companion or sign language interpreter instead. This implies that people with a disability are invisible, they do not matter, or they do not have anything meaningful to communicate. This kind of behavior reveals society's tendency to perpetrate *disability erasure*, a form of marginalization in which people with disabilities are ignored, overlooked, or rendered invisible. For example, people with disabilities are typically not recognized in Hollywood, unless they are presented as stereotypical representations. Ironically, disability is often erased, even when it is the focus, such as the Hollywood practice of hiring non-disabled actors to play the roles of people with disabilities. In an example from the fashion industry, Brazilian *Vogue's* publicity campaign for the 2016 Paralympics featured images of non-disabled models who were digitally altered to appear physically disabled.[74] A woman was photo-shopped to look as though her right arm had been amputated, while a man was given a prosthetic right leg.

Folk beliefs about disabilities can also be offensive; for example, the belief that people with disabilities have superhuman abilities to compensate for their disabilities. There is an urban legend that Blind people have exceptional hearing, although the actual explanation may be that they depend more on their sense of hearing and are, therefore, more attuned to hearing than their sighted counterparts. Another urban legend is that all Autistic people are savants, that they have extraordinary skills not exhibited by most people. (Historically, Autistic people with exceptional abilities were called *idiot savants*, which is now a highly offensive, outdated term.) This belief may have its origins in popular culture. In the 1988 movie *Rain Man*, Dustin Hoffman plays the role of Raymond Babbitt, an Autistic savant who displayed a remarkable memory for ball player statistics, memorized parts of the telephone book, and counted cards in Las Vegas. In reality, the estimated prevalence of savant abilities in autism is 10 percent (while the prevalence of extraordinary skills in the allistic community is less than 1 percent).[75] Alternatively, disabilities are construed as inabilities, and people with disabilities are portrayed as having limited skills and lacking talents or unique gifts. The accomplishments of people with disabilities are often sensationalized. They are patronizingly called *brave* and *coura-geous* or praised with *Good for you!* when they perform daily activities or tasks that would otherwise be deemed mundane. People with disabilities don't want to be treated as though they are heroic or special; they want to be treated as equal.

It can also be offensive to categorize disability as disease, imply-ing that treatment or cure is needed, although some diseases can, indeed, be disabling. Disease-related language uncovers another area of ableist language. The words used to talk about ill health, including *disease, sickness,* and *illness* carry stigma and imply infirmity, debility, and contagion. The colloquial sense of *disease* is a social problem; for example, *crime is a disease* or *gambling is a disease*. In metaphorical usage, *sick* has overtones of perver-sion, like the insult *sicko*, while an *illness* can be a bad habit or behavior, for instance *greed is an illness*. In particular, some diseases are stigmatized, because they are little understood, contagious, incurable, life-threatening, or terminal. Such dis-eases are feared and often tabooed. When a disease is discrimi-nated against, so too are the people with that disease. People with certain diseases, or those connected to these diseases, are often the targets of prejudice.

Ebola is one of these little understood, communicable diseases that has a high risk of death. Ebola, a rare but deadly virus that causes fever, muscle pain, diarrhea, and bleeding, originated in West Africa in the 1970s. In 2014, there were several major out-breaks, and the disease spread to the United States and the United Kingdom, which created panic in the West. Ebola is stigmatized by a fear of the disease, driven by high mortality rates, gruesome symptoms, and misunderstandings about the continent of origin. This has led to xenophobia and racism against people of African origin. There have been reports of attacks against African immi-grants in schools; in one case, several students were beaten and severely injured by those who called them "Ebola."[76] Ironically, the students were immigrants from Senegal, a country that has been declared free of Ebola by the World Health Organization.

The fear surrounding the emerging AIDS/HIV epidemic in the 1980s largely exists today.[77] (This is often called AIDS/HIV-phobia.) In the early years, an AIDS diagnosis was often likened to a "death sentence." The disease is still associated with death, although advances in medical research mean that it can be managed by drugs, while those with the disease can expect many years of good health. Before the introduction of the term *AIDS*, the disease was initially labeled *the gay disease*, *the gay plague*, *gay cancer*, and *the homosexual disorder*, because the first recognized cases were restricted to gay men. The press coined the term *GRID*, which stood for "Gay-related immune deficiency."[78] The disease was soon reported in other demographics too, and so the US Centers for Disease Control and Prevention adopted the *term the 4-H disease*, because the high-risk groups included "homosexuals," heroin users, hemophiliacs, and Haitians. (At one time AIDS was also known as *the Haitian disease*.) It was later realized that these terms were misleading, and the acronym *AIDS* (Acquired Immunodeficiency Syndrome) was introduced in 1982, while *HIV* (Human Immunodeficiency Virus) was named in 1986. Today, HIV/AIDS are often euphemistically called *The Virus* or *The Bug*. Because of the stigma associated with the diseases, AIDS deaths are still not typically reported as such in obituaries and memorial services, while AIDS-related conditions such as pneumonia or tuberculosis are instead given as the cause of death.[79] Myths surrounding HIV/AIDS still exist, such as misconceptions about transmission and stereotypes about people with the disease. It is often assumed that a person with AIDS is LGBTQ, an intravenous drug user, a sex worker, or a person who has committed infidelity. There is a tendency to seek meaning in disease, and AIDS is often perceived as an affliction on the sinful and those who deserve punishment for their immorality.[80, 81]

Some ways of talking about disease inspire unwanted sympathy and pity. It can be disempowering to describe someone as an HIV/AIDS *patient*, *victim*, or *sufferer*. These terms imply defeat and a lack of control. They portray the person with the disease as passive, helpless, and dependent on the care of others. Similarly, the older terms *afflicted* and *stricken*, which appear in phrases such as *afflicted with cystic fibrosis* and *stricken with tuberculosis*, suggest that the individual is a powerless object of the disease, while *suffers* (e.g., *suffers from autism*) suggests that the person is agonized by their disability. Person-first language is often preferred when talking about disease. For example, *a person with celiac disease* is preferred to *He is a celiac*, which can be an objectifying label that defines an individual as their diagnosis. The person is not the disease, the person *has* a disease, so it is preferred to say *a person who has*, *a person with*, or *a person who is diagnosed with* a chronic health condition.

Similar to hidden disabilities, some chronic diseases are known as *invisible illnesses*, because they are not always obvious to the onlooker. Invisible illnesses include fibromyalgia, arthritis, irritable bowel syndrome, thyroid diseases, sleep disorders, and chronic fatigue syndrome (CFS) (which is also known by the disparaging term *yuppie flu*). People with these diseases may display no outward signs of symptoms or suffering, and so others around them may lack understanding and empathy. People with invisible illnesses may be accused of faking or imagining their condition. They may be branded a *hypochondriac*, or be told *You don't look sick*, or *But you look so good*. They might be told that the illness is *made up* or *all in your head*. This is also experienced by some people with mental illness, whereby the severity and complexity of the condition is often minimized. Invisible illnesses are not perceived as legitimate in the same way as a visible physical condition. People with these illnesses may be judged as weak and pathetic rather than sick, treated as though it is their fault, and told flippantly that they should simply *snap out of it, live with it*, or *get over it*. In 2008, the Depression is Real Coalition developed an advertising campaign that asserted; "You'd never say, 'It's just cancer, get over it.' So why do some say that about depression?"[82]

Cancer represents more than 100 separate diseases, although it is spoken about as if it were a single condition. Despite increasing survival rates, cancer is still equated with death, while metaphors conjure up images of decay, corruption, and evil influence; for example, *a cancer on society*. Cancer is still a taboo subject for many people. Some people refer to cancer instead as a *tumor, growth, carcinoma,* or *mitotic disease,* or by the euphemism *The Big C*.[83] Others refuse to name the disease at all, and for some people there are cultural prohibitions against speaking about cancer. Superstitions about the disease are still common. Some fear that simply mentioning "cancer" can bring on the disease. In some cultures, cancer is believed to be punishment for evil deeds committed in a previous life, or it is thought that the person with cancer did something to deserve the illness. Fault and responsibility are assigned to people with certain cancers; for example, a person with lung cancer is often assumed to be a cigarette smoker, while a person with skin cancer might be blamed for not wearing sunscreen. Often to the detriment of their health, many people face taboos against talking about cancer that affects intimate parts of the body, such as breast or prostate cancer, because this may be seen as immodest in their culture, while cancers linked to sexually transmitted diseases may label them as promiscuous or irresponsible.

The taboo aspect of diseases such as cancer is wielded as an offensive weapon in curses, such as, *I hope you get cancer and die.* In a 1995 interview, Oasis guitarist Noel Gallagher said of rival band Blur, "I hope they catch AIDS and die."[84] In 2016, political activist Carl Paladino wished that then US President Barack Obama would contract "mad cow disease after being caught having relations with a Hereford."[85] Historically, syphilis, known as the dreaded *pox*, was a popular swear word, which was commonly invoked as an insult: *Poxy* and *pox-ridden*; as an interjection: *O pox!*, or as a curse: *Pox take you!*[86] In Shakespeare's *Romeo and Juliet*, Mercutio's dying words, "A plague o' both your houses," curses the Montague and Capulet families, whose rivalry leads to his death. Overall, insults and curses that wish suffering, disease, and death upon people have fallen out of usage in English.

Other linguistic relatives of English have retained this category in their repertoire of insults. In particular, death- and disease-related insults are common in the Dutch language. In the

Netherlands, tuberculosis, typhus, leprosy, smallpox, syphilis, cholera, and other dreaded diseases of the past are used as expletives in some modern dialects of Dutch.[87] One of the strongest insults is *kanker* ("cancer"). *Kankerlijer* ("cancer sufferer") is particularly offensive and emotionally charged, because it is akin to wishing the disease upon someone. *Kanker* is also used in creative compound nouns to insult people, such as *kankerhoer* ("cancer whore") and *kankeraap* ("cancer monkey"). Just as we have seen offensive words being used in a positive way among people who know each other well (such as *bitch* and *cunt*), *kanker* can be used as an intensifier with positive connotations. For example, *kankerlekker* can translate to "extremely attractive," although it is still not a word that is used in polite company. *Kanker op* is similar to "fuck off," although it is considered to be far more harsh because it not only tells someone to "go away" but also invokes a potentially deadly disease.[88]

The euphemism treadmill can affect disease names too. *Hansen's disease* attacks the nervous system and can result in permanent disfiguration of a person's face and limbs. Better known as *leprosy*, people with this contagious disease have been the targets of prejudice and ostracism since ancient times.[89] Different names for people with this disease reflect different perceptions of the illness over time. *Lazar* was derived from the biblical Lazarus of Bethany, who was the subject of a miracle in which Jesus raised him from the dead. This name reflected the belief that this group of people were holy, imitating Christ's passion, and living a life of suffering on earth so that they would go directly to heaven upon death. More derogatory terms include *leper* from Greek *lepros* ("scaly, scabby, rough") and *mesel* from Latin *misellus* ("wretched, unfortunate").[90] In this context, these people were considered unclean and sinful, their disease was believed to be a punishment from God, and they were blamed for disasters and epidemics. In medieval Europe, people with leprosy were required to wear beaver skin hats and carry bells with them to warn of their approach.[91] They were feared and avoided, and often exiled or quarantined in a *leprosarium* or *leper colony* (leading to the modern phrase *social leper* for a person who is deliberately avoided). Before their expulsion, they were deprived of legal rights, including marriage and inheritance, they were branded *tanquam mortuus*, ("as though dead"), and occasionally underwent ritual burial to signify their civic death.[92] In 1873, Dr. Gerhard Henrik Armauer Hansen discovered that leprosy was caused by a bacterium and was not the result of a curse or sin, so the disease was renamed *Hansen's disease* in an attempt to mitigate the stigma.[93]

Sometimes the name of a disease is changed when it becomes better understood. *Tuberculosis*, an infectious disease that affects the lungs, has been a scourge throughout history and known by many different names. It was initially called *phthisis* from the Greek "to waste away," and later *consumption* due to the fatigue and severe weight loss appearing to "consume" the person.[94] In the eighteenth century, it was also known as the *white plague* because of the extreme pallor seen among those infected, and to mark the prevalence of the disease. Despite the agonies endured by those with the condition, consumption was nicknamed the *romantic disease*, because the physical frailty and paleness of consumption was thought to be beautiful in the Romantic imagination. The disease claimed the lives of numerous Romantic artists, writers, and poets, including John Keats, Emily Brontë, and Ralph Waldo Emerson. This created a myth that consumption drove artistic genius. English Poet Lord Byron had a morbid desire to die from consumption, "Because the ladies would then say, 'Look at poor Byron, how interesting he looks in dying.'"[95]

The disease was little understood and believed to be hereditary, but in 1882, Robert Koch discovered that it was caused by bacteria and was highly contagious. Almost immediately, societal attitudes changed toward the illness, and it transformed from an interesting condition to a terrifying disease. "Consumption" became *tuberculosis*, and "consumptives" became *tuberculars* or *lungers*, who were confined to *sanatoriums*, and shunned by society for fear of contagion. In the United States, tuberculosis became known pejoratively as the *Jewish disease* because the peak of Jewish immigration intersected with the rise of the disease.[96] (Ironically, East European Jewish immigrants actually demonstrated a lower incidence of tuberculosis compared to other ethnic groups.[97]) As seen in previous chapters, some states that were once pathologized, such as *hysteria* and *homosexuality*, are now better understood and have lost their former classification as "diseases."

Euphemisms are often created for diseases that are considered embarrassing. Humorous scatological euphemisms for traveler's diarrhea make geographic reference to the specific city where it was caught, including the *Aztec 2-step*, *Montezuma's Revenge*, *Delhi Belly*, *Bali Belly*, *Chile waters*, *Rome runs*, *Turkey trots*, and *Bangladash*. The use of euphemisms is especially common when talking about venereal diseases. Known politely as *VDs*, *STDs* (sexually transmitted diseases), or *social diseases*, they are stigmatized because of the method of transmission. There are many slang terms available to avoid naming these diseases directly. Gonorrhea is known as *the clap*, possibly from *clapier*, the common old French word for "brothel."[98] Chlamydia is called *the clam*, an abbreviation that plays on the use of *clam* as a euphemism for female genitals. Herpes is *the gift that keeps on giving*, in reference to its characteristic repeated outbreaks and that it is currently incurable. Pubic lice are colloquially called *crabs*, *crotch crickets*, or *gentlemen's companions*. More dysphemistic and vulgar terms, like *cock rot*, *dick rot*, and *drippy dick* reveal disgust for people with venereal diseases, who are often portrayed as *diseased*, *dirty*, and *unclean*.

Catching a sexually transmitted disease is often perceived as a sign of loose morals, sexual promiscuity, or is construed as divine retribution for immoral behavior. Syphilis is one of these "immoral diseases." Known euphemistically as *the pox* for the skin pockmarks that appear in the early stages of the infection, naming the disease was an international blame game. Syphilis was called the *French Pox* among the British and Germans, the *British Disease* by the Tahitians, and the *Spanish Pox* by the Dutch and French.[99] The Russians blamed it on the Polish, who in turn called it the *German disease*. In India and Japan it was called the

Portuguese disease, in Persia it was called the *Turkish disease*, and in Turkey it was known as the *Christian disease*.[100] There is a parallel today with AIDS. Those in the Western world trace its origins to Africa. There is an urban legend that all venereal diseases originated in Africa, as revealed by *African toothache*, which is a derogatory slang term for sexually transmitted infections. Ironically, many people in Africa attribute AIDS to the West, where it is known as *the American disease.*

Some diseases are named after places, including towns, rivers, forests, mountains, and valleys. These "toponymous" disease names provide a glimpse into their discovery and history.[101] *Lyme disease* is named after the town of Old Lyme in Connecticut, following a rash of cases in 1975 that prompted scientists to investigate the cause of the unknown disease. The name *Zika virus* comes from the Zika forest in Ghana. *Ebola* was named after the Ebola River in Zaire. The *West Nile virus* was named after a district of Uganda. *Rocky Mountain Spotted Fever* was first identified in the Rocky Mountain region of the United States, while *Ross River Fever* was first isolated from a mosquito trapped along the Ross River in Townsville, Queensland, Australia.

In a few cases, an affected person's name became a symbol of a disease. Mary Mallon, an Irish-born woman working in New York City in the early 1900s, was the first known asymptomatic case of typhoid fever, a form of salmonella that can cause fever, diarrhea, and death. Immune to the disease she carried, Mallon is presumed to have infected over 50 people, 3 of whom died, over the course of her career as a cook, because typhoid fever is spread through water and food. Mallon's legend grew immediately and she was dubbed "Typhoid Mary" by the press.[102] Her name became synonymous with the spread of the disease, although there were other healthy typhoid carriers, including Italian immigrant Tony Labella, who is presumed to have caused over 100 cases, including 5 deaths. In the name of public safety, Mallon spent 26 years in forced quarantine.[103] A century later, her name is still infamous, and *Typhoid Mary* has broadened as a colloquial term for anyone who, knowingly or not, spreads a contagious disease.

The practice of naming diseases can stigmatize and demonize countries and communities. The World Health Organization recently issued a statement asking for the careful naming of new human diseases. To create appropriate names that are scientifically sound and socially acceptable, certain misleading terms are to be avoided, including geographic locations (e.g., *Spanish Flu, German Measles,* and *Middle East Respiratory Syndrome*), people's names (e.g., *Creutzfeldt-Jakob disease, Down Syndrome, Parkinson's disease,* and *Alzheimer's disease*), industry or occupational references (e.g., *Legionnaires' disease*), and species of animals (e.g., *bird flu, monkey pox*), to minimize negative effects on these groups.[104] Many of these names are misnomers, such as *swine flu,* which later came to be referred to as *H1N1.* Historically, this kind of naming has had serious consequences. In 2009, the Egyptian government ordered the culling of the country's 300,000 pigs during the H1N1 pandemic, although there were no confirmed cases of the disease within its borders.[105] Diseases named after religious or ethnic communities have also led to discrimination against these groups, creating barriers to travel, commerce, and cultural relations. At the time of writing, an outbreak of COVID-19 (SARS-CoV-2) emerged in Wuhan, China. Becoming known as the *Novel Coronavirus* and declared a pandemic in 2020, the highly contagious disease spread across the globe, inciting anti-Asian prejudice throughout Western countries and leading some people to dub it the *Chinese virus* or *Kung flu.* Others falsely linked the Coronavirus to Corona, the Mexican beer, given the phonological similarity of the two names.

Disease, disability, and mental illness are facts of the human species. Disease has always plagued living organisms, and statistically, most people will experience a disability at some time during the course of their lives, while one in four people have a mental illness. When it comes to talking about these human experiences, there is no consensus about what is acceptable or inoffensive terminology. Language evolves, and appropriate terminology changes. Ableism is often unintentional, and many people are unaware of the impact of their words. Stakeholders differ as to what they find offensive and have their own preferences for self-identifying labels that differ across country, culture, and time. It is important to empower people by giving them control over the naming of their own experiences, and to allow them to choose how they self-identify or describe themselves. In this way, we seek to treat someone who has a disease, disorder, or disability with compassion, respect, and understanding, and as a person, rather than as a label.

6   Hit by the Ugly Stick

Joseph Merrick was born in 1862 in Leicester, England. During his infancy he developed severe facial and body deformities. His skin appeared thick and lumpy, his legs and one arm were swollen, and a bony lump grew out of his forehead. Merrick is better known as "The Elephant Man," the name that was bestowed upon him by the "freak show" that exhibited him. The explanation for his disfigurement was that his mother was frightened by an elephant she saw in a street parade during her pregnancy.[1] Throughout Merrick's life, he had been described variously as a "creature," a "monstrous figure as hideous as an Indian idol," a "block of gnarled wood," and a "perverted version of a human being."[2] The police eventually closed down the exhibition, and Merrick spent the remainder of his life in London Hospital. In his hospital bed he had to sleep sitting up because of the weight of his head, but one night he attempted to lie down to sleep, and in doing so, he dislocated his neck and died of asphyxia. He was only 27 years old. According to his friend, Dr. Treves, Merrick's final act was the fatal result of his longing to "be like other people."[3]

Today, people who are different from others in their appearance are no longer displayed in freak shows; however, they often experience social prejudice. People who appear different become the targets of bullying, harassment, and hate crimes, simply because of the way they look. People define themselves, and are defined by others, in terms of their appearance. They are judged negatively because of a disfigurement, birthmark, facial scars, a crooked nose, their body size, the clothing they wear, or the color of their hair. Unlike sexism or racism, there is no common name for prejudice against people based on their physical appearance, although the term *lookism* is sometimes used.[4] Lookism has crossover with racism, sexism, ableism, ageism, and other categories of discrimination. It is no longer socially acceptable to publicly refer to a person as a *creature* or *monster*, although our modern language reveals that prejudice against appearance is still commonplace.

In the time of Joseph Merrick, people had a curiosity for difference and found physical otherness to be entertaining. This overlapped with racism. Some people of Asian and African descent and indigenous people were captured by "man-hunters" and placed in "human zoos" in which they were displayed in cages or kept in mock villages.[5] (See also Chapter 1.) Charles Dickens described a fascination with people and places that might otherwise be perceived as fearful or grotesque as "the attraction of repulsion."[6] The infamous American showman, Phineas T. Barnum, capitalized on this attraction, making a career of displaying hoaxes and *human oddities* to the paying public on the sideshow circuit. Freak shows exhibited obese people, albino people, hairy women, and other physically unusual humans, such as Charles Stratton, known as "General Tom Thumb," a little person who stood at 3.25 feet tall. *Little person, LP*, or *person of short stature* are now the preferred terms for people with achondroplasia and related genetic conditions. The older term *dwarf* is still in use, although some people find this offensive. *Pygmy* specifically refers to a member of an ethnic group whose people are of endemic short stature. The term is still used by anthropologists, although it can be offensive to these groups because of its racial and colonial connotations, and they prefer to be referred to by their ethnicity; for example, the Taron people of Myanmar. *Midget* is highly offensive because of its association with the freak show era. Another popular human attraction was the *Siamese Twins*, Chang and Eng Bunker, who were conjoined at the sternum. (*Conjoined twins* is now the preferred phrase.) The Thai-born Bunker brothers were the source of the name *Siamese twins*, because Thailand was formerly known as *Siam*.

At a time when they would otherwise have been socially ostracized, many of these people earned wealth, fame, and respectability by performing. In the London Hospital where

Joseph Merrick spent the rest of his days, he received charitable visits from the wealthy ladies and gentlemen of London society, including Alexandra, Princess of Wales. But as medical science began to explain disfigurements, along with the rise of disability rights, freak shows declined as a form of entertainment. Today, these shows are generally thought of as exploitative, degrading, and cruel. However, some commentators argue that reality TV is the modern-day equivalent of the freak show.[7] Many reality TV shows have a voyeuristic, objectifying aspect that focuses on physical otherness. The programs *The Little Couple* and *Little People, Big World* were about little people. *My Big Fat Fabulous Life* and *My 600lb Life* followed the lives of big people. Other documentaries profiled people with disabilities, such as *The Man with Half a Body*, *The Man Who Lost His Face*, *Born Without a Face*, and *Child Frozen in Time*. Many of these shows were aired on The Learning Channel (TLC) network, which is popularly referred to as *The Freak Show Channel*.

This attraction to difference is contrasted with fear, contempt, and aversion. People with physical differences are labeled as *deformed*, *disfigured*, *misshapen*, and *malformed*. They are dehumanized as *freaks*, *mutants*, *monsters*, *animals*, *beasts*, and *creatures*. They may be described as *hideous*, *disgusting*, *grotesque*, *sickening*, *repulsive*, or *ugly*, and they are often rendered social outcasts. From the eighteenth century until as recently as the 1970s, "unsightly beggar ordinances" existed in the United Kingdom and the United States. These were known colloquially as *ugly laws*. These laws prohibited people with physical disabilities, disfigurements, or visible diseases from appearing in public. The Chicago ordinance of 1881 read: "Any person who is diseased, maimed, mutilated, or in any way deformed, so as to be an unsightly or disgusting object, or an improper person to be allowed in or on the streets, highways, thoroughfares, or public places in the city, shall not therein or thereon expose himself to public view, under the penalty of a fine of $1 for each offense."[8] Nowadays, severe facial disfigurement is considered a disability, while discrimination or harassment of people with physical differences can be considered a hate crime.

Physical disability and difference are often equated with ugliness. *Ugly* refers to something or someone that is deemed to be unattractive or visually unappealing. A physical difference or flaw can be perceived as ugly, such as a scar, warts, acne, or wearing reading glasses or having braces. But it is often said that physical attractiveness is subjective, as in the adage *Beauty is in the eye of the beholder*. Ugliness is also in the eye of the beholder. *Ugly* can be a self-criticism. People, usually young women and girls, *feel ugly* and inadequate when they compare themselves to others, especially models and movie stars. At the extreme end, people with Body Dysmorphic Disorder (BDD) develop an obsessive focus on a minor or perceived flaw in their appearance that they believe makes them look ugly or deformed.[9] The most common features that people with BDD become preoccupied with include the face, skin, nose, stomach, or thighs. Symptoms of the condition include excessive exercise, undergoing repeated cosmetic surgery with no satisfaction, or believing that other people take special notice of their feature and mock them for it.

The adages *true beauty comes from within* and *true beauty is on the inside* suggest that attractiveness is based on character rather than physical appearance. Figures of speech tell us that it is more important to be *beautiful on the inside*, to have *inner beauty*, and *it's what's on the inside that counts*. The maxim that we should not *judge a book by its cover* warns against the hasty judgment of outward appearances. These sayings warn against superficiality, vanity, and shallowness. However, in fairy tales and modern pop culture, the good and the kind are always beautiful, while ugliness is equated with dislikeable personality traits. That *good is beautiful* while *bad is ugly* strikes us as just. This theory was once borne out by early science. Physiognomy is the now discredited idea that physical appearance reflects character, holding the belief that attractive people are inherently good, whereas ugly people are inherently immoral. The idioms *as ugly as sin*, *as ugly as the devil*, and *as ugly as hell* compare ugliness to evil.

Ugliness can also be metaphorical, such as having an *ugly character* or *ugly personality*. *Ugly* can be used figuratively to describe someone who is *ugly on the inside* and has an *ugly heart* or an *ugly soul*. In Oscar Wilde's novel *The Picture of Dorian Gray*, the handsome protagonist has his portrait painted and wishes that the painting would age instead of him.[10] His wish is realized. Gray leads a hedonistic lifestyle, and while his portrait ages and records his every sin, Gray himself remains youthful and good-looking. When he atones for his wrongdoings, Gray becomes withered and decrepit, while the painting is restored to its original beauty. The saying *Beauty is only skin deep* suggests that beauty is superficial, and that how we look does not always reflect who we are. This lesson is a popular theme in fiction. The fairy tale *Beauty and the Beast*, the musical *The Phantom of the Opera*, the novel *The Hunchback of Notre-Dame*, the play *Cyrano de Bergerac*, and the 1980s romantic comedy *Roxanne* all reveal the plight of the "ugly" but virtuous hero who falls in love with a beautiful woman, although he is ashamed of his own appearance.

Another popular theme in fiction is the transformation of the *ugly ducking*, a premise that originally comes from Hans Christian Anderson's 1843 fairy tale *The Ugly Duckling*. This is the story of an "ugly" baby bird that suffers abuse and rejection from the other animals around him until he eventually grows into a beautiful swan. This is also a trope in popular culture.[11] Typically, the "ugly duckling" is a woman considered awkward, uncool, plain, or unattractive, who transforms into someone pretty and popular. In the television comedy drama *Ugly Betty*, the main character, Betty, is considered to be "ugly" because of her dental braces, reading glasses, and lack of fashion sense. Her colleagues mock her appearance until it is discovered that she has a sweet nature, and she has had a makeover. Many movie plots feature a woman who is considered to be ugly and unpopular until she undergoes a makeover, including *Mean Girls*, *Clueless*, *She's All That*, and *The Breakfast Club*. There is also the concept of *ugly cute*; the belief that ugly can be considered cute, especially with regard to animals, such as dogs and cats.

Many idioms exist to describe ugliness, including *no oil painting*, *a face only a mother could love*, *a face that would stop a clock*, and *hit by the ugly stick*. Some phrases include animal metaphors: *ugly pig*, *ugly dog*, *ugly as a toad*, and *face like a horse*. In a tweet posted in October 2018, US President Donald Trump referred to adult film star Stephanie Clifford ("Stormy Daniels"), who claimed he had had an affair with her, as "Horseface."[12] Some ugly-related figures of speech are also sexist, because they suggest that a woman who is ugly is one who is considered to be sexually undesirable to men; including: *turn-off*, *boner-killer*, and the practice of rating women's looks on a scale from 1 to 10. (See also Chapter 2.) Many ugly-related terms are aimed almost exclusively at women. *Ugly* is also associated with *ordinary* or *average* in terms that typically refer to women: *homely*, *mousey*, *dowdy*, *frumpy*, *not much to look at*, *simple*, *plain*, *plain Jane*, and the *girl next door*. The word *ugly* itself can be a potent insult. In 2013, 13-year-old Rosalie Avila hanged herself in her bedroom following relentless bullying at school, where she was teased for being "ugly." In her suicide note to her family she apologized for being ugly, and wrote, "Please, don't post any pictures of me at my funeral."[13]

Several Hollywood actors report being told early in their careers that they were "not attractive enough" or "too ugly" to appear in movies or on television. Winona Ryder revealed that as a young actor she was auditioning for a role in a film. She was mid-sentence when the casting director interrupted her by saying, "Listen, kid. You should not be an actress. You are not pretty enough. You should go back to wherever you came from, and you should go to school. You don't have it."[14] Critics seem to be particularly judgmental of the appearance of women in movies or on television. In a 2012 review of Mary Beard's documentary *Meet the Romans*, British author A. A. Gill said that the Cambridge professor was too ugly for television and that "she should be kept away from cameras altogether."[15] An attractive person can be said to have *a face for television*, while an unattractive person may be said to *have a face for radio*.

Research suggests that good-looking people are more likely to be employed, to receive more pay, to have more attractive and highly educated spouses, and to generally fare better in life than the *looks-challenged*.[16] There are many cases of people, and particularly women, being discriminated against because they were considered to be "ugly." Television news anchor Christine Craft was demoted to reporter when a focus group determined she was "too old, too unattractive and wouldn't defer to men."[17] In 2013, the American clothing retailer Abercrombie and Fitch was accused of firing employees who were deemed to be "ugly" or "fat."[18] This came shortly after the company's admission that they do not stock XL or XXL sizes in women's clothing, because they do not want overweight women wearing their brand.

Being overweight or obese is often equated with being ugly.[19] "Fat and ugly" is a common body shaming insult, while some claim that "fat" and "ugly" are almost interchangeable words in modern society.[20] In 2015, men on British subways targeted women as "fat and ugly", handing them cards that read:

> Overweight Haters Ltd.
>   It's really not glandular; it's your gluttony . . .
>   Our oganisation hates and resents fat people. We object to the enormous amount of food resources you consume while half the world starves. We disapprove of your wasting NHS money to treat your selfish greed. And we do not understand why you fail to grasp that by eating less you will be better off, slimmer, happy and find a partner who is not a perverted chubby-lover or even find a partner at all. We also object that the beautiful pig is used as an insult. You are not a pig. You are a fat, ugly human.[21]

Being overweight or obese is highly stigmatized in Western society. Weight discrimination, often called *fat shaming, weightism, fatism, fatphobia*, or *sizeism*, is prejudice against larger people. Weight discrimination is pervasive in Anglophone culture, with rates close to the prevalence of race and age discrimination.[22] This kind of prejudice is even on the rise in the United States, despite the fact that most Americans are overweight.[23] It is often said that weight discrimination remains socially acceptable, and that prejudice against overweight people is the "last acceptable bigotry." Weight discrimination is rarely challenged and often ignored.[24] People with excess weight are humiliated, ridiculed, harassed, bullied, teased, and criticized, and often by members of their own family. A 2012 study revealed that 46 percent of Americans would rather give up a year of life than be obese, 30 percent reported they would rather be divorced than obese, while 5 percent said they would rather lose a limb.[25] Overweight and obese people evoke feelings of disgust, contempt, hostility, and fear in others, and everyday language reveals these negative attitudes.

In a clinical setting, the terms *overweight* and *obese* are used instead of *fat*, which instead describes dietary fats found in food. The Body Mass Index (BMI) is a measure of body fat based on height and weight that is used to categorize an individual's weight as *underweight, normal weight, overweight,* or *obese. Overweight* is defined as a person with a BMI of 25–29.9, while *obese* refers to a person whose BMI is 30 or greater.[26] *Morbidly obese* indicates a person who has a BMI of 35 or greater. The BMI has long been criticized for being inaccurate and misleading. For example, it does not distinguish fat from bone, muscle, and skeletal tissue. Furthermore, the BMI was created to measure the average weight of a population, not individuals, and it was developed on a group of men, not women. Despite these limitations and questions about its relevance, the BMI is still used widely in healthcare.

The language used by the healthcare industry and the media to talk about obesity is frequently hyperbolic. The prevalence of obesity is often described as an *epidemic*, which is the same label commonly used to describe pandemics such as the Black Death, AIDS, and smallpox. Using the term *epidemic* not only means that obesity is widespread, but also implies that it is a disease, and highly infectious. The rise of obesity is also described as an *outbreak*, which implies that it is a sudden occurrence, and likens the severity of obesity to outbreaks of dangerous diseases, such as *measles outbreak, salmonella outbreak*, or *Ebola outbreak. Outbreak* also suggests that obesity is contagious and instills a sense of immediate danger.

Overweight and obese people are often treated as a burden on society. Obesity has also been labeled a public health *crisis*, comparing it to a life-threatening emergency or urgent medical situation such as a *mental health crisis*. In terms of metaphor, achieving weight loss is often compared to a conflict, in phrases such as *the fight against flab, the battle of the bulge*, and *the war against obesity*. People are said to *fight, battle*, or *struggle* with their weight. The *enemies* of weight loss include fat, carbs, sugar, and junk food, while the numerous diet plans and fads are engaged in *the diet wars*. By stigmatizing obesity, this exaggerated language also stigmatizes larger people and contributes to the prejudice against them.

The terms *overweight* and *obese* are euphemisms that are grounded in medical discourse, although *fat* is often considered a term of abuse when it describes a person instead of a macronutrient. *Fat* appears in many common insults, including *fatty, fatso, fat slob, fat bitch, fat boy*, and *fat fuck*. There are many other offensive terms for larger people, including *chubby, chunky, bloated, dumpy, tubby, flabby, plump, pudgy, blimp*, and *butterball*. Some insults refer to "fat" body parts, specifically the backside and stomach, including *fat ass, lard ass, jelly-belly, pot-bellied, beer gut, man boobs*, and *thunder thighs*. Metaphors of "fat" animals are used commonly as insults: *pig, hog, cow, beached whale, land whale, hippo*, and *elephant*, and in phrases such as *fat pig, fat as a pig, eat like a pig*, to *make a pig of yourself*, and *fat cow*. Some overweight people reveal that they have been publicly "mooed" or "oinked" at.[27] Other idioms include to be *big as a house*, a *tub of lard*, and that the overweight person has *let themselves go*, or has *packed it on*.

There are a number of positive labels and euphemisms for being larger, including *plus size, curvy, cuddly, husky, flabulous, voluptuous, zaftig* and a *woman/man of size. Big, heavy, round, large, thick, soft*, and *solid* are also euphemistic, while *big-boned, thick-set*, *heavy-set, stout, portly, rotund,* and *corpulent* sound more euphemistic, because they are archaic. *Fat* was an affectionate nickname for actor Fatty Arbuckle, billiards player Minnesota Fats, and musicians Fats Waller and Fats Domino. Fat acceptance activists have attempted to reclaim *fat* as a neutral label, but for the most part, it is offensive because of its negative associations.[28] Anti-fat bias shows up in cultural stereotypes and negative attitudes toward people with excess weight. Larger people are perceived as morally weak, undisciplined, self-indulgent, unmotivated, and lacking willpower and self-restraint. They are seen as unhealthy, tired, and lazy, and it is thought that they must not exercise.[29] It is believed that they have poor eating habits; that they overeat or binge-eat; and that they are gluttonous, greedy, and always hungry. It is assumed that larger people have poor hygiene, and are dirty, smelly, and disgusting. They are judged as worthless, inferior, incompetent, unsuccessful, and unintelligent.[30] And they are generalized as unattractive, introverted, insecure, unhappy, and undesirable.[31] Larger people are often seen as all "the same," while being *fat* becomes their defining characteristic.

This stereotyping of larger people is ubiquitous in popular culture. Television shows about overweight people contain anti-fat messages, including the dramas *This Is Us, Insatiable,* and *Huge,* and the competitions *The Biggest Loser, More to Love,* and *Dance Your Ass Off.* Reality TV shows such as *The 650lb Virgin, One Big Happy Family,* and *Family by the Ton* present morbidly obese people as oddities, much like in the days of the freak shows. One study shows that 60 percent of Americans are overweight or obese, although this figure is not represented on television, where 24 percent of male characters are overweight and only 14 percent of female characters are overweight.[32] These overweight characters were more likely to appear in minor roles, less likely to be involved in romantic relationships, and were often the butt of jokes. Overweight and obese people are often the subjects of ridicule. A whole genre of humor known as *Yo Mamma* jokes are dedicated to mocking larger women, such as the gag, *Yo mamma so fat she went to the cinema and sat next to everyone.*

In Western societies, overweight and obese individuals are often treated with less respect and courtesy than thinner people.[33] Supporting the idea that fat shaming is still socially acceptable, some people have no qualms about expressing their dislike and hatred of larger people in public. Overtly offensive behavior includes targeting them with the insults listed above or making negative personal comments about their appearance. The abuse not only occurs face to face but also online. Cyber bullying of larger people is common on Twitter, Instagram, and other social networking sites, while the anonymity of the Internet makes it easier to harass others without repercussions. The social news aggregation and discussion website Reddit had a popular forum called "Fat People Hate." Over 150,000 subscribers mocked overweight and obese people on the forum.[34] They mined social media accounts and dating sites to find photographs of larger people (mostly women) to make fun of, and harass, and even send death threats to. In 2015, the forum was banned in response to Reddit's new anti-harassment policy, although #fatpeoplehate is still a popular hashtag online.

Overweight and obese people are made to feel shame and failure because of their size and they are blamed and held personally responsible for their weight. It is assumed that they sit around at home all day, overeating and not exercising. For these reasons, it is often believed that weight stigmatization is justifiable and that fat shaming will motivate larger people to lose weight. In a popular YouTube video, "Dear Fat People," comedian Nicole Arbour says, "Shame people who have bad habits until they fucking stop. Fat shaming. If we offend you so much that you lose weight, I'm okay with that."[35] However, evidence suggests that ridiculing larger people is counterproductive. Fat shaming does not lead to weight loss, but instead can lead to weight gain.[36] It does not encourage people to lose weight, but deters weight loss, keeping larger people away from resources that can help, such as the doctor, or the gym. Social rejection and prejudice can cause negative body image and lead to eating disorders and mental illness. These negative attitudes toward larger people assume that weight is controllable, although genetic and biological factors affect weight, as well as social and economic influences.[37] Various studies also show that most people cannot achieve long-term sustainable weight loss.[38] It is worth noting that it would not be tolerated if members of other stigmatized groups (e.g., people of color, people with disabilities) were told to change themselves if they do not want to be discriminated against.[39]

As discussed in previous chapters, microaggressions are more covertly offensive. These are subtle, everyday expressions of prejudice that are so pervasive and normalized that many people may not recognize them as stigmatizing at all.[40] Non-verbal microaggressions against larger people include staring at them at the gym, scrutinizing their food choices by monitoring what they eat in a restaurant, or checking out the contents of their shopping cart at the supermarket.[41] *Concern trolling* involves body shaming disguised as expressions of care and concern about a larger person's health. Phrases including *Do you really want to eat that much?*, *You're not going to eat that, are you?*, and, *You'll probably just want a salad, right?* suggest that larger people should always be on a diet and should be embarrassed about the food they eat. An unsolicited remark such as, *I lost weight on this diet, you should try it* or gifting someone a diet book implies impolitely that they need to lose weight. The common question asked of larger people, *Do you have a health issue?* expects that they should have an explanation for their larger weight, and that they need to justify their size to others. Similarly, strangers may assume that a woman is larger because she must be pregnant. Larger women are asked assumptive questions, such as, *Are you pregnant?*, *When are you due?*, or, *How many months along are you?*

Intended compliments can come across as judgments. Common questions and statements about weight that are meant to be flattering can have the opposite effect because of underlying assumptions about what is beautiful. The phrases, *Did you lose some weight? You look so much better*, imply that the person looked so much worse when they were larger. The replies, *You're not fat, you're beautiful*, and, *You're not fat. Don't talk about yourself like that!* are intended to be supportive, but they reinforce the idea that being fat is bad, and that fatness and beauty are mutually exclusive. The remark, *He's kind of heavy, but he's a really nice guy!* implies that a person who is larger is physically unattractive, although they can still have an attractive personality. This also invokes the trope of the *jolly fat man*, the *big, fun, lovable fat guy*, such as comedians Chris Farley and John Candy. There are many backhanded compliments made to overweight people, such as, *You're big, but you carry it well*. Sexist microaggressions target larger women, including, *You have such a pretty face*, *You'd be pretty if you just lost a few pounds*, and, *You're pretty, for a plus-sized girl*, while they suggest that their larger size puts them at a disadvantage. Some phrases are self-deprecating, such as, *Do I look fat in this?* which implies, *Do I look bad?* While *I feel so fat*, and *I'm having a fat day* reveal insecurity, and imply that being fat is undesirable.

In 2012, US blogger Melissa McEwan created the #FatMicroaggressions hashtag to document the derogatory comments directed at overweight people on a daily basis. She started the campaign after someone stole a photograph from her blog and used it to create a fake profile on the dating site, OKCupid. The photo was given a racist, sexist, and sizeist tagline: "Honestly, I just want to have sex with black guys."[42] Larger women are targets of *fat fetishism*, which is a fetishized sexual attraction to overweight or obese people. The derogatory terms *chubby chasers* and *chubby lovers* label people who are sexually attracted to larger people. The pornography industry fetishizes larger women with the indexing tag BBW ("Big Beautiful Women"), although some women use this acronym self-referentially. The euphemism originally came from *BBW Magazine*, a 1970s fashion and lifestyle publication for plus-size women. In general, fat bias is worse for women, who are twice as likely to experience weight discrimination. One study found that men start to experience weight discrimination when they reach 70 pounds over their healthy weight, whereas women can experience weight bias for gaining as little as 13 pounds.[43]

Anti-fat bias can have adverse social consequences. Larger people experience discrimination in the workplace, within the health-care industry, and even within personal relationships.[44] In schools, overweight children often experience bullying from peers, and studies have shown that teachers have lower expectations for the performance of larger students.[45] Being overweight can affect the quality of medical treatment that larger people receive from their doctors. A 2012 study found that doctors have similar levels of anti-fat bias as the general public.[46] There can be serious repercussions for this bias. Assumptions about larger people can delay diagnosis and treatment, and when the focus is on weight, it can often lead to a dismissal of the patient's concerns. At 23 years old, plus-size Canadian model Elly Mayday (Ashley Shandrel Luther) suffered severe lower back pain. Her doctors blamed her weight for her symptoms and suggested she exercise more often. After several years of persistence to find the real cause, she was diagnosed with a rare form of ovarian cancer.[47] Mayday died of the disease at the age of 30. Overweight and obese people also experience more workplace discrimination, where anti-fat bias is demonstrated by colleagues, supervisors, and employers.[48] Larger people are less likely to be hired and more likely to be unfairly terminated from their jobs. They earn less, and are promoted less, despite having comparable qualifications and experience.[49]

Prejudice aside, most people struggle with their self-image and do not feel comfortable in their bodies. Body positivity is a growing social movement that promotes size inclusivity and the acceptance and appreciation of all human body types. Several organizations are devoted to reducing weight discrimination, such as the National Association to Advance Fat Acceptance (NAAFA), the Association for Size Diversity and Health (ASDAH), and the Health at Every Size movement. Definitions of beauty and normative appearance standards vary across culture and time and are typically based on subjective preferences for female figures. In some African countries, being fat remains a symbol of status and power. In rural Jamaica, skinny or *meager* women are considered unattractive, mean, and stingy, while heaviness is a sign of happiness.[50] In Mauritania, some parents still force-feed their young girls; the process is called *Leblouh* or *gavage*, French words that describe the fattening up of geese to produce foie gras.[51] Thin women are believed to be unhealthy, whereas larger girls are perceived as beautiful and prosperous. In Nigeria, fat is a sign of wealth, and rich women stay in *fattening houses* prior to weddings, where they are encouraged to put on weight by eating large amounts of food during the day.[52] Throughout history, female fat has been a sign of fertility and sexuality, as illustrated by the famous Venus of Willendorf figurine that dates back to 30,000–22,000 BCE. Beauty in Renaissance Italy meant a full-figured body, such as the "Rubenesque" women painted by Peter Paul Rubens. Plus-sized comedian Dawn French once joked that, "If I had been around when Rubens was painting, I would have been revered as a fabulous model. Kate Moss, well she would have been the paintbrush."[53]

Today in Western society, it is said that there is a cultural obsession with thinness. *Thin is in*, as the saying goes. "You can never be too rich or too thin," is a quote attributed to several famously slender women, including Gabrielle "Coco" Chanel and Wallis Simpson, the Duchess of Windsor. The saying *nothing tastes as good as thin feels* reminds us to stay the course of the diet. It is considered normal for most people (in particular women) to be vigilant about their weight and dress size, to diet, and count calories and grams of fat.[54] These behaviors are inspired by the many positive social stereotypes of thinness. Having a thin body is linked to happiness, confidence, romantic success, and health.[55] Being slim is associated with positive traits, such as self-control and ambition, while thin people are seen as being popular, desirable, and lovable. Thin people enjoy *thin privilege*, which author Cora Harrington defines as, "The ability to move through life without people insisting you need to be a smaller size. If you don't have to think about that, it's a privilege."[56]

Throughout history, the ideal body type focuses on standards of female beauty. The modern Western "thin ideal" is of a woman with a slender physique, a small waist, and little body fat. Fashions have changed over the past 100 years. During the "Roaring Twenties," the preference was for curveless, boyish women, as typified by the familiar 1920s symbol of the *flapper*. Many actresses were famous for their thinness. The slim, boyish *gamine* actresses of the 1950s, such as Audrey Hepburn and Leslie Caron, made being thin seem graceful, elegant, and glamorous. The fashion industry made it stylish, sophisticated, and fashionable to be *model thin*. From the 1960s, the *hourglass* proportions of 36–24–36 were known as the "perfect" vital statistics for a woman. The late 1960s was also famous for its slim, androgynous models with their thin-inspired nicknames, such as Lesley Lawson, better known as "Twiggy," Jean Shrimpton, "the Shrimp," and Penelope Tree, "The Tree." The *waif* look was popular in the 1990s, and best exemplified by model Kate Moss. This was also the decade of *heroin chic*, a look characterized by a very thin body, pale skin, and an angular bone structure (with the implication these people had a "diet" of addictive drugs instead of food). While plus-sized models are becoming more popular today, the majority of models are thin because designers believe their clothes look better on thinner models. For this reason, models are often objectified as *walking coat hangers*, *clothes hangers*, and *mannequins*.

The fashion industry has been criticized heavily for creating an unattainable and unhealthy standard of beauty. Model Elly Mayday was a "plus-size" model by industry standards, although she rejected that label, arguing that her size 14 body was a normal size.[57] In 2017, 20-year-old Danish model Ulrikke Hoyer was canceled from a Louis Vuitton catwalk show in Japan for being "too fat" and was told that she was "too big and bloated," because she refused to starve herself before the show.[58] She weighed only 97 pounds (44 kilograms). Many models are pressured to starve themselves and lose weight to stay thin. It is reported that some models go to extreme lengths to lose weight, including taking laxatives, supposedly eating tissues or cotton balls to "feel full," or starving themselves. In several severe cases, this obsession with weight loss has led to grave consequences. In August 2006,

22 year-old Uruguayan model Luisel Ramos died of heart failure during a fashion show.[59] In November of the same year, Brazilian model Ana Carolina Reston died from multiple organ failure. Both deaths were attributed to complications of anorexia.

Anorexia nervosa is an eating disorder that involves self-starving and excessive weight loss, while the related disorder, bulimia nervosa, is marked by a cycle of binge-eating and purging. Both are serious, potentially life-threatening disorders. Some believe that the fashion industry is to blame for low self-esteem, the development of eating disorders, and related disorders of body image such as Body Dysmorphic Disorder. Eating disorders are thought to be a result of the social pressures on women and girls to attain the *thin ideal*, and their aspirations to *look like a model*. Seen as a consequence of vanity and superficiality, anorexia is often trivialized as a "rich, spoiled, white-girl's disease."[60] People with the disorder are criticized as victims of the media and are judged for trying to live up to unhealthy and artificial norms. However, studies show that this view oversimplifies the issue, because the risk of developing eating disorders can be affected by cultural influences but is mostly caused by genetic factors.[61] The deaths of Ramos and Reston from anorexia prompted the fashion industry to adopt healthier practices. In an effort to project the image of healthy models, *Vogue* magazine banned too-skinny models from its pages.[62] Fashion organizations in Italy and Spain have banned catwalk models with a BMI of 18 or below.[63]

There is a paradox to thin privilege and the thin ideal. As the saying goes, *thin is in*, but *not too thin*. *Thin shaming* or *skinny shaming* is the flip side to *fat shaming*. There are many negative stereotypes of thin people, and especially thin women. The thin woman is characterized as mean, vain, bitchy, conceited, and superficial. Some celebrities are criticized for their thinness. The naturally thin identical twins Lisa and Jessica Origliasso, of the pop duo The Veronicas, have been thin-shamed throughout their careers. Magazines and newspapers brand them as *sick* and blame them for "encouraging eating disorders."[64] Actor Lily James was told that in the movie *Cinderella* her "tiny waist" was "horrific," that she was bad for "young viewers' body image" and "telling young girls they look prettier anorexic."[65] But there are many reasons why someone can be thin or underweight, including lifestyle, genetics, or a medical condition. After undergoing chemotherapy, plus-size model Elly Mayday lost 60 pounds, which caused her to be skinny-shamed on social media.

There are several terms for thinness that have positive connotations of health and beauty, including: *slim, lithe, trim, lean, athletic, slender, svelte,* and *willowy*. But there are also many labels with negative connotations. *Skinny* can be offensive, implying that someone is "too thin," while it appears in insults such as *skinny bitch*. (With the exception of the reclamation in the *Skinny Bitch* series of diet books, the term implying a mean, tough-love approach to weight loss.[66]) Some thin-related words imply that thinness is associated with being awkward, ungraceful, and possibly tall, including: *gangly, gawky, lanky,* and *angular*. In a paradox to being seen as healthy, thinness is also related to being unhealthy and sickly, in such descriptors as: *gaunt, emaciated, starved, scrawny, bony, skeletal, anorexic,* and *malnourished*. A thin person may be called a *concentration camp victim,* a *corpse,* a *walking skeleton,* or *mummified*. Other insults for thin people are objectifying, such as: *twig, stick, rake, beanpole, beanstalk, string bean, lollipop head, stick insect, toothpick,* and *chicken legs*. Idioms for thinness include: to *look like a scarecrow,* to be *all skin and bone, a bag of bones, stick thin,* or *thin as a rail*.

Just as larger people experience microaggressions, thin people are on the receiving end too. These include unsolicited advice, inappropriate jokes, and comments, often made by strangers, which reference a person's thin body type and make it a talking point.[67] The questions, *Don't you eat anything?*, and *When was the last time you had a decent meal?*, and the statements *You need to eat more,* and, *You're so thin, you should eat something,* make assumptions about people's eating habits based on their looks alone. Telling a thin person to eat more is just as rude as telling an overweight person to eat less.[68] Related microaggressions include suggestions that a thin person only eats *rabbit food* or ordering them to eat: *Get her a sandwich, You should try eating a hamburger sometime,* or *Eat a donut.* These sayings imply that the person (usually a woman) is too thin, or must want to gain weight, and suggest that an immediate solution to the perceived problem is to eat something calorific. The common remarks, *Must be nice to be so thin, You're so thin you can probably eat anything you want,* and the question, *How do you stay so skinny?* are presumptuous and invasive, and may be distressing if the person has body image issues or an eating disorder. It is also offensive to make assumptions about a person's health based on their appearance. Some microaggressions suggest that someone is a drug addict or has an eating disorder because they are thin, by remarking, *You look anorexic*; or saying, *You look sick. You should see a doctor.*[69] Just as it is offensive to tell someone that they would look better if they were thinner, it is offensive to say to a thin person, *You'd look much better with some meat on your bones.* Some thin people believe they are "not allowed" to interpret thin-shaming comments as offensive because of their thin privilege. It is often argued that fat shaming is far worse than thin shaming, because thin people belong to the privileged group.

However, there is a paradox to fat shaming. Larger people often experience prejudice, but conversely, it is said that *big is beautiful.* A thin woman's femininity is insulted with the accusation, *You look like a boy,* while society talks about the physical ideal of the *real woman.* Common phrases tell us that *real women have curves, real women have breasts,* and *a real woman has child-bearing hips.* Several pop songs are famous for their body positivity, such as Sir Mix-A-Lot's "Baby Got Back (I Like Big Butts)," and Queen's "Fat Bottomed Girls"; although the positivity is only for larger bodies. Meghan Trainor's song, "All About That Bass" became a body-positive anthem, but lyrics such as, "boys they like a little more booty to hold," and, "bringing booty back and tell them skinny bitches that"[70] boost larger women by belittling thinner women. Similarly, Nicki Minaj's song "Anaconda" features the lyrics, "Say he don't like 'em bony, he want something he can grab"[71] disparages thinner women. The sayings, *men love curves, men love something to grab onto*, and *men like women with meat on their bones* praise larger women at the expense of thinner women, while *only dogs want bones* is also insulting to a thinner woman's partner. Moreover, these phrases give the idea that women can love their bodies, but only as long as men love them too.[72] These sayings body shame in that they flatter and empower one group of women by putting down other women's bodies.

Prejudice against physical appearance also extends to the outer body. This is another form of lookism, in which people are judged on the basis of their clothing and other adornments, such as body piercings or tattoos. Employers frequently create dress codes that prohibit visible tattoos, although these policies are only considered discriminatory if they are applied in a discriminatory manner; for example, if an employer prohibits the wearing of tattoos with religious significance. People who visibly identify with subcultures, for example through the safety-pinned anti-fashion of Punks, or the black Gothic style clothing worn by Goths, often experience prejudice. Occasionally, this intolerance can turn violent. In 2007, 20-year-old Sophie Lancaster and her 21-year-old boyfriend Robert Maltby, were attacked by a gang of teenage boys for being Goths. The beating was so brutal that Sophie died. As the prosecutor of the case observed, the pair was, "singled out, not for anything they did or said, but because of their dress."[73] As we have seen in previous chapters, LGBTQ people have experienced prejudice for their outward appearance and clothing choices. Prejudice against clothing style can also reflect classism, when people are judged on their work attire. Uniforms, such as janitor's outfits, can be seen as working class or *blue collar* with low social status, as opposed to business suits, which are seen as *white-collar* clothes with high social status.[74] In schools that don't have a uniform policy, some students are bullied because of their clothing, a situation that reflects a prejudice against socioeconomic status for those who can't afford the latest fashions.

Hair color is another important aspect of how people define themselves, and how other people define them.[75] Over time, specific hair colors have become associated with various person-ality traits. There are many stereotypes of blonde people, and blonde women in particular. Blonde is often perceived as attrac-tive, exciting, glamorous, and sexy. The 1933 film *Bombshell* starring Jean Harlow popularized the phrase *blonde bombshell*, describing a blonde woman with sex appeal. This is related to the *blonde babe* and the *busty blonde* stereotypes. Blonde women are also seen as popular and fun; as the famous saying goes, *blondes have more fun*. A 1960s advertising campaign for Lady Clairol hair dye asked, "Is it true that blondes have more fun?" This was followed by a slogan that became one of the most famous in advertising history, "If I've only one life, let me live it as a blonde."[76] The invention of hair dye introduced the *fake blonde*, including the *bottle blonde*, *bleach blonde*, or *suicide blonde* ("dyed by her own hand"). The fashion doll Barbie led to the image of the Barbie Doll type, a tanned, busty, blue-eyed blonde. This is the look that inspired Ukrainian model Valeria Lukyanova to trans-form herself into a "real-life Barbie doll" or "Human Barbie."[77]

Blonde hair is envied, although blonde women are also stereo-typed negatively as vain, promiscuous, easy, ignorant, naive, or "stupid." A blonde woman is said to rely on her looks rather than intelligence.[78] It is also stereotyped that men find blonde women to be more attractive than women with other hair colors. These stereotypes are exemplified by the 1953 musical comedy *Gentlemen Prefer Blondes*. In the film, Marilyn Monroe plays the role of Lorelei Lee, a gold-digging showgirl who performs an iconic rendition of the song, "Diamonds Are a Girl's Best Friend." The *dumb blonde* is a staple of Hollywood movies. In *Legally Blonde*, Reese Witherspoon's character Elle Woods earns a law degree at Harvard University, despite giving the initial appearance that she is a *blonde bimbo*, an attractive but scatter-brained woman. There is an entire genre of humor known as *blonde jokes*, which exploit the stereotype that blonde women are unintelligent, while the idiom *to have a blonde moment* is to do something unintelligent or to forget something. Blonde stereo-types are chiefly aimed at women, although there are also the *dumb blonde male* stereotypes of the *dumb jock* and the *surfer dude*.

In contrast to the *brainless blonde* is the *brainy brunette*. Brunette women are stereotyped variously as smart, sophisticated, or serious. In *Gentlemen Prefer Blondes*, Marilyn Monroe's *ditzy blonde* character is countered by her best friend Dorothy Shaw; a clever, witty, down-to-earth brunette played by Jane Russell. The brunette woman can also be perceived as a wholesome, sensible, girl-next-door type. Brown hair is the most common hair color, and so brunettes may also be characterized as plain looking and dull, with *boring, mousy-brown* colored hair. Alternatively, Hollywood has a preference for brunette men, especially the man who is *tall, dark, and handsome*. Dark hair is often seen as mysterious and exotic. In popular culture, people with very dark hair are also stereotyped as sinister, untrustworthy, and wicked. Light hair is often equated with good, while dark hair is "evil." In the Marvel Universe movies, the blonde God Thor is a virtuous hero, while his dark-haired adopted brother Loki is a villain.

Gray hair is stigmatized, because it is associated with aging. (See also Chapter 7.) Baldness is often associated with age too, although there are various reasons for hair loss. Male pattern baldness is usually linked to middle age or older age. There is the stereotype of a man attempting to retain his youth by wearing a *comb-over*, a *skullet*, a *toupee*, or other *hairpiece* to give the illusion that he still has a full head of hair. However, the image of the *old bald man* who is balding due to genetic factors is opposed to the image of the *hot stud* with the smooth head, who is bald by choice. Some younger men without signs of male pattern baldness choose to shave their heads as a fashion statement. This shaved head style is associated with several stereotypes, such as the *fitness freak*. This look is also connected to music subculture or politics. Having a shaved head is often linked to the punk movement and left-wing politics. Alternatively, *skinheads* are associated with Neo-Nazism, white supremacists, racism, and racist violence, as in the movies *Romper Stomper* (1992) and *American History X* (1998). Many nicknames are associated with baldness, including: *baldy, cue*

ball, chrome dome, shiny, Mr. Clean (named after the bald mascot of
the all-purpose cleaner of the same name), and the ironic nicknames *curly* and *hairy*. Women can experience hair loss too,
although there are fewer stereotypes of female baldness. Bald
women might be assumed to be undergoing chemotherapy for
cancer. Alternatively, they might be perceived as rebels who shave
their heads to defy gendered norms, such as supermodel Grace
Jones and singer-songwriter Sinead O'Connor.

Red hair was the inspiration of noted artists, including Titian,
Dante Gabriel Rossetti, John Everett Millais, John William
Waterhouse, and Sandro Botticelli in his famous *The Birth of
Venus* painting. Natural red hair is perceived as exotic, beautiful,
striking, unusual, and uncommon. It is statistically rare, account-
ing for only 2–3 percent of the world's population.[79]
Paradoxically, redheads have been stigmatized throughout history
and have been accused of being vampires, werewolves, demons,
and witches. During the European witch-hunts in the sixteenth
and seventeenth centuries, some women were put to death simply
because they had red hair, which was believed to be the devil's
mark.[80] This fear of red hair possibly stems from the biblical story
of Judas betraying Christ, because many artworks depict Judas
with red hair and a red beard.[81] In France until recently, people
with red hair were called *poil de Judas*, meaning "hair of Judas."[82]

Today, prejudice against people with natural red hair still exists
and has been likened to racism, while redheads have been called
"the white-skinned other."[83] Often called *gingers*, especially in the
UK, prejudice against people with red hair is known as *gingerism*.
Red hair is so stigmatized that some red-haired people prefer the
terms *strawberry blonde*, *Titian*, *auburn*, or *copper* to having their
hair labeled as *orange* or *red*. People with red hair are often
assumed to have certain characteristics on the basis of the color
of their hair. They are typified as impulsive, irrational, quick-
tempered, libidinous, and wild.[84] The personalities of people
with red hair are often believed to be imitative of their red hair,
and they are seen as fiery, hot-tempered, hot-blooded, passionate,
angry, and aggressive.

Many stereotypes exist of people with red hair and, because it is so rare, these generalizations are often a symbolic representation of famous people with red hair. Redheads are supposed to be funny, weird, and wacky, such as comedian Lucille Ball, or they are thought of as clownish, such as Ronald McDonald and Bozo the Clown.[85] Irish ethnicity is often attributed to people with red hair, even though Scotland has the highest percentage of red-haired people of any nation, at 11 percent.[86] Similarly, Irish stereotypes are attributed to people with red hair, and they are assumed to be Catholic, to be mischievous (like a *redheaded Leprechaun*), and to overindulge in alcohol. There are also generalizations about their skin; that they are a pasty white color, or albino, that they have red freckles, no eyelashes, and that they are not able to go out into the sun at all.

There are many insults and nicknames that refer to red hair, and while some are accepted, many are hated. Common terms refer to red or orange objects and include *carrot top, copper top, copperhead, Fanta pants, rusty crotch, fire crotch, blood nut, torchhead,* and *firehead.* The nickname *Red* can be seen as overly familiar or intimate. Other nicknames are based on the names of red-haired fictional characters, such as Little Orphan Annie, Pippi Longstocking, and Anne of Green Gables. In Australian English, *blue* or *bluey* are ironic nicknames for redheaded people, while the derogatory *ranga* is short for "orangutan." Other more affectionate terms include *Ginge* or *Meggsie*, taken from *Ginger Meggs*, Australia's longest-running comic strip dating back to the 1920s, which follows the adventures of a mischief-making 10-year-old redheaded boy. As noted, *ginger* is usually pejorative, although it can be used affectionately, as in the adopted name of actor Ginger Rogers, the nickname of Cream drummer Peter "Ginger" Baker, and singer Geri "Ginger Spice" Halliwell. Ginger was the name of the sultry, redheaded movie star in the 1960s television comedy *Gilligan's Island. Ginger* has also been reclaimed by some people with red hair who use it as a self-identifying label. But as observed in the comedy song "Prejudice" by Australian musician Tim Minchin, "Only a ginger can call another ginger 'Ginger.'"[87]

Red hair becomes the most significant characteristic for those who have it. People with red hair often feel that the color of their hair overpowers everything else, becoming all that people see. They may be identified as *the girl with red hair* or *the guy with red hair*. The popular stereotypes negatively affect the lives of people with red hair. They often have low self-esteem, experience insecurity, and feel a profound sense of being not only different from other people, but also inferior.[88] As implied by the phrase *red-headed stepchild*, people with red hair often feel neglected, mistreated, or unwanted. In 2011, the world's largest sperm bank, Cryos International, barred red-haired men from donating due to low demand.[89] (By 2014, it was reported that Cryos was now struggling to keep up with the demand for sperm containing the Melanocortin 1 receptor (MC1R) gene for red hair.)[90]

Anti-red bias and bullying are common problems, especially in the United Kingdom. A red-headed family in Newcastle, England, endured years of taunts and violence from neighbors. Their windows were smashed, their home was daubed in graffiti, they were punched and kicked, and they moved twice to escape the harassment.[91] "Ginger Kids," an episode of the cartoon *South Park*, was a satire of racism and prejudice. The episode description states, "After the sudden onset of the disease Gingervitis, Cartman rallies all ginger kids to rise up and assume their role as the master race."[92] The show had unintended consequences, spawning an unofficial *Kick a ginger kid day* across the United Kingdom, in which children with red hair were bullied, attacked, and kicked.[93] In recent years, there have been a number of suicides related to the bullying of red-haired people. In 2013, 15-year-old Helena Farrell took her own life because of the constant bullying she endured for having red hair.[94]

To *be yourself* is a popular motto. Apple Inc. told us to "Think different." Individualism is valued in our society. We are told to *follow your own path* and *dance to the beat of your own drum*. It is said, *You're beautiful just the way you are*. It is prized to be *unique*, *inimitable*, *distinctive*, and an *iconoclast*, while *yes men*, *followers*, *lemmings*, and *sheep* are looked down upon. But at the same time, there is immense social pressure to conform, especially when it comes to appearance. We belong to a culture that judges people based on their looks. People compare themselves to others and believe that they are supposed to *follow the crowd, toe the line,* and *play the game.* In our efforts to belong, we seek out *our tribe, our community,* and *our people.* The need to be accepted by society is so great that people try to conform, even when they cannot. Some people are different, because they were "born that way"; with a physical deformity, thin physique, or red hair. But they still want to *fit in* with everyone else. Just like Joseph Merrick, most people have a desperate desire to "be like other people".

7   God's Waiting Room

There are many positive stereotypes of later life. In some societies, older age is honored and respected. It is associated with experience, knowledge, kindness, authority, and wisdom. Older age is often celebrated as an achievement and a milestone. There is a long-established royal tradition in Britain that the reigning monarch sends the following message to centenarian subjects: "I am so pleased to know that you are celebrating your one hundredth birthday. I send my congratulations and best wishes to you on such a special occasion."[1] On NBC's *Today* show in the United States, host Al Roker and sponsor Smucker maintain a tradition of recognizing viewers turning 100 or older, and couples who've been together for 75 years or more, by displaying their photos on a jar of Smucker's jelly.[2]

Later life is often embraced as a time of fulfillment. Older people have earned the right to do and say as they please, and order kids to, "Get off my lawn!" In advertising, older people are represented as a leisure class. Retirement is portrayed as a time for playing golf and strolling along the beach. The *golden ager* is presented as active, independent, adventurous, health-conscious, well traveled, and worldly.[3] This is also seen as a time for older people to be rewarded for their contributions to society. Those over the age of 65 are often entitled to free healthcare, lower fares on public transport, and cheaper movie tickets; while proof of age is required to ensure that younger people do not try to take advantage of these age-related benefits. Older age is known as the *golden years* or, less positively, as the *declining years*.

There is a paradox in perspectives of aging. Positive stereotypes are far less common than negative ones. Television, advertisements, and greeting cards are filled with derogatory humor based on negative stereotypes about old age. Society may respect old age, but our culture can also disrespect it. The generation gap polarizes young and older people.[4] Younger people cease to identify with older people. As 24-year-old Jack Weinberg, leader of the Free Speech movement, famously said in the 1960s, "You can't trust anyone over 30."[5] Western society is a youth-centered culture. In the song "My Generation," the English rock band The Who sang, "I hope I die before I get old." Society is infatuated with youth and terrified of old age. Although often attributed to actor James Dean, in the novel *Knock on Any Door*, the hero Nick Romano's motto is to, "Live fast, die young, and have a good-looking corpse."[6]

We all want to live to a *grand old age*, although aging, and the process of getting there, is viewed with fear. Old age is mocked and ridiculed. Western society is ageist, as shown by the prevalence of ageist language. Ageism is discrimination on the grounds of age, and the concept has existed far longer than the word that describes it. *Ageism* was coined in 1967 by Robert N. Butler, former director of the National Institute on Aging, who described it as, "a process of systematic stereotyping of and discrimination against people because they are old, just as racism and sexism accomplish this with skin color and gender."[7] Although ageism cuts across all our lives in ways that other forms of difference do not.[8] Old age is something that we will all experience, if we are fortunate, but ageism is much less discussed than racism or sexism and receives less criticism than these other forms of prejudice.[9] Ageism largely remains a socially tolerated form of discrimination.[10, 11]

People do not know how to deal with ageism; often they don't even recognize it when it happens to them.[12] Recognizing ageism means paying attention to common messages that are heard all our lives and have been normalized. Identifying bias against old age is relatively recent, partly because old age is a newer phenomenon.[13] For most of history, the average human lifespan rarely reached 40, but today's society has witnessed a rise in life expectancy. With modern advances in medicine, nutrition, public health, and other factors, the United States alone gained an additional 30 years of life in the twentieth century.[14] More people are living to the age of 100 or more, and centenarians are the most rapidly increasing age group. Throughout the developed world, the population balance is changing, and people are living longer, healthier lives and having fewer children.[15]

Ageism can be aimed at younger people too. Bias toward adults and prejudice against young people has been labeled *childism* or *adultism*.[16] Examples of adultism can be situations in which adults wield their power over youths, such as child labor or child abuse.[17] On a linguistic level, adultism can be expressed in figures of speech; that children should arbitrarily *respect their elders* and that they *should be seen but not heard*. Terms of endearment for children, such as *demon, monkey*, and *monster*, might be considered verbal abuse in some usage, while more obviously derogatory terms include *brat, pest, nuisance, problem child, stupid, bastard, son-of-a-bitch*, and *little shit*. Some common phrases referring to children are viewed as lacking in compassion and understanding. For example, *the terrible twos* depicts the toddler's age or even the toddler as *terrible*, when the term actually describes the adult experience rather than the child's, which has led some child psychologists and experts to eschew the label. Adultism also manifests as negative stereotypes of adolescents; describing all teenagers as *selfish, lazy, irresponsible, obnoxious, troubled*, or *going through a phase*.[18] Other terms show outright contempt for young people, such as *delinquent* and *fucking punk*. Today, there is an intergenerational slinging match on social media. *Baby Boomers* are labeled *bigots* and blamed for climate change and the bad economy. *Generation Z* and *Millennials* are maligned as self-centered, entitled youths who squander their home deposits eating smashed avocado on toast while they play with their smart phones. Younger people dismiss criticisms from older people with *OK Boomer*. Meanwhile, *Generation X* watches the feud from the sidelines.

Some dictionaries define ageism as discrimination against people who are middle-aged or older.[19] Middle age was traditionally considered to be 35, when 70 was a benchmark for old age, although mid-life is now classified as the 40–60 age bracket.[20] Discrimination against middle-aged people is common, especially when it comes to employment. Middle age is known euphemistically as the *mid-life passage* or *second adulthood*, although the way people talk about this time of life is predominantly unflattering. People who turn 40 are said to have the best part of their lives behind them. They are now *over the hill*, and on the way into decline. Middle age evokes the concept of the dreaded *mid-life crisis*, the acute awareness that one's life is, at least, half over, and the discomforting realization that one's remaining time is less than what one has already lived.[21] Ageism affects young and old and everyone in between, although it appears that older people are still the most stigmatized age group. Prototypical ageism is discrimination against older people.

What age is considered to be *old*? There is no natural view of ageing, and so old age is constructed differently across societies and cultures, but it is often associated with the standard age of retirement.[22] Old age is defined in many contexts as beginning at 65.[23] But what was once considered old, no longer is. The definition of *old* differs, and it is a relative term. To younger people, *old* may be forties or fifties, while to middle-aged people, *old* may be eighties or nineties. There is a difference between biological or physical aging versus age as a social category. As a result, few meaningful statements can be made about people in general over age 65.[24] For this reason, some gerontologists divide the older population into more specific categories, differentiating between the *young old* person who is 60–74, to an *old old* or *very old* person aged 75–84, to the *oldest old* person aged 85 years or older.[25]

As we can see, *old* encompasses a broad age bracket, but there is still a misconception that older people are *pretty much all alike*. In light of the variation across people considered to be old, grouping terms such as *the old*, *old people*, *the aging*, and *the elderly* can be offensive. These labels are perceived as objectifying, because they create a category of people defined by a single characteristic, their

age, without acknowledging their diversity. As discussed throughout this book, collective terms lump people together. In this case,
they don't take into account the considerable differences in gender, ethnicity, health, or actual age across individuals. People are
not defined by their lifetime experiences, achievements, abilities,
and personalities, but only by their age. This separation of *the old*
further expresses the alienation of older people from the rest of
society.

Old is a descriptor that is often contrasted with *young*, but it is
not a neutral term. *Old* can be offensive when used as a dismissive
label for people, such as *old people, old folks, old person, old man,
old woman,* and *old lady*. Old intensifies many age-related insults,
such as *old codger, old fogey, old fuddy duddy,* and *silly old fart*.[26]
Oldies and *golden oldies* are fond names for classic rock music, but
oldies is a derogatory term when used to refer to older people. *Old*
also appears in many disparaging similes, such as *there is no fool
like an old fool, as old as the hills, as old as Adam,* and *as old as
Methuselah,* the man reported to have lived to the oldest age of
969 in the Hebrew Bible. *Old* appears in disparaging nicknames
such as *old man* for "father," and *olds* for "parents." In some usage,
old can be a sign of endearment showing familiarity, such as,
How's it going, you old bastard? But as a designation for people,
old has mostly negative implications. Finding an appropriate
name for this section of society is problematic, because the majority of terms are unfavorable.

In scholarly language, *gerontology* is the multidisciplinary study
of all aspects of aging, while *geriatrics* is a branch of medicine
dealing with the health of older people. *Geriatric* is a technical
term that is used in the names of medical journals and organizations, such as the American Geriatrics Society. But outside of
a clinical setting, *geriatric* is an insult when used to refer to older
individuals. Terms for ages by decade are occasionally used for
older people, including *sexagenarian* for a person aged
60–69, *septuagenarian* (70–79), *octogenarian* (80–89), *nonagenar-
ian* (90–99), and *centenarians* for people who are aged 100 or
more. These terms are generally not offensive, although they are

not in common usage and are somewhat obscure, possibly because they are derived from Latin.

Elderly person and *elderly people* are commonly used as polite terms. As a noun, *elder* has positive connotations and suggests seniority rather than being old. The word implies a sense of dignity and respect, and even power, influence, and authority, as shown in phrases such as *our elders and betters, elders of the tribe, the village elder,* and *elder brethren.* (Ironically, in the Church of Jesus Christ of Latter-Day Saints, *elder* is the lowest ranking in the priesthood and typically refers to younger men.) In early English, *elder* was the comparative of *old,* while *eldest* was the superlative form (i.e., *old, elder, eldest*), so *elder* was the equivalent to modern *older.*[27] The comparative adjectives *older* and *elder* are generally perceived as more polite than the unmarked adjectives *old* or *elderly.* While *elder* has retained positive connotations, *elderly* has now acquired ageist associations. *Older* is relative; everyone is older than someone else, so it has become the preferred term that is used in phrases such as *older person, older people, older adults,* or *older Americans,* as a general descriptor for people in later life.

Early retirement or retiring young are perceived as a sign of success in Western society. They call up stereotypes of pursuing hobbies or traveling around the world and suggest financial freedom and a large nest egg. In contrast, *retired person, retiree,* and *pensioner* connote financial hardship and living on a fixed income. These terms are often used as euphemisms for older people, but they have negative connotations of old age and withdrawing from active life. They can also be imprecise, because not all older people receive a pension or other retirement benefit. Of course, not all older people have retired from the workforce, and many continue to work into later life, often because of a lack of social security. The way that population aging is talked about reveals negative attitudes toward older people. Increased longevity is said to be causing an *aging population,* which is described as a *problem* or a *threat,* in which older people are viewed negatively as *dependents*, a *burden*, *strain*, or *drain on society*, and specifically on welfare and healthcare systems.[28] Older people are often regarded as unimportant, disposable or expendable. During the Coronavirus pandemic of 2020, Texas Republican Lieutenant Governor Dan Patrick argued that older citizens should be willing to sacrifice their lives for their country rather than allow public measures to prevent the spread of the virus to damage the US economy.[29]

There are many euphemisms for older people, but most of them are problematic. *Senior* is commonly used and is the preferred term for some stakeholders, although it is increasingly construed as ageist, because it is laden with stereotypes. It conjures up images of dentures and discounts, decline and dysfunction.[30] *Senior citizen* is also common but can be perceived as patronizing, while younger people are not differentiated as "junior citizens." Terms including *wise, respected, venerable, veteran, ageless, enduring, sage, seasoned*, and *experienced* are also popular and are favorable descriptors for older people, but this is because they are vague and do not necessarily imply old age in humans. Some words that infer old age have positive connotations, but only when they do not refer to people. In an episode of the 1980s TV sitcom *Mama's Family*, Thelma Harper asks, "Why is it that old things get more valuable with age, but old people don't?"[31] Value is placed on age when it is applied to certain items, such as antiques or wine, as shown by the idiom to *age like a fine wine*. The terms *vintage, antique, ancient, mature, old*, and *aged* carry positive implications if they refer to inanimate objects, including *vintage car, antique jewelry, ancient city, mature cheese, old lace*, and *aged wood*. In these contexts, old age is suggestive of tradition, history, rarity, and quality.

But when human old age is implied by these descriptors, the connotations are usually derogatory; for example, *She's ancient* or *He's an antique*. Old age in people is compared to old objects that are considered outdated, obsolete, useless, and "worn with age or use, decayed, deteriorated, or shabby."[32] Older people are talked about as *broken down* and *worn out*. Insulting idioms imply that older people are redundant and no longer relevant. They are perceived as past the most successful, productive period of their lives: *past his prime, over the hill, out of touch, washed up, dried up, past it,* and *behind the times.* Other expressions imply that older people are nearing the end of their lives and are close to death: *on the way out, in his twilight years, on his last leg, one foot in the grave, coffin dodgers,* and they are said to be *in God's waiting room.*

Negative stereotypes of older people are a common form of ageism that is reflected in language. Aging is often talked about as a *blessing* but also as a *curse.* In the first century CE, the Roman philosopher Seneca the Younger wrote, *Senectus morbidus est* "old age is a disease."[33] Descriptors commonly linked to older age associate aging with disease, pain, and bad health: *sickly, unwell, failing* (eyesight, hearing, or memory), *constipated, long in the tooth, hypochondriac,* and *impotent.*[34] Some terms associate older age with physical decline: *frail, fragile, slow, weak, feeble, infirm, decrepit, debilitated, impaired, deteriorating, tired,* and *incapacitated.* Other adjectives associate older age with signs of physical aging: *sagging, drooping, drooling, toothless, faded, wilted, withered, wizened, wrinkled, prune, shriveled, shrunken,* and *balding.* Gray hair is commonly associated with aging, as shown by the idiom *the old gray mare, she ain't what she used to be.* False teeth, reading glasses, hearing aids, and disability aids including wheelchairs, walking frames, and canes take on a symbolic role as signifiers of old age.[35]

Older people are represented as helpless and alone: *dependent, incompetent, child-like, recluse, lonely, neglected, poor, pathetic, worrying, sad, depressed,* and *pessimistic.*[36] They are described as bad-tempered and impatient: *irritable, cantankerous, cranky, crusty, grumpy, grouchy, crotchety, childish, bitter, angry, mumbling, muttering,* and *complaining.* They are depicted as inflexible and rigid in thought and manner: *stubborn, selfish, demanding, prejudiced, conservative, closed-minded,* and *old-fashioned.* It is said that older people are *set in their ways, living in the past,* and that *you can't teach an old dog new tricks.* The internet meme "OK Boomer" is a retort that younger people (especially Millennials and Generation Z) use to dismiss or mock the attitudes of older people (especially Baby Boomers) as being narrow-minded, judgmental, and condescending. The catchphrase is akin to the dismissive slang term *whatever*, meaning in this sense, "whatever you say" or "I don't care what you say."

Other terms used in reference to older people are suggestive of mental decline, including: *senile, dementia, disoriented, doddering, confused, muddled, foolish, stupid, crazy, rambling, forgetful, absent-minded*, and the idiom to *have a senior moment*. Cognitive impairment in older people is viewed as normative. However, only some 10 percent of people over 65 have dementia.[37] Markers associated with old age, such as memory loss and an end to sexual activity, are experienced by fewer older adults than is popularly believed. Overall, many of these behavioral traits and physical attributes are common to humans, not necessarily older people, although they are associated with and attributed to old age. Negative representations of aging portray it as a source of embarrassment. They express a pity and fear of aging (which is known as *gerontophobia*). Negative stereotypes about aging also represent our anxiety about death and dying and remind us of our own mortality.

Researchers have found that people develop these stereotypes about aging during childhood, reinforce them during adulthood, and then enter old age with internalized negative self-perceptions.[38] This "internalized ageism" affects the way that people perceive and interact with older people, but also influences the self-definitions and behavior of older people.[39, 40] This leads to discrimination against fellow older people when they disassociate themselves from *those old people*. Negative attitudes toward old age affect how people cope when they reach it. One study discovered that when older people were exposed to words like *absent-minded, feeble, shaky*, and *forgetful*, they performed significantly worse on memory and balance tests.[41] Another study found that people with an optimistic view of aging lived longer than those with a pessimistic view, with an increased lifespan of up to 7.5 years. These perceptions influenced longevity; the more positive the self-perception, the greater the will to live.[42]

The concept of healthy aging has become popular in Western society, and advocates plan for good health in their older age by way of exercise, meditation, diet, and supplements. These are the *wellderly*, older people who are in good health, as opposed to the *illderly*, older people who are in poor health. The Wellderly study researched a group of chronic disease-free people over the age of 80, in the hopes of unlocking the genetic secrets behind lifelong health.[43] The Singularity movement has taken this a step further, believing that advances in medical science will eventually allow people to protect their bodies from aging, leading to immortality.[44] Some older consumers identify as *woofies*, "Well-Off Older Folks" who are fit, healthy, and financially secure.[45] The idea of *successful aging* or *positive aging* is also promoted, the goal being to reach older age with a sufficient degree of financial, physical, mental, and emotional wellness and having a sense of control, confidence, independence, and satisfaction in their lives.[46]

The media is always dominated by extreme portrayals of older age, of negative versus positive stereotypes. But even the benevolent images of older age can be viewed as negative, because they define an entire group of people indiscriminately. While there are accounts of "exceptional" older people skydiving, bodybuilding, or running marathons in their eighties, not all individuals can live up to these expectations. These stories may have the effect of dispelling negative stereotypes and can be inspiring to younger people, although they can have an adverse effect on those in their own peer group.[47] There are positive stereotypes of older people as wise, generous, trustworthy, or doting grandparents; the kindly grandpa who takes his grandchildren fishing and offers them *grandfatherly advice*, and the caring grandmother who bakes cookies and reads stories to her grandkids. These caricatures can all have limiting, constraining effects on older people. The habit of putting all older people on a pedestal has been called *positive ageism* or *sageism*.[48]

The majority of ageist stereotypes are negative. Many of them are gender-specific, denigrating older people on the basis of both age and gender. Insults that are predominantly used against older men include *codger, curmudgeon, fogey, fossil, fool, coot, geezer, goat, goose, fuddy duddy, windbag,* and *old timer.* As discussed above, the insults are intensified if preceded by *old, boring old, silly old,* or *stupid old.* Contrary to the stereotype that older people are not sexually active, there is social disapproval toward older men who express an interest in sex, and they are seen as perverted, depraved, and disgusting: a *dirty old man, dirty old pig, old pervert,* or *old lecher.* These terms are contrasted with *old maid* and *spinster,* labels that imply celibacy in women and suggest a paradox that an older woman is ridiculed if she is not sexually active, while an older man is condemned if he is.[49]

Stereotypes portray older women as objectionable and reflect sexism as well as ageism. Older woman-specific insults include *battle-axe, shrew,* and *harridan.* These insults are also intensified when prefaced with *old,* such as *old bag, old broad,* and *old bitch.* Older women may be depicted as demanding, pushy, nagging, snappy, bossy, interfering, impatient, bitter, and busybodies. These traits are exemplified in characters on popular television shows, such as Thelma Harper from *Mama's Family,* Estelle Costanza in *Seinfeld,* Marie Barone from *Everybody Loves Raymond,* Sophia Petrillo in *The Golden Girls,* and Gladys Kravitz, the nosy neighbor on *Bewitched.* Ageism is generally trivialized in mainstream culture, and television, movies, and advertisements often create and perpetuate stereotypes of older people. Many insults assign undesirable physical features to older women, including *crone, witch,* and *hag.* Some woman-specific terms involve animal metaphors, including (old) *cow, crow, nag, sow,* and *bat.* Derogatory bird-related metaphors suggest that older women are unappealing and unattractive. Descriptions for a younger woman are (hot) *bird* or *chick,* but disparaging terms for an older woman are (old) *boiler, biddy,* or a *turkey.* She is said to be *no spring chicken* or a *tough old bird.*

It is a common saying that *beauty has no age limit,* although at the same time people don't want to *look their age* or *show signs of age.* In their attempts to *look younger* people search for the *fountain of* youth, *the secret to eternal youth*, or the *elixir of youth*. The phrase *anti-aging* reinforces the idea that aging is a disease or condition to be fixed, similar to the use of *anti-* in anti-anxiety medication, anti-fungal spray, or anti-inflammatory medicine. Aging is "treated" with anti-aging products and procedures. The beauty industry demonizes aging, and advertisements tell us that we need to *battle aging, fight aging*, and *wage a war against aging* by using *anti-aging* and *age-defying* products that promise to *erase the signs of aging* or even *reverse the aging process*. There are a few positive sayings about wrinkles, that they are *laugh lines* that *tell the story of a person's life*, but by and large, they are perceived as the major sign of aging that need to be eradicated. In this way, *anti-aging* reveals a subtle acceptance of ageism, as we do not imagine products that are *anti-* to other categories of society. In 2017, *Allure* magazine announced it would stop using the term *anti-aging* in light of these negative associations.[50]

Commentators observe that there is a double standard of aging that is harsher on women than men, suggesting that age is kinder to men than to women.[51] It is said that as men age, they become *distinguished, dignified*, and *rugged*, while their wrinkles and scars *add character*. In women they are viewed as blemishes and imperfections. Men are allowed to look older, while women are pressured to stay *forever young*. To age is to somehow fail or lose something. Changes in appearance are one of the most deeply felt aspects of aging. In particular, the loss of physical attractiveness is of great concern to many women.[52] As their youth and beauty fade, women believe that they become overlooked, ignored, and invisible in society. In their fight to stay visible, many women try to stave off the ravages of time by using anti-aging products: make-up, skin care, diets, dying their gray hair, and undergoing procedures such as injectables or plastic surgery, but they are then criticized as being vain and superficial for worrying about their looks.

Author Susan Sontag once wrote that women are, "Old as soon as they are no longer very young."[53] Women are valued for their youth and attractiveness but devalued as they age. Their sexual value drops when they are no longer *young and hot*. During a Howard Stern interview in 2002, 56-year-old Donald Trump said that he typically dumps his girlfriends when they reach the age of 35, because "it's checkout time."[54] In general, there is the stereotype that men retain their sex appeal longer than women, who quickly become *too old*. In another Howard Stern interview, actor Olivia Wilde revealed that she was rejected for a role in the movie *The Wolf of Wall Street*, because she was considered to be "too old" at the age of 28.[55] Hollywood is dominated by ageism and sexism. The industry defines female actors by their age and has a preference for young starlets. At the age of 37, American actor Maggie Gyllenhall was informed that she was considered "too old" to play the lover of a 55-year-old man.[56] It is a common complaint that female actors are no longer offered leading roles after the age of 40, while male actors are often paired with women young enough to be their daughters or granddaughters.

The terms *MILF* ("Mother I'd Like to Fuck"), *GILF* ("Grandmother I'd Like to Fuck"), *soccer mom*, and *yummy mummy* not only objectify and fetishize mothers, and middle-aged or older women, but also imply that normally, older women are no longer sexy or desirable. Calling an older person *grandpa*, *gramps*, *pops*, *grandma*, or *granny* can be offensive because the person in question may not have any children, let alone grand-children. These terms are often used as insults, to imply that some-one is old enough to be a grandparent. *Grandmother* and *grandfather* have connotations of older age, suggesting that the woman or man is old enough to have not only children, but also grandchildren. These traditional labels embody the stereotypes of old age, and some grandparents dislike using them, because they make them "feel old." Actor Goldie Hawn revealed her reluctance to be called *grandmother*, because the word has "so many connota-tions of old age and decrepitude," and so her son decided she would be called *Glam-ma* instead.[57] Many modern grandmothers prefer using trendy nicknames, such as *G-mom*, *Glamother*, *Gigi*, or *Mimi*, while some grandfathers prefer *G.P.*, *G-dad*, or *Granddude*. Foreign-language titles are popular too, such as *nonna*, Italian for "grandmother," or *bubee*, which is "grandmother" in Yiddish. Other grandparents prefer to be called by their first names, or to invent a nickname that is original and meaningful to their family.[58]

Many women over 30 experience aging anxiety when they are warned that their *biological clock* is ticking, and they are running out of time to start a family. Today, more women focus on education and career before childbearing, and then seek the help of assisted reproductive technologies such as in vitro fertilization (IVF), so many women are having children in their late thirties, early forties, and beyond. In 2017, at the age of 50, musician Janet Jackson gave birth to a boy, in what was termed a *geriatric pregnancy*.[59] Most of the terminology surrounding "older pregnancy" is unflattering. In clinical terms, a pregnant woman over the age of 35 is said to be of *advanced maternal age*. *Elderly primigravida* sounds like a serious illness, but it means "a woman who goes into pregnancy for the first time at the age of 35 or older."[60] *Elderly multigravida* means second (or more) pregnancy in a woman who will be 35 years of age or older at her expected date of delivery. Not only is there a biological deadline for childbearing, but there is also a social "deadline." Parents who have children after the age of 40 often experience social stigma.[61] They may be told they are *too old* to have children at their age, or strangers may assume that older parents are actually grandparents.

Fertility is associated with youth, and there is a social emphasis on women as child bearers. As discussed above, *spinster* and *old maid* suggest unmarried and celibate, while they also imply an older woman who has no children. As we saw in Chapter 2, women are often defined by their relationships as wife, mother, and grandmother, and are judged when they do not fulfill these traditional roles. Terms such as *childless* and *barren* inspire a sense of pity and failure, while *infertile*, *sterile*, and *fruitless* suggest that a woman is unproductive, purposeless, or somehow defective. For these reasons, *childfree* is often preferred, because it implies choice and freedom. The cessation of menstruation, the end of childbearing years, is ominously called *menopause*, and is often perceived as losing one's womanhood. Menopause is dreaded, resented for its symptoms of mood swings and hot flashes, and a woman's fears of losing her sex drive and her sexual organs becoming *dried up*, or *shriveled like a prune*. Menopause is socially tabooed and referred to by the clinical term *climacteric*, or known euphemistically as *the mid-life change, the change of life*, or *the change*.[62]

Names for single female adults without children have negative connotations. In the fourteenth century, *spinster* simply meant "A woman who spins" yarn or other materials for a living.[63] By the eighteenth century, *spinster* referred to women who were considered past an age where it was deemed appropriate for them to be married.[64] Today, *spinster, old maid, husbandless, schoolmarm, cat lady*, and related terms suggest a prudish, repressed, old-fashioned, tragic older woman who is sad, lonely, unattractive, and *on the shelf*. Rather than stating plainly that a woman is unmarried, they also imply that she is no longer wanted and undesirable. In contrast, an unmarried man is a *bachelor*, which often has positive implications. *Bachelor* also dates back to the fourteenth century. One of the first recorded usages is in Geoffrey Chaucer's *Canterbury Tales*, in which the 20-year-old Squire is described as "a lovyere and a lusty bacheler," who spends his time dancing, singing, jousting, and chasing women.[65] *Bachelor* and *eligible bachelor* (note there is no equivalent *eligible spinster*) have connotations of youth and vigor, and suggest a man who can still choose to get married, unless he is a *confirmed bachelor* who never intends to marry. (This is also a euphemism for a gay man.) However, both bachelors and spinsters may be asked, *Why aren't you married?* with the assumption there must be something "wrong" with them. Positive alternatives to spinster have been suggested, such as *unclaimed jewels, career girls*, and *bachelor girls*.[66] In 2005, the British Civil Partnership Act dropped the terms *spinster* and *bachelor* in favor of *single*. However, they are still in popular usage, as evident in the phrases *bachelor pad* and *bachelor party*, and the reality TV dating game show *The Bachelor* (which inspired the spin-off series *The Bachelorette*).

As discussed in Chapter 2, terms of address for women imply their marital status. *Mrs.* denotes a married woman, *Miss* implies a single woman, whereas *Mr.* does not reveal whether a man is married or not. For women, these honorifics can also be age markers. *Miss* usually implies a younger woman, comparable to German *Fraulein*, Spanish *Senorita*, and French *Mademoiselle*. As a form of address, *Madam* and its abbreviation *Ma'am* are often intended to be polite or deferential, but they can also be offensive, because they typically refer to older women, implying that they are no longer considered young enough to be addressed as *Miss*. In an episode of the British TV comedy *Absolutely Fabulous*, the character Patsy Stone is on a plane to France for a vacation. During the trip, a flight attendant addresses her as *Madam*. Patsy quickly corrects her with, "-*moiselle*, Mademoiselle!", offended by the suggestion that she is no longer considered to be a young woman.[67] *Ma'am* is a sign of respect and tradition in the US military, but among the non-military it can be interpreted as dismissive, distant, or even patronizing. During a committee hearing in 2010, Senator Barbara Boxer was addressed as *Ma'am* by Brigadier General Michael Walsh, to which she responded, "Could you say senator instead of ma'am? . . . I worked so hard to get that title. So I'd appreciate it."[68]

In Western society today, there is a social convention that a wife should be younger than her husband. If a woman violates that rule and finds a sexual mate who is younger than her, he is often labeled a *toy boy* and she is a *cougar* or *jaguar* who has *robbed the cradle*, which are all terms that suggest predatory behavior. The trope of *women who like older men* is more socially accepted. However, there is social stigma attached to a man who pairs up with a much younger woman when there is a significant disparity in their ages; he is said to be a *sugar daddy*, while she is a *sugar baby* with *daddy issues* or a *gold-digger*. He is a *cradle-snatche*r, who is socially admonished with *He's old enough to be her father*, while *She is young enough to be his daughter*. The pair may even be confused as father and daughter, such as married couple Courtney and Vann Thornton, who have a 25-year age gap between them and started the Instagram hashtag #HusbandNotDad in response to negative reactions to their relationship.[69]

There is also the distinctively male stereotype of a man having a *mid-life crisis* when he abandons his middle-aged wife for a younger woman. The phrase conjures imagery of a graying or balding, middle-aged man driving a red sports car with his young mistress by his side. This transitional phase is characterized by career disillusionment, anxiety, depression, desperation, regret, boredom, a loss of identity, infidelity, and divorce (although the phenomenon is less acknowledged in women).[70] Couples who separate at mid-life or later are known colloquially as *silver separators*, while divorcing at mid-life or later is often called a *gray divorce*. If a man then pairs with a younger woman it is said that he has *traded up*, and his replacement wife is perceived as a kind of prize, a *trophy wife*.

In 2011, Virgin America capitalized on the stereotype of a wife as a commodity to be replaced and upgraded to a younger model. The airline launched an advertising campaign with the slogans, "Fool around with a younger, hotter airline," and, "Dump your old airline for a younger, hotter one."[71] This is not the first time that the Virgin brand has been accused of ageism. In 2005, eight flight attendants in Brisbane, Australia, won an age discrimination case against airline Virgin Blue, who refused them jobs because of their ages. That the applicants were deemed too old for the job was positioned euphemistically as they lacked the "Virgin flair."[72] To combat this ageist reputation, in 2015, Virgin hired Katrine Haynes, 59-year-old grandmother of 11, who became a star of their TV documentary "Virgin Atlantic: Up in the Air."[73]

Prejudice against hiring older workers is a common form of institutional ageism. The airline industry is notorious for this type of ageism, where there was a former policy of hiring 20-year-old women as *stewardesses*, as they were then called, but reassigning them to different jobs, or even firing them, by the age of 32.[74] In

1967, the United States Age Discrimination in Employment Act (ADEA) was created to prevent ageism in the workplace (although mandatory retirement ages for flight attendants were not abolished until 1970). Today, these anti-discrimination laws protect applicants and employees age 40 and above from discrimination on the basis of age in hiring; promotion; termination; wages; or terms, conditions, or privileges of employment.[75] There are similar laws prohibiting age discrimination in Australia, New Zealand, Canada, and Europe.

However, ageism in the workplace is notoriously difficult to prove. Age-based employment discrimination is illegal, although subtle ageist remarks are not, and employers tend to use euphemisms to avoid using explicitly ageist language. Employees are dismissed, not for being too old, but out of a need for *fresh blood, young blood,* or to *bring in the young guns.*[76] Job advertisements state a preference for *juniors, recent graduates, new graduates,* or *digital natives,* and those who can fit in with *a younger team, a new environment, a young company,* or *a startup culture.* This terminology implies that employers are seeking similar applicants and sends a clear message that older applicants need not apply. Code words or language workarounds are also used to conceal age discrimination.[77] Rejecting job candidates or firing employees with the justifications that they are *not a good fit* or because *we're going in a different direction* can disguise all kinds of prejudice. It is clearly against the law to advertise for a "young" applicant, so to avoid mentioning age blatantly, employers seek people who are described as *vibrant, fresh, innovative, enthusiastic, dynamic, passionate, ambitious, motivated,* and *energetic.*[78]

These descriptions run counter to the stereotypes of middle-aged and older people as being *burnt out, old school, worn out, washed up, stale,* and *past their shelf life.* Another assumption about older people and the workplace is that they are unable to use technology or are even scared of it. They are dismissed as *Luddites* or *technophobes,* who are *behind the times, not up to date,* or *not current on trends.* They are compared metaphorically to outdated technology, as *redundant, out-of-date,* and *obsolete.* In contrast, younger people are perceived as *tech savvy* and are assumed to be *sharper* and *brighter* when it comes to technology. Facebook founder Mark Zuckerberg once said, "Young people are just smarter."[79] Ageism is rampant in Silicon Valley, California, where applicants find it difficult to secure employment beyond the age of 30.[80] In general, people over the age of 40 are often considered to be *too old* to be in the tech industry, while people over the age of 50 who use the Internet frequently are dubbed *silver surfers.*

You're too old is the underlying message of all ageist language. To say someone is *too old* excludes or rejects people, implying they are no longer useful or valuable beyond a certain age. They are simply *too old to matter.* The flipside of this is the upbeat saying; *you're never too old to ...* (*try something new*, etc.). Self-referentially, people say they are *too old for this sort of thing* or *getting too old for this shit*, which have implications of being "fed up" and not putting up with something bad anymore. However, the connotations of *too old* are usually negative. As already discussed, by a certain age, women are perceived as too old to be a mother, or too old to play a love interest in Hollywood. Someone can be considered too old for a particular career move, such as *too old to go back to school* or *too old to start a business*. However, what is considered *too old* is subjective, and being perceived as too old for something doesn't necessarily imply that the person is old in terms of age. Being *too old* is relative. Careers in professional sports tend to have early expiration dates, when an athlete no longer has the strength or stamina required to compete. In 2009, after 13 years of playing professional football, New England Patriot's linebacker Tedy Bruschi retired at the age of 36, because he was "simply too old" and found his "body doesn't heal as quickly."[81]

The idea that we should no longer do certain things by a certain age is another variant of being considered to be too old. *She shouldn't wear a bikini at her age*, says that the woman is considered *too old* to look good in a bikini. Western society is youth-oriented and judgmental, and there are cultural expectations of age appropriateness when it comes to fashion and behavior, which are mostly driven by the fashion industry. Fashion magazines advise women on *how to dress for your age*, and list fashion *no-nos* and style *dos and don'ts* based on age. These fashion "rules" dictate that women over a certain age (usually 40, 50, or 60) should no longer wear mini skirts, skinny jeans, or too much make-up, and they shouldn't reveal their legs or cleavage anymore; or they are said to be committing fashion faux pas. When a woman grows older, her hair length is expected to be shorter, while her dresses are expected to become longer.

There is social pressure to look younger, but also to *act your age*. People (especially women) who try to *act younger* than their years are mocked. In UK and Australian English, *mutton dressed as lamb* is a disapproving way to describe an older woman who tries to keep up with fashion by dressing in a style that is considered to be more suitable to a younger woman.[82] French fashion designer Gabrielle "Coco" Chanel is credited with the phrase, "Nothing makes a woman look so old as trying desperately hard to look young." Conversely, younger people are derided for wearing *old-looking* clothing that is considered to be frumpy and unfashionable. Light-blue, high-waisted, loose jeans worn by middle-aged men are called *dad jeans*, while a dowdy, relaxed-fit cardigan or sweater is a *grandpa sweater*. Younger women are derided for wearing high-waisted, full coverage underpants that are nicknamed *granny knickers* or *granny panties*, because they are deemed to be unflattering, unsexy, and old.

There are ageist assumptions about the appearance of older people. Older women are stereotyped as wearing their hair short, permed, and often dyed an unnatural shade of blue, as suggested by the phrases *blue rinse set*, *blue rinse crowd*, and *silver brigade*. Older men are stereotyped as bald or balding, or if they still have (presumably gray) hair, that they style it with out-of-fashion hair products such as Brylcreem or pomade. Older people are thought to only wear clothing of their time or era, and not to buy anything new or modern. There is the caricature of the *little old lady* wearing an old-fashioned dress, stockings, hat, gloves, and a string of pearls, who has a musty or stale smell about her. Even perfumes are deemed to be appropriate for certain age brackets. Sweet or fruity fragrances are perceived as *youthful*, while floral, powdery scents, such as lavender and rose, are classified as *classic* and *mature* or are derided as *old lady perfumes* that make a woman *smell like a grandmother*.[83] What is deemed a *youthful* or *old* perfume appears to be a matter of what was popular when the person came of age. In accordance with changing fashions, certain proper names are considered to "sound old" to some communities. Female names such as Ethel, Doris, and Fanny are sometimes considered to be *old lady* names, while Wilfred, Cecil, and Percival might be considered *old man* names. It appears to be the case that young-sounding names are simply names that are common for babies, children, and youths, while names that have fallen out of popular usage sound dated.

Stereotypes exist about not only the way that older people look (or should look), but also the way they sound. Age-related voice deterioration is known colloquially as *old people's voice*. An aging voice is variously described as breathy, hoarse, croaky, weak, wavering, strained, or shaky. In fact, there are some physiological effects of aging on a person's voice, which affect about 30 percent of the population.[84] An old-sounding voice often comes with changes in frequency. Pitch usually increases with older age in men, which is attributed to atrophy of the muscles in the vocal folds.[85] Pitch decreases over time with women, often due to hormonal changes. Specific conditions can make someone sound "old," such as presbyphonia, which causes decreased loudness and increased roughness and breathiness.

Despite the many negative perceptions of aging, there are several positive adages about age. It is said that age is *just a number*, while *old is a state of mind*. It is held that *you're only as old as you feel*, *age is an attitude*, and it is only *if you think old, you'll be old*. But for the most part, our language shows that age matters. We live in a society that is age-sensitive. Age is experienced most directly on our birthdays. Each birthday, but especially those round numbers ushering in a new decade, sounds a new defeat.[86] There is a desire to be *the right age*, while it is undesirable to be on the *wrong side* of 30, 40, or 50. Being a *thirtysomething* or *30-ish* can be a euphemism for being in one's late thirties, and therefore approaching 40 and close to being *over the hill*.

Birthdays are a cause for reflection on age and aging, and are often a time for being the butt of ageist jokes. Having a birthday seems to give license for others to tease, and there is an assumption that if you are close to someone, you can joke about their age. Humorous birthday cards, mugs, t-shirts, and gag gifts present ageist messages. The *Life Begins at 40* cards with positive messages cannot compete with the abundance of memes that mock waning physical and mental abilities, or a flagging sex drive.[87] One such novelty is an "Over The Hill Survival Kit In A Can," which contains "marbles – to replace the ones you've already lost," a "notepad – to write things down before you forget," a "nametag – so you don't forget who you are," "teeth – for when you lose yours," and "soap – to wash away your age."[88] Many of the perpetrators of ageist humor argue that it is not intended to be malicious, and it is defended as *only a joke*. But it is hard to imagine racist jokes being met with the same benign acceptance society extends to ageist jokes.

Growing older is often joked about, but at the same time, there is a taboo surrounding the discussion of age. At birthday parties, guests are requested to avoid mentioning the person's age. Many people of *a certain age* become self-conscious about their age and embarrassed to reveal the figure. There is a social convention to never ask, *What's your age?*, a question which is perceived as personal and impolite, especially when asked of a woman. It might elicit an indignant response such as, *Don't you know you're not supposed to ask a woman her age?* In particular, women experience growing older with a sense of shame and humiliation. As a result, age denial is common, and being dishonest about one's age is a frequent reaction to ageism in society today.[89] People are often treated differently when their true age is revealed, and some believe that they must lie about their age to obtain, or keep, a job.

American comedian Lucille Ball once said that, "The secret to staying young is to live honestly, eat slowly, and lie about your age."[90] For the purposes of seeking employment, or out of pride, some celebrities and athletes lie about their age. They occasionally represent themselves as older, but usually younger than they really are. Claiming to be 21 years old when The Spice Girls' first album *Spice* was released in 1996, Geri Halliwell, better known as "Ginger Spice," was quickly nicknamed *Old Spice* when it was revealed that she was actually 25.[91] To avoid revealing their actual age, some people joke that they are *turning 21 again* (or 29, etc.). To avoid naming age directly, 50 years of age might be expressed as *21 again but with 29 years experience*. When she married for the second time at the age of 45, American singer Aretha Franklin announced in an interview that she was "32 and holding."[92]

Some people feel they must present themselves as younger than they are in order to find a partner. Dishonesty is prevalent on online dating sites, with many people lying about their physical features, especially height, weight, and age, and often presenting themselves as taller, slimmer, and younger than they really are.[93] Other people lie about their age on social media or hide their age from view. The almost-defunct networking site Myspace insisted on displaying age, so many users set their age at the limit of 99 years. For some, this was to avoid revealing their true age, although underage users also set their age at 99 to avoid automated filters that would otherwise block them from joining.[94] Typically, people lie about their age out of insecurity, a fear of being rejected, or a belief that their age is no one else's business.

Some people misrepresent their age visually by posting outdated photographs of themselves on dating profiles or social media.[95] Others decide not to display photographs at all, but to represent themselves with a digital symbol called an avatar. This image can take any form the person chooses, and men tend to use pictures of superhero characters, while women often choose characters from fantasy, such as fairies or angels. In doing so, they are giving themselves the facade of youth by way of youthful imagery. Controlling a public image and maintaining one's apparent youth in pictures is not only a digital age trend. In historical paintings, aging monarchs are portrayed in their prime at the hunt, as youthful warriors, or as powerful sovereigns dressed in imposing robes and regalia. Portraits of Queen Elizabeth I of England (1533–1603) present her as a pearly-skinned Renaissance beauty, although in later years she suffered the loss of her hair and teeth, and pockmarks left by smallpox scarred her face. In 1596, when she was now described as "very aged," she issued a law ordering the destruction of paintings, engravings, and woodcuts that depicted her as an old woman, which were to her a "great offence."[96]

Some common expressions about appearance may be intended to be complimentary, but actually express distaste for aging. They may not be intended to offend, but they often do. *You haven't changed a bit* is a greeting to someone who hasn't been seen in a while. Although flattering on the surface, this phrase can sound insincere and further imply that growing older is something negative. Other sayings are thought to be compliments but can be perceived as ageist, because they imply that being younger is better. The popular notion of the *new old* is that people are looking and acting younger for longer nowadays, and that *40 is the new 30, 50 is the new 40,* and *60 is the new 50.* These catch-phrases suggest that the person's actual age is somehow undesirable, and they also deny years of life experience. Related expressions include *she is a young 70-year-old* and *he is 80 years young,* which can be seen as patronizing and disingenuous.

There is the idea that some people can "pass" for being younger than they actually are. For example, *She is 50 but can easily pass for 40, You could pass for much younger than 40, But you don't look that old,* and, *Can you believe she's 70?* These phrases all suggest that there is a specific way that people *should* look at their age. They also imply that looking young is good, while looking older is bad. Replying with, *You're not old* or *You're still young,* in response to people who refer to themselves as *old* also implies that being young is good, while being older is bad. The expressions *young at heart, just a kid at heart,* and *old soul, young spirit* imply younger thinking or behavior, despite an older age or appearance. This kind of backhanded praise represents a type of covert ageism that is called *benevolent ageism*.[97] On the surface, these sayings appear to be complimentary, but when the underlying meaning is scrutinized, they can be considered insulting.

Another example of benevolent ageism is the common expression; *She is beautiful . . . for an older woman*. Some might construe this as a compliment and that the person represents someone for others to admire or emulate as they age.[98] For others, the qualifier suggests that it is remarkable for an older woman to be beautiful. It also diminishes the compliment by suggesting that the bar is set lower for older women, meaning "She's beautiful, considering the fact that she is old." In the novel *Gone Girl*, heroine Amy Elliott Dunne writes in her diary that she is "closer to forty than thirty; I'm not just pretty anymore, I am *pretty for my age*."[99] If the compliment is that someone is *beautiful* or *pretty*, then the person's age should be irrelevant. The caveat *for her age* further implies that it is bad to look her age, and that if she looked the age she actually is, she would not look good. There is immense social pressure placed on people, especially women, to *age gracefully*, *age well*, *stay young*, and look younger than their "real age." Those who do not are admonished in phrases such as: *she has aged badly*, and *she looks old for her age*. *You look older than your age* is a compliment when said to someone very young, but it is an insult when said to a mature adult.[100]

The qualifier *for their age* is not only used in regards to appearance, but also to refer to skills and abilities. For example, *He is fit . . . for his age*, *Her memory is good . . . for her age*, and *He dresses well . . . for his age*. These phrases suggest that these older people are exceptions to the rule and expresses surprise at their abilities, which are considered to be uncharacteristic for their age. It is a common misconception that age somehow limits capabilities. Phrases such as: *He's still so full of life*, *She still cooks her own meals at the age of 80*, and *He's still up and around at the age of 90* suggest that routine behavior is somehow extraordinary in older people and expects that, at their age, they would be incapable of everyday activity. These expressions assume that older people are weak and fragile, simply because of their age. Age is often blamed for inability, rather than state of health or fitness, as in the comment, *I'm 70 now, so I can't drive anymore.* Decline is attributed to age when illness is instead the cause, and many so-called "old-age diseases" that manifest later in life are actually caused by behavioral or environmental exposure earlier in life.[101]

Age is a metaphor for disease associated with old age in the phrase *he died of old age*, because old age is not a cause of death in and of itself. Age is also blamed for experiences common to all people regardless of age, such as forgetfulness: *At my age, I'm allowed to forget some things.* But it can be offensive to qualify a description in terms of someone's age, such as a *quick-witted 75-year-old.* Mentioning a person's age is usually irrelevant, in much the same way that referencing race or disability is irrelevant. Many older people don't want to be recognized for their age, but for their accomplishments. Using clichéd descriptors such as *sharp-witted* or *sharp as a tack* imply that these qualities need special mention because they are unusual in people of these ages. Certain hackneyed terms are commonly used to describe older people as energetic and youthful, including *spry, sassy, spirited,* and *feisty,* which are dated words that are typically used in this context only and can be construed as mocking or patronizing.

There are many common phrases that show patronizing attitudes toward older people, including *little old lady, little old man, little old dear,* and *sweet old lady.* Calling an older woman *young lady* or an older man *young man* can be perceived as sarcastic and condescending. Describing an older person as *sweet, little, tiny, adorable,* or *cute* is demeaning and suggests that they are seen as diminished and of little importance, and also ascribes child-like attributes to them.[102] Some terms of endearment are not so endearing. Using diminutives such as *sweetie, sugar, honey, dear, darling, dearie,* and *love* with older people can be seen as overly familiar and disrespectful, especially when strangers use them. These names are often intended to be flattering or respectful, to show care, or even be playful; however, they may be construed as condescending and disrespectful.

This belittling way of talking down to older people has been called *elderspeak*. This is a form of infantilization, the treatment of old age as a *second childhood*.[103] Aside from the use of pet names, verbal infantilization may involve addressing older people as though they are children, such as *good girl* and *good boy, Did you behave yourself?*, or using the *royal we*, as in *How are we doing today?* This kind of *baby talk* is often used when speaking with older people. It features simplified speech, exaggerated pitch, speaking slowly, and in a demeaning, emotional tone.[104] Terminology associated with infants is also used, such as referring to *diapers* instead of *disposable underwear*, or *bib* instead of *smock* or *clothing protector*. Infantilization can involve conflating age with disability, by assuming older people are deaf and speaking to them at an overly high volume, supposing that older people are cognitively impaired and need to have their memories "refreshed" on each visit, or ignoring them by talking about them as if they were not there.

Infantilization is often carried out by staff members of hospitals, long-term care facilities, and other services for older people. This age-inappropriate language is often deemed to be unprofessional, because the recipients are paying clients. It is preferable to ask how a person wants to be addressed, especially for older people who may have a loss of control over their lives and are offered few choices. Treating older people as children implies they have made a backward movement to earlier developmental stages, with no recognition of the lifetime of experience that separates them from children.[105] Infantilization might appear to be caring or nurturing behavior, but it can be demoralizing, disrespectful, and humiliating. The cumulative effects of the conceptual linkage between old age and childhood can lead to social responses such as depression, a loss of identity, withdrawal, and in a self-fulfilling prophecy, it can lead to child-like behaviors.[106]

A sense of isolation and alienation are major problems for older people who have often lost friends and family and are alone. As

more people live longer, they are becoming increasingly discon-
nected from society. In the past, generations lived together or
nearby, while today, older people live separately and distantly,
and often in long-term care facilities.[107] Younger people distance
themselves from older people. For the most part, older people are
segregated from society, widening the generational gap, and inciting a fear of aging and dying. A fear of death may have its basis in
the social separation from death, which no longer happens in the
home but in hospitals and long-term care facilities, which are
unfamiliar and unsettling places. They have been called *homes*,
nursing homes, *old people's homes*, or *old folk's homes*, terms that
are now perceived as derogatory. The preferred names for these
places include *adult care homes*, *skilled nursing facilities*, *residential facilities*, *assisted living facilities*, or *older adult communities*.
Hospice care, healthcare for people who are nearing the end of life,
is renamed *comfort care*, while the words *death* and *dying* are
tabooed and avoided. Instead, caregivers talk about *transitioning*
or a patient being *imminent* in place of "dying," and *passed*,
expired, or *gone* instead of "dead."

The terminology surrounding adult care can sound cold and
clinical, so euphemistic names are often used to make these places
sound more appealing, and to ease the guilt and remorse of adult
children who abandon the care of their parents to others.[108] Some
current examples from Florida in the United States include
"Paradise Village", "Golden Age Manor," "Silver Lining Estates,"
"Sunny Days Retirement Home," and "Our Dream Retirement
Home." Some areas are traditional enclaves for retirees due to
their lower tax and crime rates, lower cost of living, access to
healthcare, good weather, and larger populations of older people.
A number of these places have become synonymous with retire-
ment, such as Queensland, Australia, or Florida in the United
States. In an episode of the sitcom *Seinfeld*, Jerry Seinfeld joked,
"My parents didn't want to move to Florida, but they turned sixty,
and that's the law."[109]

Adult care homes are stigmatized, as are the people who live in
them. Likened to inmates in prison or patients in hospital, older

people in long-term care facilities live in small, impersonalized spaces. They often lose their sense of freedom, their preferences are dismissed or ignored, and they are excluded from making decisions about their own lives. They feel dehumanized and treated as less valuable members of society. Older people are thought of as being close to the end of their lives, with their time running out, but in contradiction, they have a lot of time on their hands.[110] Many older people who are institutionalized spend this time in passive inactivity, with little communication or constructive activity. They are stereotyped as sitting around, feeling bored, watching television, playing shuffleboard, and *killing time* as they wait for death.[111] So, the end-of-life housing experience has been likened to living in *God's waiting room*.[112]

Ageism is embedded in everyday language. Ageist language reflects anxieties and beliefs about getting old and reveals that aging is viewed with disgust, contempt, and fear. As a result, older people are often viewed through this same lens. Just like racism or sexism, ageism has a detrimental impact on people. It devalues the dignity and worth of older people and leaves them feeling excluded, ignored, or rejected. Society has an obligation to be concerned about the welfare of older people, who constitute a growing proportion of our population. People are living much longer than previous generations, and as life expectancy continues to improve, it is time to rethink our attitudes and beliefs about aging to create a more age-inclusive society. Younger people usually don't see themselves as getting old, but everyone is growing older. Aging is an ongoing process that everyone experiences and is not just a label that we attach to older people. Unlike other forms of discrimination, ageism cuts across society's classifications of race, gender, sexual orientation, and religion. Ageism is the only form of prejudice that we will all encounter, if we live long enough. So it seems counterproductive to be prejudiced against a group to which we will all belong.

Conclusion

Walk a Mile in Someone's Shoes

This book is a collection of offensive words and phrases, although it does not profess to be a comprehensive catalog or an encyclopedia of offensive language. Of course, it is not intended to inspire people to be offensive by showing them how to offend, or to provide ammunition for bigots. It is a guide to recognizing offensive language, in our own words, both past and present. In particular, this book explores the ways in which discrimination and prejudice are reflected through everyday language. Racism, sexism, ableism, ageism, and other -isms in language are identified and described, along with homophobia and religious discrimination. (And we discover that there is a lot of overlap and interrelatedness across these types of prejudice.) Collectively, this kind of language is shown to be offensive, because it reflects negative attitudes and beliefs toward groups of people.

Language that is considered to be offensive changes across time, culture, and context. There are many different types of offensive language, which are of varying degrees of offensiveness. As we have discussed, racist language is considered to be especially taboo and offensive today. Some language is blatantly or overtly offensive, including insults, ethnic slurs, and hate speech. This type of language is usually intended to be insulting. (Banter is an exception, as a playful form of insulting, although this is sometimes used as an excuse to defend the use of derogatory language.) Other examples are more covertly offensive, such as outdated labels, stereotypes, generalizations, and myths about groups of people. This type of language can reveal "everyday," "casual," or "hidden" bias that is often so deeply internalized and normalized that some people do not even realize it is offensive.

In this book we look at the linguistic processes that underlie offensive language, including stereotyping, stigmatization, demonization, vilification, othering, and dehumanization. By unpacking the meaning and usage of offensive words and phrases, we gain insight into why they are considered to be offensive. We also go back in time to learn what these terms once meant, and what they mean today, especially to the communities to whom they refer. We find that language reveals social attitudes, beliefs, and values at a point in time, but often reflects those of the societies that came before us. We discover that some words and phrases that weren't offensive became so over time because of their negative associations. Less frequently, some words improve in meaning and lose their offensiveness, or the target community takes them back. (But only under certain conditions.) We also find that meaning is not permanent or fixed. Meaning is not universal. This book is simply a snapshot of our ever-evolving language, which will continue to shift and change.

This book intends to be helpful in the workplace, at school or university, within families and communities, and for people in both their public and private lives. It aims to be useful in legal and political arenas, in publishing and advertising, and to the media. Offensiveness might seem like a linguistic minefield that we must tiptoe around, but it is simply not true that we *can't say anything anymore*. This book navigates this maze, proposing inclusive and preferred terminology in response to exclusive and offensive language. Rather than limiting or restricting our vocabulary, this provides us with more choices in our communication. In individual situations, we can always ask the people involved, "What is your preferred term?" We can listen to them, and show politeness and respect with the choices we make, because the words we choose reflect our attitudes. We are responsible for not only our intentions, but also the way our words are perceived. However, this book does not engage in censorship or smother free speech. It does not prescribe "PC language" or tell people how to speak. It does not proselytize or preach. This book aims to help readers to spot offensive language and to understand why it is offensive. It also encourages us to "check ourselves" and recognize prejudice and bias in ourselves, and others. It urges us to take accountability, so we are not offenders or complicit bystanders to discrimination and prejudice. As the saying goes: Be an ally.

Despite the fact that meaning in language is not static, we actually can *keep up with what's offensive*. Human rights groups, advocates, and stakeholders constantly update us in this regard. As seen throughout this book, advancements in this area have already been made. Future readers might leaf through these pages and think, "Well, obviously we don't use this kind of language anymore!" We can only hope that one day, the prejudiced language featured in this book will be a thing of the past. But as various groups fight for their equality and acquire more rights, there is resistance, and even backlash, against change. Some people actively try to reverse the progress. They fear that equal rights for other groups means fewer rights for their group. Other people deny that discrimination exists anymore and assert that equal rights have already been achieved. However, this book shows that prejudice is still pervasive, and that it changes its appearance over time.

This book is about raising awareness of prejudice in language. In these days of compassion fatigue, it is also about prompting self-examination about the way we talk, and practicing empathy toward others. It is about walking a mile in someone else's shoes and taking a different perspective. It is about standing outside of ourselves and considering the world from the point of view of someone who is different to us: a woman, a person of color, an immigrant, a Muslim, a person with a disability, or an older person. It endeavors to understand their life experiences, challenges, and perspectives and the discrimination that happens to them. It gives a voice to people who are discriminated against. It also listens to the views of these people, because they are authorities on their own discrimination. We cannot tell them what to think and feel, but we can sympathize with them. We must also be humbled by the fact that we will all be discriminated against at some point in our lives, and that we will all be offended. Knowing this, it behooves us to be sensitive to the plight of others, just as we expect others to be sensitive to us. Before we accuse someone else of being *too sensitive*, perhaps we might ask: Are we not being sensitive enough?

Growing up, many people are reminded to *toughen up* by the children's nursery rhyme, *Sticks and stones may break my bones, but words will never hurt me.* This book shows that words can indeed hurt. Words can abuse, harm, and offend. Words have power. Words matter. Language has the ability to exclude people, to make them feel that they don't belong. Language can disadvantage and disempower, and be used to silence. Language can be divisive. It can demonize, dehumanize, and endanger. Through language, demagogues whip up the fears and prejudices of crowds, inciting hatred, persecution, and violence against minority groups of people. Offensive language can be a dangerous weapon used to justify and accompany human rights abuses. It is at the very root of mass murder, torture, enslavement, segregation, war, and genocide. Language can reveal people's inhumanity to one another.

But we must remain encouraged by the fact that words also have the power to achieve good in the world. Words have the ability to heal and comfort people. They can rebuild and reconcile society. Language can show solidarity and commonality. Language can reflect our diversity, it can be inclusive, and it can encourage a sense of community and belonging. Words can unite. Language can be empowering, giving a voice to the unheard. Language can express friendship and love and it can show kindness, compassion, and empathy toward others. Gifted orators have the skills to enlighten and inspire us to be better people. Language can be an instrument of justice and human rights, to promote freedom and peace. Language is a symbol of our shared humanity, and we can use it to nurture understanding, acceptance, and equality.

Notes

Introduction: You Can't Say Anything These Days

1. Thomason, Andy. 2017. A Bunch of Conservative Students Dressed Up as Babies to Protest Safe Spaces. *The Chronicle of Higher Education*. October 19. www.chronicle.com/blogs/ticker/a-bunch-of-conservative-students-dressed-up-as-babies-to-protest-safe-spaces/120706
2. Cohen, Dov. Culture of Honor. 2007. In *Encyclopedia of Social Psychology*, edited by Roy Baumeister and Kathleen D. Vohs. Sage Publishing.
3. Boswell, James. 2009 (1783). *Life of Samuel Johnson*. Penguin Classics, p. 48.
4. Sabine, Lorenzo. 2007 (1854). *Notes on Duels and Duelling*. Kessinger Publishing. p. 68.
5. Jay, Timothy. 1992. *Cursing in America: A Psycholinguistic Study of Dirty Language in the Courts, in the Movies, in the Schoolyards and on the Streets*. John Benjamins.
6. Gubo, Darara Timotewos. 2014. *Blasphemy and Defamation of Religions in a Polarized World: How Religious Fundamentalism is Challenging Fundamental Human Rights*. Lexington Books, p. 60.
7. BBC. 1989. Ayatollah Sentences Author to Death. *BBC News*. http://news.bbc.co.uk/onthisday/hi/dates/stories/february/14/newsid_2541000/2541149.stm
8. Allan, Keith (Ed.). 2019. *The Oxford Handbook of Taboo Words and Language*. Oxford University Press.
9. Rosenberg, Marshall. 2003. *Nonviolent Communication: A Language of Life*. Puddledancer Press.
10. Allan, Keith, and Burridge, Kate. 2006. *Forbidden Words: Taboo and the Censoring of Language*. Cambridge University Press.
11. Bauer, Laurie, Lieber, Rochelle, and Plag, Ingo. 2015. *The Oxford Reference Guide to English Morphology*. Oxford University Press.
12. Rolly, Paul. 2014. Paul Rolly: Blogger Fired from Language School over "Homophonia." *The Salt Lake Tribune*, July 30. https://archive.sltrib.com/article.php?id=58236366&itype=CMSID
13. Steinmetz, Sol. 2008. *Semantic Antics: How and Why Words Change Meanings*. Random House.

14. Pinker, Steven. 1994. The Game of the Name. *The Baltimore Sun.* http://
    articles.baltimoresun.com/1994–04-06/news/1994096202_1_dutch-words-
    language
15. Umstead, Alex. 2012. *An Introductory Guide to Disability Language and
    Empowerment.* Syracuse University. http://sudcc.syr.edu/resources/lan
    guage-guide.html

1 I'm Not a Racist, But …

1. Eckermann, Ali Cobby. 2018. *Too Afraid to Cry: Memoir of a Stolen
   Childhood.* Liveright.
2. Australian Human Rights and Equal Opportunities Commission. 1997. *Bringing
   Them Home: Report of the National Enquiry into the Separation of Aboriginal
   and Torres Strait Islander Children from Their Families.* www.austlii.edu.au/au/
   other/IndigLRes/stolen/index.html
3. Australian Human Rights and Equal Opportunities Commission. *Bringing
   Them Home 8.* 2007. www.humanrights.gov.au/our-work/bringing-them-
   home-8-history-northern-territory
4. Reilly, Thomas, Kaufman, Stephen, and Bodino, Angela. 2002. *Racism:
   A Global Reader. Sources and Studies in World History.* Routledge.
5. Schaefer, Richard, T. 2008. *Encyclopedia of Race, Ethnicity and Society.* Sage
   Publications.
6. Gannon, Megan. 2016. Race is a Social Construct, Scientists Argue. *Scientific
   American.* February 5. www.scientificamerican.com/article/race-is-a-social-
   construct-scientists-argue/
7. LaRocque, Emma. 1996. The Colonization of a Native Woman Scholar. In
   Women of the First Nations, edited by Christine Miller and Patricia
   Chuchryk. The University of Manitoba Press.
8. Leahy, Todd, and Wilson, Raymond. 2009. *The A to Z of Native American
   Movements.* Scarecrow Press., p. xxxiii.
9. Legislative Council and House of Representatives of New Zealand. 1868.
   Parliamentary Debates. Third Session of the Fourth Parliament, vol. 2.
   Wellington.
10. Blanchard, Pascal, Bancel, Nicolas, and Lemaire, Sandrine. 2009. *Human
    Zoos: Science and Spectacle in the Age of Empire.* Liverpool University Press.
11. Fernandez-Arnesto, Felipe. 2008. *Amerigo: The Man Who Gave His Name to
    America.* Random House.
12. Dwyer, Helen, and Burgan, Michael. 2012. *Inuit History and Culture.* Gareth
    Stevens Publishing.

13. Sacco, Nick. 2015. The Paradoxical Nature of the "Enslaved Person vs. Slave" Name Debate. *Exploring the Past.* July 10. https://pastexplore.wordpress .com/2015/07/10/the-paradoxical-nature-of-the-enslaved-person-vs-slave-name-debate/

14. Cashin, Sheryll. 2017. *Loving: Interracial Intimacy in America and the Threat to White Supremacy.* Beacon Press.

15. *OED Online.* s.v. mulatto, *n.* and *adj.* July 2018. Oxford University Press. www.oed.com

16. Jackson, Michelle Gordon. 2014. *Light, Bright and Damn Near White: Black Leaders Created by The One-Drop Rule.* Jackson Scribe Publishing Company.

17. Guglielmo, Thomas A. 2015. Desegregating Blood: A Civil Rights Struggle to Remember. *The Conversation.* February 12. http://theconversation.com/ desegregating-blood-a-civil-rights-struggle-to-remember-37480

18. Keevak, Michael. 2011. *Becoming Yellow: A Short History of Racial Thinking.* Princeton University Press.

19. *OED Online.* s.v. redskin, *n.* July 2018. Oxford University Press. www.oed.com

20. Nunberg, Geoffrey, 2014. When Slang Becomes a Slur. *The Atlantic.* June 23. https://www.theatlantic.com/entertainment/archive/2014/06/a-linguist-on-why-redskin-is-racist-patent-overturned/373198/

21. Bright, William. 2000. The Sociolinguistics of the "S-Word": Squaw in American Placenames. *A Journal of Onomastics,* 48 (3–4), 207–216.

22. Spears, Richard. 1990. *Forbidden American English.* Passport Books.

23. Houghton, Frank, and Houghton, Sharon. 2018. "Blacklists" and "Whitelists": A Salutary Warning Concerning the Prevalence of Racist Language in Discussions of Predatory Publishing. *Journal of the Medical Library Association,* 106 (4), 527–530.

24. *OED Online.* s.v. Negro, *n.* and *adj.* July 2018. Oxford University Press. www.oed.com

25. UPI. 2010. Census Bureau Defends "Negro" Addition. January 6. www.upi .com/Top_News/US/2010/01/06/Census-Bureau-defends-negro-addition/ 70241262798663/

26. *OED Online.* s.v. nigger, *n.* and *adj.* July 2018. Oxford University Press. www.oed.com

27. Lee, Sarah. 2006. Seinfeld Actor Lets Fly with Racist Tirade. *The Guardian.* November 22. www.theguardian.com/world/2006/nov/22/usa .danglaister

28. Heffernan, Virginia. 2006. Bewildered-Sounding Man and Bewildering Words. *The New York Times.* November 22. https://www.nytimes.com/ 2006/11/22/arts/television/22heff.html

29. Cooke, Jeremy. 2007. Racial Slur Banned in New York. *BBC News.* March 1. http://news.bbc.co.uk/2/hi/americas/6406625.stm

30. Reaney, Patricia, and Wohl, Jessica. 2013. Celebrity Chef Paula Deen Denies She Is a Racist, Dropped by Walmart. *Reuters.* June 26. www.reuters.com/article/us-pauladeen/celebrity-chef-paula-deen-denies-she-is-a-racist-dropped-by-walmart-idUSBRE95N17T20130626

31. Taylor, Kate. 2018. Paula Deen is Attempting a Comeback with a New Cooking Show – Here are the Scandalous Moments that Ruined Her Career. *Business Insider.* January 17. www.businessinsider.sg/paula-deen-scandals-cost-her-cooking-empire-2018-1

32. Musser, Charles. 2011. Why Did Negroes Love Al Jolson and The Jazz Singer? Melodrama, Blackface and Cosmopolitan Theatrical Culture. *Film History: An International Journal,* 23 (2), 196–222.

33. Williams, Lena. 1993. After the Roast, Fire and Smoke. *The New York Times.* October 14. www.nytimes.com/1993/10/14/garden/after-the-roast-fire-and-smoke.html

34. Pilgrim, David. 2012. The Tom Caricature. *Jim Crow Museum.* Ferris State University. https://ferris.edu/HTMLS/news/jimcrow/tom/homepage.htm

35. De Silva, A., and Somaweera, R. 2015. Were Human Babies Used as Bait in Crocodile Hunts in Colonial Sri Lanka?. *Journal of Threatened Taxa,* 7 (1), 6805–6809.

36. Pilgrim, David. 2012. The Tom Caricature. *Jim Crow Museum.* Ferris State University. https://ferris.edu/HTMLS/news/jimcrow/tom/homepage.htm

37. *OED Online.* s.v. Dago, *n.* July 2018. Oxford University Press. www.oed.com

38. Bruchac, Joseph. 2003. *Pocahontas.* Harcourt.

39. Porter, Tom. 2017. Trump Pocahontas Slur: The President has a long history of Insulting Native Americans. *Newsweek.* November 28. www.newsweek.com/trump-pocahontas-slur-president-has-long-history-insulting-native-americans-724204

40. Relman, Eliza. 2018. Elizabeth Warren Releases DNA Test "Strongly" Supporting Claims of Native American Ancestry in Rebuke to Trump. *Business Insider.* October 15. www.businessinsider.com/elizabeth-warren-dna-test-results-native-american-ancestry-2018-10?r=US&IR=T

41. Choi, David. 2018. "I Can No Longer Call Her Pocahontas": Trump Ribs Elizabeth Warren After Her DNA-Test Reveal Falls Short. *Business Insider.* October 23. www.businessinsider.com/trump-pocahontas-elizabeth-warren-campaign-rally-2018-10?r=US&IR=T

42. Allen, Jaclyn. 2016. Colorado Latinos Criticize Trump's "I love Hispanics" Cinco de Mayo Tweet. *The Denver Channel.* May 5. www.thedenverchannel.com/news/politics/colorado-latinos-criticize-trumps-i-love-hispanics-tweet

43. Roberts, Michael. 2001. He Got Blame. December 20. *Westword.* www.westword.com/news/he-got-blame-5068727

44. Applebome, Peter. 1992. The 1992 Campaign: Racial Politics; Perot Speech Gets Cool Reception at N.A.A.C.P. *The New York Times.* July 12. www .nytimes.com/1992/07/12/us/the-1992-campaign-racial-politics-perot-speech-gets-cool-reception-at-naacp.html

45. Hall, Karen. 2004. A Soldier's Body: GI Joe, Hasbro's Great American Hero, and the Symptoms of Empire. *Journal of Popular Culture*, 38 (1), 34–54.

46. Dowell, Ben. 2014. Don't Mention the Jerries: BBC Changes World War One Programme Title. *Radio Times.* February 18. www.radiotimescom/news/ 2014–02-18/dont-mention-the-jerries-bbc-changes-world-war-one-pro gramme-title/

47. *OED Online.* s.v. gook, *n.* July 2018. Oxford University Press. www.oed.com

48. Ramirez, Anthony. 2000. Word for Word/Asian Americans; McCain's Ethnic Slur: Gone, but Not Quite Forgotten. *The New York Times.* March 5. www.nytimes.com/2000/03/05/weekinreview/word-for-word-asian-americans-mccain-s-ethnic-slur-gone-but-not-quite-forgotten.html

49. John, Arit. 2014. Making Fried Chicken and Watermelon Racist. *The Atlantic.* February 6. https://www.theatlantic.com/national/archive/ 2014/02/heres-why-your-fried-chicken-and-watermelon-lunch-racist/ 357814/

50. Johnson, Theodore, R. 2014. Recall that Ice Cream Truck Song? We Have Unpleasant News for You. *Codeswitch*, National Public Radio. May 11. https://www.npr.org/sections/codeswitch/2014/05/11/310708342/ recall-that-ice-cream-truck-song-we-have-unpleasant-news-for-you

51. Urwand, Ben. 2016. The Black Image on the White Screen: Representations of African Americans from the Origins of Cinema to the Birth of a Nation. *Journal of American Studies*, 52 (1), 45–64.

52. Demby, Gene. 2013. Where Did That Fried Chicken Stereotype Come From? *Codeswitch*, National Public Radio. May 22. www.npr.org/sections/ codeswitch/2013/05/22/186087397/where-did-that-fried-chicken-stereo type-come-from

53. Meyer, Zlati. 2018. Starbucks Apologizes to Latino Customer for Racial Slur Written on His Drink Cup. *USA Today.* May 17. www.usatoday.com/story/ money/2018/05/17/starbucks-accused-racism-again-hispanic-mans-drink-order-had-racial-slur/619842002/

54. Moule, J. 2009. Understanding Unconscious Bias and Unintentional Racism. *Phi Delta Kappan*, 90 (5), 320–326.

55. Reilly, Katie. 2016. Here Are All the Times Donald Trump Insulted Mexico. *Time.* August 31. http://time.com/4473972/donald-trump-mexico-meeting-insult/

56. Ruz, Camila. 2015. The Battle Over the Words Used to Describe Migrants. *BBC News.* August 28. https://www.bbc.com/news/magazine-34061097

57. Centre on Migration, Policy and Society (COMPAS). 2013. Migration in the News. *The Migration Observatory.* University of Oxford. https://migrationobservatory.ox.ac.uk/resources/reports/migration-in-the-news/

58. Zimmer, Ben. 2018. "Wop" Doesn't Mean What Andrew Cuomo Thinks It Means. *The Atlantic.* April 23. www.theatlantic.com/politics/archive/2018/04/wop-doesnt-mean-what-andrew-cuomo-thinks-it-means/558659/

59. *OED Online.* s.v. wop, *n.2* and *adj.* July 2018. Oxford University Press. www.oed.com

60. New York City Commission on Human Rights. 2019. NYC Commission on Human Rights Announces New Legal Enforcement Guidance and Actions against Discrimination Based on Immigration Status and National Origin. Press release. September 25. https://www1.nyc.gov/assets/cchr/downloads/pdf/press-releases/Immigration_Guidance_Press_Release.pdf

61. Simon, Abigail. 2018. People Are Angry President Trump Used This Word to Describe Undocumented Immigrants. *Time.* June 19. https://time.com/5316087/donald-trump-immigration-infest/

62. Hund, Wulf, D., Mills, Charles, W., and Sebastiani, Silvia. 2015. *Simianization: Apes, Gender, Class and Race.* Lit Verlag.

63. Nott, Josiah Clark, and Gliddon, George, R. 1854. *Types of Mankind.* Lippincott, Grambo & Co.

64. Crawford, Adrian. 2013. Adam Goodes "Gutted" by Racial Slur but Wants AFL Fan Educated. *ABC News.* 27 May. www.abc.net.au/news/2013–05-25/goodes-gutted-but-places-no-blame/4712772

65. Cooney, Samantha. 2016. West Virginia Official Who Called Michelle Obama an "Ape in Heels" Loses Her Job. *Time.* December 28. http://time.com/4618912/michelle-obama-facebook-post-fired/

66. Reed, Anika. 2018. Roseanne Barr Shares Calmer Video after Explosive Valeria Jarrett Comments. *USA Today.* July 20. www.usatoday.com/story/life/people/2018/07/20/roseanne-barr-defends-racist-tweet-valerie-jarrett-new-video/806353002/

67. Finkelstein, Joel, Zannettou, Savvas, Bradlyn, Barry, and Blackburn, Jeremy. 2018. A Quantitative Approach to Understanding Online Antisemitism. *14th International AAAI Conference on Web and Social Media (ICWSM 2020).* https://arxiv.org/abs/1809.01644

68. Carless, Will. 2018. They Spewed Hate. Then They Punctuated It with the President's Name. *PRI.* April 20. www.pri.org/stories/2018-04-20/they-spewed-hate-then-they-punctuated-it-president-s-name

69. Rogers, Katie, and Fandos, Nicholas. 2018. Trump Tells Congresswomen to "Go Back" to the Countries They Came From. *The New York Times.* July 14. www.nytimes.com/2019/07/14/us/politics/trump-twitter-squad-congress.html

70. Dawsey, Josh. 2018. Trump Derides Protections for Immigrants from "Shithole" Countries. *The Washington Post*. January 12. www.washington post.com/politics/trump-attacks-protections-for-immigrants-from-shit hole-countries-in-oval-office-meeting/

71. Alvarez, Lizette, and Buckley, Cara. 2013. Zimmerman is Acquitted in Trayvon Martin Killing. *The New York Times*. July 13. www.nytimes.com/ 2013/07/14/us/george-zimmerman-verdict-trayvon-martin.html

72. Blow, Charles M. 2015. Stop Playing the "Race Card" Card. *The New York Times*. March 19. www.nytimes.com/2015/03/19/opinion/charles-blow-stop-playing-the-race-card-card.html

73. Rosen, James. The April 2015 Playboy Interview with Dick Cheney. *Playboy*. March 1. www.playboy.com/read/playboy-interview-dick-cheney

74. López, Ian Haney. 2015. *Dog Whistle Politics: How Coded Racial Appeals Have Reinvented Racism and Wrecked the Middle Class*. Oxford University Press.

75. Lopez, German. 2016. The Sneaky Language Today's Politicians Use to Get Away with Racism and Sexism. *Vox*. February 1. www.vox.com/2016/2/1/ 10889138/coded-language-thug-bossy

76. Bonilla-Silva, Eduardo, and Forman, Tyrone A. 2000. "I Am Not a Racist But … ": Mapping White College Students' Racial Ideology in the USA. *Discourse & Society*. January 1. doi:10.1177/0957926500011001003

77. Kuo, Rachel. 2015. 5 Ways "Asian Women Fetishes" Put Asian Women in Serious Danger. *Everyday Feminism*. December 25. https://everydayfemin ism.com/2015/12/asian-woman-fetishes-hurtful/

78. Kuo, Rachel. 2016. 4 Reasons Why Calling a Woman of Color "Exotic" is Racist. *Everyday Feminism*. January 26. https://everydayfeminism.com/ 2016/01/calling-woc-exotic-is-racist/

79. Horowitz, Jason. 2007. Biden Unbound: Lays into Clinton, Obama, Edwards. *The New York Observer*. February 5. https://observer.com/2007/ 02/biden-unbound-lays-into-clinton-obama-edwards/

80. Alim, Samy H., Smitherman, Geneva, and Dyson, Michael Eric. 2012. *Articulate While Black: Barack Obama, Language, and Race in the US*. Oxford University Press.

81. Associated Press. 2008. GOP Congressman Calls Barack and Michelle Obama "Uppity." September 5. *The Mercury* News. www.mercurynews.com/2008/09/ 05/gop-congressman-calls-barack-and-michelle-obama-uppity/

82. Springer, Anthony. 2006. Kanye West Calls Mixed Girls "Mutts". *Hip Hop DX*. December 1. https://hiphopdx.com/news/id.4685/title.kanye-west-calls-mixed-girls-mutts

83. Pomeroy, Steven Ross. 2014. "They All Look Alike": The Other-Race Effect. *Forbes*. January 28. https://www.forbes.com/sites/rosspomeroy/2014/01/28/ think-they-all-look-alike-thats-just-the-other-race-effect/#77b562743819

84. Harker, Joseph. 2014. "It's Not Just Samuel L Jackson – We've All Had Those "We All Look Alike" Moments. *The Guardian.* February 12. www.theguar dian.com/commentisfree/2014/feb/12/samuel-l-jackson-laurence-fish burne-black-outsider

85. Swarns, Rachel L. 2015. The Science Behind "They All Look Alike to Me." *The New York Times.* September 20. www.nytimes.com/2015/09/20/nyre gion/the-science-behind-they-all-look-alike-to-me.html

86. DiAngelo, Robin. 2018. *White Fragility: Why it's So Hard for White People to Talk about Racism.* Beacon Press.

87. Ross, Janell. 2017. "It's Okay to be White" Signs and Stickers Appear on Campuses and Streets across the Country. *The Washington Post.* November 3. www.washingtonpost.com/news/post-nation/wp/2017/11/03/ its-okay-to-be-white-signs-and-stickers-appear-on-campuses-and-streets- across-the-country/

88. Skutnabb-Kangas, Tove. 2015. Linguicism. In *The Encyclopedia of Applied Linguistics,* edited by Carol Chapelle. Wiley. DOI:10.1002/9781405198431. wbeal1460

89. Lippi-Green, Rosina. 1997. *English with an Accent: Language, Ideology and Discrimination in the United States.* Routledge.

90. Pilgrim, David. 2012. The Tom Caricature. Ferris State University. https:// ferris.edu/HTMLS/news/jimcrow/tom/homepage.htm

91. Broome, Richard. 1995. Enduring Moments of Aboriginal Dominance: Aboriginal Performers, Boxers and Runners. *Labour History,* 69, 171–187.

92. Levinson, Martin H. 2011. *Brooklyn Boomer: Growing Up in the Fifties.* iUniverse.

93. Hill, Jane H. 2008. *The Everyday Language of White Racism.* Wiley-Blackwell.

94. Zimmer, Ben. 2019. Why Trump Uses Mock Spanish. *The Atlantic.* June 14. www.theatlantic.com/entertainment/archive/2019/06/loco-hombres-why- trump-uses-mock-spanish/591733/

95. Hill, Jane H. 1993. Hasta la Vista, Baby. Anglo Spanish in the American Southwest. *Critique of Anthropology,* 13 (2), 145–176.

96. Unmissable Japan. 2012. Superdry. www.unmissablejapan.com/etcetera/ superdry

97. Wang, Cynthia, and Silverman, M. Stephen. 2006. Outrage Grows Over Rosie O'Donnell's Asian Joke. *People.* December 12. people.com/celebrity/ outrage-grows-over-rosie-odonnells-asian-joke/

98. Stampler, Laura. 2013. GM Pulls "Racist" Chevy Ad That Calls China "The Land of Fu Manchu." *Business Insider.* May 1. www.businessinsider.com/gm- pulls-racist-chevy-ad-that-calls-china-the-land-of-fu-manchu-2013-5

99. Chow, Kat. 2014. How "Ching Chong" Became the Go-To Slur for Mocking East Asians. *Codeswitch,* National Public Radio. July 14. www.npr.org/sections/

codeswitch/2014/07/14/330769890/how-ching-chong-became-the-go-to-slur-for-mocking-east-asians

100. Rojas, Nicole. 2018. Dunkin Donuts Asked Customers to Report Employees Speaking a Foreign Language in Exchange for Free Coffee. *Newsweek*. June 18. www.newsweek.com/baltimore-dunkin-donuts-under-fire-sign-asking-customers-out-employees

101. *Seinfeld*. 1995. The Understudy. Season 6, episode 24. Aired May 18. Shapiro/West Productions in association with Castle Rock Entertainment.

102. *OED Online*. s.v. spiggoty, *n*. (and *adj.*). July 2018. Oxford University Press. www.oed.com

103. Wolfson, Sam. 2018. New Yorker's Respond to Lawyer's Racist Rant with "Latin Party" Outside His House. *The Guardian*. May 18. www.theguardian.com/us-news/2018/may/18/aaron-schlossberg-racist-lawyer-new-york-latin-party

104. Chuck, Elizabeth. 2016. "Speak English, You're in America," Woman Tells Latina Shoppers in Rant Caught on Camera. *NBC News*. December 21. www.nbcnews.com/news/latino/speak-english-you-re-america-woman-tells-latina-shoppers-rant-n698776

105. Stevens, Matt. 2017. New Jersey Teacher Who Told Students to "Speak American" Returns to School. *The New York Times*. November 24. www.nytimes.com/2017/10/24/nyregion/speak-american-high-school.html

106. Baker, Peter, and Shear, Michael D. 2019. El Paso Shooting Subject's Manifesto Echoes Trump's Language. *The New York Times*. August 4. www.nytimes.com/2019/08/04/us/politics/trump-mass-shootings.html

107. Grabar, Henry. 2017. How "Press One for English" Became an Anti-Immigrant Meme. *Slate*. September 11. https://slate.com/business/2017/09/most-companies-dont-ask-you-to-press-one-for-english-but-that-doesnt-stop-the-right-wing-from-complaining-about-it.html

108. Stokes, Bruce. 2017. Language: The Cornerstone of National Identity. *Global Attitudes & Trends*, Pew Research Center. February 1. www.pewglobal.org/2017/02/01/language-the-cornerstone-of-national-identity/

109. National Museum Australia. White Australia Policy. 2018. http://www.nma.gov.au/defining-moments/resources/white-australia-policy

110. National Archives of Australia. 2018. Immigration Restriction Act 1901. www.naa.gov.au/collection/a-z/immigration-restriction-act.aspx

111. Mason, Keith. 2014. The Saga of Egon Kisch and the White Australia Policy. *Bar News: The Journal of the New South Wales Bar Association*. Summer, 64–67.

112. Boissoneault, Lorraine. 2017. Literacy Tests and Asian Exclusion Were the Hallmarks of the 1917 Immigration Act. *Smithsonian Magazine*.

February 6. www.smithsonianmag.com/history/how-america-grappled-immigration-100-years-ago-180962058/

113. Ault, Alicia. 2016. Did Ellis Island Officials Really Change the Names of Immigrants? *Smithsonian*. December 28. www.smithsonianmag.com/smithsonianinstitution/ask-smithsonian-did-ellis-island-officials-really-change-names-immigrants-180961544/

114. Finstad, Suzanne. 2002. *Natasha: The Biography of Natalie Wood*. Three Rivers Press.

115. Douglas, Kirk. 2007. *Let's Face It: 90 Years of Living, Loving and Learning*. Wiley.

116. Polly, Matthew. 2018. *Bruce Lee: A Life*. Simon & Schuster.

117. Simmons, Gene. 2001. *Kiss and Make-Up*. Crown Archetype.

118. Eligon, John. 2018. No "Foreign" Names for Children, Dear Abby Advised. Furious Parents Replied. *The New York Times*. October 18. www.nytimes.com/2018/10/18/us/dear-abby-whitewash-foreign-names.html?smid=fb-nytimes&smtyp=cur

119. Bear, Charla. 2008. American Indian Boarding Schools Haunt Many. National Public Radio. May 12. https://www.npr.org/templates/story/story.php?storyId=16516865

120. Cummins, Jim. 1997. Cultural and Linguistic Diversity in Education: A Mainstream Issue? *Educational Review*, 49 (2), 105–114.

121. Asmus, Sabine, and Williams, Siôn. 2014. Welsh between Stability and Fragility. In *Unity in Diversity*, vol. 2, edited by Sabine Asmus and Barbara Braid. Cambridge Scholars Publishing.

122. Human Rights and Equal Opportunities Commission of Australia. 1997. *Bringing Them Home: Report of the National Enquiry into the Separation of Aboriginal and Torres Strait Islander Children from Their Families*. www.austlii.edu.au/au/other/IndigLRes/stolen/index.html

123. Koch, Harold, and Nordlinger, Rachel. 2014. *The Languages and Linguistics of Australia: A Comprehensive Guide*. De Gruyter Mouton.

124. Zimmerman, Michael. 2017. The Importance of Preserving and Promoting Languages: A Liberal Arts Perspective. *Huffington Post*. September 20. www.huffingtonpost.com/michael-zimmerman/the-importance-of-preserv_b_12088728.html

2 Boys Will Be Boys

1. Potts, John. 2013. *The Monstrous Familial: Representations of the Unacceptable Family*. Palgrave Macmillan.

2. Cornes, Judy. 2015. *Sex, Power and the Folly of Marriage in Women's Novels of the 1920s*. McFarland.

3. Holm, Nicholas. 2016. *Advertising and Consumer Society: A Critical Introduction*. Red Globe Press.

4. Barreto, Manuela, and Ellemers, Naomi. 2013. Sexism in Contemporary Societies: How It Is Expressed, Perceived, Confirmed and Resisted. In *The Sage Handbook of Gender and Psychology*, edited by Michelle K. Ryan and Nyla R. Branscombe. Sage Publications.

5. *OED Online*. s.v. sexism, *n.2*. December 2018. Oxford University Press. www.oed.com

6. Beauvoir, Simone de. 2011 (1949). *The Second Sex*. Penguin.

7. Cameron, Deborah. 2019. *Feminism: A Brief Introduction to the Ideas, Debates and Politics of the Movement*. University of Chicago Press.

8. *Holy Bible*. 2011. New International Version. Biblica, Inc.

9. Pagels, Elaine H. 1976. What Became of God the Mother? Conflicting Images of God in Early Christianity. *Signs: Journal of Women in Culture and Society*, 2 (2), 293–303.

10. *OED Online*. s.v. patriarchy, *n*. December 2018. Oxford University Press. www.oed.com

11. Gimbutas, Marija. 1992. *The Civilization of the Goddess*. HarperCollins.

12. Davis, Elizabeth Gould. 1972. *The First Sex*. Penguin Books.

13. Matriarchy. 2017. *Encyclopedia Britannica*. Encyclopedia Britannica Inc.

14. Przeworski, Adam. 2009. Conquered or Granted? A History of Suffrage Extensions. *British Journal of Political Science*, 39 (2), 291–321.

15. Keene, Jennifer, Cornell, Saul, and O'Donnell, Edward. 2013. *Visions of America: A History of the United States*. Pearson Education.

16. Friedan, Betty. 1963. *The Feminine Mystique*. W. W. Norton & Co.

17. Humphrey, Elizabeth King. 2013. *The Feminist Movement of Today*. Mason Crest.

18. Kynaston, David. 2014. *Modernity Britain: Book Two: A Shake of the Dice, 1959–62*. Bloomsbury.

19. Suazrez, Fernando. 2008. Hecklers Want Clinton to Iron Their Shirts. *CBS News*. January 7. www.cbsnews.com/news/hecklers-want-clinton-to-iron-their-shirts/

20. Jacobson, Ivy. These 6 Male Celebrities Took Their Wives' Last Names. *The Knot*. www.theknot.com/content/male-celebrities-who-took-wives-last-names

21. Ibid.

22. *OED Online*. s.v. master, *n.1* and *adj*. December 2018. Oxford University Press. www.oed.com

23. Shariatmadari, David. 2016. Eight Words that Reveal the Sexism at the Heart of the English Language. *The Guardian*. January 27. www.theguar

dian.com/commentisfree/2016/jan/27/eight-words-sexism-heart-english-language

24. Ricker, Thomas. 2015. First Click: Elon Musk, Rockstar Savior. *The Verge*. May 1. www.theverge.com/2015/5/1/8527931/elon-musk-rockstar-savior

25. Friedan, Betty. 1963. *The Feminine Mystique*. W. W. Norton & Co.

26. Greer, Germaine. 2008. (1970). *The Female Eunuch*. Harper Perennial.

27. Hegewisch, Ariane. 2018. *The Gender Wage Gap: 2017: Earnings Differences by Gender, Race, and Ethnicity*. Institute for Women's Policy Research. https://iwpr.org/publications/gender-wage-gap-2017/

28. Marcotte, Amanda. 2016. Rudy Giuliani's Comment that Donald Trump is Better "Than a Woman" is Made Even More Sexist by the Context. *Salon*. October 3. www.salon.com/2016/10/03/giulianis-comment-that-trump-is-better-than-a-woman-is-made-even-more-sexist-by-the-context/

29. Lewis, Ruth, Rowe, Mike, and Wiper, Clare. 2019. Online/Offline Continuities: Exploring Misogyny and Hate in Online Abuse of Feminists. In *Online Othering*, edited by Karen Lumsden and Emily Harmer. Palgrave Macmillan.

30. Baugess, James S., and Allen DeBolt, Abbe (Eds.). 2011. *Encyclopedia of the Sixties: A Decade of Culture and Counterculture*. ABC-Clio.

31. Dow, Bonnie J. 2014. *Watching Women's Liberation, 1970: Feminism's Pivotal Year on the Network News*. University of Illinois Press.

32. Curtis, Scarlett. 2018. *Feminists Don't Wear Pink and Other Lies*. Ballantine Books.

33. Sommers, Christina Hoff. 1996. *Who Stole Feminism? How Women Have Betrayed Women*. Simon & Schuster.

34. Saidlear, Cliona. 2017. Feminism, Feminist Activism, and "Dissident Feminists." *The Irish Times*. October 13. www.irishtimes.com/opinion/letters/feminism-feminist-activism-and-dissident-feminists-1.3253981

35. *OED Online*. s.v. misandry, *n*. December 2018. Oxford University Press. www.oed.com

36. *OED Online*. s.v. misogynist, *n*. and *adj*. July 2018. Oxford University Press. www.oed.com

37. Davies, Lizzy. 2012. Julia Gillard Speech Prompts Dictionary to Change "Misogyny" Definition. *The Guardian*. October 17. www.theguardian.com/world/2012/oct/17/julia-gillard-australia-misogyny-dictionary

38. Muller, Denis. 2018. Sexist Abuse Has a Long History in Australian Politics – and Takes Us All to a Dark Place. *The Conversation*. July 3. http://theconversation.com/sexist-abuse-has-a-long-history-in-australian-politics-and-takes-us-all-to-a-dark-place-99222

39. Berlatsky, Noah. 2013. When Men Experience Sexism. *The Atlantic*. May 29. www.theatlantic.com/sexes/archive/2013/05/when-men-experience-sexism/276355/

40. BBC. 2018. Elliot Rodger: How Misogynistic Killer Became "Incel" Hero. *BBC News*. April 26. www.bbc.com/news/world-us-canada-43892189

41. Ibid.

42. Ibid.

43. McRae, Mike. 2018. *Unwell: What Makes a Disease a Disease?* University of Queensland Press.

44. Tasca, Cecilia, Rapetti, Mariangela, Carta, Giovanni Mauro, and Fadda, Bianca. 2012. Women and Hysteria in the History of Mental Health. *Clinical Practice and Epidemology in Mental Health*, 8, 110–119.

45. Maglaty, Jeanne. 2011. When Did Girls Start Wearing Pink? *Smithsonian*. April 7. www.smithsonianmag.com/arts-culture/when-did-girls-start-wearing-pink-1370097/

46. Frost, Amber A'Lee. 2015. No Such Cuck. *The Baffler*, 29, 106–109.

47. Shamir, Milette, and Travis, Jennifer. 2002. *Boys Don't Cry? Rethinking Narratives of Masculinity and Emotion in the U.S.* Columbia University Press.

48. Bates, Laura. 2014. *Everyday Sexism: The Project that Inspired a Worldwide Movement*. Thomas Dunne Books.

49. Brown, Kara. 2015. The Problem with Calling Women "Females." *Jezebel*. February 5. https://jezebel.com/the-problem-with-calling-women-females-1683808274

50. Ross, Janell. 2016. Trump's "Such a Nasty Woman" Comment has Sparked Something. *The Washington Post*. October 20. www.washingtonpost.com/news/the-fix/wp/2016/10/20/trumps-such-a-nasty-woman-comment-has-sparked-something

51. *OED Online*. s.v. cunt, *n*. December 2018. Oxford University Press. www.oed.com

52. Johnson, Samuel. 2004 (1755). *A Dictionary of the English Language*. Walker Books.

53. Grose, Francis. 1796. *A Classical Dictionary of the Vulgar Tongue*. Third ed. S. Hooper.

54. *OED Online*. s.v. bimbo, *n.2*. December 2018. Oxford University Press. www.oed.com

55. *OED Online*. s.v. bitch, *n.1*. December 2018. Oxford University Press. www.oed.com

56. Freeman, Jo (Joreen). 1968. The BITCH Manifesto. www.jofreeman.com/joreen/bitch.htm

57. Bareket, Orly, Kahalon, Rotem, Shnabel, Nurit, and Glick, Peter. 2018. The Madonna–Whore Dichotomy: Men Who Perceive Women's Nurturance and Sexuality as Mutually Exclusive Endorse Patriarchy and Show Lower Relationship Satisfaction. *Sex Roles*, 79 (9–10), 519–532. DOI:10.1007/s11199-018-0895-7

58. Russo, Maria Del. 2018. Mistress, Slut, "the Other Woman": The Way We Talk about Relationships is Inherently Sexist. *The Washington Post*. April 6. www.washingtonpost.com/news/soloish/wp/2018/04/06/the-way-we-talk-about-relationships-is-inherently-sexist/

59. Craik, Jennifer. 2004. *The Face of Fashion: Cultural Studies in Fashion*. Routledge.

60. Rao, Soumya. 2018. Headless Women of Hollywood: A Social Media Project Highlights the Faceless Women in Movie Posters. *Scroll in*. March 22. https://scroll.in/reel/872522/headless-women-of-hollywood-a-social-media-project-highlights-the-faceless-women-in-movie-posters

61. Moye, David. 2018. Howard Stern Tells How Trump Sexualized Ivanka and Makes David Letterman Cringe. *Huffington Post*. May 21. www.huffington post.co.uk/entry/howard-stern-donald-trump-ivanka-david-letter man_n_5b02fc36e4b07309e05aff01?ri18n=true

62. Kaplan, Katharine A. 2003. Facemash Creator Survives Ad Board. *The Harvard Crimson*. November 19.

63. Paresky, Pamela. 2016. What's Wrong with Locker Room Talk? *Psychology Today*. October 10. www.psychologytoday.com/us/blog/happiness-and-the-pursuit-leadership/201610/whats-wrong-locker-room-talk

64. United Nations. What is Sexual Harassment? *Women Watch*. www.un.org/womenwatch/osagi/pdf/whatissh.pdf

65. Bosman, Julie. 2019. A College Student was Killed by a Man Whose Catcalls She Tried to Ignore. *The New York Times*. November 27. www.nytimes.com/2019/11/27/us/chicago-college-student-killed-catcall.html

66. Equality Act 2010. The National Archives. https://www.legislation.gov.uk/ukpga/2010/15/section/26

67. Klarfeld, Jessica. 2011. A Striking Disconnect: Marital Rape Law's Failure to Keep Up with Domestic Violence Law. *The American Criminal Law Review*, 48 (4), 1819–1841.

68. McDonough, Bart R. 2018. *Cyber Smart: Five Habits to Protect Your Family, Money, and Identity from Cyber Criminals*. Wiley.

69. Fitzgerald, Louis F., and Weitzman, Lauren M. 1991. Men who Harass: Speculation and Data. In *Ivory Power: Sexual Harassment on Campus*, edited by Michele A. Paludi. SUNY Press.

70. Trades Union Congress. 2016. Still Just a Bit of Banter? Sexual Harassment Report. www.tuc.org.uk/research-analysis/reports/still-just-bit-banter

71. Kimmel, Michael S. 2018. Getting Men to Speak Up. *Harvard Business Review*. January 30. https://hbr.org/2018/01/getting-men-to-speak-up

72. Williams, Zoe. 2017. Sexual Harassment 101: What Everyone Needs to Know. *The Guardian*. October 16. www.theguardian.com/world/2017/oct/16/facts-sexual-harassment-workplace-harvey-weinstein

73. Kantor, Jodi, and Twohey, Megan. 2017. Harvey Weinstein Paid Off Sexual Harassment Accusers for Decades. *The New York Times*. October 5. www.nytimes.com/2017/10/05/us/harvey-weinstein-harassment-allegations.html

74. Birnbaum, Debra. 2017. Alyssa Milano on #MeToo Campaign: "I Wanted to Take the Focus Off the Predator." *Variety*. October 17. https://variety.com/2017/biz/news/metoo-alyssa-milano-harvey-weinstein-1202592308/

75. Vendituoli, Monica. 2014. #NotAllMen, but #YesAllWomen: Campus Tragedy Spurs Debate on Sexual Violence. *The Chronicle of Higher Education*. May 28. www.chronicle.com/article/NotAllMen-but-YesAllWomen-/146811/

76. Preves, Sharon E. 2005. *Intersex and Identity: The Contested Self*. Rutgers University Press.

77. Blackless, M., Charuvastra, A., Derryck, A., Fausto-Sterling, A., Lauzanne, K., and Lee, E. 2000. How Sexually Dimorphic Are We? Review and Synthesis. *American Journal of Human Biology*, 12 (2), 151–166.

78. Pikramenou, N. 2019. Towards Intersex Legal Protection Beyond Europe. In *Intersex Rights*. Springer.

79. Avise, John, C. 2011. *Hermaphroditism: A Primer on the Biology, Ecology, and Evolution of Dual Sexuality*. Columbia University Press.

80. Fekete, Nihoul, C. 2005. Does Surgical Genitoplasty Affect Gender in the Intersex Infant? *Hormone Research in Pediatrics*, 64 (2), 23–26.

81. Greenfield, Charlotte. 2014. Should We "Fix" Intersex Children? *The Atlantic*. July 8. www.theatlantic.com/health/archive/2014/07/should-we-fix-intersex-children/373536/

82. Mathieu, Éric, Daili, Myriam, and Zareikar, Gita. 2019. *Gender and Noun Classification*. Oxford University Press.

83. Kranz, G., Hahn, A., Kaufmann, U., Küblböck, M., Hummer, A., Ganger, S., Seiger, R., et al. 2014. White Matter Microstructure in Transsexuals and Controls Investigated by Diffusion Tensor Imaging. *Journal of Neuroscience*, 34, (46), 15466–15475.

84. Flores, Andrew R., Herman, Jody L., Gates, Gary J., and Brown, Taylor N. T. 2016. How Many Adults Identify as Transgender in the United States? The Williams Institute. https://williamsinstitute.law.ucla.edu/wp-content/uploads/How-Many-Adults-Identify-as-Transgender-in-the-United-States.pdf

85. Steinmetz, Katy. 2014. Why It's Best to Avoid the Word "Transgendered." *Time*. December 15. http://time.com/3630965/transgender-transgendered/

86. *OED Online*. s.v. cisgender, *adj.* and *n*. December 2018. Oxford University Press. www.oed.com

87. Merriam Webster. 2019. Merriam-Webster's Words of the Year 2019. www.merriam-webster.com/words-at-play/word-of-the-year/they

88. Hajela, Deepti. 2017. NYC Subway to Use Gender-Neutral Terms During Announcements. *AP News*. November 18. https://apnews.com/

499f0d7b020a432eb86825668cbbe195/NYC-subway-to-use-gender-neu
tral-terms-during-announcements

89. Web MD. 2018. When You Don't Feel at Home with Your Gender. www
.webmd.com/sex/gender-dysphoria#1

90. National Center for Transgender Equality. 2016. Questionable Questions
About Transgender Identity. September 2. https://transequality.org/issues/
resources/questionable-questions-about-transgender-identity

91. Bettcher, Talia Mae. 2007. Evil Deceivers and Make-Believers: On
Transphobic Violence and the Politics of Illusion. *Hypatia*, 22 (3), 43–65.

92. Greer, Germaine. 2009. Caster Semenya Sex Row: What Makes a Woman?
The Guardian. August 20. www.theguardian.com/sport/2009/aug/20/ger
maine-greer-caster-semenya

93. Jones, Kelsie Brynn. 2016. Trans-Exclusionary Radical Feminism: What
Exactly Is It, and Why Does It Hurt? *Huffington Post*. February 2. www
.huffingtonpost.com/kelsie-brynn-jones/transexclusionary-radical-
terf_b_5632332.html

94. Clements, K. C. 2017. What is Deadnaming? *Healthline*. October 19. www
.healthline.com/health/transgender/deadnaming

95. Smith, Gwendolyn. 2018. This New Study Debunks the "Transgender Predator"
Bathroom Myth – Again. *LGBTQ Nation*. September 12. www.lgbtqnation
.com/2018/09/new-study-debunks-transgender-predator-bathroom-myth/

96. Haas, Ann P., Rodgers, Philip L., and Herman, Jody L. 2014. *Suicide
Attempts among Transgender and Gender Non-Conforming Adults*. The
Williams Institute. http://williamsinstitute.law.ucla.edu/wp-content/
uploads/AFSP-Williams-Suicide-Report-Final.pdf

3 Not That There's Anything Wrong with That

1. Foldy, Michael, S. 1997. *The Trials of Oscar Wilde: Deviance, Morality, and
Late-Victorian Society*. Yale University Press.

2. *OED Online*. s.v. homosexuality, *n*. December 2018. Oxford University Press.
www.oed.com

3. *OED Online*. s.v. heterosexuality, *n*. December 2018. Oxford University Press.
www.oed.com

4. Stevens, Phillips, Jr. 2015. Culture and Sexuality. In *The International
Encyclopedia of Human Sexuality*, edited by Patricia Whelehan and Ann
Bolin. John Wiley & Sons.

5. Laumann, E. O., Gagnon, J. H., Michael, R. T., and Michaels, S. 1994. *The
Social Organization of Sexuality: Sexual Practices in the United States*.
University of Chicago Press.

6. Bailey, N. W., and Zuk, M. 2009. Same-Sex Sexual Behavior and Evolution. *Trends in Ecology & Evolution*, 24 (8), 439–446.

7. *OED Online*. s.v. sodomy, *n*. December 2018. Oxford University Press. www .oed.com

8. Lang, Sabine. 1998. *Men as Women, Women as Men: Changing Gender in Native American Cultures*. University of Texas Press.

9. Goldsmith, Netta Murray. 1998. *The Worst of Crimes. Homosexuality and the Law in Eighteenth Century England*. Ashgate Publications.

10. Frost, Natasha. 2017. How the 18th-Century Gay Bar Survived and Thrived in a Deadly Environment. *Atlas Obscura*. December 8. www.atlasobscura.com/ articles/regency-gay-bar-molly-houses

11. McCann, Kate. 2017. Turing's Law: Oscar Wilde among 50,000 Convicted Gay Men Granted Posthumous Pardons. *The Telegraph*. January 31. www .telegraph.co.uk/news/2017/01/31/turings-law-thousands-convicted-gay- bisexual-men-receive-posthumous/

12. The International Lesbian, Gay, Bisexual, Trans and Intersex Association. 2017. *State-Sponsored Homophobia – A World Survey of Sexual Orientation Laws: Criminalisation, Protection and Recognition*, 12th ed. https://ilga.org/ ilga-state-sponsored-homophobia-report-2017

13. Crompton, Louis. 2006. *Homosexuality and Civilization*. Harvard University Press.

14. The Holy Bible. 2001. *English Standard Version*. Crossway Bibles.

15. McNeill, J. J. 1993. *The Church and the Homosexual*. Beacon.

16. Boswell, John. 1980. *Christianity, Social Tolerance, and Homosexuality: Gay People in Western Europe from the Beginning of the Christian Era to the Fourteenth Century*. University of Chicago Press.

17. McNeill, John J. 1993. *The Church and the Homosexual*. Beacon.

18. The Holy Bible. 2001. *English Standard Version*. Crossway Bibles.

19. *OED Online*. s.v. homosexuality, *n*. December 2018. Oxford University Press. www.oed.com

20. Morrow, Deana, and Messinger, Lori. 2006. *Sexual Orientation and Gender Expression in Social Work Practice: Working with Gay, Lesbian, Bisexual and Transgender People*. Columbia University Press.

21. Ibid.

22. Subtirelu, Nicholas. 2015. Why the Word "Homosexual" is Offensive. *The Week*. June 2. https://theweek.com/articles/556341/why-word-homosexual-offensive

23. Peters, Jeremy W. 2014. The Decline and Fall of the "H" Word. *The New York Times*. March 21. www.nytimes.com/2014/03/23/fashion/gays- lesbians-the-term-homosexual.html?_r=3

24. Drescher, Jack. 2015. Out of DSM: Depathologizing Homosexuality. *Behavioral Sciences*, 5 (4), 565–575.

25. Grau, Günter, and Shoppman, Claudia. 2013. *The Hidden Holocaust? Gay and Lesbian Persecution in Germany 1933–45*. Routledge.

26. Drescher, Jack. 2015. Out of DSM: Depathologizing Homosexuality. *Behavioral Sciences*, 5 (4), 565–575.

27. Ibid.

28. Eckholm, Erik. 2012. Rift Forms in Movement as Belief in Gay "Cure" Is Renounced. *The New York Times*. July 6. www.nytimes.com/2012/07/07/us/a-leaders-renunciation-of-ex-gay-tenets-causes-a-schism.html?pagewanted=all

29. Iati, Marisa. 2019. Conversion Therapy Center Founder who Sought to Turn LGBTQ Christians Straight Says He's Gay, Rejects "Cycle of Self Shame." *The Washington Post*. September 5. www.washingtonpost.com/religion/2019/09/03/conversion-therapy-center-founder-who-sought-turn-lgbtq-christians-straight-now-says-hes-gay-rejects-cycle-shame/

30. Adams, Henry E., Wright, Lester W. Jr., and Lohr, Bethany A. 1996. Is Homophobia Associated with Homosexual Arousal? *Journal of Abnormal Psychology*, 105 (3), 440–445.

31. Ryan, Richard, and Ryan, William, S. 2012. Homophobic? Maybe You're Gay. *The New York Times*. April 27. www.nytimes.com/2012/04/29/opinion/sunday/homophobic-maybe-youre-gay.html

32. Wilson, Erin Faith. 2015. 16 Antigay Leaders Exposed as Gay or Bi. *Advocate*. May 29. www.advocate.com/politics/politicians/2015/05/29/16-antigay-leaders-exposed-gay-or-bi?pg=3

33. *The New York Times*. 2007. Senator, Arrested at Airport, Pleads Guilty. August 28. www.nytimes.com/2007/08/28/washington/28craig.html

34. Foldy, Michael S. 1997. *The Trials of Oscar Wilde: Deviance, Morality, and Late-Victorian Society*. Yale University Press.

35. Bristow, Joseph. 2009. *Oscar Wilde and Modern Culture: The Making of a Legend*. Ohio University Press.

36. *OED Online*. s.v. lavender, *n.2* and *adj.* December 2018. Oxford University Press. www.oed.com

37. Ellmann, Richard. 1988. *Oscar Wilde*. Vintage.

38. BBC. 1999. Gay Tinky Winky is Bad for Children. February 15. *BBC News*. http://news.bbc.co.uk/2/hi/entertainment/276677.stm

39. King, Gilbert. 2012. The "Latin Lover" and His Enemies. *Smithsonian Magazine*. June 13. www.smithsonianmag.com/history/the-latin-lover-and-his-enemies-119968944/

40. Plant, Richard. 2011. *The Pink Triangle: The Nazi War Against Homosexuals*. Holt.

41. Raby, Peter. 2006. *Wilde's Comedies of Society*. Cambridge University Press.

42. Crooks, Roderic N. 2013. The Rainbow Flag and the Green Carnation: Grindr in the Gay Village. *First Monday*, 18 (11). University of Illinois.

43. Baker, Paul. 2004. *Polari: The Lost Language of Gay Men*. Routledge.

44. King, Gilbert. 2012. The "Latin Lover" and His Enemies. *Smithsonian Magazine*. June 13. www.smithsonianmag.com/history/the-latin-lover-and-his-enemies-119968944/

45. Hofler, Robert. 2014. *The Man Who Invented Rock Hudson: The Pretty Boys and Dirty Deals of Henry Wilson*. University of Minnesota Press.

46. Pyron, Darden Asbury. 2000. *Liberace: An American Boy*. University of Chicago Press.

47. Van Leer, David. 1999. A World of Female Friendship: The Bostonians. In *Henry James and Homo-Erotic Desire*, edited by J. R. Bradley. Palgrave Macmillan.

48. Johnson, David K. 2006. *The Lavender Scare: The Cold War Persecution of Gays and Lesbians in the Federal Government*. University of Chicago Press.

49. Carter, David. 2010. *Stonewall: The Riots That Sparked the Gay Revolution*. St. Martin's Press.

50. Chauncey, George. 2008. *Gay New York: Gender, Urban Culture, and the Making of the Gay Male World, 1890–1940*. Basic Books.

51. GLAAD. 2019. GLAAD Media Reference Guide: Terms to Avoid. www.glaad.org/reference/offensive

52. Levon, Erez. 2016. Molly, Gay, Transsexual, Transgender: LGBT Words Transition, Too. October 24. *Financial Times*. www.ft.com/content/9f3c233a-91f7-11e6-8df8-d3778b55a923

53. *OED Online*. s.v. gay, *adj.*, *adv.*, and *n.* December 2018. Oxford University Press. www.oed.com

54. Rowe, Nicholas. 2010 (1703). *The Fair Penitent*. Gale ECCO.

55. *OED Online*. s.v. gay, *adj.*, *adv.*, and *n.* December 2018. Oxford University Press. www.oed.com

56. Wilkinson, Sophie. 2013. Are Lesbians Invisible Because They're Women? *Stylist*. www.stylist.co.uk/life/sophie-wilkinson-asks-are-lesbians-invisible-because-they-are-women/53680

57. Lerner, Gerda. 2009. *Living with History: Making Social Change*. University of North Carolina Press.

58. Livia, Anna, and Hall, Kira (Eds.). 1997. *Queerly Phrased: Language, Gender and Sexuality*. Oxford University Press.

59. King, William. 1974 (1736). *The Toast*. Garland Publications.

60. *OED Online*. s.v. lesbian, *n.* and *adj.* December 2018. Oxford University Press. www.oed.com

61. *OED Online*. s.v. tribade, *n.* December 2018. Oxford University Press. www.oed.com

62. *OED Online.* s.v. dyke, *n.* December 2018. Oxford University Press. www .oed.com

63. Ulrichs, Karl Heinrich. 1994. *The Riddle of "Man-Manly" Love.* Prometheus Books.

64. Norton, Rictor. 1992. *Mother Clap's Molly House: The Gay Subculture in England, 1700–1830.* Heretic Books.

65. Law, Jonathan. 2011. *The Methuen Drama Dictionary of the Theatre.* Bloomsbury.

66. Haggerty, George E. 2012. *Gay Histories and Cultures.* Routledge.

67. Haggerty, George E. 2000. *Encyclopedia of Gay Histories and Cultures.* Routledge.

68. Richards, Matt, and Langhorne, Mark. 2018. *Somebody to Love: The Life, Death and Legacy of Freddie Mercury.* Weldon Owen.

69. Bullock, Darryl W. 2017. *David Bowie Made Me Gay: 100 Years of LGBT Music.* Abrams Press.

70. *OED Online.* s.v. faggot, *n.* and *adj.* December 2018. Oxford University Press. www.oed.com

71. Ibid.

72. God Hates Fags. Westboro Baptist Church. www.godhatesfags.com/

73. *South Park.* 2009. "The F-Word." Season 13, episode 12. South Park Studios.

74. Preston, John. 2017. *A Very English Scandal: Sex, Lies and a Murder Plot at the Heart of the Establishment.* Other Press.

75. Collins, Ronald K. L. 2012. Comedy and Liberty: The Life and Legacy of Lenny Bruce. *Social Research,* 79 (1), 61–86.

76. Sullivan, James. 2010. *7 Dirty Words: The Life and Crimes of George Carlin.* Da Capo Press.

77. *OED Online.* s.v. queer, *n.2.* December 2018. Oxford University Press. www .oed.com

78. Robins, Ashley H. 2011. *Oscar Wilde – The Great Drama of His Life: How His Tragedy Reflected His Personality.* Sussex Academic Press.

79. *Queer Eye.* 2003–2007. TV series. Bravo Original Production and Scout Productions.

80. Williams, Walter L. 2010. The "Two-Spirit" People of Indigenous North Americans. *The Guardian.* October 11. www.theguardian.com/music/2010/ oct/11/two-spirit-people-north-america

81. Nagle, Rebecca. 2018. The Healing History of Two-Spirit, A Term That Gives LGBTQ Natives A Voice. *Huffington Post.* June 30. www.huffingtonpost.com/ entry/two-spirit-identity_us_5b37cfbce4b007aa2f809af1

82. Allen, Samantha. 2018. Why Bisexuals Feel Ignored and Insulted at LGBT Pride. *Daily Beast.* June 22. www.thedailybeast.com/why-bisexuals-feel-ignored-and-insulted-at-lgbt-pride?

83. Lesbian, Gay, Bisexual, Transgender, Queer, Intersex, Asexual Resource Center. 2018. Words that Hurt. UC Davis. https://Lgbtqia.ucdavis.edu/edu cated/words

84. Baumgardner, Jennifer. 2008. *Look Both Ways: Bisexual Politics*. Farrar, Straus, and Giroux.

85. Holden, Dominic. 2018. Who Are LGTBQ Americans? Here's A Major Poll on Life, Sex, and Politics. *BuzzFeed News*. June 13. www.buzzfeednews.com/ article/dominicholden/lgbtq-in-the-us-poll#.vclv7Z9AVw

86. Deevey, Sharon. 1990. Older Lesbian Women An Invisible Minority. *Journal of Gerontological Nursing*, 16 (5), 35–39.

87. Rieger, Gerulf, Savin-Williams, Ritch C., Chivers, Meredith L., and Baily, Michael J. 2015. Sexual Arousal and Masculinity-Femininity of Women. *Journal of Personality and Social Psychology*, 111 (2), 265–283.

88. King, Thomas A. 2008. *The Gendering of Men, 1600–1750*, vol. 2: *Queer Articulations*. University of Wisconsin Press.

89. Mack, Sara, and Munson, Benjamin. 2012. The Influence of /s/ Quality on Ratings of Men's Sexual Orientation: Explicit and Implicit Measures of the "Gay Lisp" Stereotype. *Journal of Phonetics*, 40 (1), 198–212.

90. Goldman, Russell. 2007. Ahmadinejad: No Gays, No Oppression of Women in Iran. ABC News. September 24. https://abcnews.go.com/US/story? id=3642673

91. Swift, Jonathan. 2016. *Gulliver's Travels and A Modest Proposal*. Simon & Schuster.

92. Wagner, John. 2018. Trump Calls California's Sanctuary Laws a "Ridiculous, Crime Infested & Breeding Concept." *The Washington Post*. April 18. www .washingtonpost.com/news/post-politics/wp/2018/04/18/trump-calls-cali fornias-sanctuary-laws-a-ridiculous-crime-infested-breeding-concept

93. Ayres-Deets, Andrea. 2013. Ben Carson Compares Homosexuality to Bestiality and Pedophilia. *Mic*. March 30. www.mic.com/articles/31809/ben- carson-compares-homosexuality-to-bestiality-and-pedophilia

94. *Seinfeld*. 1993. The Outing. Season 4, episode 17. Aired February 11. Shapiro/West Productions in association with Castle Rock Entertainment.

95. Mackie, Drew. 2018. Gayest Episode Ever: "Seinfeld" Killed It With "Not That There's Anything Wrong With That." *Hornet*. November 3. https://hornet .com/stories/seinfeld-not-that-theres-anything-wrong-with-that-two/

96. Brown, J. R. 2011. No Homo. *Journal of Homosexuality*, 58 (3), 299–314.

97. *OED Online*. s.v. Ganymede, *n*. December 2018. Oxford University Press. www.oed.com

98. Haramis, Nick. 2018. Welcome to the Age of the Twink. *The New York Times*. May 14. www.nytimes.com/2018/05/14/t-magazine/age-of-the- twink.html

99. Don't Ask, Don't Tell is Repealed. 2011. US Department of Defense. http://archive.defense.gov/home/features/2010/0610_dadt/

100. Perper, Rosie. 2017. The 28 Countries Around the World Where Same-Sex Marriage Is Legal. *Business Insider.* www.businessinsider.com/where-is-same-sex-marriage-legal-world-2017-11?r=US&IR=T

101. Deevey, Sharon. 1990. Older Lesbian Women An Invisible Minority. *Journal of Gerontological Nursing,* 16 (5), 35–39.

102. Adams, Maurianne, Bell, Lee Anne, and Griffin, Pat (Eds.). 2007. *Teaching for Diversity and Social Justice.* Routledge.

103. Jimenez, Stephen. 2013. *The Book of Matt: Hidden Truths About the Murder of Matthew Shepard.* Steerforth Press.

4 Don't Be a Jew

1. Laqueur, Walter. 2008. *The Changing Face of Anti-Semitism: From Ancient Times to the Present Day.* Oxford University Press.

2. Cohen, Mark. 1995. *Under Crescent and Cross: The Jews in the Middle Ages.* Princeton University Press.

3. Brustein, William. 2003. *Roots of Hate: Anti-Semitism in Europe Before the Holocaust.* Cambridge University Press.

4. Lewis, Bernard. 1984. *The Jews of Islam.* Princeton University Press.

5. Schweitzer, Frederick M., and Perry, Marvin. 2002. *Antisemitism: Myth and Hate From Antiquity to the Present.* Palgrave Macmillan.

6. United States Department of State. 2008. *Contemporary Global Anti-Semitism: A Report Provided to the United States Congress.* https://2009-2017.state.gov/documents/organization/102301.pdf, p. 5.

7. Pew Research Center 2012. *Rising Tide of Restrictions on Religion.* http://assets.pewresearch.org/wp-content/uploads/sites/11/2012/09/RisingTideofRestrictions-fullreport.pdf

8. Pew Research Center. 2012. *The Global Religious Landscape.* http://assets.pewresearch.org/wp-content/uploads/sites/11/2014/01/global-religion-full.pdf

9. Lugo, Luis, and Cooperman, Alan. 2012. *Rising Tide of Restrictions on Religion. Pew Research Center.* http://assets.pewresearch.org/wp-content/uploads/sites/11/2012/09/RisingTideofRestrictions-fullreport.pdf

10. Jewish Telegraphic Agency. 2016. US Anti-Semitism Worst Since 1930s, ADL Leader Says. *Times of Israel.* November 17. www.timesofisrael.com/us-anti-semitism-worst-since-1930s-adl-leader-says

11. Schwarz-Friesel, Monika, and Reinharz, Jehuda. 2017. *Inside the Antisemitic Mind: The Language of Jew-Hatred in Contemporary Germany*

(The Tauber Institute Series for the Study of European Jewry). Brandeis University Press.

12. The Holy Bible: King James Version. 2013. Christian Art Publishers.

13. *OED Online.* s.v. Semite, *n.* March 2018. Oxford University Press. www .oed.com

14. Schäfer, Peter. 1998. *Judeophobia: Attitudes towards the Jews in the Ancient World.* Harvard University Press.

15. The Holy Bible: King James Version. 2013. Christian Art Publishers.

16. Paul VI. 1965. Nostra Aetate: Declaration on the Relation of the Church to Non-Christian Religions. October 28. http://www.vatican.va/archive/hist_ councils/ii_vatican_council/documents/vat-ii_decl_19651028_nostra-aeta te_en.html

17. Trachtenberg, Joshua. 2002. *The Devil and the Jews: The Medieval Conception of the Jew and its Relation to Modern Antisemitism.* The Jewish Publication Society.

18. United States Department of State. 2008. *Contemporary Global Anti-Semitism: A Report Provided to the United States Congress.* https://2009-2017.state.gov/documents/organization/102301.pdf, p. 28.

19. Schwartz, Madeleine. 2016. The Origins of Blood Libel. *The Nation.* January 28. www.thenation.com/article/the-origins-of-blood-libel/

20. Pew Research Center. 2012. The Global Religious Landscape. http://assets .pewresearch.org/wp-content/uploads/sites/11/2014/01/global-religion-full .pdf, p. 9.

21. Lahey, Kate. 2009. Race Hate Attack on Jewish Teen. News.com.au. March 17. www.news.com.au/national/race-hate-attack-on-jewish-teen/news-story/2981e2c43e3dc3f3fe60eb4c9b29981b

22. Cortellessa, Eric. 2018. ADL Study Finds 4.2 Million Anti-Semitic Tweets Posted in Year. *The Times of Israel.* May 7. www.timesofisrael.com/adl-study-finds-4-2-million-anti-semitic-tweets-posted-in-year/

23. *OED Online.* s.v. Yid, *n.* March 2018. Oxford University Press. www.oed.com

24. Crace, John. 2012. Are Tottenham Hotspur Fans Really OK to Use the Word Yid at Matches? *The Guardian.* November 9. www.theguardian.com/foot ball/blog/2012/nov/09/tottenham-hotspur-fans-yid-chants

25. United States Department of State. 2008. Contemporary Global Anti-Semitism: A Report Provided to the United States Congress. https://2009-2017.state.gov/documents/organization/102301.pdf, p. 16.

26. Bamber, David, and Hastings, Chris. 2000. Errol Flynn "Spied for Allies, Not the Nazis." *The Telegraph.* December 31. www.telegraph.co.uk/ news/uknews/1379907/Errol-Flynn-spied-for-Allies-not-the-Nazis.html

27. *OED Online.* s.v. Hymie, *n.* March 2018. Oxford University Press. www .oed.com

28. Ben-David, Calev. 2016. Snap-Judgment: Shot Down In "Hymie-Town". *Jerusalem Post*. April 21. www.jpost.com/Opinion/Snap-Judgment-Shot-down-in-Hymie-town-451977

29. Ibid.

30. Liberman, Anatoly. 2009. Another Derogatory Name for the Jew: *Kike*. Oxford University Press blog. October 14. https://blog.oup.com/2009/10/ethnic-slurs-kike/

31. *OED Online*. s.v. Kike, *n*. March 2018. Oxford University Press. www.oed.com

32. Rosten, Leo. 1968. *The Joys of Yiddish*. Pocket Books.

33. Burston, Bradley. 2016. I Hadn't Been Called a Kike Since Fourth Grade. Donald Trump Changed All That. *Haaretz*. October 5. www.haaretz.com/opinion/i-hadn-t-been-called-a-kike-in-years-trump-changed-that-1.5446176

34. Foxman, Abraham. 2010. *Jews and Money: The Story of a Stereotype*. Palgrave Macmillan.

35. *OED Online*. s.v. Jew, *n*. March 2018. Oxford University Press. www.oed.com

36. Donadio, Rachel. 2018. The Meaning of France's March Against Anti-Semitism. *The Atlantic*. March 29. www.theatlantic.com/international/archive/2018/03/the-murder-of-mireille-knoll-in-france-might-be-the-last-straw-for-french-jews/556796/

37. The Holy Bible: King James Version. 2013. Christian Art Publishers.

38. Fox, Pam. 2016. *The Jewish Community of Golders Green: A Social History*. The History Press.

39. Farano, Adriano. 2006. Don't Be a Jew. *Café Babel*. February 22. www.cafebabel.co.uk/culture/article/dont-be-a-jew.html

40. Whine, Michael. 2010. Short History of the Definition. In *Proceedings of the 10th Biennial Seminar on AntiSemitism: The Working Definition of Antisemitism – Six Years After*. Paris, August 30–September 2. The Stephen Roth Institute for the Study of Contemporary Antisemitism and Racism.

41. Phillips, Melanie. 2007. Britain's Anti-Semitic Turn. *City Journal*. August. www.city-journal.org/html/britain%E2%80%99s-anti-semitic-turn-13046.html

42. Jacobs, Steven L., and Weitzman, Mark. 2003. *Dismantling the Big Lie: The Protocols of the Elders of Zion*. KTAV Publishing House.

43. Weiner, Allison Hope. 2006. Mel Gibson Apologizes for Tirade After Arrest. *The New York Times*. July 30. www.nytimes.com/2006/07/30/us/30gibson.html

44. Gillan, Audrey. 2006. Mel Gibson Apologises for Anti-Semitic Abuse. *The Guardian*. July 31. www.theguardian.com/world/2006/jul/31/arts.usa

45. Pappademas, Alex. 2011. Winona Forever. *GQ*. January issue. www.gq.com/story/winona-ryder-forever-black-swan-star-trek

46. Kaleem, Jaweed, and Jarvie, Jenny. 2017. Neo-Nazi Website Unleashed Internet Trolls against a Jewish Woman, Lawsuit Says. *Los Angeles Times.* April 18. www.latimes.com/nation/la-na-neonazi-website-lawsuit-20170418-story.html

47. Gambino, Lauren. 2016. Journalist Who Profiled Melania Trump Hit with Barrage of Anti-Semitic Abuse. *The Guardian.* April 28. www.theguardian.com/us-news/2016/apr/28/julia-ioffe-journalist-melania-trump-antisemitic-abuse

48. Steinweis, Alan E. 2009. *Kristallnacht 1938.* Harvard University Press.

49. Ibid.

50. Schwarz-Friesel, Monika, and Reinharz, Jehuda. 2017. *Inside the Antisemitic Mind: The Language of Jew-Hatred in Contemporary Germany.* Brandeis University Press.

51. Campaign Against Antisemitism. Recognizing Antisemitism: Antisemitic Language. https://antisemitism.uk/recognising-antisemitism/antisemitic-language/

52. United States Department of State. 2008. Contemporary Global Anti-Semitism: A Report Provided to the United States Congress. https://2009–2017.state.gov/documents/organization/102301.pdf, p. 22.

53. Tapper, Jake. 2007. Like Father, Like Son? *ABC News.* November 2. https://abcnews.go.com/Entertainment/story?id=2256719&page=1

54. Usborne, Simon. 2013. Exclusive: David Irving: The Hate that Dare not Speak Its Name. *The Independent.* August 30. www.independent.co.uk/news/uk/home-news/exclusive-david-irving-the-hate-that-dare-not-speak-its-name-8792411.html

55. Ibid.

56. Tharoor, Ishaan. 2016. Iran Revs Up for Its Latest Holocaust Cartoon Contest. *The Washington Post.* May 12. www.washingtonpost.com/news/worldviews/wp/2016/05/12/iran-revs-up-for-its-latest-holocaust-cartoon-contest/?noredirect=on&utm_term=.efa145a65544

57. Lohmann, Paulgerhard. 2014. *The Anti-Jewish Racist Mania of Hitler, The Jews in Fritzlar, and Its Boroughs, and Their Few Friends.* Books on Demand.

58. Cornell, Saul. 2008. *A Well-Regulated Militia: The Founding Fathers and the Origins of Gun Control in America.* Oxford University Press.

59. Fogelman, Hugh. 2012. *Christianity Uncovered: Viewed Through Open Eyes.* Author House.

60. Allert, Tilman. 2013. *The Hitler Salute: On the Meaning of a Gesture.* Henry Holt & Company.

61. Ibid.

62. Sehmer, Alexander. 2015. In Which Countries is it Illegal to Perform the Nazi Salute? *The Independent.* July 20. www.independent.co.uk/news/uk/home-news/queen-nazi-salute-countries-where-gesture-is-illegal-10401630.html

63. Dearden, Lizzie. 2016. White Supremacists Chant "Hail Trump" while Performing Hitler Salutes at Alt-Right Conference. *The Independent.* November 22. www.independent.co.uk/news/world/americas/donald-trump-president-elect-alt-right-white-supremacists-nazi-hitler-salutes-richard-b-spencer-a7431216.html

64. *OED Online.* s.v. swastika, *n.* March 2018. Oxford University Press. www.oed.com

65. Panati, Charles. 1996. *Sacred Origins of Profound Things.* Penguin Books.

66. Schmidt, Natasha. 2005. Reclaiming the Symbol. *Index on Censorship,* 34 (2), 52–53.

67. Regan, Mike. 2007. Jewish Graves Desecrated in New Zealand – Again. *The Jerusalem Post.* October 30. www.jpost.com/Jewish-World/Jewish-News/Jewish-graves-desecrated-in-New-Zealand-again

68. Schwarz-Friesel, Monika, and Reinharz, Jehuda. 2017. *Inside the Antisemitic Mind: The Language of Jew-Hatred in Contemporary Germany* (The Tauber Institute Series for the Study of European Jewry). Brandeis University Press.

69. Herbst, Phillip. 2003. *Talking Terrorism: A Dictionary of the Loaded Language of Political Violence.* Greenwood.

70. *OED Online.* s.v. Jew, *n.* March 2018. Oxford University Press. www.oed.com

71. Burston, Bradley. 2016. I Hadn't Been Called a Kike Since Fourth Grade. Donald Trump Changed All That. *Haaretz.* October 5. www.haaretz.com/opinion/i-hadn-t-been-called-a-kike-in-years-trump-changed-that-1.5446176

72. Bruce, Lenny. 2016. *How to Talk Dirty and Influence People: An Autobiography.* Da Capo Press.

73. Martin, Daniel. 2014. John Prescott Accused of "Trivialising the Holocaust" after Comparing the Gaza Strip to a Concentration Camp. *Daily Mail.* July 30. www.dailymail.co.uk/news/article-2711447/John-Prescott-accused-trivialising-Holocaust-comparing-Gaza-strip-concentration-camp.html

74. Hammer, Reuven. 2007. The Chosen People. *The Jerusalem Post.* October 10. www.jpost.com/Jewish-World/Judaism/The-chosen-people

75. Meierrieks, Danie, and Gries, Thomas. 2018. "Pay for It Heavily": Does U.S. Support for Israel Lead to Anti-American Terrorism? *Defence and Peace Economics,* 31 (2), 160–176.

76. Wilson, Jeff. 2016. Buddhism in America. *Oxford Research Encyclopedia of American History.* http://americanhistory.oxfordre.com/view/10.1093/acrefore/9780199329175.001.0001/acrefore-9780199329175-e-320.

77. Robinson, Greg. 2009. *A Tragedy of Democracy: Japanese Confinement in North America.* Columbia University Press.

78. Lee, Jonathan H. X. 2015. *History of Asian Americans: Exploring Diverse Roots*. Greenwood, p. 78.

79. Pew Research Center. 2012. *The Global Religious Landscape*. http://assets .pewresearch.org/wp-content/uploads/sites/11/2014/01/global-religion-full .pdf, p. 9.

80. Bailey, Sarah Pulliam. 2010. American Zenophilia. *Humanities*, 31 (2).

81. Weaver, Heather L. 2014. Buddhist Student, Religious Liberty Prevail in Louisiana. American Civil Liberties Union. March 14. www.aclu.org/ blog/religious-liberty/buddhist-student-religious-liberty-prevail-louisiana

82. Gunasekara, V. A. 2003. Hinduism in Buddhist Perspective. The Buddhist Society of Queensland. www.budsas.org/ebud/ebdha255.htm

83. Pew Research Center. 2012. The Global Religious Landscape. http://assets .pewresearch.org/wp-content/uploads/sites/11/2014/01/global-religion-full .pdf, p. 9.

84. People v. Murphy. 1977. *The Leagle*. March 16. www.leagle.com/decision/ 197733398misc2d2351294

85. Rajan, Valli J. 1995. Using TV, Christian Pat Robertson Denounces Hinduism as "Demonic." July. *Hinduism Today*. https://www.hinduism today.com/modules/smartsection/item.php?itemid=3502

86. Ibid.

87. Roy-Chowdury, Sandip. 1999. From Dotbusters to Cool Dots. *India Currents*. March 1. https://indiacurrents.com/from-dotbusters-to-cool-dots/

88. Kumar, Amitava. 2017. Being Indian in Trump's America. *The New Yorker*. March 15. www.newyorker.com/news/news-desk/being-indian-in-trumps-america

89. Takaki, Ronald. 1998. *A History of Asian Americans: Strangers from a Distant Shore*. Back Bay Books.

90. Shaw, Rosalind. 1990. The Invention of African Traditional Religion. *Religion*, 20 (4), 339–353.

91. US Equal Employment Opportunity Commission. Religious Discrimination. 12–1 Coverage (2). www.eeoc.gov/policy/docs/religion.html

92. *USA Today*. 2010. "No God" Comment Adds Up to No Job for Fired Math Teacher. June 1. http://usatoday30.usatoday.com/news/religion/2010-05-29-fired28_st_n.htm

93. Jillette, Penn. 2012. *Every Day Is an Atheist Holiday! More Magical Tales from the Author of God, No!* Penguin.

94. Goodnough, Abby. 2012. Student Faces Town's Wrath in Protest Against a Prayer. *The New York Times*. January 26. www.nytimes.com/2012/01/27/ us/rhode-island-city-enraged-over-school-prayer-lawsuit.html? pagewanted=all&_r=0

95. Burgess, Katherine. 2018. Atheists Take Official's "Go to Hell" Remark with Humor, Disappointment. March 16. *The Wichita Eagle*. www.kansas.com/news/local/article205591684.html

96. Pew Research Center. 2014. How Americans Feel About Religious Groups. www.pewforum.org/2014/07/16/how-americans-feel-about-religious-groups/

97. Pew Research Center. 2012. *The Global Religious Landscape*. http://assets.pewresearch.org/wp-content/uploads/sites/11/2014/01/global-religion-full.pdf, p. 9.

98. Pew Research Center. 2012. *Rising Tide of Restrictions on Religion*. Pew Research Center. http://assets.pewresearch.org/wp-content/uploads/sites/11/2012/09/RisingTideofRestrictions-fullreport.pdf

99. Limbaugh, David. 2003. *Persecution: How Liberals Are Waging War Against Christians*. Regnery Publishing.

100. Dowty, Alice. 2012. Hodges Now Leery of Jindal Reform. *The Livingston Parish News*. June 29. www.livingstonparishnews.com/news/hodges-now-leery-of-jindal-reform/article_6c2da5fe-c1e5-11e1-ae3b-0019bb2963f4.html

101. Stack, Liam. 2016. How the "War on Christmas" Controversy was Created. *The New York Times*. December 19. www.nytimes.com/2016/12/19/us/war-on-christmas-controversy.html

102. Aldrich, Jeremy. 2011. The History of "Happy Holidays." December 23. www.hburgjeremy.com/2011/12/history-of-happy-holidays.html

103. Kumar, Anugrah. 2013. NY State Senator Wants Atheist "Nobody Needs Christ" Christmas Ad Removed from Times Square. *The Christian Post*. December 22. www.christianpost.com/news/ny-state-senator-wants-atheist-nobody-needs-christ-christmas-ad-removed-from-times-square-111339/

104. *USA Today*. 2018. Church Leader Wants People to Stop Using "Mormon" and "LDS" as Substitutes for Full Name. August 18. www.usatoday.com/story/news/nation-now/2018/08/18/russell-m-nelson-mormon-not-substitute-full-name-church/1032948002/

105. Eltagouri, Marwa. 2018. Joy Behar Publicly Apologizes for Calling Pence's Christianity a "Mental Illness." *The Washington Post*. March 14. www.washingtonpost.com/news/acts-of-faith/wp/2018/03/13/vice-president-pence-is-right-joy-behar-publicly-apologizes-for-mocking-christianity/?utm_term=.bc47ca8beb05

106. US Constitution. 1791. Amendment 1. Cornell Law School. www.law.cornell.edu/constitution/first_amendment

107. Pew Research Center. 2012. *The Global Religious Landscape*. http://assets.pewresearch.org/wp-content/uploads/sites/11/2014/01/global-religion-full.pdf, p. 45.

108. Ibid.
109. Esposito, John L. 1999. *The Oxford History of Islam*. Oxford University Press.
110. *OED Online*. s.v. Islam, *n*. March 2019. Oxford University Press. www .oed.com
111. *OED Online*. s.v. Muslim, *n*. and *adj*. March 2019. Oxford University Press. www.oed.com
112. Kunnummal, Ashraf, and Abbasi, Alexander. 2017. The Islamophobia of Buddhist Terror? Why Language Matters. *ReOrient: The Journal of Critical Muslim Studies*. https://www.criticalmuslimstudies.co.uk/the-islamopho bia-of-buddhist-terror-why-language-matters/
113. Hippler, Jochen, and Lueg, Andrea (Eds.). 2007. *The Next Threat: Western Perceptions of Islam*. Pluto Press.
114. Mamdani, Mahmood. 2005. *Good Muslim, Bad Muslim: America, the Cold War, and the Roots of Terror*. Three Leaves Press.
115. *OED Online*. s.v. Islamophobia, *n*. March 2019. Oxford University Press. www.oed.com
116. *OED Online*. s.v. Germanophobia, *n*. March 2019. Oxford University Press. www.oed.com
117. *OED Online*. s.v. Francophobia, *n*. March 2019. Oxford University Press. www.oed.com
118. *OED Online*. s.v. xenophobia, *n*. March 2019. Oxford University Press. www.oed.com
119. Mohideen, Haja, and Mohideen, Shamimah. 2008. The Language of Islamophobia in Internet Articles. *Intellectual Discourse*, 16 (1), 73–87.
120. Media Matters for America. 2006. Robertson Labeled Islam a "Bloody, Brutal Type of Religion." May 1. www.mediamatters.org/video/2006/05/ 01/robertson-labeled-islam-a-bloody-brutal-type-of/135543
121. Elmasry, Mohamad. 2019. New Zealand Mosque Attacks and the Scourge of White Supremacy. *Al Jazeera*. March 15. www.aljazeera.com/indepth/ opinion/zealand-mosque-attacks-scourge-white-supremacy-190315090752857.html
122. Abdelaziz, Rowaida, Ahmed, Akbar Shahid, and Robins-Early, Nick. 2019. Islamophobia is a Global Crisis – And It's Time We View It That Way. *Huffington Post*. March 17. www.huffpost.com/entry/islamophobia-is-a-glo bal-crisis-and-its-time-we-view-it-that-way_n_5c8e5867e4b0db7da9f48156
123. *The Guardian*. 2001. Blair meets British Muslims. September 21. www .theguardian.com/world/2001/sep/27/september11.usa
124. Ostroy, Andy. 2017. "Muslims Killed Us on 9/11?" *Huffington Post*. December 6. www.huffingtonpost.com/andy-ostroy/muslims-killed-us-on-911_b_764784.html

125. Mohammad, Noor. 2015. The Doctrine of Jihad: An Introduction. *Journal of Law and Religion*, 3 (2), 381–397.
126. Said, Edward. 1978. *Orientalism*. Pantheon Books.
127. Bowen, John R. 2012. *Blaming Islam*. MIT Press.
128. Tayyen, Sana. 2017. "Good" Muslim, "Evil" Islam Dichotomy. *Huffington Post*. February 26. www.huffpost.com/entry/good-muslim-evil-islam-di_b_9297142
129. Bonotti, Matteo. 2017. *Partisanship and Political Liberalism in Diverse Societies*. Oxford University Press.
130. Johnson, Boris. 2018. Denmark Has Got It Wrong. Yes, the Burka is Oppressive and Ridiculous – but That's Still No Reason to Ban It. *The Telegraph*. August 5. www.telegraph.co.uk/news/2018/08/05/denmark-has-got-wrong-yes-burka-oppressive-ridiculous-still/
131. Perry, Barbara. 2014. Gendered Islamophobia: Hate Crimes against Muslim Women. *Social Identities*, 20 (1), 74–89.
132. Hartman, Todd K., and Newmark, Adam J. 2012. Motivated Reasoning, Political Sophistication, and Associations between President Obama and Islam. *PS: Political Science & Politics*, 45 (3), 449–455.
133. Adamson, Bryan. 2011. The Muslim Manchurian Candidate: Barack Obama, Rumors, and Quotidian Hermeneutics. *Journal of Civil Rights and Economic Development*, 25 (4), 581–624.
134. Suebsaeng, Asawin, and Gilson, David. 2012. Chart: Almost every Obama Conspiracy Theory Ever. *Mother Jones*. November 2. www.motherjones.com/politics/2012/11/chart-obama-conspiracy-theories/
135. Block, Ray, and Onwunli, Chinonye. 2010. Managing Monikers: The Role of Name Presentation in the 2008 Presidential Election. *Presidential Studies Quarterly*, 40 (3), 464–481.
136. Tashman, Brian. 2012. The Ultimate Obama-Islam-Sharia-Agenda21-Immigration Debt Conspiracy. *Right Wing Watch*. May 23. www.rightwingwatch.org/post/the-ultimate-obama-islam-sharia-agenda-21-immigration-debt-conspiracy/
137. Show Racism the Red Card (SRTRC). 2014. *To What Extent Do Young People Share Potentially Damaging Attitudes with Far Right Groups and where do these ideas Come From? What Are the Opportunities and Risks that This Presents?* http://srtrc.s3-eu-west-1.amazonaws.com/The-Attitudes-of-Young-People—SRtRC-study.pdf
138. Webb, Whitney. 2019. The Christchurch Shooting and the Normalization of Anti-Muslim Terrorism. *MintPress News*. March 15. www.mintpressnews.com/the-christchurch-shooting-and-the-normalization-of-anti-muslim-terrorism/256295/
139. Sonmez, Felicia, and DeBonis, Mike. 2019. Trump Tells Four Liberal Congresswomen to "Go Back" to Their Countries, Prompting Pelosi to

Defend Them. *The Washington Post*. July 14. www.washingtonpost
.com/politics/trump-says-four-liberal-congresswomen-should-go-back-
to-the-crime-infested-places-from-which-they-came/2019/07/14/

140. Dziedzic, Stephen. 2017. Pauline Hanson's Anti-Islam Post in Wake of
London Attack Slammed by Bill Shorten. *ABC News*. June 4. www.abc.net
.au/news/2017–06-04/pauline-hanson-london-bridge-islam-tweet-
slammed-bill-shorten/8588120

141. Johnson, Jenna. 2015. Trump Calls for "Total and Complete Shutdown of
Muslims Entering the United States." *The Washington Post*. December 7.
www.washingtonpost.com/news/post-politics/wp/2015/12/07/donald-
trump-calls-for-total-and-complete-shutdown-of-muslims-entering-the-
united-states

142. Yilmaz, Ihsan. 2016. The Nature of Islamophobia: Some Key Features. In
Fear of Muslims? International Perspectives on Islamophobia, edited by
Douglas Pratt and Rachel Woodlock. Springer.

143. Baker, Nick. 2019. Outrage as Fraser Anning Blames NZ Attacks on
"Muslim Immigration." *SBS News*. March 15. www.sbs.com.au/news/
outrage-as-fraser-anning-blames-nz-attacks-on-muslim-immigration

144. Kwai, Isabella. 2018. Australian Senator Calls for "Final Solution" to
Muslim Immigration. *The New York Times*. August 14. www.nytimes
.com/2018/08/14/world/australia/final-solution-fraser-anning.html

145. Middle East Policy Council. Arab, Middle Eastern, and Muslim? What's the
Difference?! *TeachMideast*. http://teachmideast.org/middle-east-policy-
council/

146. Hamm, Mark S. 1994. *Hate Crime: International Perspectives on Causes and
Control*. Routledge.

147. Engel, Matthew. 2002. Naïve Bush Slights Pakistanis with a Short-Cut. *The
Guardian*. January 8. www.theguardian.com/world/2002/jan/09/usa
.matthewengel

148. Hankir, Ahmed Zakaria, Ali, Sayeeda, Siddique, Usman, Carrick, Frederick
R., and Zaman, Rashid. 2019. Islamophobia: A British Muslim Perspective.
In *Islamophobia and Psychiatry*, edited by H. Steven Moffic, John
Peteet, Ahmed Zakaria Hankir, and Rania Awaad. Springer.

149. Woodall, Bernie. 2017. Florida Man Sentenced to 15 Years in Prison for
Vandalizing Mosque. *Reuters*. December 6. www.reuters.com/article/us-
florida-islam-hatecrime/florida-man-sentenced-to-15-years-in-prison-
for-vandalizing-mosque-idUSKBN1E02Z9

150. Owen, Tess. 2015. Sikh Man is Brutally Beaten After Being Called "Bin
Laden" and "Terrorist." *Vice News*. September 10. https://news.vice.com/
article/sikh-man-is-brutally-beaten-after-being-called-bin-laden-and-
terrorist

151. Bever, Lindsey. 2015. Police: 7th-Grader Calls Muslim Schoolmate "Son of ISIS," Threatens to Shoot and Kill Him. *The Washington Post.* December 14. www.washingtonpost.com/news/morning-mix/wp/2015/ 12/14/police-7th-grader-calls-muslim-schoolmate-son-of-isis-threatens-to-shoot-and-kill-him/

152. Lewis, Charlton T., and Short, Charles. 1879. *A Latin Dictionary.* Clarendon Press.

153. Schaub, Michael. 2015. ISIS Bookstore in Colorado Rebrands after Vandalism. *Los Angeles Times.* December 30. www.latimes.com/books/ jacketcopy/la-et-jc-colorado-bookstore-isis-rebrands-20151230-story. html

154. Lourgos, Angie Leventis. 2016. People Named Isis Share Tales of Ignorance. *Chicago Tribune.* January 25. www.chicagotribune.com/news/ ct-people-named-isis-met-20160123-story.html

155. Ionis Pharmaceuticals. 2015. Isis Pharmaceuticals Changes Name to Ionis Pharmaceuticals. Press Release. December 18. http://ir.ionispharma.com/ news-releases/news-release-details/isis-pharmaceuticals-changes-name-ionis-pharmaceuticals

156. Workman, Karen. 2015. When You're Named Isis for the Goddess, Not the Terror Group. *The New York Times.* November 20. www.nytimes.com/ 2015/11/21/world/europe/when-youre-named-isis-for-the-goddess-not-the-terror-group.html

157. Khan, Zeba. 2014. Words Matter in "ISIS" War, So Use "Daesh." *Boston Globe.* October 9. www.bostonglobe.com/opinion/2014/10/09/words-mat ter-isis-war-use-daesh/V85GYEuasEEJgrUun0dMUP/story.html

158. Pullella, Philip. 2016. Pope Says It's Wrong to Identify Islam with Violence. *Reuters.* July 31. www.reuters.com/article/us-pope-islam/pope-says-its-wrong-to-identify-islam-with-violence-idUSKCN10B0YO

159. Temple-Raston, Dina. 2014. Prominent Muslim Sheikh Issues Fatwa Against ISIS Violence. *National Public Radio.* September 25. www.npr.org/ 2014/09/25/351277631/prominent-muslim-sheikh-issues-fatwa-against-isis-violence

160. Skutnabb-Kangas, Tove. 2015. Linguicism. In *The Encyclopedia of Applied Linguistics,* edited by Carol Chapelle. Wiley. DOI:10.1002/9781405198431. wbeal1460

161. El Gayar, Neamat, and Suen, Ching Y. 2018. *Computational Linguistics, Speech and Image Processing for Arabic Language.* World Scientific Publishing Company.

162. Antoon, Sinan. 2016. Why Speaking Arabic in America feels Like a Crime. *The Guardian.* April 19. www.theguardian.com/commentisfree/2016/apr/ 19/why-speaking-arabic-america-feels-like-crime

163. Jobrani, Maz. 2012. A Saudi, an Indian and an Iranian Walk into a Qatari Bar. TEDxSummit. www.youtube.com/watch?v=9kxL9Cf46VM

164. George, Nick. 2015. I Was Arrested for Learning a Foreign Language. Today, I Have Some Closure. American Civil Liberties Union. January 23. www.aclu.org/blog/speakeasy/i-was-arrested-learning-foreign-language-today-i-have-some-closure

165. *The Times of Israel*. 2015. Hebrew Sign Mistaken for Islamist Banner in Louisiana. August 23. www.Timesofisrael.Com/Hebrew-Sign-Mistaken-For-Islamist-Banner-In-Louisiana

166. KCBD. 2016. LPD investigates Arabic Flag Hanging from Citizens Tower. *KCBD News*. February 15. www.kcbd.com/story/31224081/lpd-investi gates-arabic-flag-hanging-from-citizens-tower

167. Kunzmann, Kevin. 2016. Cookie Box Causes a Stir at Marshalls Creek Gulf Station. *Pocono Record*. September 19. www.poconorecord.com/news/20160919/cookie-box-causes-stir-at-marshalls-creek-gulf-station

168. Wemple, Erik. 2015. Parody Islamic State Flag Creator: "I'm Still Waiting for an Apology" from CNN. *Washington Post*. July 3. www.washington post.com/blogs/erik-wemple/wp/2015/07/03/parody-islamic-state-flag-creator-im-still-waiting-for-an-apology-from-cnn

169. Winsor, Ben. 2016. The Arabic on This Tote Bag is Hilariously Edgy. May 19. SBS. www.sbs.com.au/topics/life/culture/article/2016/05/18/ara bic-tote-bag-hilariously-edgy

170. Nagesh, Ashitha. 2016. Arabic Billboard Trolls Donald Trump Beautifully. *Metro*. October 18. http://metro.co.uk/2016/10/18/arabic-billboard-trolls-donald-trump-beautifully-6199384/

5 That's Crazy

1. Bly, Nellie. 2015(1887). *Ten Days in a Mad-house*. Golgotha Press.

2. Riva, M., Tremolizzo, L., Spicci, M., Ferrarese, C., De Vito, G., Cesana, G., and Sironi, V. 2011. The Disease of the Moon: The Linguistic and Pathological Evolution of the English term "Lunatic." *Journal of the History of the Neurosciences*, 20, (1), 65–73.

3. Chantrell, Glynnis. 2002. *The Oxford Dictionary of Word Histories*. Oxford University Press, p. 134.

4. *OED Online*. s.v. mad, *adj*. January 2018. Oxford University Press. www.oed.com

5. *OED Online*. s.v. crazy, *adj*. January 2018. Oxford University Press. www .oed.com

6. Coon, Dennis, and Mitterer, John O. 2008. *Introduction to Psychology: Gateways to Mind and Behavior*. Wadsworth Publishing.

7. Reaume, Geoffrey. 2002. Lunatic to Patient to Person: Nomenclature in Psychiatric History and the Influence of Patients' Activism in North America. *International Journal of Law and Psychiatry*, 25 (4), 405–426.

8. American Psychiatric Association. 2013. *Diagnostic and Statistical Manual of Mental Disorders* (5th ed.).

9. Steven Pinker. 1994. The Game of the Name. *The Baltimore Sun*. http://articles .baltimoresun.com/1994-04-06/news/1994096202_1_dutch-words-language

10. Millington, Michael J., and Leirer, Stephen J. 1996. A Socially Desirable Response to the Politically Incorrect Use of Disability Labels. *Rehabilitation Counseling Bulletin*, 39, 276–283.

11. Kerschberg, Benjamin. 2014. *101 "Insanely Great" Resources – Big Data*. BK Literary Enterprises.

12. Burridge, Kate. 2015. "Taboo Words." In *The Oxford Handbook of the Word*, edited by John R. Taylor. Oxford University Press.

13. Rauch, Jonathan. 2016. How American Politics Went Insane. *The Atlantic*. July/August issue.

14. Pierce, Chester M. 1995. Stress Analogs of Racism and Sexism: Terrorism, Torture and Disaster. In *Mental Health, Racism and Sexism*, edited by Charles Vert Willie, Patricia Perri Rieker, Bernard M. Kramer, and Bertram S. Brown. Taylor & Francis.

15. Umstead, Alex. 2012. An Introductory Guide to Disability Language and Empowerment. Syracuse University Disability Cultural Center. http://sudcc .syr.edu/LanguageGuide/index.html

16. Schumaker, Erin. 2015. It's Time to Stop Using These Phrases when It Comes to Mental Illness. *Huffington Post*, April 17.

17. Silverman, Morton M. 2006. The Language of Suicidality. *Suicide and Life-Threatening Behavior*, 36 (5), 519–532.

18. Botticelli, Michael P., and Koh, Howard K. 2016. Changing the Language of Addiction. *JAMA*, 316 (13), 1361–1362.

19. Bonkers Bruno Locked Up. 2003. *The Sun*. September 23.

20. Maisel, Albert Q. 1946. Bedlam 1946. Most U.S. Mental Hospitals are a Shame and a Disgrace. *Life Magazine*. May 6, pp. 102–118.

21. Rai, Tage. 2017. The Myth that Mental Illness Causes Mass Shootings. *Behavioral Scientist*. October 13. http://behavioralscientist.org/myth-men tal-illness-causes-mass-shootings/

22. Gold, Liza H. (Ed.). 2016. *Gun Violence and Mental Illness*. American Psychiatric Association.

23. Michael Jackson: How He Came to be Known as Wacko Jacko. 2009. *The Telegraph*. June 26. www.telegraph.co.uk/culture/music/michael-jackson/ 5644026/Michael-Jackson-how-he-came-to-be-known-as-Wacko-Jacko .html

24. *OED Online.* s.v. crazy, *adj.* January 2018. Oxford University Press. www .oed.com

25. Allan, Keith, and Burridge, Kate. 2006. *Forbidden Words: Taboo and the Censoring of Language.* Cambridge University Press.

26. *OED Online.* s.v. idiot, *n.* and *adj.* January 2018. Oxford University Press. www.oed.com.

27. Cockerham, William C. 2017. *Sociology of Mental Disorder.* Routledge.

28. *OED Online.* s.v. imbecile, *adj.* and *n.* January 2018. Oxford University Press. www.oed.com

29. Gelb, Steven A. 1987. Social Deviance and the "Discovery" of the Moron. *Disability, Handicap & Society,* 2 (3), 247–258.

30. Goddard, Henry H. 1910. What Can the Public School Do for Subnormal Children? *Journal of Proceedings and Addresses of the National Education Association of the United States,* p. 913.

31. *OED Online.* s.v. cretin, *n.* January 2018. Oxford University Press. www .oed.com

32. Allan, Keith, and Burridge, Kate. 2006. *Forbidden Words: Taboo and the Censoring of Language.* Cambridge University Press, p. 215.

33. Silver, Michael G. 2004. Eugenics and Compulsory Sterilization Laws: Providing Redress for the Victims of a Shameful Era in United States History. *George Washington Law Review,* 72 (4), 862.

34. Lindert, Jutta, Stein, Yael, Guggenheim, Hans, Jaakkola, Jouni J. K., and Strous, Rael D. 2012. How Ethics Failed: The Role of Psychiatrists and Physicians in Nazi Programs from Exclusion to Extermination, 1933–1945. *Public Health Reviews,* 34 (8).

35. Durham, Michael. 1992. Political Correctness: Mencap Vows to Keep Its Name Despite Row. *Independent.* July 19. www.independent.co.uk/news/uk/politics/ political-correctness-mencap-vows-to-keep-name-despite-row-1534423.html

36. Gopalan, Rejani Thudalikunnil. 2016. *Handbook of Research on Diagnosing, Treating and Managing Intellectual Disabilities.* Information Science Reference.

37. Definition of Intellectual Disability. American Association of Intellectual and Developmental Disabilities. http://aaidd.org/intellectual-disability/definition

38. *OED Online.* s.v. stupid, *adj.* and *n.* January 2018. Oxford University Press. www.oed.com

39. ischemgeek. 2014. The Case Against Stupid. https://ischemgeek.wordpress .com/2014/02/15/the-case-against-stupid/

40. Wawrzyniak, Agnieszka. 2012. The Influence of Contextual Factors upon the Semantics of *Selly. Kwartalnik Neofilologiczny,* 59, 85–97.

41. *OED Online.* s.v. fool, *n.1* and *adj.* January 2018. Oxford University Press. www.oed.com

42. *OED Online.* s.v. dumb, *adj.* and *n.* January 2018. Oxford University Press. www.oed.com

43. Turner, David, M. 2012. *Disability in Eighteenth-Century England: Imagining Physical Impairment.* Routledge.

44. *About for Dummies.* www.dummies.com/about-for-dummies/

45. BBC. 2006. Osborne's Autism Jibe Criticized. *BBC News.* October 2. http://news.bbc.co.uk/2/hi/uk_news/politics/5399072.stm

46. Sharkie, Fiona. 2017. Don Burke's Words an Assault on Autistic People. *Herald Sun.* November 28. https://www.perthnow.com.au/opinion/rendez view/don-burkes-words-an-assault-on-autistic-people-ng-1105f34f4946137 b8318f77895836929

47. Brown, Lydia Z. X. 2011. The Significance of Semantics: Person-First Language: Why It Matters. www.autistichoya.com/2011/08/significance-of-semantics-person-first.html

48. Umstead, Alex. 2012. An Introductory Guide to Disability Language and Empowerment. Syracuse University Disability Cultural Center. http://sudcc .syr.edu/LanguageGuide/index.html

49. Down, John Langdon H. 1866. Observations on an Ethnic Classification of Idiots. *London Hospital Reports*, 3, 259–262.

50. Mégarbané, André, Ravel, Aimé, Mircher, Chloe, Sturz, Franck, Grattau, Yann, Rethoré, Marie-Odile, Delabar, Jean-Maurice, and Mobley, William C. 2009. The 50th Anniversary of the Discovery of Trisomy 21: The Past, Present, and Future of Research and Treatment of Down Syndrome. *Genetics in Medicine*, 11, 611–616.

51. BBC. 2017. Author Libby Weaver Apologises over "Mongolism" in Book. *BBC News.* November 6 www.bbc.com/news/world-australia-41882083

52. Orr, Gillian 2014. Why Are the Words "Mongol," "Mongoloid" and "Mongy" Still Bandied About as Insults? *Independent.* November 23. www.independent.co.uk/arts-entertainment/tv/features/why-are-the-words-mongol-mongoloid-and-mongy-still-bandied-about-as-insults-9878557.html

53. Linton, Simi. 1998. *Claiming Disability: Knowledge and Identity.* New York University Press.

54. Brown, Steven E. 1995. *The Chart: Disability Culture/Rights/Pride Paradigm.* Institute on Disability Culture.

55. Olkin, Rhoda. 2002. Could You Hold the Door for Me? Including Disability in Diversity. *Cultural Diversity and Ethnic Minority Psychology*, 8 (2), 130–137.

56. Brown, Lydia X. Z. 2013. How "Differently Abled" Marginalizes Disabled People. www.autistichoya.com/2013/08/differently-abled.html

57. Sol, Saporta, and R. R. B. 1991. Old Maid and Dirty Old Man: The Language of Ageism. *American Speech*, 66 (3), 333–335.

58. *OED Online.* s.v. cripple, *n.* and *adj.* January 2018. Oxford University Press. www.oed.com

59. Rose, Damon. 2006. The S-Word. *BBC News.* April 12. news.bbc.co.uk/2/hi/uk_news/magazine/4902432.stm

60. Scope. Our History. www.scope.org.uk/about-us/history

61. *OED Online.* s.v. lame, *adj.* January 2018. Oxford University Press. www.oed.com

62. Ibid.

63. Aaron, Jessi Elana. 2015. "Lame," "Stand Up," and Other Words We Use to Insult the Disabled without Even Knowing It. *The Washington Post.* www.washingtonpost.com/posteverything/wp/2015/05/13/lame-stand-up-and-other-words-we-use-to-insult-the-disabled-without-even-knowing-it/

64. Daugherty, Megan, and Macdonald, Marian. 2004. Deaf is Dandy: Contrasting the Deaf and Hearing Cultures. *Intercultural Communication Studies,* 13 (2), 111–117.

65. Jankowski, Katherine, A. 1997. *Deaf Empowerment: Emergence, Struggle, and Rhetoric.* Gallaudet University Press.

66. Royal National Institute of Blind People. Our History. www.rnib.org.uk/who-we-are/history-rnib

67. Goffman, Erving. 1963. *Stigma.* Penguin, p. 14.

68. Personal correspondence with the author.

69. Mingus, Mia. 2017. Forced Intimacy: An Ableist Norm. *Leaving Evidence.* August 6. https://leavingevidence.wordpress.com/2017/08/06/forced-intimacy-an-ableist-norm/

70. Diebelius, Georgia. 2017. Amputee War Hero Told to "Prove He Is Disabled" by Virgin Train Staff. *Metro.* September 8. http://metro.co.uk/2017/09/08/amputee-war-hero-told-to-prove-he-is-disabled-by-virgin-train-staff-6913674/

71. Del Real, Jose. 2015. Trump Draws Scornful Rebuke for Mocking Reporter with Disability. *The Washington Post.* November 26. www.washingtonpost.com/news/post-politics/wp/2015/11/25/trump-blasted-by-new-york-times-after-mocking-reporter-with-disability

72. Hanson, Hilary. 2015. Trump Mocking Physical Disabilities is Nothing New. *Huffington Post.* November 26. www.huffingtonpost.com/entry/trump-mocks-disabled-reporter_us

73. Resnick, Gideon, and Suebsaeng, Asawin. 2016. Donald Trump called Deaf Apprentice Marlee Matlin "Retarded," Three Staffers Say. *The Daily Beast.* April 13. www.thedailybeast.com/donald-trump-called-deaf-apprentice-marlee-matlin-retarded-three-staffers-say

74. BBC. 2016. Disabled Models and Athletes Outraged by Brazilian Vogue Paralympic Campaign Photo. *Newsbeat.* August 26. www.bbc.co.uk/news

beat/article/37194585/disabled-models-and-athletes-outraged-by-brazi
lian-vogue-paralympic-campaign-photo

75. Edelson, Stephen. n.d. Research: Autistic Savants. Autism Research Institute. www.autism.com/understanding_savants

76. Sanburn, Josh. 2014. Ebola Brings Another Fear: Xenophobia. *TIME.* October 29. http://time.com/3544130/ebola-panic-xenophobia/

77. Avert. HIV Stigma and Discrimination. www.avert.org/professionals/hiv-social-issues/stigma-discrimination

78. Lettau, Ludwig A. 2000. The Language of Infectious Disease: A Light-Hearted Review. *Clinical Infectious Diseases,* 31 (3), 734–738.

79. Allan, Keith, and Burridge, Kate. 2006. *Forbidden Words: Taboo and the Censoring of Language.* Cambridge University Press.

80. Sontag, Susan. 1978. *Illness as Metaphor and AIDS and Its Metaphors.* Penguin.

81. Anderson, Veanne N. 1992. For Whom Is This World Just? Sexual Orientation and AIDS. *Journal of Applied Social Psychology,* 22 (3), 248–259.

82. Depression is Real Coalition. 2006. www.depressionisreal.org (website discontinued).

83. Allan, Keith, and Burridge, Kate. 2006. *Forbidden Words: Taboo and the Censoring of Language.* Cambridge University Press, p. 221.

84. BBC. 1995. Timeline: Blur v Oasis after Britpop. *BBC News.* August 14. http://news.bbc.co.uk/2/hi/entertainment/4151510.stm

85. Goodman, J. David. 2016. Carl Paladino, Trump Ally, Wishes Obama Dead of Mad Cow Disease in '17. *The New York Times.* December 23. www.nytimes.com/2016/12/23/nyregion/carl-paladino-trump-ally-wishes-obama-dead-and-aims-racial-insults-at-michelle-obama.html

86. Mohr, Melissa. 2016. The Profanity of Disease. Oxford University Press blog. https://blog.oup.com/2016/06/profanity-disease-pox-leprosy/

87. Burridge, Kate. 2002. *Blooming English: Observations on the Roots, Cultivation and Hybrids of the English Language.* Cambridge University Press.

88. "Cancer Sufferer" and Other Strange Dutch Insults. 2013. *Pet Hates* blog. April 29. https://pethatesblog.wordpress.com/2013/04/29/cancer-sufferer-and-other-strange-dutch-insults/

89. Masato, Ishii. 2016. Hansen's Disease in Japan: The Lingering Legacy of Discrimination. Nippon.com. https://www.nippon.com/en/features/c02703/

90. Whitney, William Dwight. 1890. *The Century Dictionary of the English Language.* Century Company.

91. Aldahan, Adam, Shah, Vidhi V., Mlacker, Stephanie, Aldahan, Suzanne M., and Nouri, Keyvan. 2016. Discrimination against People with Dermatologic Diseases. *JAMA Dermatol,* 152 (2), 140.

92. Allan, Keith, and Burridge, Kate. 2006. *Forbidden Words: Taboo and the Censoring of Language.* Cambridge University Press, p. 208.

93. Ghosh, Sangita, and Chaudhuri, Soumik. 2015. Chronicles of Gerhard-Henrik Armauer Hansen's Life and Work. *Indian Journal of Dermatology*, 60 (3), 219–221.

94. Frith, John. 2014. History of Tuberculosis: Part 1 – Phthisis, Consumption and the White Plague. *Journal of Military and Veterans' Health*, 22 (2), 29–35.

95. Ibid.

96. Kraut, Alan. 2010. Immigration, Ethnicity and Epidemic. *Public Health Reports*, 125, 123–133.

97. Abrams, Jeanne. 2009. *Dr. Charles David Spivak: A Jewish Immigrant and the American Tuberculosis Movement.* University Press of Colorado.

98. Taylor, Robert. 2017. Medical Words Linked to Places. In *The Amazing Language of Medicine.* Springer.

99. Allan, Keith, and Burridge, Kate. 2006. *Forbidden Words: Taboo and the Censoring of Language.* Cambridge University Press.

100. Haubrich, William S. 1997. *Medical Meanings: A Glossary of Word Origins.* Philadelphia. American College of Physicians.

101. Appuhamy, Ranil D., Tent, Jan, and Mackenzie, John S. 2010. Toponymous Diseases of Australia. *Medical Journal of Australia*, 193 (11–12), 642–646.

102. Soper, George A. 1939. The Curious Career of Typhoid Mary. *Bulletin of the New York Academy of Medicine*, 15 (10), 698–712.

103. Leavitt, Judith, W. 1997. *Typhoid Mary: Captive to the Public's Health.* Beacon Press.

104. World Health Organization. 2015. WHO Issues Best Practices for Naming New Human Infectious Diseases. www.who.int/mediacentre/news/notes/2015/naming-new-diseases/en/

105. Ballantyne, Coco. 2009. Will Egypt's Plans to Kill Pigs Protect It from Swine – Sorry, H1N1 Flu? *Scientific American.* May 1. https://blogs.scientificamerican.com/news-blog/will-egypts-plans-to-kill-pigs-prot-2009-05-01/

6 Hit by the Ugly Stick

1. Ford, Peter, and Howell, Michael. 2010. *The True History of the Elephant Man: The Definitive Account of the Tragic and Extraordinary Life of Joseph Carey Merrick.* Skyhorse Publishing.

2. Koven, Seth. 2006. *Slumming: Sexual and Social Politics in Victorian London.* Princeton University Press.

3. Ibid.

4. Ayto, John. 1999. *20th Century Words.* Oxford University Press.

5. Blanchard, Pascal, Bancel, Nicolas, and Lemaire, Sandrine. 2009. *Human Zoos: Science and Spectacle in the Age of Empire.* Liverpool University Press.

6. Allen, Rick. 1999. John Fisher Murray, Dickens, and "The Attraction of Repulsion." *Dickens Quarterly*, 16 (3), 139.

7. Williams, Jessica L. 2017. *Media, Perfomative Identity, and the New American Freak Show*. Palgrave Macmillan.

8. Schweik, Susan M. 2009. *The Ugly Laws: Disability in Public*. New York University Press.

9. Phillips, Katharine A. 1991. Body Dysmorphic Disorder: The Distress of Imagined Ugliness. *The American Journal of Psychiatry*, 148 (9), 1138–1149.

10. Wilde, Oscar. 1993(1890). *The Picture of Dorian Gray*. Dover.

11. Raiten-D'Antonio, Toni. 2010. *Ugly as Sin: The Truth About How We Look and Finding Freedom from Self-Hatred*. Health Communications.

12. Sullivan, Eileen, and Haberman, Maggie. 2018. Trump Calls Stormy Daniels "Horseface" in Gloating Twitter Post. *The New York Times*. October 16. www.nytimes.com/2018/10/16/us/politics/trump-stormy-daniels-horse face-women.html

13. Adams, Char. 2017. Bullied Teen Who Killed Herself Apologized for Being Ugly, Didn't Want Any Photos at Funeral. *People*. December 20. https://people.com/human-interest/bullied-teen-suicide-photo-funeral/

14. Bahadur, Nina. 2017. Winona Ryder Interview: Actress Was Once Told "You Are Not Pretty Enough." *The Huffington Post*. December 6. www .huffingtonpost.com/2013/05/07/winona-ryder-interview-you-are-not-pretty-enough_n_3229779.html

15. Rojas, John-Paul Ford. 2012. Mary Beard Hits Back at AA Gill after He Brands Her "Too Ugly for Television." *The Telegraph*. April 24. www.tele graph.co.uk/news/picturegalleries/celebritynews/9223149/Mary-Beard-hits-back-at-AA-Gill-after-he-brands-her-too-ugly-for-television.html

16. Hamermesh, Daniel, S. 2013. *Beauty Pays: Why Attractive People Are More Successful*. Princeton University Press.

17. Crisler, Joan, and Ghiz, Laurie. 1993. Body Image Issues of Older Women. *Women & Therapy*, 14 (1–2), 67–75.

18. Lutz, Ashley. 2013. Former Abercrombie Manager Alleges That Workers Were Fired for Being Too Fat. *Business Insider*. May 17. www.busines sinsider.com/abercrombie-allegedly-fired-fat-people-2013-5

19. Greenhalgh, Susan. 2015. *Fat-Talk Nation: The Human Costs of America's War on Fat*. Cornell University Press.

20. Elliptical Reviews. 2016. Weight Haters: A Look at Fat Shaming on Twitter. www.ellipticalreviews.com/weight-haters/

21. Hastings, Deborah. 2015. Police are Investigating Cards Saying "You are Fat, Ugly" Handed to Women on British Subway. *Inside Edition*. November 30. www.insideedition.com/headlines/13287-police-are-investigating-cards-say ing-you-are-fat-ugly-handed-to-women-on-british-subway

22. Puhl, Rebecca M., Andreyeva, Tatiana, and Brownell, Kelly D. 2008. Perceptions of Weight Discrimination: Prevalence and Comparison to Race and Gender Discrimination in America. *International Journal of Obesity*, 32 (6), 992–1000.

23. Gay, Kathlyn. 2013. *Bigotry and Intolerance: The Ultimate Teen Guide (It Happened to Me)*. Scarecrow Press.

24. Schwartz, Marlene, Vartanian, Lenny, Nosek, Brian, and Brownell, Kelly. 2006. The Influence of One's Own Body Weight on Implicit and Explicit Anti-Fat Bias. *Obesity*, 14, 440–447.

25. Ibid.

26. Centers for Disease Control and Prevention. 2016. *Health*. National Center for Health Statistics. www.cdc.gov/nchs/data/hus/hus16.pdf#053

27. FashionMeCurvy. 2017. Bullied for Being a Fat Girl at School, They Mooed at Me in High School! August 18. www.youtube.com/watch?v=tL8KC9RvFoM

28. Munro, Lauren. 2018. Everyday Indignities: Using the Microaggressions Framework to Understand Weight Stigma. *The Journal of Law, Medicine and Ethics*, 45 (4), 502–509.

29. Puhl, Rebecca M., and Heuer, Chelsea A. 2010. Obesity Stigma: Important Considerations for Public Health. *American Journal of Public Health*, 100 (6), 1019–1028.

30. Carels, R. A., Domoff, S. E., Burmeister, J. M., Koball, A. M., Hinman, N. G., Davis, A. K., Wagner Oehlhof, M., Leroy, M., Bannon, E., and Hoffmann, D. A. 2013. Examining Perceived Stereotype Threat among Overweight/Obese Adults Using a Multi-Threat Framework. *Obesity Facts*, 6, 258–268.

31. Blaine, B. Evan, and McClure Brenchley, Kimberly, J. 2017. *Understanding the Psychology of Diversity*. Sage Publications.

32. Greenberg, Bradley S., Eastin, Matthew, Hofschire, Linda, Lachlan, Ken, and Brownell, Kelly D. 2003. Portrayals of Overweight and Obese Individuals on Commercial Television. *American Journal of Public Health*, 93 (8), 1342–1348.

33. Puhl, Rebecca M., Andreyeva, Tatiana, and Brownell, Kelly D. 2008. Perceptions of Weight Discrimination: Prevalence and Comparison to Race and Gender Discrimination in America. *International Journal of Obesity*, 32 (6), 992–1000.

34. Abad-Santos, Alex. 2015. Why Reddit's Ban on Fat People Hate Is Ripping It Apart. *Vox*. June 11. www.vox.com/2015/6/11/8767035/fatpeoplehate-reddit-ban

35. Ross, Ashley. 2015. "Dear Fat People" Comedian Nicole Arbour: "I'm Not Apologizing FOR This Video." *Time*. September 10. time.com/4028119/dear-fat-people-nicole-arbour/

36. Blaine, Evan, B., and McClure Brenchley, Kimberly, J. 2017. *Understanding the Psychology of Diversity.* Sage Publications.

37. Puhl, Rebecca M., Andreyeva, Tatiana, and Brownell, Kelly D. 2008. Perceptions of Weight Discrimination: Prevalence and Comparison to Race and Gender Discrimination in America. *International Journal of Obesity*, 32 (6), 992–1000.

38. NAAFA: The National Association to Advance Fat Acceptance. www.naa faonline.com/dev2/education/faq.html

39. Meadows, Angela. 2018. Discrimination against Fat People Is So Endemic, Most of Us Don't Even Realize It's Happening. *The Conversation.* May 9. http://theconversation.com/discrimination-against-fat-people-is-so-ende mic-most-of-us-dont-even-realise-its-happening-94862

40. Ibid.

41. Tischner, Irmgard, and Malson, Helen. 2008. Exploring the Politics of Women's In/Visible "Large" Bodies. *Feminism & Psychology*, 18, 260–267.

42. McEwan, Melissa. 2012. Adventures in Blogging, Part Wev. Shakesville. May 17. http://www.shakesville.com/2012/05/adventures-in-blogging-part-wev.html

43. Puhl, Rebecca M., Andreyeva, Tatiana, and Brownell, Kelly D. 2008. Perceptions of Weight Discrimination: Prevalence and Comparison to Race and Gender Discrimination in America. *International Journal of Obesity*, 32 (6), 992–1000.

44. Puhl, Rebecca M., and Heuer, Chelsea A. 2010. Obesity Stigma: Important Considerations for Public Health. *American Journal of Public Health*, 100 (6), 1019–1028.

45. O'Brien, Kerry S., Latner, Janet D., Halberstadt, Jamin, Hunter, John A., Anderson, Jeremy, and Caputi, Peter. 2008. Do Antifat Attitudes Predict Antifat Behaviors? *Obesity*, 16, Supplement 2, S87–S92.

46. Sabin, Janice, A., Marini, Maddalena, and Nosek, Brian A. 2012. Implicit and Explicit Fat-Bias among a Large Sample of Medical Doctors by BMI, Race/Ethnicity and Gender. *PLos ONE*, 7 (11), e48448.

47. Cosgrove Baylis, Sheila. 2015. Plus-Size Model Elly Mayday Says Doctors Dismissed Her Cancer Symptoms, Blamed Her Weight. *People.* October 24. https://people.com/bodies/plus-size-model-elly-mayday-says-doctors-dis missed-her-cancer-symptoms/

48. Rudolph, Cort W., Wells, Charles L., Weller, Marcus D., and Baltes, Boris B. 2009. A Meta-Analysis of Empirical Studies of Weight-Based Bias in the Workplace. *Journal of Vocational Behavior*, 74 (1), 1–10.

49. O'Brien, Kerry S., Latner, Janet D., Halberstadt, Jamin, Hunter, John A., Anderson, Jeremy, and Caputi, Peter. 2008. Do Antifat Attitudes Predict Antifat Behaviors? *Obesity*, 16, Supplement 2, S87–S92.

50. Sobo, Elisa J. 1997. The Sweetness of Fat: Health, Procreation and Sociability in Rural Jamaica. In *Food and Culture: A Reader,* edited by Carole Couniha and Penny Van Esterik. Routledge.

51. Ouldzeidoune, Nacerdine, Keating, Joseph, Bertrand, Jane, and Rice, Janet. 2013. A Description of Female Genital Mutilation and Force-Feeding Practices in Mauritania: Implications for the Protection of Child Rights and Health. *PLoS One,* 8 (4), e60594.

52. Stewart, Claire. 2017. *As Long As We Both Shall Eat: A History of Wedding Food and Feasts.* Rowman & Littlefield Publishers.

53. Robson, David. 2015. The Myth of Universal Beauty. *BBC Future.* June 23. www.bbc.com/future/story/20150622-the-myth-of-universal-beauty

54. Maurer, Donna, and Sobal, Jeffrey (Eds.). 1995. *Eating Agendas. Food and Nutrition as Social Problems.* Walter de Gruyter.

55. Tiggemann, Marika, Polivy, Janet, and Hargreaves, Duane. 2009. The Processing of Thin Ideals in Fashion Magazines: A Source of Social Comparison or Fantasy? *Journal of Social and Clinical Psychology,* 28, 73–93.

56. Barr, Sabrina. 2018. "Thin Privilege": Writer Explains Meaning in Twitter Thread. *The Independent.* July 23. www.independent.co.uk/life-style/thin-privilege-explained-discrimination-body-size-fat-shaming-cora-harring ton-a8459761.html

57. Boesveld, Sarah. 2019. Plus-Size Model Elly Mayday on Facing Cancer. *Chatelaine.* March 4. www.chatelaine.com/health/plus-sized-model-elly-mayday-cancer/

58. *New Zealand Herald.* 2017. 44kg Model Deemed "Too Fat" for Louis Vuitton Fashion Show. May 23. www.nzherald.co.nz/lifestyle/news/article.cfm? c_id=6&objectid=11861502

59. Taber, Kimberly Conniff. 2006. With Model's Death, Eating Disorders Are Again in Spotlight. *The New York Times.* November 20. www.nytimes.com/2006/11/20/world/americas/20iht-models.3604439.html

60. Bordo, Susan. 2009. Not Just a "White Girl's Thing": The Changing Face of Food and Body Image Problems. In *Critical Feminist Approaches to Eating Dis/Orders,* edited by Helen Malson and Maree Burns. Routledge, p. 47.

61. Fassino, Secondo, Amianto, Federico, Gramaglia, Carla Maria, Facchini, Federico, and Abbate-Daga, Giovanni. 2004. Temperament and Character in Eating Disorders: Ten Years of Studies. *Eating and Weight Disorders,* 9, 81–90.

62. Critchell, Samantha. 2012. Vogue Bans Too-Skinny Models from Its Pages. *The Washington Times.* May 3. www.washingtontimes.com/news/2012/may/3/vogue-bans-too-skinny-models-from-its-pages/

63. Ibid.
64. Sanghani, Radhika. 2017. Holly Willoughby and the Thin-Shaming Trend That Shames Us All. June 20. www.telegraph.co.uk/women/life/holly-wil loughby-thin-shaming-trend-shames-us/
65. Ibid.
66. Freedman, Rory, and Barnouin, Kim. 2005. *Skinny Bitch: A No-Nonsense, Tough Love Guide for Savvy Girls Who Want to Stop Eating Crap and Start Looking Fabulous.* Running Press Adult.
67. Loughlin, Bronagh. 2017. Skinny Shaming: "I'm Told I'd Look Better with Meat on My Arse." *Irish Times.* May 23. www.irishtimes.com/life-and-style/people/ skinny-shaming-i-m-told-i-d-look-better-with-meat-on-my-arse-1.3091811
68. Bingham-Smith, Kate. 2017. Skinny-Shaming Is a Thing Too, and It's Not Taken (Or Given) as a Compliment. February 7. *Scary Mommy.* www .scarymommy.com/skinny-shaming/
69. Arora, Taniya. 2017. Skinny Shaming: It's Real and It Needs to Stop. *Swirlster.* October 23. https://swirlster.ndtv.com/wellness-mother/skinny- shaming-1765961
70. Trainor, Meghan. 2014. All About That Bass. AZ Lyrics. www.azlyrics.com/ lyrics/meghantrainor/allaboutthatbass.html
71. Minaj, Nicki. 2014. Anaconda. AZ Lyrics. www.azlyrics.com/lyrics/nickimi naj/anaconda.html
72. McKinney, Kelsey. 2014. "All About That Bass" Isn't Actually Body Positive. *Vox.* September 12. www.vox.com/2014/9/12/6126429/ban-meghan-trainor
73. Scott, Jennifer. 2017. Sophie Lancaster Murder: Are Young People Still Scared to be Goths? *BBC News.* August 24. www.bbc.com/news/uk-40628457
74. Freeman, Jonathan B., Penner, Andrew M., Saperstein, Aliya, Scheutz, Matthias, and Ambady, Nalini. 2011. Looking the Part: Social Status Cues Shape Race Perception. *PLoS ONE,* 6 (9), e25107.
75. Heckert, Druann Maria, and Amy Best. 1997. Ugly Duckling to Swan: Labeling Theory and the Stigmatization of Red Hair. *Symbolic Interaction,* 20 (4), 365–384.
76. Pitman, Joanna. 2008. *On Blondes.* Bloomsbury.
77. Idov, Michael. 2017. This Is Not a Barbie Doll. This Is an Actual Human Being. *GQ.* July 12. www.gq.com/story/valeria-lukyanova-human-barbie-doll
78. Sherrow, Victoria L. 2006. *Encyclopedia of Hair: A Cultural History.* Greenwood.
79. Heckert, Druann Maria, and Best, Amy. 2011. Ugly Duckling to Swan: Labeling Theory and the Stigmatization of Red Hair. *Symbolic Interaction,* 20 (4), 365–384.
80. Cooper, Wendy. 1971. *Hair: Sex, Society, and Symbolism.* Stein and Day.
81. Ibid.

82. Rifelj, Carol. 2010. *Coiffures: Hair in Nineteenth-Century French Literature and Culture*. University of Delaware Press.
83. Harvey, Jacky Coliss. 2015. *Red: A History of the Redhead*. Black Dog & Leventhal.
84. Heckert, Druann Maria, and Best, Amy. 2011. Ugly Duckling to Swan: Labeling Theory and the Stigmatization of Red Hair. *Symbolic Interaction*, 20 (4), 365–384.
85. Ibid.
86. Ibid.
87. Minchin, Tim. 2009. Prejudice. Genius lyrics. https://genius.com/Tim-min chin-prejudice-lyrics
88. Heckert, Druann Maria, and Best, Amy. 2011. Ugly Duckling to Swan: Labeling Theory and the Stigmatization of Red Hair. *Symbolic Interaction*, 20 (4), 365–384.
89. Harvey, Jacky Coliss. 2017. *Red: A History of the Redhead*. Black Dog & Leventhal.
90. Ibid.
91. BBC. 2007. Red-Haired Family Forced to Move. June 2. *BBC News*. http://news.bbc.co.uk/2/hi/uk_news/england/tyne/6714735.stm
92. *South Park*. 2005. Ginger Kids. Season 9, episode 11. South Park Studios. http://southpark.cc.com/full-episodes/s09e11-ginger-kids
93. O'Carroll, Sinead. 2013. Irish Father of Suicide Victim Calls for More Action on Red-Haired Bullying. *The Journal*. November 29. www.thejournal.ie/girl-bullied-suicide-red-hair-1197689-Nov2013/
94. Ibid.

7 God's Waiting Room

1. Vernikos, Joan. 2004. *The G-Connection: Harness Gravity and Reverse Aging*. iUniverse, Inc., p. 248.
2. TODAY. Celebrate with TODAY! Ask Al Roker to Wish Your Loved Ones a Happy Birthday or Milestone. NBC. www.today.com/series/today-celebrates/celebrate-today-ask-al-roker-wish-your-loved-ones-happy-t69606
3. Cozma, Raluca, and Dahmen, Nicole S. 2008. *Media Takes: On Ageism*. International Longevity Center. www.issuelab.org/resource/media-takes-on-aging.html
4. Nuessel, Frank. 1999. Old Age Needs a New Name: But Don't Look for It in Webster's. In *Reflections on Language*, edited by Stuart Hirschberg and Terry Hirschberg. Oxford University Press.

5. Benet, James. 1964. Growing Pains at UC. *San Francisco Chronicle.* November 15, p. 6.

6. Motley, Willard. 1947. *Knock on Any Door.* D. Appleton-Century, p. 157.

7. Butler, Robert. 1969. Age-ism: Another Form of Bigotry. *The Gerontologist,* 9, 243–246.

8. Woodward, Kathleen. 1991. *Ageing and Its Discontents: Freud and Other Fictions.* Indiana University Press.

9. Bytheway, Bill. 1995. The Imbecility of Old Age: The Impact of Language. In *Ageism.* Open University Press.

10. Robertson, Guy. 2017. Ageing and Ageism: The Impact of Stereotypical Attitudes on Personal Health and Well-Being Outcomes and Possible Personal Compensation Strategies. *Self & Society,* 45 (2), 149–159.

11. North, Michael S., and Fiske, Susan T. 2012. An Inconvenienced Youth? Ageism and Its Potential Intergenerational Roots. *Psychological Bulletin,* 138 (5), 982–997.

12. Gullette, Margaret. 2010. *Agewise: Fighting the New Ageism in America.* University of Chicago Press.

13. Read, Katy. 2017. Ageism is Everywhere. Here's What We Can Do About It. *Chicago Tribune.* www.chicagotribune.com/lifestyles/sns-tns-bc-srs-age ism-20171020-story.html

14. Cozma, Raluca, and Dahmen, Nicole, S. 2008. *Media Takes: On Ageism.* International Longevity Center. www.issuelab.org/resource/media-takes-on-aging.html

15. Ibid.

16. Myles, Aleisa. 2015. Casting Light on Childism: Recognizing, Resisting, and Transforming Prejudice and Oppression against Children. Dissertation. Widener University.

17. Flasher, J. 1978. Adultism. *Adolescence,* 13 (51), 517–523.

18. Arnett, Jeffrey, J. 2007. Suffering, Selfish, Slackers? Myths and Reality about Emerging Adults. *Journal of Youth and Adolescence,* 36 (1), 23–29.

19. *Webster's Dictionary,* s.v. ageism. 2018. www.webster-dictionary.org/defini tion/ageism

20. Cozma, Raluca, and Dahmen, Nicole S. 2008. *Media Takes: On Ageism.* International Longevity Center. www.issuelab.org/resource/media-takes-on-aging.html

21. Bering, Jesse. 2011. Half Dead: Men and the "Mid-Life Crisis." Bering in Mind. *Scientific American.* https://blogs.scientificamerican.com/bering-in-mind/half-dead-men-and-the-mid-life-crisis/#

22. Wilson, Gail. 2000. *Understanding Old Age: Critical and Global Perspectives.* Sage Publications.

23. World Health Organization. 2004. *A Glossary of Terms for Community Health Care and Services for Older People: Ageing and Health Technical Report, vol. 5*, p. 42.

24. Haber, David. 2013. *Health Promotion and Aging: Practical Applications for Health Professionals*. Springer Publishing Company.

25. World Health Organization. 2004. *A Glossary of Terms for Community Health Care and Services for Older People: Ageing and Health Technical Report, vol. 5*, p. 42.

26. Burridge, Kate. 2015. Taboo Words. In *The Oxford Handbook of the Word*, edited by John R. Taylor. Oxford University Press.

27. *OED Online*. s.v. elder *adj.* and *n.3*. January 2018. Oxford University Press. www.oed.com

28. Warnes, Anthony M. 1993. Being Old, Old People and the Burdens of Burden. *Ageing and Society*, 13 (3), 297–338.

29. Nowlin, Sanford. 2020. San Antonio Mayor Rips Texas Lt. Gov. Dan Patrick for Saying Old People Should Sacrifice Themselves for the Economy. *San Antonio Current*. March 25. www.sacurrent.com/the-daily/archives/2020/03/25/san-antonio-mayor-rips-texas-lt-gov-dan-patrick-for-saying-old-people-should-sacrifice-themselves-for-the-economy

30. Trafford, Abigail. 2004. Who Are You Calling "Senior"? *The Washington Post*. August 9. www.washingtonpost.com/wp-dyn/articles/A52898-2004Aug9.html

31. *Mama's Family*. 1988. TV series. Mama's Girls. Season 4, episode 18. Joe Hamilton Productions.

32. *OED Online*. s.v. old, *adj.* January 2018. Oxford University Press. www.oed.com

33. Silverstein, Merril, Bengston, Vern, Putnam, Michelle, Putney, Norella, and Gans, Daphna. 2008. *Handbook of Theories of Aging*. 2nd ed. Springer.

34. Palmore, Erdman B. 1999. *Ageism: Negative and Positive*. Springer.

35. Bytheway, Bill., Ward, Richard, Holland, Caroline, and Peace, Sheila. 2007. *Too Old: Older Peoples' Accounts of Discrimination, Exclusion and Rejection: A Report from the Research on Age Discrimination Project (RoAD)*. Help the Aged. http://oro.open.ac.uk/7281/

36. Osgood, N. J. 1996. Society Does Not Respect the Elderly. In *An Aging Population: Opposing Viewpoints*, edited by Charles P. Cozic. Greenhaven Press.

37. Jacoby, Susan. 2011. *Never Say Die: The Myth and Marketing of the New Old Age*. Pantheon.

38. Levy, Becca R., Slade, Martin D., Kunkel, Suzanne R., and Kasl, Stansilav V. 2002. Longevity Increased by Positive Self-Perceptions of Aging. *Journal of Personality and Social Psychology*, 83, 261–270.

39. Brubaker, Timothy H., and Powers, Edward A. 1976. The Stereotype of "Old": A Review and Alternative Approach. *Journal of Gerontology*, 31 (4), 441–447.

40. Nussbaum, Jon F., Pitts, Margaret J., Huber, Frances N. Krieger, Janice L. Raup, and Ohs, Jennifer E. 2005. Ageism and Ageist Language Across the Life Span: Intimate Relationships and Non-Intimate Interactions. *Journal of Social Issues*, 61 (2), 287–305.

41. Levy, Becca R., Pilver, Corey, Chung, Pil H., and Slade, Martin D. 2014. Subliminal Strengthening: Improving Older Individuals' Physical Function over Time with an Implicit-Age-Stereotype Intervention. *Psychological Science*, 24 (12), 2127–2135.

42. Levy, Becca R., Slade, Martin D., Kunkel, Suzanne R., and Kasl, Stansilav V. 2002. Longevity Increased by Positive Self-Perceptions of Aging. *Journal of Personality and Social Psychology*, 83, 261–270.

43. Scripps Research Translational Institute. www.scripps.edu/science-and-medicine/translational-institute/translational-research/genomic-medicine/wellderly/index.html

44. Kurtzweil, Ray. 2005. *The Singularity Is Near*. Penguin.

45. Kaye, Lenard W., and Butler, Sandra. 2005. *Gerontological Social Work in Small Towns and Rural Communities*. Routledge.

46. Powell, L. 1992. Successful Aging: Our Common Future? *Australasian Journal on Ageing*, 11 (1), 36–41.

47. Dionigi, Rylee A. 2015. Stereotypes of Aging: Their Effects on the Health of Older Adults. *Journal of Geriatrics*, 2015, 1–9. DOI:10.1155/2015/954027

48. Minichiello, Victor, Browne, Jan, and Kendig, Hal. 2000. Perceptions and Consequences of Ageism: Views of Older People. *Ageing and Society*, 20 (3), 253–278.

49. Saporta, Sol, and R. R. B. 1991. Old Maid and Dirty Old Man: The Language of Ageism. *American Speech*, 66 (3), 333–335.

50. Lee, Michelle. 2017. Allure Magazine Will No Longer Use the Term "Anti-Aging." *Allure*. August 14. www.allure.com/story/allure-magazine-phasing-out-the-word-anti-aging

51. Sontag, Susan. 1972. The Double Standard of Aging. *The Saturday Review*. September 23, pp. 29–38.

52. Muhlbauer, Varda, and Chrisler, Joan C. 2007. *Women over 50: Psychological Perspectives*. Springer Science and Business Media.

53. Sontag, Susan. 1972. The Double Standard of Aging. *The Saturday Review*. September 23, pp. 29–38.

54. Abcarian, Robin. 2018. How Much More Humiliation Can Melania Trump Take? *LA Times*. February 20. www.latimes.com/local/abcarian/la-me-abcarian-melania-20180220-story.html

55. Hannum, Claire. 2016. Olivia Wilde Was Deemed "Too Old" For A *Wolf of Wall Street* Role. *Self*. March 16. www.self.com/story/olivia-wilde-was-deemed-too-old-for-a-wolf-of-wall-street-role

56. Sieczkowski, Cavan. 2015. Maggie Gyllenhaal, 37, Told She's "Too Old" To Play Love Interest of 55-Year-Old. *Huffington Post.* May 25. https://www .huffingtonpost.com/2015/05/21/maggie-gyllenhaal-too-old-55_n_7350960 .html

57. Hawn, Goldie, and Holden, Wendy. 2006. *A Lotus Grows in the Mud.* Berkley Books.

58. Wellford, Lin, and Pifer, Skye. 2009. *The New Grandparents Name Book: A Lighthearted Guide to Picking the Perfect Grandparent Name.* ArtStone Press.

59. BBC. 2017. Janet Jackson, 50, Gives Birth to a Boy, Eissa Al Mana. *BBC News.* January 3. www.bbc.com/news/world-us-canada-38503168

60. Eleje, George Uchenna, Igwegbe, Anthony Osita, Okonkwo, Jon E. N., Udigwe, Gerald O., and Eke, Ahizechukwu Chigoziem. 2014. Elderly Primigravidae Versus Young Primigravidae: A Review of Pregnancy Outcome in a Low Resource Setting. *Nigerian Journal of Medicine,* 23 (3), 220–229.

61. Billari, F. C., Goisis, A., Liefbroer, A. C., Settersten, R. A., Aassve, A., Hagestad, G., and Spéder, Z. 2010. Social Age Deadlines for the Childbearing of Women and Men. *Human Reproduction,* 26 (3), 616–622.

62. Greer, Germaine. 1993. *The Change: Women, Aging and The Menopause.* Ballantine Books.

63. *OED Online.* s.v. spinster, *n.* January 2018. Oxford University Press. www .oed.com

64. Eschner, Kat. 2017. "Spinster" and "Bachelor" Were, Until 2005, Official Terms for Single People. *Smithsonian Magazine.* September 14. www.smith sonianmag.com/smart-news/where-did-spinster-and-bachelor-come-180964879/

65. Chaucer, Geoffrey. 2005 (1387). *The Canterbury Tales: Fifteen Tales and the General Prologue.* W. W. Norton & Company, p. 46.

66. Brown, Lisa. 2015. "Get a Man, While You Can!" Celebrating Old Maid's Day. University Libraries. February 16. https://blogs.library.unt.edu/unt125/2015/ 02/16/get-a-man-while-you-can-celebrating-old-maids-day-in-denton/

67. IMDb. 1992. *Absolutely Fabulous.* TV Series. Season 1, episode 3: France. Quotes. www.imdb.com/title/tt0504669/quotes

68. Ludden, Jennifer. 2010. Please Don't Call Me "Ma'am." *Talk of the Nation.* September 8. National Public Radio. www.npr.org/templates/story/story .php?storyId=129727777

69. Horn, Nick. 2017. #HusbandNotDad: What Experts Say About Relationships with Large Age Gaps. *Healthy Way.* November 17. www .healthyway.com/content/husbandnotdad-what-the-experts-say-about-rela tionships-with-large-age-gaps/

70. Conway, Jim. 1997. *Men in Midlife Crisis.* David C. Cook.

71. Church, Emily Musil. 2011. No Comment: A "Younger, Hotter" Virgin. *Ms. Magazine*. September 12. http://msmagazine.com/blog/2011/09/12/no-com ment-a-younger-hotter-virgin/

72. Todd, Mark. 2005. Virgin Blue Loses Age Discrimination Case. *The Age*. October 10. www.theage.com.au/news/business/virgin-blue-loses-age-dis crimination-case/2005/10/10/1128796447967.html

73. Smith, Oliver. 2015. Meet Virgin's Newest Flight Attendant – A 59-Year-Old Grandmother of 11. *The Telegraph*. July 7. http://www.telegraph.co.uk/travel/ news/Meet-Virgins-newest-flight-attendant-a-59-year-old-grandmother-of-11/

74. Fredman, Sandra, and Spencer, Sarah. 2003. *Age as an Equality Issue: Legal and Policy Perspectives*. Hart Publishing.

75. The Age Discrimination in Employment Act of 1967. US Equal Employment Opportunity Commission. https://www.eeoc.gov/laws/statutes/adea.cfm

76. Nelson, Todd, D. 2002. *Ageism: Stereotyping and Prejudice against Older Persons*. MIT Press.

77. Kennedy, Joyce Lain. 2014. Identifying Age Discrimination Traps when Searching for Jobs. *The Telegram*. March 30. www.telegram.com/article/ 20140330/COLUMN72/303309971

78. Fox Rothschild. 2014. We're on the Hunt for Young, Fit and Competent Employees. *Employment Discrimination Report*, blog. October 17. https:// employmentdiscrimination.foxrothschild.com/2014/11/articles/general- employment-discrimination/age-discrimination-another-category/were- on-the-hunt-for-young-fit-and-competent/

79. DePillis, Lydia. 2016. Baby Boomers are Taking on Ageism – and Losing. *The Washington Post*. August 4. www.washingtonpost.com/lifestyle/maga zine/baby-boomers-are-taking-on-ageism–and-losing

80. Kalkat, Vikram, and Gruenenfelder, Reto. 2017. *Digital Spine: A Study in Business Strategy*. Amazon Digital Services.

81. National Football League. 2009. Patriot's Bruschi Announces Retirement after 13 Seasons. August 31. www.nfl.com/news/story/ 09000d5d812455f9/article/patriots-bruschi-announces-retirement-after- 13-seasons

82. *Cambridge Advanced Learner's Dictionary and Thesaurus*. s.v. mutton dressed as lamb. Cambridge University Press. https://dictionary.cambridge .org/us/dictionary/english/mutton-dressed-as-lamb

83. Krause, Rachel. 2016. An Unironic Ode to "Old Lady" Perfumes – and Why They're Worth a Try. *StyleCaster*. http://stylecaster.com/beauty/old-lady- perfumes/

84. Johns, Michael M., III, Arviso, Lindsey C., and Ramadan, Fadi. 2011. Challenges and Opportunities in the Management of the Aging Voice. *Otolaryngology – Head and Neck Surgery*, 145 (1), 1–6.

85. Ward, Paul H., Colton, Ray, McConnell, Fred, Malmgren, Leslie, Kashima, Haskins, and Woodson, Gayle. 1989. Aging of the Voice and Swallowing. *Otolaryngology – Head and Neck Surgery*, 100 (4), 283–286.
86. Sontag, Susan. 1972. The Double Standard of Aging. *The Saturday Review*. September 23, pp. 29–38.
87. Demos, Vasilikie, and Jache, Anne. 1981. When You Care Enough: An Analysis of Attitudes towards Aging in Humorous Birthday Cards. *The Gerontologist*, 21 (2), 209–215.
88. Amazon. Humorous Over the Hill Birthday Survival Kit in A Can. https://www.amazon.co.uk/Humorous-Birthday-Survival-Kit-Novelty/dp/B007P5KJQS
89. Palmore, Erdman B., Branch, Laurence, and Harris, Diane. 2005. *Encyclopedia of Ageism*. The Haworth Press.
90. Adams, Abby. 1989. *An Uncommon Scold*. Simon & Schuster.
91. Cookney, Francesca. 2014. From "Old Spice" Geri Halliwell to Joseph Stalin: Top Ten Cases of Famous People Fibbing about Their Age. February 15. *The Mirror*. www.mirror.co.uk/3am/celebrity-news/old-spice-geri-halliwell-joseph-3147390
92. Moore, Trudy S. 1987. Aretha Franklin Finds Happiness with New Love in Her Life. *Jet*. April 27, p. 30.
93. Finkel, Eli J., Eastwick, Paul W., Karney, Benjamin R., Reis, Harry T., and Sprecher, Susan. 2012. Online Dating: A Critical Analysis from the Perspective of Psychological Science. *Psychological Science in the Public Interest*, 13 (1), 3–66.
94. Dean, Stephen. 2007. *Sexual Predators: How to Recognize Them on the Internet and on the Street. How to Keep Your Kids Away*. Silver Lake Publishing.
95. Knafo, Danielle, and Bosco, Rocco Lo. 2017. *The Age of Perversion: Desire and Technology in Psychoanalysis and Culture*. Routledge.
96. Archer, Jayne Elisabeth, Goldring, Elizabeth, E., and Knight, Sarah S. 2007. *The Progresses, Pageants, and Entertainments of Queen Elizabeth I*. Oxford University Press.
97. Bytheway, Bill. 1995. The Imbecility of Old Age: The Impact of Language. In *Ageism*. Open University Press.
98. Rodale, Maria. 2017. For Her Age. *Huffington Post*. December 6. www.huffingtonpost.com/maria-rodale/for-her-age_b_5499612.html
99. Flynn, Gillian. 2012. *Gone Girl*. Crown Publishing Group, p. 204.
100. Bytheway, Bill, Ward, Richard, Holland, Caroline, and Peace, Sheila. 2007. *Too Old: Older Peoples' Accounts of Discrimination, Exclusion and Rejection: A Report from the Research on Age Discrimination Project (RoAD)*. Help the Aged. http://oro.open.ac.uk/7281/

101. Cozma, Raluca, and Dahmen, Nicole, S. 2008. *Media Takes: On Ageism.* International Longevity Center. www.issuelab.org/resource/media-takes-on-aging.html

102. Gendron, Tracey L., Welleford, Ayn E., Inker, Jennifer, and White, John T. 2016. The Language of Ageism: Why We Need to Use Words Carefully. *The Gerontologist,* 56 (6), 997–1006. DOI:10.1093/geront/gnv066

103. Salari, Sonia Miner, and Rich, Melinda. 2001. Social and Environmental Infantilization of Aged Persons: Observations in Two Adult Day Care Centers. *The International Journal of Aging and Human Development,* 52 (2), 115–134.

104. Hummert, Mary Lee, and Shaner, Jaye L. 1994. Patronizing Speech to the Elderly as a Function of Stereotyping. *Communication Studies,* 45 (2), 145–158.

105. Gresham, Mary L. 1976. The Infantilization of the Elderly. *Nursing Forum,* 15 (2), 196–209.

106. Hockey, J., and James, A. 1993. Infantilization as Social Discourse. In *Growing Up and Growing Old: Ageing and Dependency in Life Course.* Sage Publications.

107. Read, Katy. 2017. Ageism Is Everywhere. Here's What We Can Do About It. *Chicago Tribune.* October 18. www.chicagotribune.com/lifestyles/sns-tns-bc-srs-ageism-20171020-story.html

108. Nuessel, Frank. 1999. Old Age Needs a New Name: But Don't Look for it in Webster's. In *Reflections on Language,* edited by Stuart Hirschberg and Terry Hirschberg. Oxford University Press.

109. Novak, William. 2016. *Die Laughing: Killer Jokes for Newly Old Folks.* Touchstone.

110. Scourfield, Peter. 2012. Defenders against Threats or Enablers of Opportunities: The Screening Role Played by Gatekeepers in Researching Older People in Care Homes. *The Qualitative Report,* 17 (14), Article 2. https://nsuworks.nova.edu/cgi/viewcontent.cgi?article=1788&context=tqr

111. Owen, Tom, and NCHRDF (Eds.). 2007. *My Home Life: Quality of Life in Care Homes.* Help the Aged with The National Care Homes Research and Development Forum.

112. Shemmings, Yvonne. 1998. Death and Dying in Residential Homes for Older People. In *Residential versus Community Care,* edited by Raymond Jack. Palgrave.

Index

Johnson, Samuel, 4, 75
Jolie, Angelina, 137
Jolson, Al, 22
Jones, Grace, 218
Judaism, 34, 57, 124–136

Keats, John, 191
Kelly, Megyn, 72
Kent State University, 4
Khomeini, Ayatollah, 5
King, Martin Luther, 18
King, William, 109
Kisch, Egon, 51
Koch, Robert, 191
Korean, 28, 29, 41, 49
Kovaleski, Serge, 184
Krauthammer, Charles, 184
Kristallnacht, 131
Ku Klux Klan, 29, 35, 36
Kubrick, Stanley, 39

Latino, 25, 26, 30, 46, 47, 49
lavender marriages, 105
Lavender Panthers, 103
Lawson, Lesley, 211
Lee, Bruce, 52
Legionnaires' disease, 194
Lejeune, Jerome, 175
Lennon, John, 60
leprosy, 31, 190
lesbian, 65, 81, 96, 100, 105–110, 113,
    114, 115, 117, 118, 121
Lesbos, Greek island, 109
LGBTQ, 10, 90, 107, 109, 115, 117, 119,
    120, 121, 122, 123, 131, 187, 215
Liberace, Vladziu Valentino, 105, 112
Limbaugh, Rush, 73
linguicism, 44, 46, 53, 155
Linneaus, Carl, 16
lookism, 196–221
Lopez, George, 30
Lucas, George, 137

Lyme disease, 193
lynching, 20, 21, 24

Macpherson, Elle, 78
Mad Pride, 162
Maharishi Mahesh Yogi, 137
male fragility, 87
male privilege, 86, 122
Mallon, Mary ("Typhoid Mary"), 193
Mandarin, 16, 47
Manosphere, 67, 68, 72, 73
mansplaining, 64
marginalization, 38, 39, 42, 65, 139, 151,
    162, 170, 185
Mária Kertbeny, Károli, 100
marital rape, 81
marriage bars, 63
Martin, Trayvon, 36
Matlin, Marlee, 184
Mayday, Elly, 209, 211, 213
McCain, John, 28
Me Too movement, 85
medical model of disability, 176
Men's Rights Activists, 67, 68, 72
Men's Rights movement, 67
Mencap, 169, 173
Mencia, Carlos, 30
Mensch, Louise, 74
mental illness, 92, 101, 142, 159–169,
    172, 174, 175, 188, 194, 206
Mercury, Freddie, 112
Merrick, Joseph, 166, 196, 197, 198, 221
Mexican people, 26, 29, 30, 31, 42, 46,
    47, 49
Mexico, 31, 79
Michael Jackson, 166
microaggressions, 38, 92, 207, 208, 213
Middle Ages, 109
Middle East, 118, 124, 125, 144, 147, 149,
    152, 194
Middle English, 8, 172
migration, 12, 13, 31